OUT OF LINE, OUT OF PLACE

OUT OF LINE, OUT OF PLACE

A GLOBAL AND LOCAL HISTORY OF WORLD WAR I INTERNMENTS

EDITED BY ROTEM KOWNER AND IRIS RACHAMIMOV

CORNELL UNIVERSITY PRESS
Ithaca and London

First published 2022 by Cornell University Press

Library of Congress Cataloging-in-Publication Data

Names: Kowner, Rotem, editor. | Rachamimov, Iris, 1964– editor.
Title: Out of line, out of place : a global and local history of World War I internments / edited by Rotem Kowner and Iris Rachamimov.
Description: Ithaca, New York : Cornell University Press, 2022. | Includes bibliographical references and index.
Identifiers: LCCN 2022005432 (print) | LCCN 2022005433 (ebook) | ISBN 9781501765421 (hardcover) | ISBN 9781501765902 (paperback) | ISBN 9781501765438 (epub) | ISBN 9781501765445 (pdf)
Subjects: LCSH: World War, 1914–1918—Concentration camps. | World War, 1914–1918—Prisoners and prisons. | Internment camps—History—20th century.
Classification: LCC D627.A2 O88 2022 (print) | LCC D627.A2 (ebook) | DDC 940.4/72—dc23/eng/20220203
LC record available at https://lccn.loc.gov/2022005432
LC ebook record available at https://lccn.loc.gov/2022005433

In loving memory of

***Nancy Fitch** (1946–2020)—A distinguished historian of modern Europe, the French Revolution, French antisemitism, and the First World War, who was loved by her colleagues and students as well as by her family and friends*

***Dan Tomáš Spira** (1932–2020)—A child in the concentration camp of Nováky, who survived the Holocaust to become a respected scientist and a loving father, grandfather, and great grandfather*

***Leon Kowner** (1927–2021)—A youth internee at the Łódź Ghetto and the Auschwitz concentration camp, who survived the Holocaust to become an accomplished seaman, inspiring teacher, and marvelous father*

Contents

Acknowledgments

This volume represents the end result of a prolonged project that involved extended collaborative research, an international workshop, numerous meetings, and the formation of an extensive network of scholars interested in various topics related to internment and captivity during World War I. We could not have developed this joint research project or completed the preparation of this specific volume without the generous support and cordial assistance of several organizations and numerous individuals. We are particularly grateful to the Israel Science Foundation (Grants ISF 1152/12 and ISF 2262/16) for supporting this entire project since its inception, as well as the Research Authority at the University of Haifa and the Institute of Advanced Studies at Tel Aviv University for generously supporting the international workshop. We are also grateful to Emily Andrew of Cornell University Press for her broad vision and constructive guidance. Finally, we thank the authors of this volume, many of whom are the leading authorities in their respective fields, for their cooperation and their cordial response to the demands raised by editorial needs.

The Editors

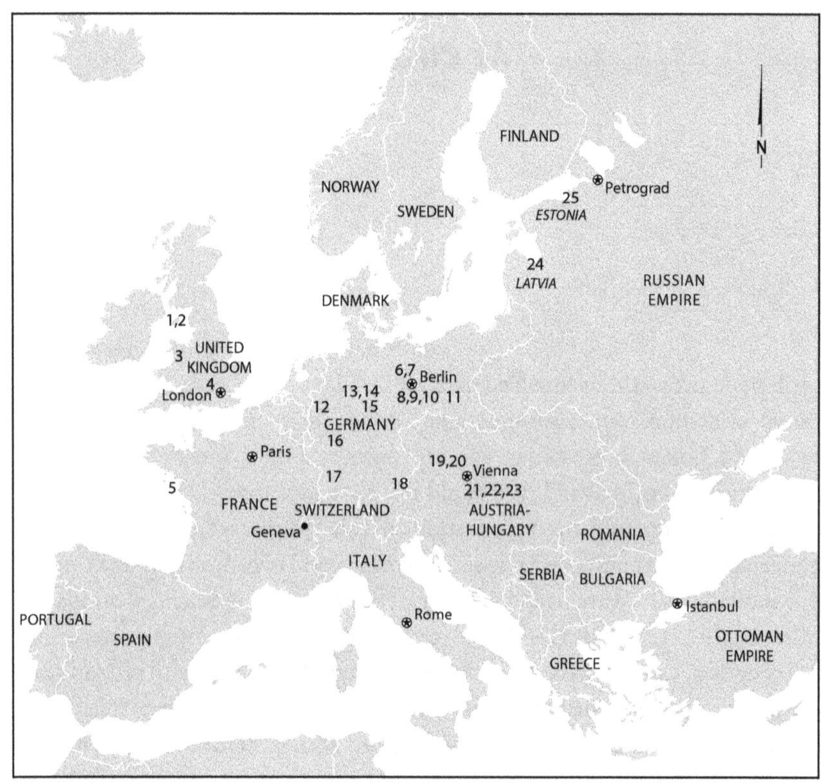

Map 1. Location of internment camps in Europe (mentioned in this book)

United Kingdom: 1. Knockaloe Internment Camp, Isle of Man; 2. Douglas Aliens Detention Camp, Isle of Man; 3. Frongoch Internment Camp, Wales; 4. Alexandra Palace Camp, London. **France**: 5. Île de Noirmoutier Internment Camp ("Black Monastery"), Department of Vendée. **Germany**: 6. Havelberg Camp, Saxony-Anhalt; 7. Ruhleben Internment Camp, Berlin; 8. Altengrabow POW Camp, Saxony-Anhalt; 9. Zossen-Weinberge POW Camp, Brandenburg; 10. Halbmondlager Camp ("Crescent Camp"), Wünsdorf, Brandenburg; 11. Frankfurt-an-der-Oder Civilian and POW Camp, Brandenburg; 12. Friedrichsfeld POW Camp, Voerde, North Rhine-Westphalia; 13. Senne Civilian and POW Camp, Bielefeld, North Rhine-Westphalia; 14. Holzminden Internment and POW Camp, Lower Saxony; 15. Erfurt Civilian and POW Camp, Thuringia; 16. Limburg-an-der-Lahn Civilian and POW Camp, Hesse; 17. Rastatt Civilian and POW Camp, Baden-Württemberg; 18. Traunstein Civilian Camp, Upper Bavaria. **Austria-Hungary**: 19. Gmünd Refugee Camp, Lower Austria; 20. Steinklamm Refugee Camp, Lower Austria; 21. Mittendorf Refugee Camp, Lower Austria; 22. Bruck an der Leitha Refugee Camp, Lower Austria; 23. Nézsider/ Neusiedl am See, at the time Hungary (present-day Austria); **Russian Empire**: 24. Riga Transit Camp, Latvia; 25. Narva Transit Camp, Estonia.

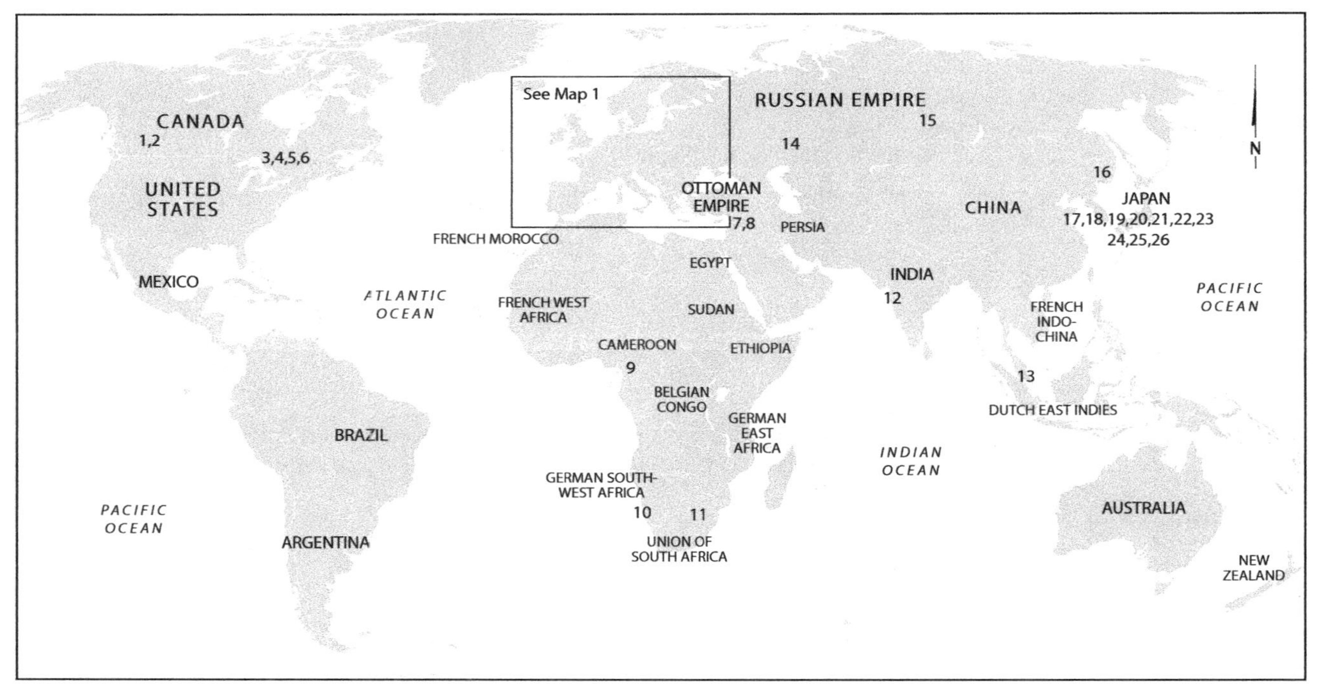

Map 2. Location of internment camps outside Europe (mentioned in this book)

Canada: 1. Castle Mountain Internment Camp, Banff National Park, Alberta; 2. Banff Internment Camp, Alberta; 3. Petawawa Internment Camp, Ontario; 4. Kapuskasing Internment Camp, Ontario; 5. Spirit Lake Internment Camp, Ontario; 6. Valcartier Internment Camp, Québec. **Ottoman Empire**: 7. Bab Camp, Syria; 8. Meskenah Camp, Syria. **German Empire**: 9. Mbanga-Mujuka Internment Camp, Mbanga, Cameroon; 10. Lüderitz Internment Camp ("Shark Island"), German South West Africa (present-day Namibia). **British Empire**: 11. Pretoria Internment Camp, South Africa; 12. Ahmednagar Internment Camp, Maharashtra, India; 13. Tanglin Prison Camp, Singapore. **Russian Empire**: 14. Totskoe Camp, Orenburg Oblast, Russia; 15. Tomsk Internment Camp, Tomsk Oblast, Russia; 16. Nikol'sk-Ussuriĭsk Camp, Primorsky Krai, Russia. **Japan**: 17. Kurume POW Camp, Fukuoka Prefecture; 18. Ninoshima POW Camp, Hiroshima Prefecture; 19. Himeji POW Camp, Hyogo Prefecture; 20. Aonogahara POW Camp, Hyogo Prefecture; 21. Osaka POW Camp, Osaka Prefecture; 22. Nagoya POW Camp, Aichi Prefecture; 23. Narashino POW Camp, Chiba Prefecture; 24. Matsuyama POW Camp, Ehime Prefecture; 25. Marugame POW Camp, Kagawa Prefecture; 26. Bandō POW Camp, Tokushima Prefecture.

OUT OF LINE, OUT OF PLACE

Introduction

Military, Civilian, and Political Internments: Examining Great War Internments Together

Iris Rachamimov and Rotem Kowner

Mass internment has long been recognized as a defining experience of World War II. The mere mention of a few well-known episodes or the naming of a few prison camps are enough to elicit recognition from specialists and nonspecialists alike: Drancy and Westerbork, the Siam-Burma Railway, the internment of Japanese-Americans, and, of course, the vast camp complex at Auschwitz-Birkenau, which included dozens of affiliated camps and which served simultaneously as a concentration camp, a prisoner-of-war camp, a labor camp, and an extermination camp. It is estimated that as many as thirty-five million soldiers became prisoners of war (POWs) during World War II and its aftermath and that many millions of civilians found themselves behind barbed wire all over the world.[1]

In contrast, it is only in the last three decades that historians have come to recognize mass internment as a fundamental experience of World War I.[2] Although it was already clear during the war itself that about eight million soldiers had become prisoners (about one of every nine soldiers to put on a uniform), and although the term "barbed-wire disease" (Ger. *Stacheldraht-krankheit*) was coined at the time by the Swiss psychiatrist Adolf Vischer to describe the mental anguish suffered by inmates, these prisoners' ordeals were not integrated into the war's historiography until the first decade of the twenty-first century. While the war itself had been studied in great detail by historians, the phenomenon of imprisonment does not possess the same public resonance as other aspects of the conflict. Thus, it is still not seen as an emblematic experience of the war on par with chemical warfare or shell shock and as a major cause of individual trauma.[3] The fact that a great majority of military prisoners fell into enemy hands on the Eastern Front, and not on the better-known Western Front, has undoubtedly contributed to its historiographical marginalization and its omission as a central legacy of the war.[4]

When the war broke out on July 28, 1914, none of the belligerents was prepared for the large number of casualties that included a vast number of captured soldiers. The situation on the Eastern Front was particularly grave in this regard. The mobile nature of warfare in the east resulted in a number of cases in the encirclement of large military formations and ensuing mass capture. Thus, for example, during the Battle of Tannenberg (August 26–30, 1914), the Russian army lost 120,000 men, of whom 95,000 were taken prisoner by German forces. By 1915 Germany had already captured a million soldiers, mostly from Russia. Further south, the Austro-Hungarian fortress of Przemyśl surrendered to the Russians on March 22, 1915, and 119,000 soldiers were led into captivity. A year later, during the Brusilov offensive of June 1916, an entire section of the Austro-Hungarian front collapsed near Lutsk, and roughly 200,000 soldiers were captured by the Russians in merely three days. Overall, some five million soldiers would become POWs on the Eastern Front alone.[5]

The massive expansion of the conflict resulted in unprecedented death and suffering that greatly exceeded most people's worst nightmares. With more than 70 million military personnel mobilized, some 8.5 million combatant deaths, and 13 million civilian deaths as a direct result of the war, the Great War, as it was known at the time, soon became the largest armed conflict in history to that date.[6] It was also a total war in the sense that entire populations and all the resources of the combatants were "committed to complete victory and thus become legitimate military targets."[7] As the war dragged on, some belligerents turned sides, and the general state of affairs deteriorated; the notions of who counted as what changed over time: friend, foe, alien, colonial, and so on. In these circumstances, the boundaries between civilians and combatants became increasingly porous as well.

Indeed, captured soldiers were not the only ones who found themselves in camps and other holding facilities during World War I. Civilians of various categories were also placed under guard and subjected to a range of restrictions and internment regimes. With the commencement of hostilities in August 1914, hundreds of thousands of refugees fled the war zones in

Belgium and in Galicia (Austria-Hungary), creating the first wave of what would eventually become an unrelenting swell of displaced people. By 1918 this swell amounted to about ten million individuals who could not return to their previous homes either temporarily or permanently.[8] They now resided in other areas within their own countries or under foreign jurisdiction, and their presence was viewed at the very least as a sanitation problem, if not a political, social, and economic menace. As Doina Anca Cretu shows in her analysis of the first refugee camps in Austria-Hungary in this book, some of these displaced people, especially the indigent, were placed in "sites of securitizations" and subjected to spatial and social controls. These people were not only "out of place" in the sense of being away from their homes, but also outside existing bureaucratic classificatory categories that gave meaning to their travails. They embodied Mary Douglas's dictum of dirt "as matter out of place" and were treated at times as such.[9]

As the war dragged on, its destabilizing influences were felt by other noncombatants as well. As Assaf Mond shows in his chapter in this book, civilians who had been present on enemy territory when the war began—some residing there for many years and considering themselves local—were registered as "enemy aliens" and gradually interned in camps. Paul Cohen-Portheim's story is a case in point. A German journalist and painter who had been vacationing in England initially, Cohen-Portheim found the fingerprinting and the constant surveillance awkward yet manageable.[10] Within a few months, however, he "had a nervous breakdown" upon realizing internment was imminent.[11] While enemy aliens and refugees were placed in camps on account of being "out of place," others were imprisoned behind barbed wire because they were seen as "out of line." Ethnic groups labeled as "disloyal"—such as Armenians in the Ottoman Empire, or Serbs and Italians in Austria-Hungary and in its occupied territories—were subjected to a range of disciplinary measures that included, among others, internment in camps.

The proliferation of internment camps as a biopolitical tool of governance must count in our minds as one of the salient legacies of World War I. Although the camp as a technology of containment, control, and punishment emerged first in the latter part of the nineteenth century mainly in colonial settings, it truly became universal and global during the war. None of the belligerent countries had been equipped to deal with the massive movement of people, military and civilian, that the war engendered, and many regimes also took the opportunity to settle old scores against real or perceived foes. Thousands of camps now dotted the globe from Western Europe to East Asia, from North America to South Africa. They were everywhere, and they became a fixture of modern governance.

Overall, World War I was an important stage in the long-term evolution of the internment camp and is still crucial for understanding why it remains the default space for holding millions of people who seem to be either "out of place" or "out of line." Throughout the twentieth century the internment camp has been used by many political powers: imperial and national states, militaristic monarchies and democratic republics, and internationally recognized governments and newly formed revolutionary regimes. Although there are differences among different kind of camps, and although the logic of internment in individual countries varied, there are also striking similarities in the way the camps operated during the Great War that warrant—even necessitate—a common investigation.

Categories for Analysis

In the past few decades historians have made great strides in filling the many research lacunae regarding World War I internments. A quick look at the crop of new books on the war suggests that a remarkable expansion of scholarly interest has taken place in this respect, initially with regard to military imprisonment and subsequently with regard to the study of civilian internment during the Great War and its aftermath.[12] Until quite recently historians estimated the number of civilian internees at a few hundred thousand at the most, primarily enemy aliens who found themselves in the wrong place at the wrong time and wound up behind barbed wire as a consequence.[13] However, the latest volume to be published on civilian internment—*Internment during the First World War: A Mass Global Phenomenon*, edited by Stefan Manz, Panikos Panayi, and Matthew Stibbe—places the number of interned civilians in the range of one to two million, a figure based on the assessment of the Red Cross International Prisoners of War Agency.[14]

The new historiography reflects a greater awareness of the widespread reliance on the forced labor of civilians during the war, especially, but not exclusively, by imperial Germany. In addition, it acknowledges the internment in camps and the subsequent murder of hundreds of thousands of Ottoman Armenians and the prevalence of non-European internments in North America, Africa, India, East Asia, Australia, and New Zealand. Moreover, the British Empire has been suggested as playing a central role as an originator—perhaps the originator—of the modern practice of the mass internment of civilians in the latter part of the nineteenth century, although British primacy has been debated by historians. Some have ascribed it instead to the actions of the Spanish army in Cuba in 1896, while others point to earlier internment practices developed by the United States during the expulsion of the

Cherokees from the southeastern United States in the 1830s and by General Sherman in the latter part of the Civil War.[15]

Although the term "concentration camp" was well established by 1914 to describe the internment of civilians during times perceived by the interning powers as "emergencies," it was not used widely during World War I. The most probable reason for this terminological preference is its negative image—a legacy of the Second South African War (1899–1902) and of German genocidal policies in southwest Africa toward the Herero and Nama people (1904–1907). Thus, belligerents and nonbelligerents alike (such as Switzerland and the Netherlands, who maintained neutral camps during the war) tended not to use the term in relation to the military and civilian prisoners held on their territory, preferring such terms as "prisoner-of-war camp," "detention camp," or "internment camp." This preference also characterized the camps operated by the International Red Cross Society in the postwar years.

However, contemporaries did occasionally use the term "concentration camp" during the war and its aftermath, and it seems that the authorities did not refrain from calling their own facilities by this name despite its negative image. Thus, for example, local police authorities in Scotland repeatedly requested that the expenses arising from arresting, guarding, and escorting enemy aliens to camps be covered by the state in 1914–15. The chief constable of Ross and Cromarty sent a request to the secretary of state for Scotland on September 20, 1915, wishing to "draw attention to the number of alien enemies that have been handed over to the Police Authorities, escorted by them to Dingwall and thereafter to various Concentration Camps. [He] submits that the expenditure incurred should not come out of local rates but be borne by Imperial Funds."[16] It is interesting to note that the ensuing discussions in the Scottish office at Whitehall used both the terms "detention camps" and "concentration camps" interchangeably but preferred to allude to specific camps as "concentration camps," as was the case in referring to the "Concentration Camps in Liberton, Edinburgh, or Stobs.[17] Similar requests were made by other Scottish chief constables but to no avail—the British Exchequer refused to cover the costs.

The designation "concentration camp" (Rus. *Kontsentratsionnyi lager* from the German) was widely employed by imperial Russia, and that usage seem to have carried over to the nascent Soviet regime. The newly established Bolshevik government first used the term *Kontslager* in June 1918, initially in connection with the escalating confrontation between the communist military forces and the Czechoslovak Legion, a military force made up of mostly Czech military prisoners from Austria-Hungary who switched sides and joined the Entente. Within weeks Trotsky and Lenin were suggesting the creation of concentration camps for class enemies and political adversaries, and approximately eighty such *Kontslageria* were established by the end of the Russian Civil War in 1922.[18] The term continued to be used during the interwar years, most notably by Nazi Germany, but even there it was used alongside such terms as "detention camp, work service camp and transit camp. . . [that] shared a common purpose: to break the opposition."[19] As Tetsuden Kashima has shown, even President Franklin D. Roosevelt (1882–1945) was not averse to using the term to refer to preparations for the internment of Japanese-Americans in the case of war with Japan. Writing to the chief of naval operations in August 1936, he suggested the creation of a "special list" on the island of Oahu "of those who would be the first to be placed in a concentration camp in the event of trouble."[20] Eventually, during World War II itself, the United States preferred to employ other official designations, such as "relocation camps," "assembly centers," and "evacuation camps," although, as Kashima stresses, we believe that "the most accurate overall descriptive term is concentration camp—that is, a barbed-wire enclosure where people are interned or incarcerated under armed guard."[21]

Historically speaking, we see that camps were called by different names before, during, and after World War I. Captive soldiers during World War I were likely to be put in a facility called a "POW camp" but could just as likely spend a significant part of their captivity in other internment facilities or in unguarded facilities—working and living in the countryside.[22] Civilian prisoners of various categories—enemy aliens, members of suspect nationalities, and political prisoners—could find themselves in "internment camps" but also in "POW camps," regardless of whether they contained actual soldiers. German and Austro-Hungarian inmates in the camp known as Knockaloe (Isle of Man)—one of the largest internment facilities in World War I, with a population of 23,000 prisoners—regularly referred to their camp as a "POW camp" (Ger. *Kriegsgefangenenlager*), a "civilian prisoners camp" (*Zivilgefangenenlager*), or simply a "prisoners camp" (*Gefangenenlager*). In other words, when contemporaries talked about "camps," they could mean different things, and the exact meaning of each term was not as precisely defined as later historiography assumed. There was good reason for this imprecision as internment regimes, legal rights, and camp layouts fluctuated and overlapped a great deal during the war.

Historians dealing with World War I internments have tended to examine camps within a legal framework, distinguishing three broad categories of internment: military, civilian, and political.

1. *Military prisoners*. The first and best-known category is relatively straightforward and deals with enemy soldiers captured by a belligerent

state during the war. Historically, armies have always waged war according to certain practices and norms.[23] These might have differed among cultures and epochs yet tended as a rule to include outright killing, enslavement, incarceration, release on parole, or unconditional release. The emergence of the European state system in modern times anchored a fundamental premise regarding the treatment of military prisoners, namely that they are in the power of the state whose army has captured them—and not in the possession of the individual or group to whom they had fallen.[24] The state bears responsibility for ensuring that POWs are treated according to accepted norms. The history of international legal thinking about the treatment of military POWs can be seen as the elaboration of this fundamental premise under changing historical circumstances. The Lieber Code of 1863 is often seen as a turning point in this regard.[25] Signed by President Lincoln in the midst of the American Civil War for the use of the Union forces, it defined the ways that soldiers should conduct themselves in battle. Among other things, the code forbade the killing or torturing of enemy prisoners and urged the humane, ethical treatment of populations in occupied areas.

The Lieber Code did little, however, to prevent occasional atrocious treatment.[26] During the entire American Civil War—the biggest conflict since the Napoleonic Wars and before World War I—no fewer than 674,045 soldiers fell prisoner. Tens of thousands of them died in captivity.[27] Prison camps were often horrific sites of death even after the code had been signed. In use during the final fourteen months of the American Civil War, Andersonville prison in Georgia, for example, was one of the most notorious POW camps. In this Confederate camp nearly 13,000 of approximately 45,000 Union prisoners perished, mostly due to scurvy, diarrhea, and dysentery.[28] Further attempts to codify the treatment of POWs in a multilateral treaty began in the latter part of the nineteenth century and continued with increased vigor during the first half of the twentieth century. These attempts drew from the two main traditions of international law: the Hague law, relating to the conduct of hostilities, and the Geneva law, dealing with the treatment of war victims.[29] The fact that the most important treaties relating to prisoners of war were signed in the Hague (1899, 1907) and in Geneva (1929, 1949) attests to the dual status of POWs as both neutralized combatants and potential victims. When historians discuss military prisoners, they usually mean captured combatants in a declared conflict.

2. *Civilian prisoners*. This second category usually refers to subjects of an enemy state who did not put on uniforms and who were never members of its military force. They could be males of a military age who would have been liable for enlistment had they been in their home countries, and who

were therefore considered a potential asset to the enemy or a security threat in their place of residence. The civilian internees held in Knockaloe, Ruhleben near Berlin, the "Black Monastery" on the Île de Noirmoutier in the French Vendée, and in hundreds of other locations throughout the world, including European colonies and dominions, belonged to this subgroup. "Civilian internees" could also mean enemy subjects who were not necessarily liable to be drafted by the enemy but who were perceived as useful workers by the detaining power, and who consequently became forced laborers. The French and Belgian forced laborers in Germany, some of whom were women, fall into this category. In recent years historians have begun paying increased attention to another type of "civilian" camp that emerged during World War I and its aftermath: the refugee camp. Although one might debate whether these refugee camps should be classified as "camps of containment" or full-fledged internment facilities, they nonetheless had the same liminal qualities of other civilian camps.[30]

3. *Political prisoners*. The third category often referred to subjects of the interning state itself, who were nonetheless suspected of aiding the enemy in one way or another or of refusing to support the war effort to the expected extent. As André Keil shows in his chapter in this volume, they either belonged to a recognizable organization that opposed or was inimical to the policies of its own government, as were, for example, the socialist Karl Liebknecht (1871–1919) of the Spartacus League or the nationalist Karel Kramář (1860–1937) of the Young Czech party. Political prisoners might also belong to a larger group labeled collectively as "suspect" in the eyes of the authorities without necessarily belonging to a specific organization (as, for example, were Italian and south Slav civilians in Austria-Hungary, Armenians in the Ottoman Empire or Alsatians and Poles in Germany). These people were often interned pursuant to emergency wartime legislation.

From a legal point of view, this division makes perfect sense. After all, each category of prisoner was subjected to a different legal (or extralegal) regime. Military prisoners were recognized combatants of a sovereign country whose treatment should have theoretically complied with the articles of the 1907 Hague Convention on the Laws and Customs of War on Land. Although the seventeen articles relating to POWs therein were far from perfect, they did envision a specific internment regime.[31] Civilian internees found themselves behind barbed wire without necessarily having committed any clear offense according to any existing legal category. Their threat was a potential one, deemed to be serious enough to require confinement. Civilians also found themselves interned for opportunistic reasons during the war because they lacked the legal and political protection of a state—as was the case with the hundreds of thousands of foreign laborers who toiled in Germany. These were vulnerable people whose treatment did not necessarily align with any preexisting legal regimes. In addition, there were political prisoners, some of whom had done something that contravened established laws. Others belonged to organizations that actively pursued goals viewed as contrary to those of the warring state and who were subjected to conventional forms of supervision, confinement, or incarceration. The rest belonged to a collectivity perceived as a political threat. These prisoners are usually covered by the national histories of each country or national group, and their histories are usually not discussed in the framework of the history of mass internment.

The Actual Experience of Prisoners and the Limitations of Existing Categories

While the analytical approach has generated excellent work, this volume demonstrates the great deal of overlap in the actual experience of internment undergone by the different categories. In reality, as Matthew Stibbe, Bohdan Kordan, and André Keil show in their respective chapters, many civilian and political internees experienced "militarized" internment during the war. On the other hand, military prisoners found their daily lives "civilianized" to such an extent that they occasionally had to explain to their families that they were actually prisoners. Moreover, and despite the fact that the legal frameworks influencing the life of prisoners were different and distinct, it is clear that in many cases the interning power used more than one framework vis-à-vis a particular group of prisoners to legitimate its actions. The following episode seems to illustrate this argument well.

On Thursday, November 19, 1914, a "disturbance" took place in the Aliens Detention Camp in Douglas on the Isle of Man.[32] At two in the afternoon, after the main meal of the day was served, the inmates refused to vacate the dining hall and began overturning tables and chairs. The prisoners' anger had been building in the weeks leading up to this incident. They protested the severe overcrowding in the camp, which, on the day of the incident, contained over 3,300 detainees, about eight hundred more than the stated maximum occupancy, which in itself was considerably higher than the maximum occupancy of the facility's former purpose—a camp for young working-class men advertised as "novel, delightful, economical and sociable"—and operated by a certain Mr. Cunningham dubbed "Schlauschinken" (a cunning ham) by the inmates.[33] The detainees also objected to the quantity and quality of the food, which was reportedly dirty and infested with insects. The guards, who feared losing control of the situation, opened fire, killing four prisoners in the dining hall itself, while a fifth inmate later died from his wounds in the hospital.

In investigating the incident to determine whether the shooting was justified, the appointed coroner of inquests summoned the camp commander, Colonel Madoc, a jury of residents of the Isle of Man, as well as a group of witnesses: detainees, guards, and doctors. One of the main issues under investigation was the legal status of the Alien Detention Camp, which had been established in September 1914 under the aegis of the Aliens Restriction Act, passed by the British government a month earlier. What, for example, were the criteria for determining whether the shooting and the killings were lawful? The internees were obviously not lawbreakers in a regular sense, as they had done nothing wrong except for being in the wrong place (i.e., under British control) at the wrong time (the commencement of hostilities). They were civilians interned in camps, but as such, did they have a right to protest overcrowding and bad food? They were all of military-service age but were not yet soldiers. Indeed, had they resided in their country of origin, they might have been conscripted to fight against Britain.

However, does their status as potential soldiers mean that they were governed by the Hague Convention of 1907? After all, this convention stipulated (in article 8) that "prisoners of war shall be subject to the laws, regulations, and orders in force in the army of the State in whose power they are. Any act of insubordination justifies the adoption towards them of such measures of severity as may be considered necessary." This view was corroborated by the coroner of inquests, who addressed the jury with the following statement:

> I may be right or I may be wrong, but in my opinion these aliens detained in the camp were prisoners of war, and as such were subject to the rules of the camp and subject to such military regulations as prescribed there. I know that the popular idea that a prisoner of war is a man who is captured from the enemy during military or naval operations. These men, as we know, were not so captured, but for the exigencies of wartime and the necessities of operations in times of war I am very much inclined to advise you that they are Prisoners of War.[34]

The jury concurred with this counsel and validated the legality of the shooting—something that the prisoners deeply resented. Consequently, the camp and the much larger Knockaloe Camp, which opened a few weeks later, were often referred to as "civilian POW camps" or "POW camps," alongside other designations such as "internment camps" (see figure I.1). This hybridity was by no means a coincidence. It emanated from the contradictory logic of regarding people as prisoners of war in a literal sense, i.e., they are prisoners because of the war, but only occasionally as "prisoners of war" in the sense envisioned by the Hague Convention. The Douglas incident was no exception during World War I.

The three categories of imprisonment often become blurred when examined from below. Thus, when we examine the question of labor we see that severe shortages in working hands led to the deployment of millions of prisoners in the economies of the belligerent states. The 1907 Hague Convention had authorized the use of rank-and-file labor "in tasks deemed to be not excessive and. . . [with] no connection with the operation of the war." It prohibited the forced labor of officers and called for remuneration based on the existing rates of working soldiers in the captor's army (allowing deductions for maintenance).

France and Germany began to employ POWs in their economy in winter of 1914–15 with Austria-Hungary, Russia, and finally Britain following suit within a year. POWs were to be found in agriculture, industry, transportation, and a plethora of different services, as well as in vast construction projects. "All of Europe's major belligerents," argued Richard Speed, "became heavily dependent on war prisoners to replace workers who had been sent to the front."[35] If a belligerent state could find additional sources for much needed labor, it would recruit individuals to their war economies, as was the

FIGURE I.1. Civilian POW Camp Knockaloe, Isle of Man, Britain (1917–19). Watercolor by prisoner George Kenner. Courtesy of Christa Bedford.

case with Polish, French, Belgian, and Russian civilians who were employed by the Central Powers, or with the Allied powers' use of Chinese laborers on the Western Front and the large number of Chinese laborers working in Russia. As noted by the historian Guoqi Xu, "Chinese workers came primarily under military management and were usually organized into military-type units commanded by officers. If they broke rules, they could be court-martialed and, in fact, at least ten Chinese laborers under British control were executed under military law during the war."[36]

Some prisoner laborers fared better and their lives resembled those of civilians. Austria-Hungary employed as many as half the prisoners on farms and in small enterprises, where they lived among the civilian population without being greatly restricted in their freedom of movement. As historians Verena Moritz and Julia Walleczek-Fritz have observed, this intermingling caused the military authorities to be very apprehensive "about fraternization between prisoners and people."[37] Consequently, a warning was issued to the civilian population in Upper Austria and published in the *Linzer Post* on December 22, 1915:

> In many instances, the civilian population has not respected the rules that are naturally demanded in contact between the local population and enemy prisoners of war, not from a patriotic sense of duty but particularly for morality and propriety. There have been many cases in which women and girls have been unmindful of nationality, race and family honor in interacting with POWs. For this reason, every interaction . . . between civilians and prisoners that is not necessary for the work relationship is forbidden. In particular, women and girls are warned not to enter into a love affair or to maintain forbidden contact.[38]

As a rule, prisoner-laborers had a greater chance to be integrated into the household and to interact with civilian men and women in smaller farms. In Russia, many prisoners who worked on farms and in agriculture developed meaningful relationships with the local peasants, and this also applied to some of those who were employed in other branches of the economy. The Austro-Hungarian censorship collected from letters the names of several thousand POWs who either married local women or intended to do so. Thus, for example, Julius Marxiser wrote the following from a camp near the city of Tomsk in Siberia in October 1917: "I would like to inform you that I married a Japanese woman here. I am doing well. I thought to myself, I am here already three years in captivity, why shouldn't I make my life more pleasant when I can? At home nobody really cares what happens here to the good soldiers, even the state takes care of no one."[39]

The life of many other working prisoners, military and civilian alike, hardly resembled the life of a working family member of a rural household but was reminiscent of that of a plantation hand, an exploited industrial laborer, or a penal-colony deportee. German and Austro-Hungarian POWs in France, for instance, worked in diverse locations such as locomotive and automotive factories, stone quarries, ports and quays. In August 1915, an inspection team found 618 prisoners living in tents and warehouses on the outskirts of Rouen, most of them employed as stevedores on barges and ships. They worked between forty-eight and fifty-four hours a week and, like most prisoners, received their wages as coupons that were only redeemable in camp canteens. This was the experience of no fewer than 500,000 Polish seasonal workers who were subjects of the Russian empire and happened to be in Germany when war broke out. They were invariably forbidden to return home, and many found themselves in barrack-style camps with their freedom of movement extremely limited. As Christoph Jahr and Jens Thiel have recently argued, the treatment of many of them was extremely bad: "As a rule, the civilians were held alongside military prisoners of 'other rank' (i.e., in so-called *Mannschaftlager* [enlisted men camps])."[40] Traunstein Camp in southeastern Bavaria, for example, included both enemy aliens and internal political prisoners of imperial Germany among its inmates. As Jahr and Thiel observe, "The boundaries between 'inner' and 'outer' enemies became blurred during the war."[41]

The worst conditions of any working environment during the Great War prevailed along the Murman railway line which connected the Petrograd region with the ice-free port of Murmansk. Traversing Karelia and the Kola Peninsula, the Murman railway became a top priority of the Russian army at the beginning of the war when the routes across the Baltic and Black Seas were cut off by the Central Powers. To expedite the construction of the railway, the Russian government sent an estimated seventy thousand prisoners of war to reinforce the existing workforce between July 1915 and October 1916. Although funds had been allocated by the Russian government for housing, maintenance, and clothing, most of the money was embezzled by the guards and engineers. Thus, the laboring prisoners had no proper accommodations and often slept in branch huts or even on the bare ground. The great distances along the line (over 950 miles) and its limited accessibility meant that fresh food reached the prisoners only rarely. The combination of hard labor in extremely difficult conditions led to many deaths among the POWs: Elsa Brändström estimated that twenty-five thousand POWs died on the Murman railway, while the official Russian figures confirmed a mere 379 deaths. Historian Reinhard Nachtigal, who published the most detailed monograph on the subject, found Brändström's account more plausible, calling the project "the epitome of the horror of captivity."[42]

Another type of internment that emerged during the war functioned as a self-managing homosocial town. This type, which Manz and Panayi have referred to as "humane" internment, was not always characterized by its "humaneness" (a vague term in any case).[43] This model was most prevalent among interned officers, who were exempted from compulsory work and among civilian internees. Because interned officers received pay from the captor state on the same level as officers in the captor army and because civilian internees in many camps were allowed access to their prewar funds, everyday life inside these camps had the rich quality of an active urban community with theaters, sporting teams, gardens, workshops, and a very clear sense of domesticity within barracks. Knockaloe had twenty-eight different theatres that operated between 1914 and 1919, and that offered no fewer than four hundred different productions in German, as well as plays in French, English, Spanish, Turkish, and Italian. Prisoner theaters (*Plennytheater*) in the German language existed in forty-six different officer camps, some with ensembles of more than a hundred actors and musicians, employing dozens of carpenters, electricians, and stagehands. Prisoners bought season tickets, dined at an adjacent restaurant, wrote reviews, and argued about which internee best portrayed the female roles.[44]

At least 150,000 prisoners lived in such an environment. Their level of integration into the captor society was significantly lower than that of working prisoners. The prisoners had control over their daily schedule and were busy with camp life. J. Davidson Ketchum, a civilian internee at the camp of Ruhleben (near Berlin), and later a professor of psychology at the University of Toronto, wrote that "the men created for themselves a unique social world so complete and many-sided that its existence in a prison camp is almost unbelievable."[45] For these prisoners the internment camp possessed a liminal quality where time itself appeared to stop. Their pasts and previous lives seemed distant and inaccessible while their futures seemed uncertain. Paul Cohen-Portheim, called his captivity memoirs *Time Stood Still* and thought this sense of "uncertainty made all plans and movements in any direction appear senseless."[46] His homecoming to Berlin at the end of the war was a shock:

> I found that a new adaptation was demanded from me, that it was quite impossible to slip back to where I stood before my internment. Not only were all the outside circumstances changed, but I myself was no longer the same man. . . . What had followed was not a return to

> the existence formerly familiar to me, or to anything like my pre-war life. . . . It was impossible for me to slip back to where I stood before my internment. It was my return from war to peace; it seemed more like a return from peace to war.[47]

The Globalization of Great War Internments

World War I was also the first global war in terms of its internments. Although the armed conflict was largely confined to the European continent and its periphery, the identity of the interned and the locations of their internment extended far beyond Europe. The globalization of different kinds of internment and the impact on unifying the standards of captivity were novel features. Thereafter, captivity in wars and armed conflicts would never be the same. Indeed, this form of globalization exerted far-reaching repercussions on the way that military, civil, and political internments would be interpreted in the interwar period; it would eventually determine the use, misuse and, regretfully, the abuse of internments in all subsequent wars, especially in World War II.

The war can be seen as a watershed in the globalization of international law. The internment of a huge number of prisoners of all sorts within Europe and beyond prompted the implementation of the rules, norms, and standards that had been ratified by all major belligerents a few years earlier. Indeed, it was only shortly before the war that these standards were conceived during the Hague Conventions of 1899 and 1907, which specified the treatment of prisoners of war, both combatants and noncombatants.[48] These conventions laid the foundations for the global humanitarian treatment of internees, regardless of their category. As early as 1904–1905, both Japan and Russia tended to follow the stipulation of the Hague Convention of 1899 in their nineteen-month conflict, treating each other's prisoners decently, but this conflict was far from global.[49] In 1914, however, the existence of a body of rules, together with the unprecedented dimensions of the conflict, the number of prisoners, and the fears of reciprocity acted as a catalyst for the greater spread, both within Europe and beyond, of the norms of international law and the standardization of the humanitarian treatment of internees. This globalization notwithstanding, compliance with these rules and evolving norms was not necessarily uniform or strict, as several chapters in this volume demonstrate.

As Nancy Fitch, Hazuki Tate, Naoko Shimazu, and Mahon Murphy discuss in their respective chapters, the multiethnic and racial character of the interned is one of the most salient features of the globalization of the Great War. The participants in this war not only included soldiers from every corner of Europe—Russians, Turks, Britons, Germans, and French, to mention only a few of the major groups—but also many non-Europeans. Some of these were of European ancestry (e.g., most of the American, Canadian, Australian, New Zealander, and South African soldiers), but many were not.[50] Among the belligerents the Allied powers made extensive use of the subjects of their colonies and empires. France, for example, mobilized its North African and sub-Saharan subjects; Britain deployed a large number of subcontinental Indians, and tsarist Russia called soldiers from its Far East and Muslim districts.[51] Alongside these non-European combatants, the Allies also recruited some 140,000 Chinese workers who served on the Western Front.[52]

By the end of the war, the Allies employed over 300,000 non-European workers, including the Chinese, along with some 100,000 Egyptians, 21,000 Indians, 20,000 native South Africans, and others.[53] The presence of these soldiers and civilians among the prisoners of World War I has recently received scholarly attention, but there is still need for a detailed examination of the attitudes toward them and the impact on stereotypes and prejudice.[54] At the same time, the presence of prisoners of so many nationalities and ethnicities in the conflict, let alone the number of non-Europeans among them, does not mean that the conflict became a race war—certainly not to the extent that World War II would become. Despite the existence of a steep global hierarchy based on race, the Great War can be seen as nothing but a prelude to the horrors of the subsequent global conflict more than two decades later. More specifically, and apart from the Armenian genocide that took place in 1915–1917, World War I did not witness the mass killing or extreme abuse of internees because of race or ethnicity in the manner that so characterized their treatment by some belligerents in both the European and the Asiatic-Pacific theaters of World War II.

The wide geographical spread of internment locations is another remarkable feature of the Great War's globalization. Since the war was not limited to Europe alone, both combatants and civilians captured in other continents were rarely brought back to core conflict zones. In fact, the opposite was more common. In many cases soldiers captured and civilians arrested in Europe were transferred to camps in other continents. In Britain, for example, enemy residents (e.g., Germans, Austro-Hungarians, Turks, and Bulgarians) who had settled in the home islands or in overseas territories were often interned on the grounds of being a potential danger. Some were incarcerated in Britain, but others were sent as far as South Africa and India.[55] Non-European members of the Allied powers also participated in the endeavor to keep enemy residents behind bars. In this respect, the United States, Canada, Australia, and New Zealand invariably interned enemy citizens during the war.[56] Combatants also spent their captivity far from their home countries. German and Austrian soldiers, for example, were interned in Japan, as discussed in Naoko Shimazu's chapter.[57] This geographical range is a testimony to how ubiquitous and truly global World War I internment was, but very little research has delved into its deeper meaning. For instance, what was the impact on the formation of global norms for the treatment of prisoners of war and civilian internees? What was the effect on postwar attempts to institute such norms? What was the impact on European racial prejudice on one hand, and on anticolonial movements on the other hand?

Determinants of Treatment during Internment

The status of prisoners of war and other internees in modern conflicts has been uncertain. As Matthew Stibbe discusses in his chapter, this uncertainty arises from the interplay of various factors: the official adherence to international conventions by the state and its functionaries; the specific circumstances of becoming a prisoner; economic considerations and a myriad of local and regional considerations that may tilt treatment one way or another. As a violent site of action where the struggle for life and death may overcome any norms and etiquette, wars do not offer the ideal setting for protecting human lives. This war zone predicament is evident in the first moments after soldiers surrender, when their captors face the age-old dilemma of whether to kill their prisoners or spare their lives.[58] Despite the emergence of various humanitarian conventions before World War I, the motivation to kill surrendered enemy personnel, or to abuse them at a later stage to the point of death, did not vanish. If any, this "total war" demonstrated that the motivation to eliminate prisoners remained strong. After all, eliminating prisoners undermines the long-term war potential of the enemy and allows captors to avoid allocating manpower to guard them and resources to accommodate and feed them. Moreover, killing prisoners deliberately or letting them die by other means affects the enemy's fighting spirit and satisfies the need for revenge.

Nonetheless, the fact that millions of POWs and internees survived captivity in World War I suggests that there are also strong motives for sparing the lives of surrendered enemy soldiers and captured civilians. Sparing their lives helps to maintain the image of a civilized and moral nation and denies ammunition for enemy propaganda, limiting both foreign and internal criticism. POWs can also be used as forced labor for assisting the captor's war effort (which is more relevant to "total wars" and extended conflicts), especially in such strategic domains as mining and agriculture. In addition, sparing the lives of POWs may expedite a belligerent's victory. Niall Ferguson, for example, has argued that the surrender rate, rather than the mortality rate, of enemy soldiers was a primary determinant of defeat in the Great War, since sparing surrendered soldiers encouraged the surrender of their fellow soldiers.[59] Finally, holding POWs may provide leverage in wartime negotiations and in postwar negotiations, especially when the other side is sensitive to their fate.

This optimistic view of the Great War notwithstanding, the captives in this conflict were not meted the same treatment with evident outcomes. Indeed, in some states, and in a number of notable camps in particular, internment conditions were relatively good and mortality rates low, whereas in other states—and in certain notorious camps, such as Totskoe in Russia or Nézsider in Austria-Hungary—conditions were extremely harsh and mortality rates atrociously high. By and large, these differences were not fortuitous but rather reflected disparate national agendas, economic capacities, attitudes to specific national and ethnic groups, and positions within the conflict. Although no study has examined the quantitative data and qualitative evidence for differential treatment during the entire war, some have probed the motivation for specific treatment and its outcomes in a single front, or have examined certain aspects of it.[60] Based on these studies, a preliminary analysis of internment during this war suggests that there were still conflicting motivations relating to whether prisoners should be treated well or abused, even when enemy prisoners were spared.

The most prominent of these motivations was probably associated with economic capacity and needs. As Lena Radauer discusses in her chapter, ideological motives, at least in this conflict, were marginal for the most part. Mistreatment was often the result of a shortage or a desire to prevent a shortage of food supplies, guard manpower, and medical supplies. Cruelty, on the other hand, was based on the premise of deterring POWs from insubordination and thereby saving manpower. That said, there were also several motives for treating POWs well. First and foremost, good treatment ensured reciprocity and increased the survival rate of the captors' own POWs held by the enemy. Treating POWs well also helped to maintain order and decreased the need for a great deal of manpower to guard them. Certain aspects of the treatment remain unclear. For example, was there any difference in the treatment meted to civilian and combatant internees? Did the changing status of the internees (from internees to prisoners and vice versa) lead to a change in their treatment? Was there a gender difference in the treatment? Were there certain prewar professions that provided their holders with an advantage? And were there any broad national patterns of internment that characterized this conflict?

Main Questions and Lines of Investigation

Altogether, the narrative offered by this book is bound by a number of novel observations and perspectives on several aspects of World War I internment. The eleven thematic chapters seek, individually and collectively, to elaborate upon the following lines of investigation:

1. *Categories of internment.* The conventional categories that distinguish between military, civilian, and political internments do not offer a sufficiently nuanced description of the complexity found in World War I. We propose that these ostensibly different forms of internment were fluid and at times even overlapping. For this reason, a comprehensive analysis of internment during World War I requires us not only not to steer clear of these a priori distinctions but rather try to examine them together in order to discover broad trends and reactions that transcend, for example, nationality, specific groups of prisoners, and locations of internment. Furthermore, as Neville Wylie and Sarina Landefeld discuss in their chapter, this insight was clearly understood at the time, evidenced by the fact that postwar jurists and officials proposed constructing a single legal framework capable of meeting the interests of military prisoners, enemy aliens, and internally displaced refugees

2. *The global dimension of internment.* The wartime global mass internment should not be seen as merely a geographical phenomenon but rather a political, social, and legal event with far-reaching repercussions. It affected the increasing standardization of norms of internment during the war and the endeavors to form universal norms of internment, but it also amplified racial stereotypes, prejudice, and ethnic strife. This transformation of racial stereotypes occurred both within Europe and far beyond. On the one hand, exposure to colonial prisoners in Europe and their use of anti-enemy propaganda was a source of augmented racism. On the other hand, exposure to European prisoners and internees in the colonial world was another testimony to their vulnerability and a stimulus for future liberation.

3. *The determinants of treatment during internment.* As this volume will show, internees were not treated equally during World War I, either on individual and collective levels, or with respect to combatants and civilians. This is attested to subjectively by countless memoirs as well as in unequivocal statistics, such as the highly divergent mortality rates for different groups. In

attempting to explain this observed differential treatment, we assume that several determinants played a significant role, often while interacting with each other. These determinants include the identity of the captors and their military and moral legacy of treatment; the identity of the captive's nation and its image; the point in time at which the captives were interned; and the reciprocal relations between the two belligerents.

4. *Internment and the end of the war.* Although the war ended officially in November 1918, the internment, and thus the actual "war" experience of many internees, ended much later. In essence, we assume that the greater a war is—in terms of manpower, the number of captives, and the geographical spread of internment—the wider the gap between the official date on which the war ends and the actual denouement of the internees' plight, regardless of their civil status. Large-scale wars are also bound to generate local conflicts and minor wars that do not necessarily terminate once the main conflict ends. These impediments tend to sustain internment or at least to hamper repatriation. In this sense, World War I may serve as the quintessential example of this gap.

5. *Impact on future treatments.* The unique features and unprecedented scale of internment during World War I influenced the entire concept of wartime internment throughout the twentieth century. More specifically, the mass internment of combatants, civilians, and political prisoners; the deterioration of distinction between these categories; and the ubiquitous presence of prisoners throughout the globe required the institution of a new and widely accepted standard of treatment for prisoners and facilitated the emergence of new conventions on their behalf.

Notes

1. See, e.g., Mackenzie 1994; Rachamimov 2012b; Polian 2005; Wachsmann 2015; Kashima 2003.
2. See, e.g., Davis 1983; Speed, 1990; Rachamimov 2002; Leidinger and Moritz 2003; Hinz 2006; Nachtigal 2003; Vance 2006; Stibbe 2008b; Jones, H. 2011a; Murphy 2017; Manz, Panayi, and Stibbe 2019.
3. Vischer 1919.
4. Rachamimov 2002; Moritz and Walleczek-Fritz 2017.
5. Rachamimov 2002, 38. There is a vast literature on the Great War and its chronology. For recent overviews, see Strachan 2001; Sondhaus 2011.
6. Keegan 1998, 8.
7. Bicheno 2004.
8. Gatrell 2013.
9. Douglas 1966, 47.
10. Cohen-Portheim 1932, 12.

11. Cohen-Portheim 1932, 15.
12. See note 2 in this chapter.
13. Stibbe 2006, 5; Stibbe 2008b.
14. Manz, Panayi, and Stibbe 2019.
15. Forth 2016; Hyslop 2011; Pitzer 2017; Madley 2005.
16. National Records of Scotland file HH31–10–20.
17. National Records of Scotland file HH31–10–20.
18. Applebaum 2003, 8–9.
19. Wachsmann 2015, 33.
20. Kashima 2003, 16.
21. Kashima 2003, 8.
22. Rachamimov 2002.
23. See, e.g., Best 1994, 16; Levie 1978; Beaumont 1983, 1996; Roberts 1994; Reisman and Antoniu 1994; Vance 2006.
24. Levie, 1978, 5.
25. See Kramer, Arnold 2008, 88–96.
26. For the treatment of POWs during the American Civil War, see Pickenpaugh 2009; Springer and Robins 2015; Kutzler 2019; Schlotterbeck et al. 2019; Silkenat 2019.
27. Among the prisoners, some 264,437 (39.2 percent) were paroled in the field, and among the remaining at least 56,194 (13.7 percent) died in captivity. See Rhodes 1904, 507–8.
28. For an eyewitness testimony of the conditions in this camp, see Kellogg 1867, 56.
29. The harbinger of these multilateral humanitarian treaties was the First Geneva Convention. Signed on August 22, 1864, by representatives of twelve European states, it focused on "the Amelioration of the Condition of the Wounded in Armies in the Field." This convention was replaced by the more detailed Geneva Convention on Wounded and Sick, 1906. For the two conventions, see the International Committee of the Red Cross: Treaties, States Parties and Commentaries, https://ihl- https://ihl-databases.icrc.org/applic/ihl/ihl.nsf/vwTreatiesHistoricalByDate.xsp. Prior to World War I the Hague Convention of 1899 had been associated with the relatively benevolent treatment of POWs during the Russo-Japanese War of 1904–1905. See Kowner 2008, 48, and Naoko Shimazu's chapter in this volume.
30. McConnachie 2016, 1–4.
31. Howard, Andreopolous, and Shulman 1994; Best 1994; Levie 1978; Rachamimov 2002; Jones, H. 2011a; Rachamimov 2012b.
32. *Disturbance at the Aliens Detention Camp: Official Report* 1914; Fyson 2000.
33. Creswell 2010.
34. *Disturbance at the Aliens Detention Camp: Official Report* 1914, 5.
35. Speed 1990, 103.
36. Xu 2014, 2–3.
37. Moritz and Walleczek-Fritz 2017, 3; Walleczek-Fritz 2017, 273–74.
38. Cited in Walleczek-Fritz 2017, 273.
39. Rachamimov 2002, 151.
40. Jahr and Thiel 2019, 43.

41. Jahr and Thiel 2019, 47.

42. Nachtigal 2001.

43. Manz and Panayi 2020, 32.

44. Rachamimov 2006.

45. Ketchum 1965, 3.

46. Cohen-Portheim 1936, 98.

47. Cohen-Portheim 1936, 214, 235.

48. For the text of the two Hague Conventions, see Avalon Project at Yale Law School on the Laws of War, https://avalon.law.yale.edu/subject_menus/lawwar.asp.

49. See Kowner 2000, 2001; Naoko Shimazu's chapter in this volume.

50. See, e.g., Pegram 2020.

51. See, e.g., Levine 1998; Omissi 1999; Zehfuss 2005; Thilmans 2012; Van Galen Last, Futselaar, and de Jager 2016; Cardozo 2019.

52. See, e.g., Zhong 2017; Dornel 2018; Black 2019.

53. See, e.g., Vu-Hill 2011.

54. See, e.g., Caglioti 2018.

55. Panayi 1993b; Manz and Panayi 2020. Cf. Murphy 2017.

56. Nagler 2018; Barkhof 2018; Semchuk and Budney 2018; Monteath 2018.

57. See, e.g., Kowner 2009; Kordan 2018.

58. See, e.g., Crawford 2010; Roberts 2011; Scheipers 2011.

59. Ferguson 2004.

60. See, e.g., Davis 1983; Rachamimov 2002; Cook 2006; Spoerer 2006; Jones, H. 2011a.

Part I

Internments in Europe

Chapter 1

(Dis)entangling the Local, the National, and the International

Civilian Internment in Germany and in German-Occupied France and Belgium in Global Context

Matthew Stibbe

Since the 1990s, an increasing body of scholarly work has addressed the complex issue of civilian internment during World War I in different local, national, regional, and imperial settings.[1] Scholars are also beginning to explore the interconnected and global nature of this phenomenon[2] and its links to a broader "dynamic of destruction" incorporating economic blockades, forced migration, violence against enemy soldiers and prisoners of war, the use of gas, air, and submarine attacks, the deliberate targeting of cultural treasures by invading armies, and the 1915 Turkish genocide against the Ottoman Armenians.[3] Yet there are still some important gaps in our understanding of particular camp systems, including, as Uta Hinz noted in 2003, in the case of imperial Germany, where the exact motives for the internment of more than 100,000 enemy civilians over the course of the war, most of them French and Belgian nationals, remain obscure and unexplained.[4] This is even more surprising given the prominent place of internment in the propaganda war between Germany and its enemies during the years 1914 to 1918.[5]

Previous literature has dwelt on three aspects of the internment question. First it has been interpreted as a means by which nation-states sought to monitor and persecute alien minorities in wartime. The lead here was taken by France and Britain, which were the first states in 1914 to implement measures against enemy citizens living in their midst, including expropriations, expulsions, and incarceration. Similar ordinances were also introduced in their respective colonies and dominions, as well as in German overseas territories in Africa and the Pacific overrun by Allied troops in the opening months of the conflict.[6] Second, the development of internment into a worldwide phenomenon during the war has been attributed to two main factors, retaliatory measures introduced by Germany and Austria-Hungary in autumn 1914 affecting British and French nationals living there, and the decision made by countries that subsequently joined the Allied camp—including Italy in 1915, Portugal and its Atlantic and African possessions in 1916, the United States, Panama, and Brazil in 1917, and Siam and Haiti in 1918—to follow the Anglo-French example when it came to the treatment of enemy aliens, albeit with certain local variations.[7] Finally, things came full circle when France and Britain took the lead again in permanently expelling former German and Habsburg internees in 1919–20, including from their overseas colonies and dominions, a process that went hand in hand with French *épuration* (purification) measures in the "regained" border provinces of Alsace and Lorraine.[8]

This metaview of civilian captivity in World War I is not necessarily unique. In fact, it is very close to the narrative put forward by the German Reichstag's Committee of Investigation into the causes and consequences of the war in its final report, published in 1927, which held Britain and France responsible for instigating mass internment in 1914 and portrayed German measures as purely reactive.[9] It also explains the focus on Ruhleben, the camp near Berlin used by the German authorities to house British civilian internees during the war, in subsequent historiography.[10] Over and over again, the German Foreign Office made clear that the Reich was holding these prisoners in retaliation for the alleged mistreatment of German nationals in Britain and the British empire, and that they were in effect bargaining counters. In November 1916 Johannes Kriege (1859–1937), the head of the Foreign Office's legal department, even offered an "all for all" exchange of civilian prisoners between Germany and Britain in a speech in the Reichstag, a proposal that was subsequently rejected by the Imperial War Cabinet in London.[11]

However, while Ruhleben makes a very good case study for understanding the experience of World War I captivity, not least as its inmates left behind so many written sources, it was not at all typical of internment camps in Germany.[12] Its proximity to the German capital, the comparatively low turnover of prisoners, and the protection from abuse offered by the fact that Britain and its overseas colonies and dominions held up to ten times as many Germans, meant that this camp developed a remarkably rich cultural life, with sports, theater, educational courses, and a range of other "national" pursuits marking it out as the site of a particularly vibrant "community at war."[13] Above all, though, Ruhleben stood out because its inmates were relatively well fed, even in 1917–18, and were not required, at any stage in the war, to perform forced labor. This placed it at the positive end of a long continuum of different types of camp and camp experience.

More to the point, the four to five thousand British internees held here represented only a tiny fraction of the total number of civilian prisoners in Germany and German-occupied parts of Europe during the war. According to John Horne and Alan Kramer, for instance, at least ten thousand French civilians and thirteen thousand Belgians had already been deported from occupied regions to camps in Germany by the end of 1914.[14] The numbers increased significantly in 1915 and continued to rise thereafter, not least as enemy civilians were now also being deported from conquered territories in the east—from the Government-General in Warsaw and the area known as Ober Ost.[15] France and Belgium nonetheless remained the principal source of internees. In most cases deportation orders appear to have come from military commanders on the ground, with little coordination between the districts assigned to particular armies in the areas behind the front line. The International Committee of the Red Cross (ICRC), in a report published in October 1918, painted a picture of mounting chaos, with no central authority in charge of German internment policy, no evidence of rational planning, little concern to ensure compliance with international conventions or preexisting customs of war, and a complete breakdown in accurate record keeping:

> Some civilian detainees in Germany appear to have been transferred to prisons in Belgium and occupied France, where they can neither communicate with their families in unoccupied France, nor receive aid parcels, nor have visits from representatives of the neutral powers charged with their protection. We regret that up till now it has proved impossible to obtain any kind of information on the conditions those prisoners are being held in.[16]

Using a variety of sources, including the files of the legal department of the German Foreign Office in Berlin, Red Cross publications, and military records held in the Bavarian War Archive in Munich, this chapter will look at the motivations for internment and deportation of civilians from German-occupied northern France and Belgium as a specific case study. A central argument will be that if we want to understand German internment practices, and why they differed in particular contexts, we have to look beyond internment itself as simply being shaped by the requirements of "grand strategy" (Ger. *große Politik*), state-directed labor, and migratory policies or the subjective need to respond in kind to the worldwide internment of German civilians by Allied countries. Rather, the views of military commanders operating in the occupied rear areas, and their assessment of the changing material, psychological, and security interests of their troops, were also significant determinants. The concluding section will address some of the conceptual implications of these findings for writing the history of World War I captivity specifically as global history. First, though, it will be necessary to offer a general overview of German attitudes towards French civilians in the invaded territories.

German Internment Policies in Occupied France and Belgium

German internment and deportation policies in occupied northern France and that part of Belgium subject to direct military rule were determined to some extent by the administrative structures set up by the German army in the field. Once the initial fighting had ended, a distinction was made between the immediate front-line area (Ger. *Operationsgebiet*), from which almost all French and Belgian civilians were compulsorily evacuated, and the rear area (Ger. *Etappengebiet*, Fr. *étape*), which was divided into six separate districts (*Etappen*) of different size and population density, corresponding to the six German armies operating on the Western Front. Each district was ruled by a rear-area inspectorate (*Etappeninspektion*) and a series of rear-area commanders (*Etappenkommandanten*), who were responsible for labor procurement, policing local communities, and ensuring the security of the occupation troops. The *Etappeninspektionen* in turn were answerable to the army supreme command, the *Oberste Heeresleitung* (OHL).[17]

The initial wave of deportations, from September to December 1914, was, as Horne and Kramer rightly note, carried out as a "localized response" to a variety of imagined threats, including fear of spies and irregular fighters (Ger. *Franktireurs*; Fr. *franc-tireurs*) and a perceived need to deter or punish would-be resistance by taking hostages. Since women, children, and men above military age were included among the ten thousand French civilians and the thirteen thousand Belgians sent to camps in Germany at this time, the rounding-up of men capable of bearing arms cannot be regarded as the only motive, although it certainly played a part.[18] Meanwhile, a similarly confused mixture of concerns was behind the parallel deportation of domestic political suspects from Alsace and Lorraine by the harsh new military regime imposed on these border provinces from the beginning of the war. As many as four hundred German nationals—mostly political leaders, lawyers, and journalists suspected of pro-French sentiments—were expelled from Lorraine alone, with some held in internment camps and others subjected to forced residency (Ger. *Zwangsaufenthalt*) in the German interior.[19] Members of the Roma and Sinti communities were likewise forcibly removed, first from the fortress area around Strasbourg and then from the whole of Alsace-Lorraine; some of them subsequently ended up in Baden, Bavaria, and other parts of western and southern Germany, where they soon became a target for local prejudice and persecution.[20]

In the meantime, as far as these initial deportations are concerned, there is little evidence of a coordinated policy directed from the top. The German Foreign Office intervened only when it discovered that Swiss nationals were also being expelled from Upper Alsace, fearing that this could harm relations with an important neutral state.[21] Otherwise, it preferred not to know about the actions of German military commanders in occupied France and the Belgian étape, particularly as the Reich authorities at this point were attempting to draw international attention to atrocities committed by Russian troops in East Prussia in 1914–15, when some thirteen thousand German civilians, including women and children, were rounded up and expelled into the interior of the tsarist empire.[22] Similarly, the decision to intern all British males of military age resident in Germany and German-occupied territory on November 6, 1914, was officially presented in the German press as a legitimate act of retaliation for the internment or mistreatment of Germans living in Britain and its colonies.[23] The German Foreign Office, then, had good reason not to involve itself directly in these early deportations of hostages and "suspect" civilians from France, Alsace-Lorraine, and Belgium, even if it knew something about them from Swiss and other sources.[24]

The Prussian War Ministry in Berlin, and its Bavarian counterpart in Munich, were even less inclined to reveal details about civilian deportees being held in camps on the German home front. As early as December 1914, the chairman of the Central Committee of German Red Cross Associations, which in October 1914 had been designated as the central inquiry office (*Zentral-Nachweise-Bureau*) for POWs in Germany, wrote to the Prussian War Ministry to protest about the "inadequate" nature of its lists of civilian prisoners, noting that it had received complaints from the ICRC on this score.[25] Even when the lists began to improve after March 1915, the age, gender, and nationality of the internees were still (deliberately?) omitted, although nationality (as well as rank and number) were included for military prisoners. Drawing attention to the fact that the German field armies in France and Belgium were deporting women, children, and elderly men, as well as civilian males of draft age, to camps in the interior, was something that the German military authorities wished to avoid. In line with this, the *Unterkunftsdepartement*, the section of the War Ministry that was responsible for compiling the lists, did not even seek to define the term "civilian prisoner" until April 1916. According to a circular issued by Colonel (later General) Emil Friedrich, the head of the *Unterkunftsdepartement*, to senior military commanders, the war ministries of Bavaria, Saxony, and Württemberg, and the heads of various branches of the civilian government, "Zivilgefangene" were "enemy civilians . . . who were not serving in a hostile army when the war broke out and have not enlisted since, but who have nonetheless been placed in a German prisoner-of-war camp—regardless of whether they are still of arms-bearing age and whether they have been found to be permanently unfit for active service or not." Even then, he was at pains to stress that this definition was provisional and not a "definitive answer to what is essentially a question of international law."[26]

In fact, rather than the War Ministry, it was the rear-area commanders in northern France and Belgium who first cultivated a more sophisticated knowledge of the legal aspects of civilian internment and deportation. Imperial Germany's military leaders, both before and after 1914, were strong advocates of a concept of wartime occupation, partly enshrined in the Hague Conventions of 1899 and 1907, that made civilian resistance illegal and put the onus on local inhabitants to buckle down and accept the authority of the hostile army.[27] In 1914–15 this assumption was made easier by the American decision to feed the population of occupied Belgium and France in a scheme organized by the businessman and future US president Herbert Hoover. As far as the German military were concerned, this meant that there could be no legitimate reasons for hunger protests.[28] Occupied civilians accused of harming the German army's combat readiness, spying, hiding weapons, inciting public disorder, stealing from military stores, or assisting Allied soldiers on the run could be tried and sentenced to death or long periods in prison by special military courts, as were indeed hundreds of French and Belgian men and women. Otherwise, in meeting its legal obligation to "ensure, as far as possible, public order and safety," Germany military rule would respect the "laws in force in the country" prior to the occupation, as stipulated under article 43 of the 1907 Hague Convention on the Laws and Customs of War on Land (*Haager Landkriegsordnung*, HLKO).[29]

Very quickly, though, a new problem arose. Under article 52 of the HLKO, occupied populations could be required to contribute to the day-to-day functioning of municipalities, for instance through the maintenance of roads, buildings, and public utilities, provided that they were not forced to take part in "military operations against their own country" and were paid at customary local rates.[30] But what happened if they refused? Could this be punished as an (unlawful) form of resistance? As time went on, the rear-area commanders and field police were faced with more and more cases of "work refusal" (Ger. *Arbeitsverweigerung*), and they looked for guidance from the rear-area inspectorates on how to react.[31] For the latter, as Philippe Nivet puts it, "the security of the occupation troops and respect for order" were a "constant concern."[32] Recognition of patriotism as a legitimate motive for "work refusal" was off the cards, because it did not fit with the German military's cultural conception of how occupied civilians should behave. Yet ignoring the problem was also not an option, given the increasing labor shortages in the occupied zones, and the supposed damage done to the morale of the occupation troops themselves, and even ordinary Germans on the home front, when faced with "recalcitrant" and "work-shy" French and Belgian civilians.[33]

Instead, three different solutions presented themselves. First, some of those who had been deported to Germany in the early phase of the war might be brought back to occupied France or the field army zones of Belgium, on the understanding that they would work, and that refusal to work might result in their being deported (and thus separated from their families) again. In this way persons who were increasingly described in radicalized language as "useless eaters" (Ger. *unnütze Esser*)—as they had to be fed in camps in Germany, and yet did not contribute to the domestic war economy—might be made to earn their own keep.[34] In the district administered by the Sixth Army, individual rear-area commanders were given responsibility from December 1915 for making requests for specific individuals to be returned. The ability to bear arms was not considered a barrier to release, but those originally deported because they were suspected of spying or because they had "made a social nuisance of themselves" (Ger. *sich lästig gemacht haben*), for instance through petty criminality, drunkenness, or unregulated prostitution, were to remain in captivity.[35]

How many were discharged from camps in Germany is difficult to determine, given the loss of the relevant Prussian military records during Allied bombing raids on Potsdam in early 1945, but individual case files in the Bavarian War Archive certainly indicate that a considerable number were returned.[36] Later in the war those released and sent home might be required to sign work contracts with the German army. The commander of the third Bavarian army corps (attached to the Sixth Army) even had an answer to those Frenchmen who refused to sign such contracts out of fear that they might be labeled as "traitors" to France and called to account after the war. According to a suggestion he circulated to other corps commanders, they might be issued with a written affidavit testifying that "the work was performed against their wishes on the orders of the occupation authorities."[37] On the other hand, as the commander of the second Bavarian army corps also made clear in March 1917, "those unfit for work can only be permitted to return to the occupied zone in exceptional circumstances."[38]

A second solution to the problem of labor shortages and *Arbeitsverweigerung* in the *Etappengebieten* of occupied France and Belgium was the use of direct force. As Annette Becker has shown, this happened for the first time on a grand scale at Easter 1916, when roughly twenty thousand women and teenage girls from the French industrial towns of Lille, Roubaix, and Tourcoing, many of middle-class background, were rounded up on the orders of the Sixth Army's rear inspectorate and transported to rural areas, where they were put to temporary work on agricultural projects. These deportations were accompanied by compulsory gynecological examinations in an attempt to undermine the victims' class and gender identities (by treating them like prostitutes and dehumanized "objects" available to be used at any time for military ends).[39]

Worse was to follow in October 1916, when, coinciding with the appointment of Paul von Hindenburg and Erich Ludendorff to the third OHL, a series of forced labor battalions (*Zivil-Arbeiter-Bataillone* or ZABs), twenty-five in total by spring 1918, each composed of four companies of five hundred workers, were set up in occupied France and in the Belgian étape. The targets this time were unemployed but able-bodied men of various nationalities, who were moved around in gangs to work on infrastructure, agricultural, or forestry projects and were sometimes deployed directly behind the front lines, within the range of Allied gunfire.[40] The men were paid, but unlike "free" laborers, they were forced to wear special colored brassards, were not permitted leave to visit their families other than in "exceptional" circumstances, and were under armed guard twenty-four hours a day.[41]

Third, from 1917 enemy civilians held in internment camps in Germany might be directly transferred to the ZABs operating with the field armies in northern France and Belgium, either immediately upon their release or after they refused to sign work contracts following their return home. Now the impetus came from the OHL itself, which took over and centralized what had previously been a more localized effort and in so doing also adopted and rendered acceptable a radicalized language when talking about civilian prisoners. On February 24, 1917, for instance, the Prussian War Ministry in Berlin received a telegram from the Quartermaster General, Ludendorff, which read:

> In order to relieve prison camps on the home front of the burden of useless eaters and to provide a new source of labor for the armies [in

> the field] we propose to return all French and Belgian civilian prisoners who were deported from the occupied areas to the same, so long as they are physically fit and are not currently employed in Germany. [The purpose is] to exhort them to work [*sie zur Arbeit anzuhalten*]. We request that all acting corps commanders be instructed to deliver prompt information on the number of civilian prisoners being held in their districts who would fall into the category of suitable returnees.[42]

Again, because of the loss of the relevant Prussian military records, it is impossible to say how many persons were affected, but in the Bavarian War Archive there is evidence of forced return being imposed on a number of male French civilian prisoners.[43] The ICRC and the Spanish embassy in Berlin, which was charged with protecting French and Belgian interests in Germany for the duration of the war, also regularly complained that they could do nothing to help civilian prisoners who had been transferred back to occupied France or the Belgian étape. The German authorities would only grant them permission to inspect camps on the home front and neither the Prussian or Bavarian War Ministries, nor individual camp directors, had the authority to compel the field armies to account for the welfare and whereabouts of (former) civilian prisoners in their districts. A Spanish embassy official, for instance, informed an ICRC delegation to Berlin in spring 1917 that French and Belgian internees who had been returned to occupied territories administered by the field armies were not able to correspond with their families and that their names did not appear on recent lists of prisoners handed on via the German Red Cross. He also alleged that some of them had been forced, contrary to international law, to take part, alongside Russian POWs, in demolition work on the Somme sector of the Western Front in association with the German army's strategic withdrawal to the heavily fortified Hindenburg line.[44] This is but one reason for being skeptical about what it actually meant when civilian deportees from occupied territories were discharged from internment camps in Germany. In other contexts, too, as we shall see in more detail below, "release" could simply mean being transferred from one form of war captivity to another.

Internment on the German Home Front

How many French civilians were deported to Germany during the period from 1914 to 1918? As the Prussian ministry of war's final figure of 111,879 enemy civilians interned on the home front by October 1918 was a cumulative total only and was not broken down according to nationality or release date, it is impossible to say how many of these officially acknowledged internees were French or Belgian (as opposed to nationals of other enemy countries).[45] The ICRC, which remained distrustful of German record keeping, believed that by 1916 the German army was in effect operating a revolving-door policy when it came to civilian prisoners from France and Belgium. Fresh deportations were thus matched by releases of detainees already in Germany, some of whom were sent back to the occupied territories as an additional labor resource, some of whom "voluntarily" signed contracts with German employers on the home front and were therefore recategorized by the Prussian War Ministry as "*former* civilian prisoners" (see below), and some of whom were allowed to travel to nonoccupied France via Switzerland under exchange agreements reached with the French government. According to the ICRC's final estimates, at least 100,000 French and Belgian civilians were deported to Germany during the war, 96,337 of whom had already entered the home-front camp system before the end of 1917. This represented an average of 350–400 new civilian prisoners each week.[46]

As in 1914, so again after 1915, the German motives for using deportation as a weapon of war were mixed. At times, considerations of *große Politik* played a role, especially when it came to ordering targeted reprisals against occupied French and Belgian civilians in response to the Allies' global war against German imperial holdings and property interests overseas. In 1915 all German civilians and soldiers held in West Africa following the joint Anglo-French occupation of German colonies there in 1914 were deported en masse to camps in French North Africa (in defiance of the German demand that they be released from captivity altogether or sent on to mainland France). They were joined in North Africa by tens of thousands of German combatants captured in Europe. Germany's ability to retaliate in kind was severely limited, not least as the only prisoners it held outside Europe were a few hundred British and Belgian nationals arrested in 1914–15 in German East Africa. Even the latter had to be abandoned to advancing Anglo-Belgian forces in early 1916.[47]

Targeted reprisals in Europe promised more immediate results. Thus, in April 1916 a series of temporary deportation measures were successfully initiated that forced the French authorities to agree to transfer Germans held in Morocco, Algeria, and Tunisia to camps in metropolitan France (where, as was loudly proclaimed in the German press, they would no longer be guarded by nonwhite African troops). Altogether 250 French civilians, as well as 30,000 military POWs, were sent to work in the marshes in German-occupied Latvia and were only brought back to Germany once France had agreed to German demands.[48] Similar forms of reprisal were also instigated in November 1916 against a select group of French notables; in June 1917 against 200 Belgian civilians; and in January 1918 against 1,000 French civilians, 600 of them men and 400 of them women, all in connection with the alleged abuse of German civilians in colonial contexts or the ongoing refusal to release German nationals deported by the French army from the small part of Alsace it had managed to occupy in August 1914.[49]

Meanwhile, hostage taking at the local level also continued to play a role in deportations, reflecting the priority that the German army gave to ensuring the security of its own troops in the occupied zones by seizing notables (men and women) as a guarantee for the good behavior of particular towns and villages.[50] Nonetheless, by the second half of 1916 at the latest, the competing needs of different sections of the German war economy for labor, the growing success of the Allied naval blockade, and a desire to overcome the negative effects of "work refusal" at home and in occupied territories, had come to take priority over other factors. This was seen, most notoriously, in the case of the sixty thousand unemployed Belgian workers forcibly sent from the civilian-administered parts of occupied Belgium (i.e., the area beyond the étape) to Germany between October 1916 and March 1917. The policy ran against the wishes of the German governor-general in Brussels, General Moritz von Bissing, but it had the approval of the OHL and several leading German industrialists, including Carl Duisberg, Alfred Hugenberg, Walther Rathenau, and Hugo Stinnes.[51]

The aim was to persuade the deportees to sign "voluntary" work contracts, thus transforming them into "free" workers. However, in the end only 13,376 of them complied, and the rest—more than three-quarters of the total—were eventually returned to Belgium following protests from German Reichstag deputies and neutral states, including the Vatican, Spain, and the United States.[52] In fact, as far as enforced foreign labor was concerned, the German domestic economy benefited much more from the 500,000–600,000 Russian-Polish seasonal workers who were trapped in the country when the war broke out and were refused permission to return home, or who were "voluntarily" recruited for labor in Germany from German-occupied Russian Poland after 1915;[53] and from the roughly 2.5 million military POWs of all nationalities who were held in camps on the home front and were required to work, unless they were invalids or officers.[54]

How did French and Belgian deportees experience their internment in Germany? While figures from the Prussian ministry of war suggest that by October 1918 as many as eighty camps on the German home front held some civilian prisoners (alongside military POWs), only a handful held more than five hundred civilians: Frankfurt-an-der-Oder (634); Havelberg (1,820); Holzminden (4,240); Limburg-an-der-Lahn (1,174); Rastatt (1,223); Ruhleben

(2,318); Senne (2,462); and Traunstein (623).[55] Apart from Ruhleben, which was for British nationals only, it is likely that French and Belgian civilians together made up the largest group in most of these camps. Certainly this was the case with Holzminden, in the duchy of Brunswick (today in Lower Saxony), which according to figures from May 1916, included 2,535 French men, ninety-six French women, and thirty French children, together with 991 Belgian men, fifty-four Belgian women, and twelve Belgian children among its 5,866 civilian inmates.[56] Inspectors from the Spanish embassy in Berlin expressed concerns about overcrowding in the civilian compound there and the fact that "upright" French and Belgian women were housed together with prostitutes.[57] It was also alleged that male prisoners and guards had access to the female barracks at night. Both claims were hotly contested by the Prussian ministry of war.[58]

The allegation that the German camp system on the home front forced civilian prisoners to work against their will was also denied by the German military authorities, both during and after the war. Zivilgefangene, like officer POWs, were supposedly only ever recruited for labor outside the camps on a voluntary basis.[59] This matched international agreements reached with the British, French, and Russian governments at an early stage in the war, adherence to which was considered crucial by the German Foreign Office in order to protect the interests of German civilians in Allied hands.[60] The Belgian deportations of 1916–17, which anyway were halted in March 1917, subsequently looked like an unfortunate exception. In April 1918, for instance, the Prussian War Ministry reassured the German Foreign Office, in response to a series of negative reports in the pro-French Swiss press, that "the former civilian prisoners who are working in German industries are all volunteers. They are hired and paid on the same basis as German workers."[61] The use of the phrase "*former* civilian prisoners" is significant here, as it suggests that some internees were being "released" (and therefore removed from the lists forwarded to the German Red Cross and from the protections offered by the accord with the Allies on the nonuse of civilian internee forced labor) after "agreeing" to work in the German domestic war economy. Officially they were no longer captives but "free" laborers who had "chosen" to accept offers of industrial or agricultural employment in exchange for their liberty.

Reports from neutral inspectors nonetheless suggested something rather different. At the end of April 1917, for instance, Spanish embassy officials who had visited the Havelberg camp, then in the Prussian province of Brandenburg (today in Saxony-Anhalt), noted that "the 150 French civilian prisoners who volunteered to work in the Hahn'sche works in Grossenbaum [Duisburg] in exchange for the promise of being allowed to visit their families in occupied France after a period of four months, are still waiting for this promise to be met."[62]

A few weeks later, a report on civilian prisoners at Holzminden claimed that "the French and Belgian civilians sent to the Hannover-Hainholz works are living under conditions which leave much to be desired. . . . The prisoners are granted only a limited amount of freedom, causing them to suffer from low morale. . . . If they refuse to work or make complaints they run the risk of being beaten."[63]

And in August 1917 similar accusations came from Russian civilian prisoners at Holzminden who had been forced to work in a communal kitchen and a local factory: "They told us that if they refused to work they were threatened with being sent to clear marshes or being conscripted into labor details in Lichtenhorst or Verdener Moor, places known for the terrible conditions which the prisoners are expected to endure."[64]

Just how many "former" enemy alien civilian prisoners were recruited into the German workforce after 1916, and how many experienced the varying degrees of coercion detailed above, is difficult to say due to the loss of the relevant Prussian military files. Admittedly, much larger groups of enemy POWs and migrant laborers—notably Russians, Russian Poles, Dutch nationals, Belgians who "voluntarily" signed contracts, and Italians—worked in the German war economy on the home front, with "former" civilian internees therefore only representing a small proportion of the total foreign workforce.[65]

The global economic context is also important in understanding why the conflict was increasingly seen in Germany, particularly but not only among extreme right-wingers, as a "war of work" between nations and races.[66] When it came to the use of labor resources, nationalists asserted, German "quality" and "cultural creativity" would triumph over the Allies' access, through colonies and overseas commerce, to the endless, undifferentiated mass of racially or culturally inferior "human material" (Ger. *Menschenmaterial*) supposedly on offer for hire from outside Europe.[67] From late 1916 the pressure on *all* able-bodied, patriotic civilians in Germany to work grew stronger, especially after the passage of the Auxiliary Service Law (*Gesetz über den vaterländischen Hilfsdienst*) on December 5. The latter introduced labor conscription for every German male aged sixteen to sixty who was not serving in the armed forces or working in essential industries in an ultimately unsuccessful bid to eradicate "malingering."[68] It was around this time, too, that Hindenburg famously insisted that the war economy should operate according to the principle that "whoever does not work shall not eat."[69] It is even possible that the willingness of the supreme military authorities to endorse the substantial exchange agreement reached with the French government at Bern in April 1918 was conditioned by the knowledge that those prisoners still left in the camps—the so-called "useless eaters"—were of no economic value to Germany, given that most of them were too sick (or of too high a social standing) to be pressured into offering themselves as "free" workers.[70]

Even so, the move toward what Hinz calls the "economic totalization of the war" after 1916[71] should not blind us to the fact that many of the original decisions about the use of deportations and forced labor in the war against enemy civilians were taken not by the third OHL under Hindenburg and Ludendorff, or by government ministries in Berlin and Munich, but by individual camp directors in the German interior and army commanders on the ground in occupied France and the Belgian étape. The implications of this, and the possibility of a significant transfer of cultural attitudes toward civilian "enemies" from the occupied zones to the home front and back again, will now be addressed.

Internment in Occupied Territories and on the Home Front

In spring 1915, according to Helen McPhail's work, a group of French civilian deportees from Péronne returned to occupied France with tales of having been incarcerated somewhere near Frankfurt-am-Main, where they were forced to perform heavy labor, including stone breaking and road mending.[72] This was probably the camp at Limburg-an-der-Lahn, which held mainly military, and some civilian detainees from 1914 onwards. For this particular group of returnees, though, and many like them, "release" and repatriation were mixed blessings. True, they might now be reunited with their families and businesses. However, particularly if they were unemployed, they might also be expected to engage in "emergency maintenance work" (Ger. *Notstandsarbeiten*) on public amenities under the direction of the local rear army commander. Even before the introduction of the ZABs in October 1916, evading such service, or encouraging others to do so, could result in a three-year jail sentence imposed by a German military court, or huge fines of up to six thousand marks (for those who were able to pay them).[73]

More generally, by 1915 German field commanders had moved beyond simply outlawing, punishing, and deterring *active* civilian resistance to the occupation. Rather, *passive* resistance in the form of "work refusal" was now also criminalized and its perpetrators treated as "incorrigible laggards" (Ger. *böse Bummler*), irrespective of their class background.[74] They were labelled "work-shy persons," who supposedly feigned patriotism as a "cover-story" to enable them to "continue their idle lifestyles undisturbed while cozily pocketing their municipal unemployment benefits (*gemeindliche Arbeitslosenunterstützung*)."[75] A regulation issued from army general headquarters in October 1916 ordered rear-area commanders in charge of rounding up "able-bodied persons" for *Notstandsarbeiten* to include those who led purposeless lives "as a result of gambling, drinking, idleness, unemployment or work-shyness."[76] Men recruited into the ZABs were not only to be screened for their "fitness to work," but from January 1917 they were also required to undergo medical checks for sexually transmitted infections, a deliberate act of degradation which—as in the case of the women and teenage girls caught up in the Easter deportations of 1916—confirmed their status as legal nonentities and disenfranchised "objects" at the mercy of a foreign military power, rather than occupied civilians with rights as well as obligations guaranteed under the prevailing laws and customs of land warfare.[77] And those who were unable to work on health or other grounds were often disparaged in biological terms as "useless eaters" (Ger. *unnütze Esser*),[78] or singled out as "inferior specimens" (*minderwertiges Menschenmaterial*).[79]

French and Belgian civilians, in other words, were divided into two groups—"orderly" subjects, who were willing to accept the legitimacy of the occupation under international law and thus the need to maintain a correct attitude toward work and a consistent *Leistungsbereitschaft* (willingness to perform), and those more "alien" or "criminal" elements, who represented a danger to military security, community harmony, and the well-being of the field armies. Furthermore, the harsh, repressive measures directed against the latter were legitimized by reference to the supposed benefits of compulsory labor and "German work" as a prophylactic tool against joblessness and the "chaos" of urban life, and not just by particular interpretations of international law.[80] The rear-area inspectorate for the Sixth Army even complained in December 1916 that those French civilians forcibly assembled into the initial ZABs were not made of the strongest "human material" (*Menschenmaterial*) because they "are drawn almost exclusively from the urban population" and were "often in poor health as a result of the unhygienic conditions in working-class quarters." By contrast, "the stronger rural population cannot be recruited into the ZABs because they are not unemployed and are urgently needed for agricultural work."[81] Yet it was precisely these prejudices against the city poor—which probably pre-dated the war but were radicalized by imagined and real wartime encounters with French and Belgian civilians, including with the much feared but largely mythical *Franktireurs* at the start of the occupation[82]—that made the German army feel that the ZABs were a crucial part of their current military struggles and an essential means of making the German nation more resilient in the face of further (biological) trials of strength and nerve ahead. In other words, for commanders on the ground, the argument that urban unemployment was a danger to "order" was not simply a legal subterfuge—as it was for those lawyers in the German Foreign Office in autumn 1916, who cited article 43 of the HLKO as a means of justifying their support for deportations *within* the occupied zones—but a matter of genuine conviction and cultural belief.[83]

The transfer of such ideas by the German military to the invaded territories administered by the field armies, and from there back to the home front, can be seen most vividly in a little-known, planned social intervention that was drawn up in the localized context of southern Bavaria in the last months of the war, where prejudice against the "unemployed" and "big city scum" (*Großstadtgesindel*) was also rife.[84] Through an agreement between the public authority responsible for the promotion of rural infrastructure, soil conservation, and water supply systems in the Munich region (the *Kulturbauamt München*) and the acting commander of the first Bavarian army corps district (covering most of southern Bavaria), a scheme was hatched in summer 1918 to send a group of carefully selected "work-shy and criminally-inclined adult males" from Munich to a "productive construction site" (Ger. *Kulturbaustelle*) belonging to the Wielenbach community enterprise scheme (the "Genossenschaft Wielenbach") in the town of Weilheim. Here they would be "compel[led] . . . to work . . . at the appropriate rate (minimum five marks per day) minus their food and accommodation costs."[85]

Initially a total of two hundred inmates was envisaged, with a guard of fifty soldiers.[86] By September 1918 the camp was ready to receive 160 prisoners.[87] Unfortunately, there is little information about the specific criteria that were to be used to select prisoners from among the bigger population of petty criminals and the unemployed in Munich. More significant was the self-consciously experimental nature of this project, and the early statement from the senior official in charge of POW camps in southern Bavaria that "the inner life of the *Baustelle* should follow the model of a POW work camp."[88] Here, then, we can see the "traces of a totalitarian war ideology" that both Hinz and Becker refer to, albeit this time directed not at enemy civilians, aliens, or POWs but at "internal enemies."[89] At the same time it is possible to identify crossovers with the Eastern Front as well as the Western Front, for it was in the occupied east, as Vejas Gabriel Liulevicius has shown, that "notions of 'German work' and 'cultural [or productive] work' were fused"—with military officials casting themselves as "bringers of *Kultur*" to foreign "lands and peoples."[90] Indeed, viewed from rural and small-town southern Bavaria, the poorer, inner-city districts of Munich might also appear as a "foreign" space, exemplifying all the negative traits of an unproductive, globalized, and massified *Unkultur* and, worse still, inhabited by a "criminal" or "parasitic" underclass in need of German "cultivation."[91]

Further north, the acting commanders of the second and third Bavarian army corps districts were likewise aware of the plans to create a camp at Weilheim and pushed for a policy of concentrating "gypsies from all the [Bavarian] army corps districts" there, thereby transforming a project with a local focus into one with larger, regional dimensions.[92] "The inclusion of women" was considered "impossible for the time being" but was not ruled out for the future.[93] Plans were also mooted to build two further "productive work camps" (or *Kulturbaustellen*) at Schlehdorf and Herzogsägmühle near Peiting, both of them again in southern Bavaria (Oberbayern administrative district).[94] On October 11, 1918, the acting commander of the first Bavarian army corps even wrote to his counterparts in the second and third army corps districts, asking them to begin identifying suitable candidates to send to Weilheim: "In the first instance the persons selected should be given a thorough medical examination to ascertain their ability to work, since only those who are fully fit for labor are of any use in Weilheim."[95]

There is no evidence that any prisoners actually arrived at Weilheim before November 1918. If they did, they would have been there for a matter of two to three weeks at most. In any case, a letter of January 1919 from the acting commander of the first Bavarian army corps to the other Bavarian army commanders indicates that "the work camp [*Arbeitslager*] at Weilheim-Wielenbach" had had to be closed "owing to the revolution."[96] Nonetheless the project, even if it had insufficient time to get off the ground, points to an interest shown by Bavarian military and police officials on the home front in drawing "lessons" from the experience of work units in POW camps and occupied territories and their willingness to appropriate the same kind of brutalized language to describe what they were doing and why—for instance, via references to "hygienic measures" against "criminal vermin" (Ger. *verbrecherisches Gesindel*);[97] the categorization of Gypsies as a "pest" (Ger. *Plage*);[98] or the constantly expressed desire to force "tramps" and "work-shy persons" to sign up for construction and other jobs as an appropriate means of supporting the war effort and providing local communities with improvements to their infrastructure.[99]

The very notion that social "undesirables" at home could be cast, in effect, as prisoners of war and exploited for their labor on the same basis and for the same ends as enemy POWs is itself a good illustration of one of the central features of civilian captivity in World War I Germany, namely its combination of improvisation and radicalization. Also evident in the "Weilheim project" was the strong emphasis on finding new and locally effective ways (Ger. *wirksame . . . Zwangsmaßnahmen*),[100] to (re)establish order in the midst of the increasing economic, social, and human chaos of war, a chaos that returned to Germany with the revolution of 1918–19, the hyperinflation crisis of 1923, and the Great Depression from 1929. At the political level there were certainly some echoes of the recent past in the program that the Nazis developed for governing Munich in case their putsch in November 1923 succeeded. Point 16 of this program called for the detention of "security risks and useless eaters" in "collection camps" (*Sammellager*), where they would be required to work. Those who refused would face the death penalty, in line with the punishment facing military deserters (but not yet civilians) during the war.[101] And in respect to "experiments" in social policy, while it would be wrong to see a direct line or linear path to the German concentration camps of the 1930s in any of the developments discussed here, it is worth bearing in mind Jane Caplan's point that "there are no *ex nihilo* creations in complex bureaucratic states." In particular, for local administrative bodies keen to cooperate with the self-styled "emergency" directives of the Hitler regime in 1933–1936, "the issue of labor . . . provided one of the principal public legitimations for the camps."[102]

Returning to the plans for a work camp at Weilheim in 1918, the most striking parallel with experiences on the Western Front lies in the close attention paid to how the prisoners in Bavaria were to be supervised, with a strong emphasis on preventing escapes and ensuring the "maintenance of security."[103] As with the ZABs in northern France and the Belgian étape, then, the armed military guards were to be carefully selected and trained, while concern for their physical and moral welfare dictated that they should take all steps necessary to prevent and deter violence from the "persons dangerous to public order" (Ger. *gemeingefährliche Personen*) in their custody.[104] This included the denial of visits or communication between prisoners and their friends or relatives on the outside, as well as regular searches of prisoners for knives and other weapons, and a ban on smoking or drinking alcohol during working hours. More to the point, "infringements of the work regulations and of orders and instructions issued by the military director or the site management will constitute an offence under the state-of-siege law."[105] This meant that any kind of resistance to forced labor, active or passive, was criminalized and turned into an act of deliberate sabotage against the German war effort, as was already the case for some of the French (and Belgian) civilians of working age living in the étape.

(Dis)entangling the Local, the National, and the International

The different strands of German internment policy discussed in this essay confirm Annette Becker's finding that while there were various kinds of camps for enemy civilians on the home front and in occupied France and Belgium, there was as yet no fully fledged "concentration camp system" in World War I.[106] Rather, the motives for internment were too complex and too contradictory to speak of a coherent approach. True, the lawyers of the German Foreign Office had decided that, from the end of 1914 onward, civilian prisoners might be legitimately used as hostages in order to put pressure on the Allies to release the tens of thousands of German nationals that they were holding at the global level. This policy was also endorsed by the Prussian and Bavarian ministries of war, by Reich Chancellor Bethmann Hollweg, and at one point even by the kaiser, Wilhelm II.[107] Yet, on its own it cannot explain why more than 100,000 enemy subjects were interned in Germany between 1914 and 1918. Retaliation at the international level was not the only motive, nor was "national" outrage at the treatment of German minorities abroad.

One possible solution to this conundrum is to apply the notion of a dual POW system operating within several of the belligerent states during the war to the case of French and Belgian civilian deportees and internees in German captivity. According to Heather Jones, this dual system evolved when camps were divided into two different types: "on the one hand, the home front camp and working unit network, and, on the other, a largely separate [and even harsher, M.S.] system of army-run prisoner of war labor companies which remained at or near the front area as a permanent labour force, working directly for armies."[108] Yet while this model works convincingly for explaining the violence experienced by military POWs in western Europe—as Jones's comparative findings ably demonstrate[109]—to apply it to the German treatment of civilian prisoners would assume a level of centralized design and coordination not evident in the sources.

What the materials available in the Bavarian War Archive do tell us, on the other hand, is that much of the thinking behind the deportation and internment policies implemented by military commanders on the ground was based on a particular war culture and response to dealing with enemy civilians and "internal enemies" that lay at the complex intersection between local, national, and international developments and between the home front and multiple fighting fronts, including *Ober Ost* as well as the *Etappengebieten* in occupied France and Belgium. At the national level some of this thinking may have emerged out of earlier cultural attitudes and practices within the German military that predated World War I. Isabel Hull, for example, has argued that the German general staff derived one particularly important "lesson" from the wars of 1866 and 1870–71: that violence constrained by extramilitary factors, such as diplomacy or international law, while still potentially sufficient for overpowering the enemy's conventional military forces, might be ineffective in the face of popular insurgency and guerrilla warfare. These "lessons" were then applied to the treatment of enemy civilians in colonial wars (including the genocidal campaigns against the Herero and Nama in German South West Africa in 1904–1908) and to the inhabitants of European territories invaded by German troops during World War I.[110]

However, such continuities offer a partial explanation at best. To a much greater degree the German field armies' thinking in late 1914 was connected to specific experiences in Belgium and France. This included both the initial *Franktireur* scare of August–October and the way it triggered an unanticipated sense of alarm that colored and radicalized responses to subsequent challenges. Among these challenges, the new and unfamiliar situation that German commanders faced when confronted with the phenomenon of patriotic work refusal on the part of the local population, and the existential anxieties this produced concerning the morale, comfort, and physical safety of their own troops as well as the resolve of the home front and the troops fighting on the front line, stood out in particular.

Contrary to Hull's findings, then, German army commanders were able to think in strategic, extramilitary, and even domestic-political terms.[111] In many ways they had to, given what they faced, namely the unexpected (and disorientating) combination of static trench warfare in northern France and Belgium, global economic blockade and inability to defend overseas colonies and markets, and multiple occupations in eastern and western Europe, with their incredibly high labor demands. This produced a set of dilemmas that their more confident forebears during the Franco-Prussian war of 1870–71 and the colonial conflicts of the late nineteenth century had not encountered and could not have imagined. In short, by the beginning of 1916 at the latest, the commanders on the ground in the *Etappengebieten* could not see how they could continue to run an orderly, self-sufficient occupation regime in a modern industrial society such as northern France and Belgium—and in the midst of a global, industrialized conflict like the Great War—without introducing radical and innovative measures to combat the modern, urban "disease" of idleness and work-shyness. The only alternative to conscripting enemy civilians was to displace the burden of provisioning the occupation troops wholly onto the home front, an option that the German field armies in northern France and

Belgium were not willing to consider—even if they might have hoped or foreseen that some of their policies aimed at combatting work-shyness among occupied civilians would eventually be taken up on the home front too.

Finally, what are the implications of these findings for our understanding of the relative importance of local, national, and international factors—and the complex links between them—when considering civilian internment as a global phenomenon during World War I? Tammy Proctor has rightly argued that from 1914 onward internment developed into a "deliberate state policy" aimed at civilian "outsiders" within particular countries. Equally it was a means by which opposing states sought to wage war against each other on the European and worldwide stages.[112] Nonetheless, as the German example suggests, it was also a policy that states could easily lose control of, particularly when local and regional factors were also brought into the equation. At the national and international levels, the Prussian war ministry and the imperial government in Berlin had signaled that they had more or less given up on securing any worthwhile material advantages for the home front from civilian internment, or even achieving a better bargaining hand with the Allies, when, admittedly at a very late stage in the war, they negotiated the wide-reaching Bern and Hague exchange agreements with France and Britain in April and July 1918 respectively.

Under these schemes, thousands of eligible civilian internees and military POWs were repatriated, although repeated delays in implementation meant that thousands more were still waiting to be released as the war came to an end. Similarly, recruitment to the ZABs in occupied France and Belgium was supposedly halted in spring 1918, with the existing battalions marked for disbandment.[113] Yet on the ground in the last months and weeks of the war, enemy civilians were still being held in German military custody, in the East as well as the West. They were also being moved between the home front and the rapidly disintegrating German lines in the still-occupied parts of France and Belgium, and between established camps, civilian and military prisons, abandoned warehouses, and other makeshift places of incarceration, none of which were accessible to ICRC inspectors.[114] At the same time, ad hoc plans were being laid by the military authorities in Bavaria for the internment of "gypsies" and "petty criminals" as a local solution to the supposed problem of "work-shyness" and "disorderly" lifestyles.

German policy at home and in occupied northern France and Belgium was not, of course, made in a vacuum. Integrating the diverse and typically unbordered strands of local case studies such as this into a global framework for understanding World War I captivity raises new and exciting conceptual challenges. In particular, it forces us to rethink what might be called the "connectivity conundrum" and the key historical-political assumptions that go with it.[115] Too often comparative histories of the internment phenomenon are written in terms of a simplistic binary division between top-down global and international processes (such as migration flows or the development of a common set of laws on the rules of land warfare) and what are sometimes cast as "provincial," inward-looking or "micro" responses at the subnational and local levels. A more comprehensive view needs to factor in and make visible the reciprocal interplay between different spatial levels that lies hidden beneath the surface of the constant movement of ideas, practices, and mentalities, as well as peoples, across rapidly changing (wartime and postwar) borders and jurisdictions. Only thus can we begin to identify—and bring together—the many different ways in which World War I was a turning point in the global use of prison camps—both as sites of mass incarceration for combatants and noncombatants, and as imagined spaces existing at the increasingly fluid intersection of the local, the national, and the international.

Notes

I would like to thank Heather Jones, Alan Kramer, and Kim Wünschmann for their very helpful comments on an earlier draft of this chapter.

1. For examples of the most recent scholarship, see Manz, Panayi, and Stibbe 2019; Stibbe 2019; Manz and Panayi 2020; Bauerkämper 2021; Caglioti 2021.
2. Stibbe 2013a.
3. Kramer, Alan 2007; Jones, H. 2011a.
4. Hinz 2003.
5. Hinz 1999.
6. Panayi 2014; Murphy 2017.
7. Stibbe 2013a, 161–62.
8. Panayi 2014, 24–25; Boswell 2000, 141.
9. Deutscher Reichstag 1927, 719–855.
10. Jahr 1999; Stibbe 2008a.
11. Stibbe 2008a, 139, 143.
12. As argued most recently by Jahr and Thiel 2019, 41–42.
13. Stibbe 2004.
14. Horne and Kramer 2001, 166.
15. On Ober Ost, see Liulevicius 2000.
16. Stibbe 2006, 16.
17. For a concise overview of the administrative structure of the German military occupation, see Wilkin 2016, 230–31.
18. Horne and Kramer 2001, 166.
19. Boswell 2000, 133.
20. See, e.g., Munich Police Inspectorate to the Bavarian State Ministry of Interior, July 6, 1915. Copy in Bayerisches Hauptstaatsarchiv Munich, Abteilung IV:

Kriegsarchiv (henceforth BayHStA-KA), Stellvertretendes Generalkommando I. Bayerisches Armeekorps (WK) 986.

21. See the legal department's extensive correspondence about this issue in Bundesarchiv Berlin-Lichterfelde (henceforth BArch), R 901/82914.

22. Watson 2014b.

23. Stibbe 2008a, 40.

24. See, for example, Bureau international féministe de renseignements en faveur des victims de la guerre, Lausanne, to the German envoy in Bern, December 26, 1914, in BArch, R 901/82914.

25. Central Committee of German Red Cross Associations, Department for POW Welfare, to the Prussian Ministry of War, December 8, 1914, in BArch, R 901/82913.

26. Begriff: "Kriegs- und Zivilgefangene"—communiqué issued by the Prussian War Ministry, April 17, 1916. Copies in BayHStA-KA, Infanteriedivisionen (WK) 4379, and BArch, R 901/82917.

27. Gumz 2014, 72–73.

28. On the Hoover-administered Committee for Relief in Belgium (CRB), which operated in Belgium from October 1914 and in northern France from March 1915, see McPhail 2000, 61–88. Hunger was nonetheless a common feature of life under German occupation by early 1916, especially in big cities like Lille.

29. Liszt 1920, 476.

30. See Commander of the Sixth Army, "Grundsätze für die Verwendung von freien Arbeitern aus der Zivilbevölkerung des besetzten Gebietes," October 17, 1916, which makes explicit reference to article 52, in BayHStA-KA, Generalkommando III. Bayerisches Armeekorps (WK) 2315.

31. See, for instance, Geheime Feldpolizei, Zweigstelle Valenciennes, to the Rear Area Inspectorate of the Sixth Army, September 2, 1916, in BayHStA-KA, Etappenformationen (WK), 146.

32. Nivet 2011, 52.

33. Geheime Feldpolizei, Zweigstelle Valenciennes, September 2, 1916 (as note 31 above). Connolly 2018, 254–58, notes that work refusal in the occupied Nord "was rare" and "successful refusals even rarer," but he still gives many examples where it happened. For the German military, imagined or "attempted" episodes were in any case as important as real ones.

34. See, for instance, the use of the phrase "useless eaters" in Commander of the second Bavarian army corps, Korpstagesbefehl, November 12, 1915, in BayHStA-KA, Generalkommando II. Bayerisches Armeekorps (WK) 693, Bd. 2: Kriegsgefangene, 1915–17.

35. Supreme Commander of the Sixth Army to all army corps commanders, December 17, 1915, in BayHStA-KA, Generalkommando II. Bayerisches Armeekorps (WK) 693, Bd. 2: Kriegsgefangene, 1915–17.

36. See the dozens of case files in BayHStA-KA, Generalkommando II. Bayerisches Armeekorps (WK) 693, Bd. 5: Rückkehr von Zivilgefangenen 1917.

37. Commander of the third Bavarian army corps to the commanders of the fifth and sixth Bavarian army corps, November 20, 1916, in BayHStA-KA, Generalkommando III. Bayerisches Armeekorps (WK) 2315.

38. Commander of the second Bavarian army corps, March 2, 1917, in BayHStA-KA, Generalkommando II. Bayerisches Armeekorps (WK) 693, Bd 5: Rückkehr von Zivilgefangenen 1917.

39. Becker, A. 1998, 68–77.

40. Watson 2014a, 404; Hull 2014, 138–40. Five ZABs were also set up in the territory administered by Ober Ost in the east. See Watson 2014a, 402; and Liulevicius 2000, 73–74.

41. See also Supreme Commander of the Sixth Army to all army corps commanders, November 12, 1916, in BayHStA-KA, Infanteriedivisionen (WK) 4074.

42. Quartermaster General to Prussian Ministry of War, February 24, 1917. Copy in BayHStA-KA, Generalkommando I. Armeekorps (WK) 2005.

43. See the examples in BayHStA-KA, Generalkommando II. Bayerisches Armeekorps (WK) 693, Bd. 5: Rückkehr von Zivilgefangenen 1917.

44. Missions d'Etude: Mlle Cramer et M. Boissier à Berlin, Copenhague et Stockholm (March–April 1917), in Archives du Comité International de la Croix-Rouge, Geneva, C G1/419/XI. On the demolition work on the Somme in early 1917, see Geyer, Michael 2006.

45. Doegen 1919, 29.

46. CICR 1921, 136–37. See also Becker, A. 1998, 233.

47. Stibbe 2013a, 165.

48. The figure of 250 civilians sent to German-occupied Russia in April 1916 is cited in Prussian War Ministry to German Foreign Office (*Auswärtiges Amt*, henceforth AA), November 6, 1916, in BArch, R 901/82917. On the thirty thousand military POWs deported at the same time, see Jones, H. 2011a, 136–7.

49. AA to the Dutch Legation in Berlin, June 28, 1917, in BArch, R 901/84337. See also Nivet 2011, 129–32; Stibbe 2013a, 165–66; *Bulletin International des sociétés de la Croix-Rouge*, no. 194, April 1918, 221–22.

50. Nivet 2011, 127–29; McPhail 2000, 38; Becker, A. 2014a, 275–77; Connolly 2018, 20. See also the many individual examples in BayHStA-KA, Generalkommando II. Bayerisches Armeekorps (WK) 707; and BayHStA-KA, Stellvertretendes Generalkommando I. Bayerisches Armeekorps (WK) 2137.

51. The key study on this episode is Thiel 2007.

52. Watson 2014a, 386–87.

53. Herbert 1986, 91.

54. Oltmer 2006, 68–69.

55. Jahr and Thiel 2019, 43. See also Kriegs- und Zivilgefangene in Gefangenenlagern, Lazaretten und Austauschstationen (zahlenmäßige Aufstellungen nach dem Stand vom 10. Mai und 10. Oktober 1918), in BArch, R 67/525.

56. See Bestand Holzminden, May 13, 1916, in Evangelisches Zentralarchiv Berlin, 51 C III g 2.

57. Spanish embassy in Berlin to AA, June 19, 1916, in BArch, R 901/82917.

58. Prussian War Ministry to AA, September 4, 1916, in BArch, R 901/82917. Even so, the Spanish embassy's complaints are corroborated by other sources. See, e.g., the report drawn up on December 4, 1916 by Adelaide Livingstone, head of the British government's Committee on the Treatment by the Enemy of British Prisoners of War, after interviewing six British women who had recently returned from Holzminden, in the National Archives, Kew, London, FO 383/210.

59. Doegen 1919, 175.

60. Hull 2014, 132.

61. Prussian Ministry of War to AA, April 2, 1918, in BArch, R 901/84319.

62. Spanish Embassy in Berlin to AA, April 30, 1917, in BArch, R 901/84319.

63. Spanish Embassy in Berlin to AA, May 24, 1917, in BArch, R 901/84337.

64. Spanish Embassy in Berlin to AA, August 16, 1917, in BArch, R 901/84337.

65. Herbert 1986, 84 and 100; Watson 2014a, 388–92.

66. Conrad 2010, 363.

67. Trarore 2014, 61. On the use of the brutish term "Menschenmaterial," see also Mosse 1990, 179.

68. McElligott 2014, 12 and 16–17.

69. Watson 2014a, 381.

70. On the Bern accords of April 26, 1918, see Becker, A. 1998, 255–66.

71. Hinz 2006, 359.

72. McPhail 2000, 39.

73. See, for instance, Proclamation of the Rear Inspectorate of the Sixth Army, June 4, 1916, in BayHStA-KA, Etappeninspektion (WK) 146.

74. See also Thiel 2007, 126, 179.

75. Geheime Feldpolizei, Zweigstelle Valenciennes, to the Supreme Commander of the Sixth Army, September 2, 1916, in BayHStA-KA, Etappenformationen (WK) 146. According to Connolly 2018, 18, it was not uncommon in some of the industrial towns in the occupied north for more than 43 percent of the population to be in receipt of unemployment benefits paid out from municipal insurance funds, although how much of this was due to German requisitioning of materials and how much to "work refusal" is difficult to determine. On the functioning of French municipalities under the German occupation, and their continued responsibility for ensuring the "welfare of the population," including the payment of benefits to those on the unemployment register, see also Nivet 2011, 42–52.

76. Ordannance concernant la restriction des charges publiques de secours et l'aide à porter en cas de calamité publique, Großes Hauptquartier, October 3, 1916, in BayHStA-KA, Etappenformationen (WK) 147.

77. Quartermaster General, "Neuaufstellung von Z.A.B.s und Einziehung von Ersatzarbeitern," January 2, 1917, in BayHStA-KA, Etappenformationen (WK) 147.

78. See notes 34, 35, and 42 above.

79. Rear Inspectorate of the Sixth Army to the Quartermaster General, December 27, 1916, in BayHStA-KA, Etappenformationen (WK) 172.

80. On the value-laden term "Deutsche Arbeit" or "German work" as a category denoting supposedly "superior" national characteristics and social "inclusion"/"exclusion" on the basis of "performance" (*Leistungsbereitschaft*), and, equally importantly, its emergence as a discursive tool in welfare policies and "preventive social policing," see Campbell 1989, Caplan 2005, and Hörath 2014. For the "interconnectedness" of this concept, in other words its development in global, international, and transnational contexts, as well as within Germany itself, see also Conrad 2010, 334–79; and for its wartime "fusion" with the idea of German "cultural work" in the occupied East (Ober Ost), see Liulevicius 2000, 45–47.

81. Rear Inspectorate of the Sixth Army, December 27, 1916 (as note 79 above).

82. Horne and Kramer 2001. Prewar fears of urban degeneracy and the "corrupting effects of city life," including sexual deviance and associated threats to German "manhood," are also emphasized by Crouthamel 2014, 17.

83. On the "tortured construction of Hague article 43" put together by the AA's legal department in September 1916 to support its contention that deportations within the occupied zones for purposes of recruitment into the ZABs could be lawful if they were presented as a means of safeguarding "public order and security," see Hull 2014, 133.

84. On the largely hostile attitude of Bavarian peasants toward impoverished city dwellers, both during and after the war, see Ziemann 2007, 191–209; and Geyer, Martin H. 1998, 184–86.

85. Acting commander of the Bavarian first army corps to various departments, October 2, 1918, in BayHStA-KA, Stellvertretendes Generalkommando I. Bayerisches Armeekorps (WK) 678.

86. Inspectorate for POW camps of the first Bavarian army corps to the acting commander of the Bavarian first army corps, June 19, 1918, in BayHStA-KA, Stellvertretendes Generalkommando I. Bayerisches Armeekorps (WK) 678.

87. Acting commander of the Bavarian first army corps to the Inspectorate for POW camps of the Bavarian first army corps, September 7, 1918, in BayHStA-KA, Stellvertretendes Generalkommando I. Bayerisches Armeekorps (WK) 678.

88. Inspectorate for POW camps of the first Bavarian army corps to the acting commander of the Bavarian first army corps, June 19, 1918, in BayHStA-KA, Stellvertretendes Generalkommando I. Bayerisches Armeekorps (WK) 678.

89. Hinz 2006, 363; Becker, A. 2014a, 258, 280. On German (mis)treatment of other kinds of "internal enemy," this time political suspects as well as "social undesirables" such as vagrants, prostitutes and homosexuals, see André Keil's contribution to this volume.

90. Liulevicius 2000, 26, 45–46.

91. Liulevicius 2000, 46, 71; Conrad 2010, 364.

92. Acting commander of the Bavarian first army corps to the Inspectorate for POW camps of the Bavarian first army corps, September 7, 1918, in BayHStA-KA, Stellvertretendes Generalkommando I. Bayerisches Armeekorps (WK) 678.

93. Acting commander of the Bavarian first army corps to various departments, October 2, 1918, in BayHStA-KA, Stellvertretendes Generalkommando I. Bayerisches Armeekorps (WK) 678.

94. Acting commander of the Bavarian first army corps to the Inspectorate for POW camps of the Bavarian first army corps, September 7, 1918, in BayHStA-KA, Stellvertretendes Generalkommando I. Bayerisches Armeekorps (WK) 678.

95. Acting commander of the Bavarian first army corps to the acting commanders of the second and third army corps, the State Ministry of Interior and the Munich Police Inspectorate, October 11, 1918, in BayHStA-KA, Stellvertretendes Generalkommando I. Armeekorps (WK) 986.

96. Acting commander of the Bavarian first army corps to the acting commanders of the second and third army corps, January 11, 1919, in BayHStA-KA, Stellvertretendes Generalkommando I. Armeekorps (WK) 986.

97. Acting commander of the Bavarian first army corps to the Inspectorate for POW camps of the Bavarian first army corps, September 14, 1918, in BayHStA-KA, Stellvertretendes Generalkommando I. Bayerisches Armeekorps (WK) 678.

98. Acting commander of the Bavarian first army corps to the Bavarian State Ministry of Interior, May 26, 1917, in BayHStA-KA, Stellvertretendes Generalkommando I. Bayerisches Armeekorps (WK) 986.

99. Bavarian War Ministry to the acting commanders of all three Bavarian army corps, February 17, 1917, in BayHStA-KA, Stellvertretendes Generalkommando I. Bayerisches Armeekorps (WK) 986; Acting commander of the Bavarian first army corps to the Inspectorate for POW camps of the Bavarian first army corps, August 18, 1918, in BayHStA-KA, Stellvertretendes Generalkommando I. Bayerisches Armeekorps (WK) 678.

100. Inspectorate for POW camps of the first Bavarian army corps to the acting commander of the Bavarian first army corps, June 19, 1918, in BayHStA-KA, Stellvertretendes Generalkommando I. Bayerisches Armeekorps (WK) 678.

101. Evans, R. 2003, 346.

102. Caplan 2005, 26, 31.

103. Inspectorate for POW camps of the first Bavarian army corps to the acting commander of the Bavarian first army corps, June 19, 1918, BayHStA-KA, Stellvertretendes Generalkommando I. Bayerisches Armeekorps (WK) 678. On the similar concern to prevent escapes and "unrest" among the ZABs in France and the operational and rear areas of occupied Belgium, see Thiel 2007, 127.

104. Acting commander of the Bavarian first army corps to various departments, July 11, 1918, in BayHStA-KA, Stellvertretendes Generalkommando I. Bayerisches Armeekorps (WK) 678.

105. Vorläufige Dienstanweisung für den militärischen Leiter der Baustelle Weilheim, n.d. [September 1918], in BayHStA-KA, Stellvertretendes Generalkommando I. Bayerisches Armeekorps (WK) 678.

106. Becker, A. 2014a, 281.

107. Stibbe 2008a, 31–37.

108. Jones, H. 2008a, 30.

109. See also Jones, H. 2011a, 374–75.

110. Hull 2014, 289. See also Hull 2005, 117–30.

111. Hull 2005, 115.

112. Proctor 2010, 204–5.

113. Thiel 2007, 129–30.

114. Stibbe 2006, 16.

115. Some of these assumptions are usefully unpicked in Douki and Minard, 2007.

Chapter 2

The Captives of the Kaiser

Schutzhaft and Political Prisoners in Germany

André Keil

World War I witnessed the large-scale internment of civilians by almost all belligerents. This affected diverse groups, ranging from so-called "enemy aliens" to political prisoners and social "undesirables" who were perceived as threats to the "will to endure" at the home fronts. In Germany, approximately 100,000 civilians were detained as "citizens of enemy states."[1] There were, however, also up to 5,500 persons, who were detained in so-called *Schutzhaft* (protective custody) under the state of siege legislation, most of them without proper trials.[2] The latter category consisted of a diverse group of radical socialists, among them the prominent antiwar activists Karl Liebknecht and Rosa Luxemburg, but also members of "unreliable" ethnic groups, such as Alsatians and Poles. The sheer number of political prisoners makes the German case particularly relevant. Only the Austro-Hungarian empire interned more of its own citizens on political grounds or because of their questioned allegiance to the state.

Although it is difficult to establish the exact numbers from the surviving records, we can assume that the authorities in the Habsburg empire arrested and interned several thousand individuals. The majority of them were Italian "Irredentists" and Czech nationalists, who were detained on a large scale for their political activities.[3] In Britain eighteen hundred Irish Republicans were interned at the Frongoch internment camp in North Wales after the Easter Rising of 1916.[4] The majority of internees in Frongoch—a derelict distillery that was previously used to intern German POWs—were not combatants but Irish civilians arrested under Defence of the Realm Regulation 14B, which allowed for the incarceration of enemy aliens as well as of those of "hostile association."[5] Almost all these Irish prisoners were, however, released from captivity in December 1916 when David Lloyd George became prime minister. Apart from Irish Republicans, who were arrested and interned in large numbers, there were just under one hundred political prisoners detained under Defence Regulation 14B during the war. However, this comparatively small number changes when the significant number of conscientious objectors in British prisons and internment camps after 1916 is also considered as part of the wider group of those interned on political grounds.[6] Detention without trial to deal with "unreliable" elements of the population and political dissenters was practiced in varying degrees by all belligerents, yet research on the issue remains rather patchy and more national case studies should offer new perspectives on the extent of these practices during the war.

While detention without trial and the internment of political prisoners in the German empire were not unique developments, there were features that made them stand out. Particularly during the later stages of the war, there were attempts to use the instrument of Schutzhaft to remove social "undesirables," including homosexuals, vagrants, and prostitutes, from the wartime *Volksgemeinschaft*. This problem is also discussed by Matthew Stibbe in his contribution to this volume with his discussion of plans for the creation of work camps by the Bavarian authorities during the war. Yet there were also significant continuities between the wartime practices of political captivity and the large-scale use of Schutzhaft by Weimar governments between 1919 and 1924.[7] Against this backdrop it is also necessary to mention that the Nazi regime resorted to the instrument of Schutzhaft to detain over two hundred thousand political opponents almost immediately after its ascent to power in 1933 alone.[8]

Within a brief period the Nazis combined political captivity with mass incarceration in prison camps—both of which were rooted in practices of internment during World War I. These points highlight the historical significance of the phenomenon of detention without trial and underline its importance for understanding the dynamics of German home front politics that shaped the regime under the state of siege. Yet the large quantity of Schutzhaft prisoners also highlights its importance for understanding the phenomenon of civilian internment at large during the war. The subject of protective custody has hitherto been almost completely absent in the historiography of the German home front during World War I. One reason for this neglect is the rather limited source base, since many protective custody orders (Ger. *Schutzhaftbefehle*) have not survived in the archives. Moreover, if the subject is discussed in the literature it is usually treated as a footnote in the debates about political dissent during the war.[9]

The engagement with the problem of civilian captivity during World War I must go beyond the internment of enemy aliens and needs to address the treatment of the significant number of "political prisoners" in almost all belligerents as well. The situation in Germany during the during war is well suited as a case study for this issue. Political prisoners have to date not played a prominent role in debates about civilian captivity during the war, which mainly focuses on so-called "enemy aliens." However, despite the different reasons for their captivity, the experiences and effects of captivity were strikingly similar for those subjected to it. Most Schutzhaft detainees experienced challenges very similar to other civilian prisoners, such as coping with isolation, uncertainty, and boredom. There were, however, also significant differences from the internment of enemy aliens or prisoners of war. Detainees were legally neither treated as criminal nor as civilian prisoners of war; instead they were by definition subject to special detention because they allegedly posed a threat to public order and security. They were dealt with under wartime emergency powers and placed in a distinct legal category that deprived them of most of their constitutional rights and almost made them "nonpersons" in a juridical sense. Schutzhaft was ordered by local military commanders under their emergency powers of the state of siege.

Initially, there were no legal restrictions on how long suspects could be kept in custody. In some cases Schutzhaft lasted only a few hours or days; in other cases, however, detention could last for years.[10] The arbitrariness of the Schutzhaft set it apart from other forms of civilian internment that were at least in part regulated by international and humanitarian conventions, albeit in no legally binding form. The phenomenon also outlasted the Kaiserreich and World War I. The first Weimar governments made excessive use of emergency powers, including Schutzhaft, to combat revolutionary movements. Particularly in the immediate postwar period, Schutzhaft also became associated with brutal violence and even killings of prisoners. This chapter argues that political incarceration must be seen as a relevant part of the history of civilian captivity during World War I. It highlights how notions of alleged "enemies within" shaped who was targeted and interned by the authorities. The gradual extension of the use of Schutzhaft during the war to social undesirables—often simply referred to by the authorities as "urban scum"—also exemplifies the process of the brutalization of German wartime society. What is more, its continued use after 1918 also sheds light on continuities between World War I and the postwar period—or as historian Robert Gerwarth put it, on a "war that failed to end."[11]

State of Siege and Protective Custody in German Prewar Planning

Schutzhaft was no innovation of World War I. The concept dated back to the middle of the nineteenth century. In 1850 the Prussian Law about the Freedom of the Person (*Gesetz zum Schutz der persönlichen Freiheit*) introduced the instrument of Schutzhaft as a means to arrest persons without a warrant.[12] This was limited to cases of immediate danger to public security or the personal safety of the detainee (hence "protective custody") and was subject to confirmation by a judge. A year later the Prussian Law about the State of Siege of 1851 (*Gesetz betreffend den Belagerungszustand von 1851*) incorporated the concept of protective custody as a prerogative of the authorities in cases of public emergencies—however without the legal restrictions and judicial reviews.[13] The siege law was a direct response to the revolutionary uprisings of 1848–1849 and designed to provide legal cover for military action against domestic unrest.[14] After the declaration of a state of siege, the commanding generals of the individual army corps districts were to take over the executive powers, including the right to arrest and detain any person indefinitely. Essentially, this provision of the state of siege was designed to enable the military authorities to remove undesired persons, such as alleged spies or political agitators from the public.

The state of siege was not restricted to use in wartime but entailed more general emergency powers in case of a national crisis, such as civil unrest or large-scale strikes. The power to declare it remained the exclusive prerogative of the king, and later the kaiser, when it was included in the Imperial Constitution of 1871 as article 68. Despite the abundance of domestic crises before 1914, the full state of siege was only declared twice—on the occasion of metalworkers' strikes in the Silesian town of Königshütte in 1884 and Bielefeld in 1885.[15] However, the use of emergency powers was only limited to specific localities, often only lasting for a few days or weeks. There was no practical knowledge as to how to govern a whole country under a semi-permanent state of exception. This also meant that protective custody itself was a rare occurrence before 1914. Nonetheless, designs for the declaration of the state of siege and the use of emergency powers became a crucial part of military contingency plans. Domestic policies became such an important part of strategic planning because leading generals were convinced that a future war would not only have to be fought against external forces but also against potential "enemies within." This centered on the assumption that a confrontation between the Social Democrats and the state was anyway inevitable.[16] The 1912 conference of the Socialist International in Basle and its pledge to oppose any imperialist war only reinforced this belief.[17] Plans to crack down on social democratic organizations immediately before or after the outbreak of hostilities were consequently implemented in mobilization orders.

Since the early 1900s several service regulations and memoranda had been circulated within the officer corps that explained the systematic procedure for the declaration of the state of siege and planned measures for use against potential enemies within. The March 30, 1907, order of the commander of the Seventh Army Corps, General Moritz von Bissing, is a relevant case in point.[18] In this very detailed instruction to all commanders and staff officers, von Bissing laid out the planned actions in case of an uprising or war, which included the preemptive declaration of a state of siege. Bissing's contingency plan demanded the swift and ruthless suppression of any unrest and the use of Schutzhaft against known socialist agitators and leaders. Even the preemptive detention of Reichstag MPs in defiance of their immunity was included in this plan. All captured ringleaders and armed persons were to be "finished off with the weapon."[19]

These orders were based on strategic analyses of the general staff and its department of military history. In studies such as *Kampf in Insurgierten Städten* (Combat in Insurgent Cities), the general staff laid down the main principles to be applied to gain control over a hostile urban environment.[20] The study analyzed all major insurgencies in European cities since 1848, including the Paris Commune of 1871 and the Russian revolution of 1905. It concluded that the actual fighting necessarily had to be accompanied with preemptive measures such as establishing control over the press, the suppression of political agitation, and particularly the use of protective custody for alleged agitators and ringleaders. The study delivered a blueprint for counterinsurgency plans for the case of the declaration of the state of siege for all army corps commands. The basic principles—the swift and brutal suppression of armed resistance combined with the extensive use of Schutzhaft—shaped the approach of the German military toward counterinsurgency warfare. The actions in occupied Belgium in September and October 1914, and also the violent suppression of the revolutionary unrest in Germany in 1919, followed the code of practice laid out in these orders almost to the letter.

The preparations for the state of siege also entailed the collation of arrest lists, which contained the names of persons who were to be taken into

Schutzhaft after the declaration of the state of siege. In correspondence from 1913, for instance, Saxon authorities requested updated lists of persons who were to be "detained because of political or security police considerations."[21] This document is one of the few surviving pieces of evidence that the war plans were accompanied by extensive contingency planning for the preemptive detention of social democratic leaders and agitators. The practice of maintaining "black lists" of political activists was, however, not a unique feature of the German case. In France, the ministry of the interior had maintained the so-called "Carnet B" since 1886. After 1909 the Carnet was used in preparation for the detention of "the most militant anarchists and antimilitarists" in case of a war or domestic emergency.[22] This highlights that the notion of an "internal war" against socialists, anarchists, and dissidents was a widespread feature of prewar military planning in Europe. The use of emergency powers, and particularly the extensive use of detention without trial, in the German case the use of the so-called Schutzhaft, were essential parts of these designs.

Protective Custody and the Regime under the State of Siege, 1914–1918

The developments during the July Crisis of 1914 seemed initially to confirm the expectations of the authorities that a clash with the Social Democratic Party of Germany (*Sozialdemokratische Partei Deutschlands*; SPD) was imminent. July 1914 saw the biggest series of public meetings during the imperial period in Germany.[23] Overall, at least 485,000 persons attended antiwar rallies and far outnumbered the occasional patriotic pro-war demonstrations.[24] The actions of the Social Democrats clearly fitted into scenarios for which contingency plans had been prepared by the military. The peace meetings vividly demonstrated that the SPD had considerable potential to mobilize its rank and file against the war. However, after secret negotiations between the SPD and the imperial government, the military authorities eventually decided against the planned crackdown. In exchange for a guarantee of their personal freedom and the vague promise of political reforms, the SPD agreed to a political truce—the so-called "Burgfrieden."[25] Already on July 25, 1914, the Prussian minister of war, Erich von Falkenhayn, recommended a generally lenient handling of the state of siege and advised against the planned preemptive detention of SPD officials.[26] Yet, it seems that this was merely superficial. Already days after the outbreak of the war, the Berlin Police had intensified its efforts to monitor the SPD in the city, and particularly the political branch, Department VII, continued to work against the "enemies of the realm." Police spies were, for instance, employed in large number to infiltrate and monitor political meetings despite the dwindling manpower of the police and the new additional task to combat espionage. The new emergency powers under the state of siege also allowed the authorities to intercept and censor postal communications of activists.[27]

Initially, there were only very few cases of Schutzhaft. While military and police were reluctant to detain political opponents, so-called "enemy aliens" and alleged spies were arrested much more readily. During the first months of the war, however, most local military commanders used their emergency powers under the state of siege mainly to regulate the practicalities of daily life. The issued decrees predominantly covered matters such as food supply, consumption, and price controls, as well as measures relating to the short-term surge in unemployment during August and September 1914.[28] There were, however, also first signs of the harsh repression that would dominate the handling of the state of siege during the war. Defending the moral order of the home front became a major concern for the authorities. Harsh sentences were, for instance, passed against women who had had "inappropriate" contact with prisoners of war.[29] Particularly the "spreading of false news" soon became code for all kinds of critical opinion, ranging from spreading rumors to openly questioning the war and its conduct by the military.[30]

The use of Schutzhaft became a convenient instrument for the authorities to silence dissent and remove undesirables from the wartime community. At the same time detention without trial helped to avoid public scrutiny and possible further protests. A rather diverse group that became the first target of out-and-out repressive measures during the early months of the war were the so-called "citizens of enemy states" (Ger. *feindliche Fremdstaatangehörige*).[31] The legal status of this group came only vaguely under international and humanitarian law, for instance in the Martens' Clause of the Hague Conventions.[32] Most measures against enemy aliens were therefore based on the emergency powers under the state of siege that allowed detention without trial, based on the right to take any person into protective custody or the synonymous military security detention (*militärische Sicherheitshaft*). These measures set the precedent for the use of protective custody against other groups that were later also defined as "enemies within." Another group that caused concerns for the authorities was the population of Alsace-Lorraine. The general mistrust of the allegedly pro-French Alsatians was nurtured by reports of emphatic welcomes for advancing French troops in the early weeks of the war.[33] The existing tensions between military authorities and the civilian population of Alsace-Lorraine were now aggravated by the state of siege. Military commanders exercised their emergency powers particularly harshly here, leading to a high number of Alsatians, at least 850, being put before courts martial or held in Schutzhaft.[34]

By mid-1915 the arbitrary handling of the state of siege and protective custody by the military commanders was increasingly scrutinized in the Reichstag. SPD deputies began to demand a repeal of the state of siege for those parts of the empire that were not directly affected by combat operations. A motion brought forward by the Social Democratic parliamentarian Adolf Albrecht in July 1915 demanded the restoration of the suspended civil liberties and the return to civilian government by repealing the state of siege.[35] In the budget committee the Social Democrats threatened to boycott further negotiations should there be no changes to the current regime under the state of siege. Due to the limited constitutional powers of the Reichstag, the adoption of the budget was one of the few occasions where political concessions could be demanded from the imperial government.[36]

The stance of the Social Democrats in the Reichstag budget committee was symptomatic of the growing public discontent with the regime under the state of siege. In particular, the arbitrary use of Schutzhaft was increasingly seen as an excess of emergency government. During the Reichstag sessions of 1916, deputies of SPD, Liberals, and even the catholic Zentrum began to criticize its excessive use by the military commands.[37] For example, military commanders had ordered protective custody against individuals who were acquitted by the civil courts. In other cases protective custody was used to prolong already spent prison sentences. The case of the prominent socialist dissenter Rosa Luxemburg highlighted this practice. After spending almost two years in prison for insulting the German Army, Luxemburg was released in July 1916 and then immediately taken into protective custody, where she remained until October 1918.

In strictly legal terms protective custody was not a form of punishment but an instrument of security policy that was not subject to judicial control by the judges. Its application was entirely within the discretion of the local military commanders, who often based it on arbitrary definitions of state security interests and potential threat. There were no effective legal means for detainees to demand a review or to challenge their imprisonment.[38] The imperial government reacted only reluctantly to these criticisms, although internal assessments backed most of the claims made in the Reichstag.[39] A first concession to the critics was the establishment in Berlin in March 1916 of a central authority for complaints regarding the actions of the local military commanders. The so-called Supreme Military Commander (*Obermilitärbefehlshaber*) had no powers in the actual chain of command but could be addressed to review decisions of the local commanders. This minor reform was enacted as a royal decree (*königlicher Erlass*) to avoid the impression of success for the parliamentary campaign.[40]

But the threat of obstruction in the budget committee put additional pressure on the imperial government to undertake further reforms. Protective custody remained the key issue for the parties, and the pressure for its reform was maintained. Not until December 1916 was a first draft of a Law Regarding the State of War (*Gesetz über den Kriegszustand vom 6. Dezember 1916*) presented before parliament. The draft remained far from banning the instrument of protective custody but merely gave detainees the right to consult legal counsel and to appeal their detention. For the first time, the possibility of compensation for illegal detention was introduced, but detainees had a right to be freed only after the war had ended. Nonetheless, the power of the local military commanders to detain any person without trial was not abolished. The Protective Custody Law (*Schutzhaftgesetz*) was passed by the Reichstag on December 2, 1916 and became effective on December 4, 1916.[41] The actual background of this concession was the desire of the new Third Supreme Command under Hindenburg and Ludendorff for a swift enacting of the Auxiliary Service Law, which introduced industrial conscription for all German men between the ages of sixteen and sixty.[42] The public debate about protective custody seems to have strained the negotiations so that at least a minor victory was conceded to the Reichstag parties.[43] The actual handling of the new legal provisions soon proved to be an ineffective protection against arbitrary detention by the military authorities. The courts rejected almost all legal challenges to decisions by local military commanders. The judges tended to follow the arguments of the military and police even when the evidence provided by them was thin. In many cases protective custody was ordered on the basis of vague allegations by police officers or after anonymous denunciations.[44]

Beginning in April 1917, waves of strikes swept through Germany. Led by prominent activists of the Spartacus Group and USPD—a radical antiwar party that had split from the SPD in the same month—the strikes soon combined economic demands and antiwar messages and caused considerable anxiety among police and military leaders. Despite the restrictions introduced with the Schutzhaftgesetz, preemptive detention of political activists and strike leaders was extended. Particularly after the mass strikes of April 1917 and January 1918, the number of persons in protective custody surged.[45] In addition, known socialist activists were now targeted and drafted into the army to put them under military discipline. In Berlin alone the military authorities began to draft 500–600 workers daily. Yet, about 10 percent of them evaded the draft and went underground.[46] In an analysis from February 1918, Department VII concluded that the strikes could only be suppressed because the powers under the state of siege were rigorously exercised. It became apparent that the preparation of repressive responses was the main concern for the authorities.

The war was effectively lost for Germany in June 1918. It took, however, until the end of September for the Supreme Command to officially acknowledge the fact of military defeat. On September 26, Ludendorff confessed that the war could not be won and negotiations for a truce should be commenced under the auspices of the SPD. As part of the makeshift "parliamentarization" of the empire in the last months of the war, the regime under the state of siege was hastily reformed. As early as September 25, 1918, the Imperial Home Office concluded that "without a reform of the state of siege no effective calming down of the parliamentary situation will be achieved."[47] But whereas an immediate reform of the law itself would be impossible, its handling should be softened. A first step in this direction would be to abandon the arbitrary administration of Schutzhaft by the individual military commanders and transfer their emergency powers to the Supreme Military Commander. On October 15 a royal decree was issued subsuming the local military commanders under the control of General Groener, the head of the War Office. At the same time, leading socialist antiwar activists such as Wilhelm Dittmann, Karl Liebknecht, Rosa Luxemburg, and Kurt Eisner were released after a general amnesty. This was supposed to be a sign of goodwill and opened up the way for the negotiations about constitutional reform with the representatives of the Reichstag parties.[48] The new revolutionary government of the Council of the People's Deputies officially repealed the state of siege by decree on November 12, 1918, and with it, at least for the time being, the use of Schutzhaft.[49]

Case Study: The Handling of Protective Custody by the Berlin Police

During World War I Berlin was a microcosm of German wartime society. As the biggest city of the German empire, it featured all developments that could also be observed in other urban and industrial centers on the German home front. Berlin is thus a prime case study for the handling of Schutzhaft by the authorities and their eventually futile attempts to use it as a repressive instrument to manage the German wartime society. The key actors in the city were the commanding officers of the High Command of the Marken District (*Oberkommando in den Marken*) and the Berlin police. Although the military was nominally in charge, most of the day-to-day activities were controlled by the police force. Only occasionally did the military directly intervene, often in cases of national importance and large-scale strikes. Initially, the activities of the dissident Social Democrats and concerns about the moral order of the home front and the neglect of youth were a priority for the authorities. By August 1914 the leadership of the Berlin police, in a circular to its officers, had emphasized that despite the Burgfrieden policy the Berlin socialists still followed "the golden thread of internationalism" and they had to be kept under close surveillance.[50]

The use of emergency powers, such as protective custody, brought its challenges for the police. On the one hand, the authorities hoped for an intimidating effect of harsh repression. For this purpose some degree of publicity for cases of protective custody was desired and indeed intended. Schutzhaft arrests because of "seditious speeches," "undermining of the civilian and military morale," lèse-majesté, or most frequently the "spreading of wrong news" were regularly reported in the newspapers. On the other hand, reports about the most serious cases against political activists were often censored and curtailed.[51] The authorities were interested in giving their repressive measures enough publicity to have a deterring effect, but at the same time they sought to avoid providing additional material for further protest. Protective custody and systematic intimidation were a crucial part of the management and control of dissent. The tension between intimidation and avoiding too much unwanted public scrutiny is also visible in the sources.

As early as 1915, the Prussian minister of war, Adolf Wild von Hohenborn, ordered the Berlin police to avoid prosecutions under the provisions of the Imperial Penal Code (especially article 89, "treason in wartime") because of the publicity that open court trials would create. Instead, the instrument of Schutzhaft was to be used to deal with such matters without attracting too much public scrutiny.[52] The power to keep people in prolonged custody without a trial was a convenient option for the authorities to silence dissenting voices. Yet, in many cases, the police were far from being a mere executive agency of the military commanders but acted according to their own agenda. The various departments of the Berlin police—particularly the Criminal Investigations Department (*Kriminalpolizei/Abteilung III*) and Department VII—often conducted investigations and observations on their own initiative. In most cases the military commanders were only involved when warrants for protective custody had to be issued. This changed only in 1918, when the policing of the home fronts became increasingly militarized because of the escalating domestic crisis. There were, of course, always cases where the police acted on orders and on behalf of the local military commanders, but it seems that the police undertook most of these proceedings proactively in their own capacity.[53]

Detaining people in protective custody was not always the result of proceedings by the police alone. In many cases, the police only initiated their investigations and prosecutions after receiving information from members of the public. A surge of denunciations and accusation letters is documented in the files for the period immediately after the outbreak of the war. The omnipresent patriotic propaganda created a climate in which even the slightest careless remark could bring people into trouble. The Berlin police regularly received letters with accusations regarding offenses against decrees under the state of siege or general "hostile behavior." These files also highlight the evolution of certain concepts of "enemies within." Initially, denunciations and accusations mainly concerned alleged and actual "enemy aliens" as well as people from Alsace-Lorraine. However, during the later course of the war, all kinds of critical or dissenting talk could lead to denunciations. It seems that anonymous allegations were often used to settle old accounts: landlords accused unruly tenants; people wrote letters about their neighbors; shop owners denounced competitors, employers their employees, and vice versa.[54]

Some examples illustrate the emergence of this culture of accusations and denunciations in wartime Berlin: In September 1916 the factory supervisor Arndt Reuther was taken into protective custody after a female worker had accused him of "hostile propaganda." After almost two months in solitary confinement (*Isolierungshaft*), Reuther was released without ever being charged.[55] In November 1915 the worker Emma Nehring was arrested and taken into protective custody for "illegal contacts with prisoners of war" after a denunciation. She had passed on photos, letters, and socks to a French prisoner.[56] Mere suspicion was often sufficient for the authorities to apply protective custody. The fact that these methods were legally barely restricted and insufficiently controlled facilitated their arbitrary use. The language of the denunciations also reflects how deep-rooted certain stereotypes and concepts of domestic enmity were within the population. In a letter to the Berlin police from November 1916, a Mrs. Hoffmann complained about "French and Russian Jews" who allegedly regularly met in the flat of a Dr. Eisner to "incite hatred against the Emperor and Germany."[57]

In another letter a dismissed cook complained about his former employer's "inherent affection for all things French" (*Franzosentümelei*). What caused suspicion in many cases was not concrete evidence for offences, such as belonging to certain groups or showing an allegedly hostile attitude. The frequent reference in accusation letters to certain personal features of suspects rather than their actual actions reveals the widespread conception of "enemies within." From the evidence in the sources, it can also be inferred that the denunciators came, with few exceptions, from the middle classes, whereas the accused were often workers or belonged to socially marginalized groups.[58]

The political and moral policing of the home front occupied the best part of the available police resources throughout the war in Berlin. Protective custody was used to exercise social control and to monitor the population. Departments traditionally concerned with fighting crime adjusted their activities to the wartime necessities of the political and moral policing of the home front. The Criminal Investigations Department of the Berlin police, for example, began to concentrate on prosecuting activities that were perceived as prejudicial to the war effort. A report of the department from May 1916 names very distinctive categories of persons taken into protective custody at the request of the police, representing the entirety of the "enemies within."[59] The report also emphasized the significant efforts undertaken by the department and the close collaboration between police and military authorities in this matter.

The report stressed that the initiative for these prosecutions lay with the police. Most remarkable, however, is the fact that the exceptional instrument of protective custody was not only used to quell political dissent; it became the main instrument to deal with all kinds of deviant behavior during the war. In May 1915, for example, the High Command of the Marken District issued an order, after a suggestion by the Berlin police, that all "pederasts in women's clothing" (Ger. *Päderasten in Weiberkleidung*) and homosexuals in the province were to be taken into protective custody for the duration of the war. Although eventually not enforced, this remarkable order demanded the wholesale detention of an entire social group.[60] The *Sittenpolizei*, or vice squad, also used the Schutzhaft to detain alleged prostitutes. Usually suspected women were arrested by officers at the beginning of the night and kept in custody until the next morning. The extent of this practice is unknown, but a report from May 1916 notes it as a key instrument to deal with the rampant prostitution in the city.[61]

Even after the hesitant reform of protective custody in December 1916, the number of cases did not fall significantly. Another report from 1916 reveals the full extent to which the police meanwhile used detention without trial. It lists eleven categories of offenders against which protective custody was ordered, including "fortune tellers, pederasts, peace protestors, participants of food riots, army insulters, vagrants, charlatans, pimps, prostitutes. . ., [and] persons who had unauthorized contact with prisoners of war."[62] The variety of affected groups demonstrates that the originally exceptional measures for the case of an emergency had become a regular instrument for exercising social control on the home front. The excessive use of emergency powers was possible and accepted because it could build on prevalent negative stereotypes and conceptions of "enemies of the realm." Many of these concepts had already been shaped before World War I but were aggravated by the war situation and gradually extended to other groups defined as being outside the national collective.

By targeting groups perceived as threats to the unity and moral order of the home front, the police established the boundaries of the imagined wartime *Volksgemeinschaft*. Whereas those inside these imagined boundaries could expect at least a degree of rule of law and even leniency when faced with the authorities, those outside it where often deprived of the most basic legal protections. Against this backdrop the police acted not only as an executive agency for the military and the government, but it also exercised exceptional powers at its own discretion. Police officers acted according to their self-assigned role as guardians of the home front. As Belinda Davis argues, this self-perception of the police also meant that they saw themselves as acting on behalf of the wartime Volksgemeinschaft and reacting to their justified grievances by removing undesirables, deviants, and subversives from its midst.[63] These police activities protected the patriotic sections of the nation against the perceived threats of subversion and moral decline. With the increase of Schutzhäftlinge after 1916, debates began within the military and the police about more efficient ways to detain large numbers of inmates.

In April 1917 a conference was held in Berlin to discuss the establishment of "labor camps" for "vagrants and antisocial elements."[64] Eventually, the ministry of justice advised against the establishment of such camps on legal grounds.[65] Rounding up such a large number of persons and their internment in labor camps would anyway have stretched insufficient resources and manpower. But the discussions reveal that the concepts of protective (political) custody and detainment in camps were already entwined during World War I. It was now perceived as a convenient instrument to deal with the problem of social undesirables, often referred to in the documents, as Matthew Stibbe shows in his contribution to this volume, as the "scum of the cities" (Ger. *Großstadtgesindel*) and other "useless eaters." Moreover, the authorities saw the extrajudicial detention in combination with the disciplinary regime of internment camps as an appropriate method to force the alleged "work shy" into "doing their bit" for the war effort.[66]

The actual experience of captivity for so-called Schutzhäftlinge differed significantly depending on local circumstances. Political prisoners were usually detained in "isolation custody" in *Zuchthaus* jails, where they were closely monitored and their correspondence censored. More prominent prisoners were often transferred to detention in fortresses (Ger. *Festungshaft*). These internees usually received more favorable treatment, including access to newspapers and books and visits from friends and relatives. They were also allowed to supplement their food by purchasing additional items from outside suppliers. In more low-profile cases, detainees were usually held in police prisons, which were used to keep defendants in custody before trials. In Berlin, the jail in Moabit and the cells in the building of the Berlin Police Presidency, the notorious "Rote Burg," were used for this purpose.

More high-profile detainees, such as Rosa Luxemburg, were regularly moved between prisons to avoid the establishment of solidarity networks between political prisoners. The treatment of most prisoners in protective custody did not differ significantly from that of regular inmates. They were, however, usually spared forced labor and other chores that regular prisoners were required to perform. Release from protective custody often came as unexpectedly as the arrest itself. In many cases detainees were left in the dark as to why they had been arrested or why they were released. The arbitrary handling of protective custody was part of a deliberate strategy that added to feelings of anxiety and uncertainty for detainees. For some, particularly those with little or no experience with the authorities, the experience of protective custody was certainly traumatic. Physical violence against Schutzhaft prisoners was nevertheless a rare occurrence. This can be explained as an attempt by the authorities to prevent the escalation of already heightened tensions with the SPD and the radical opposition. There was a certain fear among the authorities that the use of violence might fuel a radicalization of the antiwar opposition. In most cases removing the suspects from their communities and suppressing their ability to communicate with the outside world proved to be sufficient in the eyes of the authorities. Nonetheless, this self-constraint disappeared after the November revolution, when the military and Freikorps acted, at least nominally, on behalf of the SPD-dominated government. By 1919 Schutzhaft had become synonymous with excessive violence and brutality against detainees.[67]

Aftermath

The new revolutionary Council of People's Deputies was initially extremely reluctant to use any emergency powers under the state of siege, particularly Schutzhaft arrests, despite the turmoil of November and December 1918. This was due to the fact that particularly the representatives of the independent socialists of the USPD wanted a clean break with the repressive practices of the old regime. This sentiment was also shared by many grassroots activists of the SPD. There were also, however, very practical reasons for the reluctance to use emergency powers. Immediately after the successful November Revolution, there was a lack of clarity as to whether the old laws, including the state of siege and the Protective Custody Law of 1916, were still in force. This legal uncertainty did, however, end with the Law concerning the Provisional Powers of the Reich of February 1919, which reestablished the state of siege powers and the Schutzhaft.

When revolutionary unrest broke out in the country in March 1919, the authorities made excessive use of the Schutzhaft again. Although reliable numbers are hard to establish, it is estimated that in 1919 and 1920 alone several thousand persons were taken in Schutzhaft, which now also became associated with extreme brutality and even killings of prisoners, something that had been largely absent during the war. For instance, there were several reports of beatings and executions of Schutzhaft prisoners during the so-called March Fights in Berlin and after the crushing of the Munich Soviet.[68] This was done under the state-of-siege legislation that evolved throughout the war. Schutzhaft remained a key feature of the state of exception during the early years of the Weimar Republic and only gradually disappeared after 1923. The use of protective custody in the early years of the Weimar Republic clearly highlights the continuity of repressive practices between the old and new political orders.

Nonetheless, immediately after the breakdown of the old order, there were also remarkable attempts to redress the worst excesses of the regime under the state of siege during the war. Already in November 1918, the Council of People's Deputies deliberated about the possibility of compensation payments for those held in protective custody. For this purpose, the Reichsjustizamt (Office for National Justice) compiled a comprehensive overview of the extent of protective custody. This included approximately 5,500 persons who were held in protective custody during the war (including 850 Alsatians) and an additional 1,200 persons who were the subject of banning orders (Ger. *Aufenthaltsverbot*).[69] The report concluded that 1,032 individuals had to be considered "political" prisoners with a claim to compensation.[70] At the same time, a Council of Former Schutzhaft-Prisoners (*Rat Ehemaliger Schutzhaft-Gefangener*) was established in Berlin to lobby the new government. On February 17, 1919, the chairman of the council, a certain Mohammed Zeki Bey, addressed a letter to the minister of justice.[71] Zeki Bey complained that his lawyer had been denied access to the secret files relating to his protective custody and that the new government was protecting "those officers . . . who under the old order committed so many crimes against us."[72] It concluded that if the new socialist government failed to address the suffering of the Schutzhaft prisoners, it would essentially betray the ideas of the revolution.[73]

The subsequent discussions within different Weimar governments about the issue of compensation for legal yet illegitimate "political" protective custody during the war eventually concluded with a decision that no compensation payments should be made.[74] The funds necessary as calculated by the ministries of finance and justice would have put significant strain on the already weak finances of the young republic.[75] Similarly, the demands for legal prosecution of those responsible for the most drastic abuses of emergency powers under the state of siege were denied as well. Government lawyers insisted that almost all actions of military commanders during the war were legal under the state-of-siege legislation and that there were no legal grounds for prosecution.[76] This was not a mere legalistic argument but a political one as well. With the reestablishment of the state of siege and Schutzhaft after February 1919, such prosecutions and the ensuing public debates would necessarily also have raised questions about why the new government was resorting to the same repressive methods. Political considerations soon replaced the initial desire to distance the new republic from the old order. Political activists such as Zeki Bey, on the other hand, appealed to moral categories by emphasizing the injustices they suffered during the war as victims of the abuses of Schutzhaft.

The postwar debate about the compensation of former Schutzhaft prisoners highlights the tension between the concepts of legality and legitimacy of state agency during the war. Yet, it also raises bigger questions about the political identities of former Schutzhaft prisoners in the postwar period. Despite the comparatively large number of detainees during the war, they did not form a collective identity in the interwar period, comparable to developments after World War II. The Council of Former Schutzhaft-Prisoners, for instance, turned out to be rather short-lived and ceased to exist in 1920. Radical socialists, and particularly members of the new communist party KPD, integrated their experiences of Schutzhaft into narratives of resistance against the war. Similarly, Alsatians and Poles were able to frame their detention as part of the struggle for national unification and independence. The significant number of "social undesirables" who were subjected to Schutzhaft, however, remained mostly silent and invisible in these narratives.

The phenomena of Schutzhaft and political captivity in general were relevant parts of the experience of civilian captivity during World War I. The character changed gradually between 1914 and 1918. Initially designed to be used against dissenters, Schutzhaft also became essential to the attempts to establish social control on the home front and to protect the moral standards of the population. It was used to control and suppress all forms of behavior defined as deviant and dangerous to the collective "will to victory." As the detention list of the Berlin police highlights, protective custody gave the authorities the power to remove those persons from the wartime Volksgemeinschaft who were perceived as "enemies within." The definition of those who belonged to this category, and were thus subject to emergency measures such as Schutzhaft, was within the discretion of the military authorities. This added an element of arbitrariness to end barely limited emergency powers. What connected these often disparate categories of Schutzhaft prisoners was their perception of being outside the national collective.

The idea of the state of siege and the state of exception more generally continued to influence political thought in the interwar years. Theorists such as Carl Schmitt, for instance, made the state of exception the centerpiece of their conception of the state. The political culture of the interwar years was in many ways shaped by an uncritical celebration of unrestrained state power.[77] When looking at the phenomenon of protective custody during the war, it is hard not to draw parallels to the Nazi regime and its use of Schutzhaft as an instrument of terror and persecution. The legal basis for detention without trial after the Reichstag Fire Decree in February 1933 was indeed modeled after the original provisions in the Prussian state-of-siege legislation without the limitations introduced after 1916. Moreover, the categories of "enemies within" were clearly derived from the established notions of "'enemies of the realm" that were extended, radicalized, and racialized during the war.[78] Nonetheless, the extreme violence of the SA, the SS, and the Gestapo after 1933 was almost completely absent in the experience of political prisoners during World War I. It was the combination of the concept of "enemies within," the legal framework of Schutzhaft and the creation of "spaces of exception," for instance, the concentration camp system that facilitated brutalization of captivity. It is undeniable that World War I represents the starting point of these developments. But this process should not be seen as direct and linear. It is probably best to understand it in the terms of the Italian philosopher Giorgio Agamben as a "laboratory for the state of exception."[79]

Notes

1. Speed 1990, 216.

2. Bundesarchiv [henceforth BArch] R3001/6664, minutes of a meeting regarding the use of Schutzhaft, January 16–17, 1919.

3. Stibbe 2013b, 87–106.

4. Mahony 1987.

5. Simpson 1994, 1–33.
6. Rae 1970.
7. Keil and Stibbe 2020.
8. Wachsmann 2015, 42.
9. See, for instance, Carsten 1992.
10. BArch R3001/6664, minutes of a meeting regarding the use of Schutzhaft, January 16–17, 1919.
11. Gerwarth 2016.
12. *Gesetzsammlung für die Königlichen Preußischen Staaten* 1850, 45.
13. *Gesetzsammlung für die Königlichen Preußischen Staaten* 1851, 451.
14. Schudnagies 1994.
15. Funk 1985, 153.
16. Miller 1974, 44–46; Kruse 1994, 50–52.
17. *Manifest der Internationale zur gegenwärtigen Lage. Resolutionen am Basler Kongress*, November 24–25, 1912, 23–27.
18. Gutsche 1977, 115.
19. Gutsche 1977, 115.
20. Deist 1991, 103–52.
21. BArch R1501/112215, p. 185, letter by the Saxon Ministry of State regarding the detention of political activists, March 31, 1913.
22. Becker and Kriegel 1968; Becker, J.-J. 1973.
23. Kruse 1994, 31–36.
24. The Berlin police reported over thirty thousand participants in a meeting in Tiergarten, after which several groups marched through the city singing the "Internationale," shouting "down with the war" and occasionally clashing with police and patriotic demonstrators. Several arrests were made on this day: LAB, A Pr. Br. Rep. 030 Nr. 11361, p. 228, report about the peace demonstrations by the Berlin police president, July 28, 1914; Kruse 1994, 36.
25. Kruse 1994, 36; Miller 1974, 42–43.
26. Deist 1970, 188–92.
27. BArch R1501/112254, Kriegszustand. Postkontrolle, 1916–18.
28. Landesarchiv Berlin [henceforth LAB] A Pr. Br. Rep. 030 no. 1465, 1914–15.
29. BArch R3001/6655; BArch R3001/6656.
30. The case of the Berlin-based tailor Ernst Sporny is exemplary: he was charged with the "spreading of false news" in October 1915, acquitted by a civil court but then taken into protective custody by the commander of the Marken district from November 25, 1915, until January 15, 1916. In another trial for compensation for illegal detention, the Marken commander argued that although Sporny's public remarks were technically not "false news," they were suitable to cause disaffection with the war effort. This gave enough reason to detain him under protective custody. BArch 1501/112253, 285–7, case file Ernst Sporny, November 1915–December 1916.
31. Stibbe 2008a, 2–51; Stibbe 2008b.
32. Schircks 2002.
33. Kramer, Alan 1997, 105–21.
34. A number of cases against Alsatians, particularly those heard before the Imperial Military Court and Reichsgericht, are documented in the files of the Imperial Office of Justice; see for example: BArch R3001/6667.
35. *Verhandlungen des Reichstags, Stenographischer Bericht*, vol. 316, no. 140, 202.

36. *Verhandlungen des Reichstags, Stenographischer Bericht*, vol. 316, no. 132, 189; Reichsgesetzblatt 1915, No. 179: 813.

37. *Verhandlungen des Reichstags, Stenographischer Bericht*, vol. 319, no. 431, 865.

38. *Verhandlungen des Reichstags, Stenographischer Bericht*, vol. 307, 54. Sitz., p. 1278; see also BArch R3001/6666; Dittmann 1917.

39. BArch R3001/6662, 148–55.

40. BArch R3001/6662, 248–56.

41. Reichsgesetzblatt 1916, pp. 1329–31.

42. Feldman 1966, 197–235.

43. Deist 1970, 442–44.

44. LAB A Pr. Br. Rep. 030 Nr. 15706, Majestätsbeleidigungen aus Arbeiterkreisen, 1911–15; LAB A Pr. Br. Rep. 030 Nr. 15707, Majestätsbeleidigungen aus Arbeiterkreisen, 1915–18.

45. The Berlin Police noted over ninety cases of protective custody in the city in January 1918 alone. The alleged offenses included incitement to strike, resistance against police officers, rioting, disturbing the peace. LAB A Pr. Br. Rep. 030 Nr. 15842.

46. LAB A Pr. Br. Rep. 030 Nr. 15842.

47. BArch R1501/112262, 3–4.

48. Christoph 1988, 24–25.

49. BArch R3001/6663, 283.

50. LAB A Pr. Br. Rep. 030 Nr. 11360, 360.

51. An example illustrating this is the attempt of the Berlin police to curtail the distribution of the pamphlet "Belagerungerszustand und Zensur" by the SPD parliamentarian Wilhelm Dittmann, in which the excessive use of emergency power was criticized. Various party offices and publishers were raided to seize the pamphlet before it could be distributed; LAB A Pr. Br. Rep. 030 Nr. 15903, 248.

52. LAB A Pr. Br. Rep. 030 Nr. 15854, 4–5.

53. LAB A Pr. Br. Rep. 030 Nr. 15854; LAB A Pr. Br. Rep. 030 Nr. 15903; LAB A Pr. Br. Rep. 030 Nr. 15715.

54. LAB A Pr. Br. Rep. 030 Nr. 15706; LAB A Pr. Br. Rep. 030 Nr. 15707.

55. LAB A Pr. Br. Rep. 030 Nr. 15715.

56. LAB A Pr. Br. Rep. 030 Nr. 15713.

57. LAB A Pr. Br. Rep. 030 Nr. 15713, letter from Ms. Hoffmann to Berlin Police Presidency, November 1916.

58. LAB A Pr. Br. Rep. 030 Nr. 15707; see also LAB A Pr. Br. Rep. 030 Nr. 15648.

59. LAB Berlin A Pr. Br. Rep. 030 Nr. 11361, 343, 4 May 1916: "A large number of culprits was taken into protective custody at the request of the department such as: fortune tellers, pederasts, pimps, army insulters, etc."

60. LAB A Pr. Br. Rep. 030 Nr. 15803, 14.

61. LAB Berlin A Pr. Br. Rep. 030 Nr. 11361, 349–50.

62. LAB Berlin A Pr. Br. Rep. 030 Nr. 11361, 350.

63. Davis 2000, 126–29.

64. BArch R3001/6663, minutes of a conference regarding the use of Schutzhaft, April 11, 1917.

65. BArch R3001/6663, minutes of a conference regarding the use of Schutzhaft, April 11, 1917.

66. BArch R3001/6663, minutes of a conference regarding the use of Schutzhaft, April 11, 1917.

67. Jones, M. 2016.

68. Thoß 2012.

69. BArch R3001/6664, minutes of a meeting regarding the use of Schutzhaft, January 16–17, 1919.

70. BArch R3001/6664, minutes of a meeting regarding the use of Schutzhaft, January 16–17, 1919.

71. BArch R3001/6664, p. 51, letter from Mohammed Zeki Bey to Justice Minister Dr Landsberg, February 17, 1919.

72. BArch R3001/6664, p. 51, letter from Mohammed Zeki Bey to Justice Minister Dr Landsberg, February 17, 1919.

73. BArch R3001/6664, p. 51, letter from Mohammed Zeki Bey to Justice Minister Dr Landsberg, February 17, 1919.

74. BArch R3001/6664.

75. BArch R3001/6664.

76. BArch R3001/6664.

77. Hoffmann 2005.

78. Raithel and Strenge 2000, 41–60.

79. Agamben 2005, 7.

Chapter 3

Securitized Protection

Health Work in Wartime Austria-Hungary and the Making of Refugee Camps

Doina Anca Cretu

On August 27, 1914, the Russian army invaded Austria-Hungary in the east, generating the immediate forced displacement of people living in Galicia and Bukovina. By 1915 an Italian invasion in the south further destabilized civilians' lives in this part of the empire, leading to their immediate flight to the hinterland. War clashes generated waves of mass displacement of the population. Notably, numerous Jews, primarily from Galicia, fled because of fear of pogroms as the Russian army was advancing in the east.[1] At the same time, the government, in collaboration with the military, developed a program of formal evacuation of civilians living in and around the main war zones. Given the varied motivations behind people's forced displacement, Austria-Hungary saw over one million internally displaced civilians over the course of the war.[2] In response, the authorities placed some refugees in districts in and around major cities and towns. However, the basis of the refugee policy in its early days was built primarily on the immobilization of this population on the move and its placement into a few quickly built refugee camps, far from the war zone.

Refugee camps (Ger. *Flüchtlingslager*) were part of a broader *Lager* network that represented the crux of the Austro-Hungarian wartime policy. Besides refugees, prisoners of war and internees were placed in similar sites of securitization. Formally, the authorities differentiated refugees from the others, due to the low political danger they represented. Indeed, from the officials' vantage point, refugees were those politically harmless people who had been forced to flee. With men being conscripted to fight in the military, refugees were, for the most part, women, children, and the elderly. Vulnerable, most of them without means or a home, these refugees became the object of the welfare scheme of a protective state.[3]

The history of refugee camps, their establishment, security implications, and refugees' own experiences, has gained some attention during the last few years. Still, the periodization, as well as the shifts and turns regarding the policy of refugee confinement and related practices, remain vague. Some recent work has connected the establishment of camps in the aftermath of World War I to the "making of the modern refugee" during this period. This literature has pointed to the development of an international refugee regime through the rise of the League of Nations and of related bureaucratic measures to manage forced displacement.[4] However, much of the scholarship has remained focused on the aftermath of the Second World War and the decolonization period as watershed moments in the establishment of modern refugee camps; this was arguably shaped by Hannah Arendt's recorded reflections on the camp as a political and juridical microcosm, "a routine solution for the problem of domicile of the 'displaced persons.' "[5] Thus, historians have interpreted the use of camps as objects of national, transnational, and international governance during the post-1945 period. In these narratives, the actions of sovereign states, as well as of nongovernmental and international organizations intersected to assist refugees.[6] In the exploration of the making of refugee camps in this post-1945 period, the historiography has highlighted the use of scientists, volunteers of various professions, and media channels as modern *modi operandi* to assist mechanisms of containment of displaced populations living in these spaces.

The process of confinement in refugee camps in Austria-Hungary during World War I was, however, similarly sustained through the deployment of local administrators, professionals, and visual and narrative media forms. Containment of forcefully displaced people was nothing new. The European revolutions of 1848 and the case of African-American slaves during the Civil War in the United States are examples of how forced migration was restricted through refugee camps prior to World War I.[7] In Austria-Hungary state officials used earlier models of internment of prisoners of war and of politically dangerous populations when establishing refugee camps as a temporary emergency measure to halt the war-generated mass displacement crisis that hit the empire.[8]

Born out of the officials' belief in a short war, the design of refugee camps was an expedient measure from the outset. However, as the war continued, refugee camps gradually became permanent structures of the home front. Moreover, officials rallied new and external resources to administer and ensure the security of these sites, as well as to aid and mobilize refugees in view of broader aspirations to consolidate the state. Altogether, refugee camps in Austria-Hungary during World War I were laboratories of professionalization and expertise. There, administrators, doctors, psychologists, and educators used scientific standards, empirically tested and adapted methods to relieve and rehabilitate the hungry or the sick; in the process, they augmented the control and regulation of refugees' minds and bodies.

This chapter looks at one dimension of professionalized refugee camp management in Austria-Hungary: the organization of health-care assistance and the workers involved. It highlights the conclusion that the apparatus of health experts and on-site professionals enabled camp confinement as an instrument of population management during the war. Ultimately, the lens of health workers reveals World War I as the moment when modern refugee camps took shape through the meshing of agendas and practices of containment of seemingly foreign and unwanted populations and their state-driven relief. I treat here the concept of "health workers" as a collective protagonist. It is made of a network of Vienna-based scientific experts, supervisors of health and hygiene conditions, medical officers, and local health professionals, as well as practitioners in the camps. In practice, these individuals acted as relief workers, as they observed and evaluated the state of the camps, assisted ill refugees, and improved the health and hygiene conditions on the ground. At the same time, they reinforced the systematic securitization and containment measures that state officials devised and attempted to implement in the management of refugee camps. In this account, they were onsite mediators between state officials and the refugees. This chapter tells the story of these health workers, their designed role in the broader state policy of refugee camp management, their practices, and their experiences on the ground.

Austria-Hungary's Spaces of Refugeedom

In September 1914, immediately after the Russian invasion in the east, the Ministry of Interior in Vienna released a document designed to map the bureaucratic and practical mechanisms that represented the basis of refugee confinement as wartime policy of civilian protection. In this memorandum officials set out the criteria for sorting and classifying refugees at evacuation stations, at intermediate stations between the front and the hinterland, and on arrival in the camps or in various districts of the main urban centers. In theory, refugees deemed to be without means (Ger. *mittelos*) were selected for transport to camps, while those who had sufficient financial capacity to support themselves were sent to the larger cities of the monarchy.[9] Those refugees who could sustain themselves were then sorted by nationality and confession, which created the backbone of the organizational nature of the refugee camp system in Austria-Hungary. Early on Ruthenians[10] were sent to camps in Carinthia and Lower Austria, Christian Poles to Bohemia and Styria, whereas Jews were placed in Moravia and Bohemia. As the war went on, Italians, Slovenians, Croatians, and Romanians were placed in different camps that were progressively built and organized in Upper and Lower Austria.[11]

The question of inclusion and belonging was intrinsic to the establishment of refugee camps from an early stage. For one, most refugees were formally relocated to camps established within the Austrian part of the Habsburg monarchy. The authorities from Budapest claimed that refugees were Austrian citizens, rather than Hungarian, and so the responsibility fell on the officials in Vienna. Refugee camps had also been built in the Hungarian part, but they were transitory, with many people being rerouted to Austria.[12] Accordingly, refugees' formal citizenship shaped the early strategies of confinement organization. The issue of belonging was also present in the categorization that followed based on nationality and confession. Indeed, the state officials argued early on that this classification had practical and psychological undertones, as it represented an effort to recreate the feeling of community and home (Ger. *Heimat*) among refugees.[13]

However, confinement of refugees was also an avenue through which these insiders through citizenship became outsiders on the ground. Categorization and placement in refugee camps also meant more control over large groups of seemingly foreign individuals. Concerns over the flight of populations from the peripheries of the empire were found in official claims stating that "flood flowing into the hinterland created a new social and ethnic problem, the solution of which presides over much more than just the individual fate of the individual refugees."[14] In the authorities' perspective, the camps were not just sites to infuse welfare in aid of largely homogeneous communities but also a way to contain the dangers of foreigners' mass intrusion into the hinterland.

The intertwining of refugee containment and the humanitarian nature of the state's management of these sites was a fundamental feature of

Austria-Hungary's refugee camps. At first, the government designed refugee camps as constructions under the guise of securitized protection of displaced populations coming from the east. However, as the war went on, the number of refugees grew and the notion of a short conflict dissipated. The increased needs of refugees living in these spaces and the prolongation of the conflict brought about a shift in the agendas and the establishment and management of refugee camps. If at first the camps meant quickly built and temporary barracks, the ever expanding number of refugees and the war-generated health, food, and workforce crises precipitated the expansion of a technology of population management.[15] Thus, the camps became permanent structures where state authorities implemented short- and medium-term relief and rehabilitation measures to heal, feed, educate, and employ refugees on behalf of the local economy or for the war effort. In the long term, officials used refugee camps as sites where they could mobilize the population living in the barracks on behalf of a vision of postwar state building.

The state's short-, medium-, and long-term agendas of refugee welfare (Ger. *Flüchtlingsfürsorge*) were implemented in the camps by local administrators, religious leaders of all denominations, educators, and health workers. In this sense, the camps were veritable spaces of refugeedom, where a circuit between Vienna-driven planning and on-site implementation of refugee assistance and their overall control involved multiple actors and held different political, social, and cultural implications. Taking this multiplicity of voices into consideration, the next two sections of this chapter analyze one category that was part of the making of refugee camps—the matrix of health workers.

Blueprints of Health Work

News of the 1914 Russian invasion in the east was unsettling for Vienna's political and medical spheres. The dread of military collapse was coupled with concerns about potential contagion caused by the probable arrival of refugees from Galicia and Bukovina. Fear of disease coming from the east had long been a leitmotif of political discourse in Viennese circles.[16] As information from the front line poured in, doctors joined the chorus of distress, claiming that transports from Galicia posed an "imminent danger of infection for Vienna" unless the "political unreliable" coming from the east were placed somewhere else.[17] Thus, while refugees were Austrian citizens and, in fact, insiders, fears regarding their politics and health overlapped. It was in this fragile context that the idea of the camps emerged as a method to control this initial wave of displaced populations. The authorities then believed that this was a practical avenue to halt any potential epidemiological danger and its spread to the population. As a September 1914 Ministry of Interior memorandum on general refugee policy advised, unless camps were established and refugees placed there, "in big cities or rural areas . . . every type of control, especially those of a sanitary nature, [will] become impossible."[18] A series of emergency and preventive measures as part of a sanitary welfare (Ger. *Sanitätsfürsorge* (program followed.

Stopping disease and its potential carriers emerged as a core rationale behind the organization of refugee camps in the early days of the displacement crisis in Austria-Hungary. Officials' and doctors' fears therefore translated into the early efforts to put in place a mechanism of health-oriented work. For one, the transportation and reception of refugees were organized around sanitary measures to combat illnesses. For example, in order to prevent refugees from spreading war epidemics, the authorities established some so-called observation stations (Ger. *Beobachtungstationen*) in Hungarisch-Hradisch / Uherské Hradiště and Mährisch-Trübau / Moravská Třebová in Moravia, with the purpose of a sanitary inspection of those arriving. According to this plan, the refugees were transported to the camps or other host communities only after an appropriate medical examination. This scheme of transportation was a staple of the organization of refugee camps. However, transportation resources became scarce as the war dragged on and invasions in the south, coupled with the forced displacement of people across the empire, strained Austria-Hungary's military acumen and material capacity.[19] Consequently, many refugees continued on foot, as the trains were used for military purposes. This led to further concerns regarding the threat posed by the refugees to the broader population.

The seemingly chaotic and continuous movement of refugees from all parts of the empire continued to cause anxiety among the authorities, as well as among the locals. As more established modes of transportation remained intermittent, many refugees were left to their own devices, causing public apprehension regarding their possible encounters with the locals; these, in turn, questioned the state's efforts to address the refugees' movements and their potential to spread disease. A note on public complaints addressed to the *Österreichische Land-Zeitung*, a newspaper published in Lower Austria, gives an insight into the locals' fears of the diseased refugee:

> People write to us: For some time now, the 3rd class waiting room has been used to accommodate refugees on the night trains. As praiseworthy as this care is on the one hand, it seems questionable on the other hand, with regard to the travelling public, which is dependent on using

> this waiting room as well. As is well-known, the war refugees came from areas that are partly contaminated and the risk of transmitting infectious diseases is therefore very obvious. . . . Far worse is the fact that refugees use the same toilets, which are available to travelers. . . . It is downright strange that the sanitary conditions are here so completely disregarded, while the authorities are working with laudable zeal for the strictest of health regulations. If they are already moving the refugees at night time into the barrack camps, then they should be at least able to make sure that the people are protected and the travelers have no contact with each other, to prevent the possibility of getting sick.[20]

Medical care in Austria-Hungary on both the military front and the home front was often overstretched and constrained by a limited work force. In the early days, in and around the main battlefields, the scarcity of human resources was largely due to the authorities' perception that the war would be short. That said, by October 1914 almost one-third of physicians had been conscripted.[21] However, against the backdrop of a lasting conflict, medical efforts were enhanced with additional doctors, nurses, and material infrastructure.[22] With many resources going directly into the war effort, the home front and its various structures of civilian assistance suffered. In this context, private relief associations emerged and extended assistance to civilians in need, many of whom were women, children, and elderly refugees. Nevertheless, these private relief mechanisms functioned primarily in the major cities of the monarchy, such as Vienna, Prague, and Budapest.[23] In the refugee camps, however, it was the state that took the reins of organizing healthcare. As seen in the early reactions in Vienna and in the complaints forwarded to the newspaper *Österreichische Land-Zeitung*, protracted fears of disease pervaded Austrian society. To deal with perceptions of incapacity or incoherence, the authorities sought to position the state's efforts for health work vis-à-vis the refugees as a well-oiled mechanism of resounding success. Thus, officials designed and publicly presented a state-sustained apparatus of health workers as a modern tool to contain and potentially suppress flare-ups of disease among refugees living in camps.

Early on, the blueprint of health work highlighted the establishment of a network of personnel, based on collaboration between the center in Vienna and the camp as a site of practical action. The synchrony envisioned by officials implied the collaboration of health workers employed in camps with those working within host communities and with experts based in Vienna. Further, this cooperation was to extend to camp administrators, including representatives of the police and the military. At the heart of this collaboration, however, was precisely the wartime lacunae in personnel. This was evidenced in a document circulated in December 1914, which claimed a necessary operational flexibility, according to existent capacity in resources, in order to "ensure that perceived sanitary inconsistencies are eliminated as soon as possible."[24]

In this formal planning, the relationship between the health worker and the refugee was to be driven by the former's role in the process of camp confinement; in this understanding, the health worker was to be an agent of the state-ordained measures of securitization and movement control. From the vantage point of bureaucrats in Vienna, refugees were objects of supervision and, when needed, intervention within the health-work agenda.[25] Initially, the authorities sought to reinforce the classification used in the organization of refugee camps. As these sites were organized around the concept of *Heimat* and with ambitions of communitarian homogeneity among the confined populations, officials sought to use health workers who were able to communicate with refugees.[26] In this scheme, experts involved in the supervision of refugees and professionals working on site became interlocutors of the state in the management of camps.

The state's efforts to design and implement health work in refugee camps also became the object of public propaganda of various types. In 1915 the Ministry of Interior published a program describing various refugee policies, including the aforementioned sanitary-welfare scheme. The program put significant emphasis on sanitary difficulties in the refugee camps and described in detail the plan of health work that the state had implemented. This official publication emphasized the need for professionalization of sanitary welfare through the employment of doctors and nurses, of different ranks, and with the specific agenda to monitor refugees' health and behavior, and treat and combat disease.

This publication was further accompanied by an exhibition that aimed to offer a visual insight into the state's efforts to assist refugees in camps. This collection of photographs was yet another effort to bring the war to an audience from the home front through the public display of refugee suffering and the state's heroic efforts to alleviate it.[27] This particular exhibition presented the image of a robust system of health care in the camps, sustained by infrastructure development that, the authorities claimed, made the control of sensitive epidemiological situations possible. These images (see figures 3.1–3.2) showed a complex system of health work, involving large, well-lit, and spacious hospital barracks for ill refugees, observation hospitals and clinics, disinfection stations, pharmacies, and infant welfare clinics, as well as so-called dairy kitchens for infants and nursing homes for children and mothers alike. Ultimately, these photographs told a success story. "Thanks to the improvements in the accommodation and catering. . ., it was possible to get the epidemics under control in a relatively short period of time and, in particular, to completely prevent it from spreading to the local population,"[28] claimed the document published with the stamp of the Ministry of Interior.

Officials designed on paper and presented to the public a story of the mobilization of all possible resources and of an overarching success regarding the capacity of health work in camps. The workers on the ground were at the center of this formal show-and-tell of a seemingly modern health-care system sustained by capacious infrastructure and the use of professionals and experts. However, this organization of health work designed early on in the refugee crisis, and formally presented to the public in 1915, also coexisted with the many deficiencies that pervaded the experience on the ground. There, health workers faced epidemics that ravaged the refugee population in a context of scarce resources. At the same time, as representatives of the state in the camps, the health workers used the conditions of these sites to advance agendas of containment and to implement modern technologies for management of these seemingly backward refugee populations.

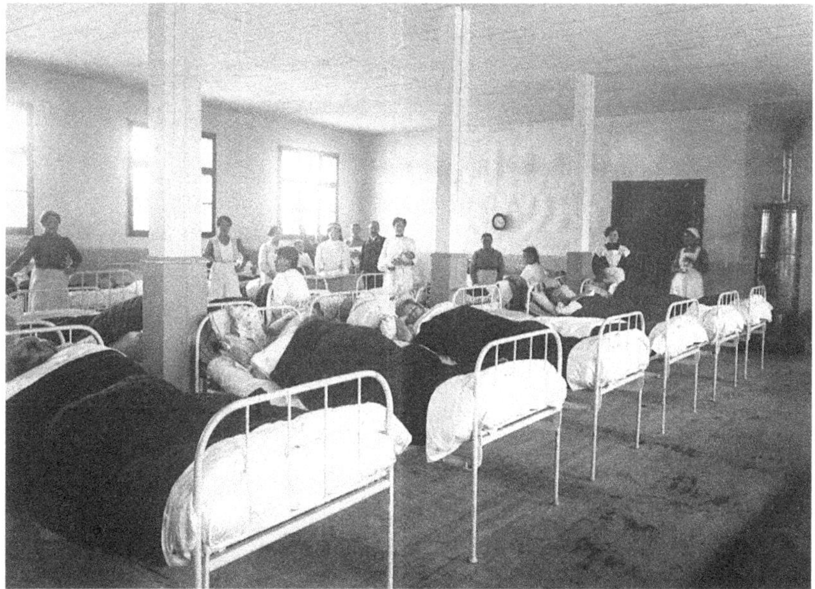

FIGURE 3.1. Hospital Interior in Gmünd Refugee Camp. Credit: Austrian National Library/Vienna, Call number Pk 3148, 190 (Flüchtlingsfürsorge).

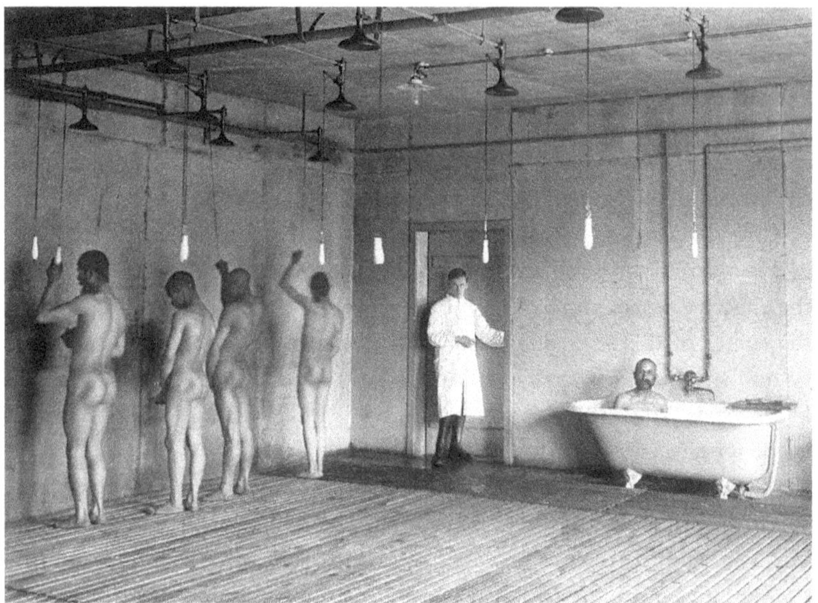

FIGURE 3.2. Disinfection Station, Gmünd Refugee Camp. Credit: Austrian National Library/ Vienna, Call number Pk 3148, 193 (Flüchtlingsfürsorge).

Experiences on the Ground

In 1915 the Romanian-born medical student Jacob Levy Moreno (1889–1974) arrived in Mitterndorf, a camp established in Lower Austria for refugees of Italian nationality displaced after the invasions in the south. Almost sixty years later, by then a distinguished psychiatrist famous for pioneering sociometry and group therapy, Moreno would reminisce about his experience in the camp:

> It was a regular Sodom and Gomorrah. . . . The women were particularly abused—so many abortions and illicit pregnancies! The [German-speaking] police were the worst in this respect. They were harsh and vulgar men. . . . It is amazing that I wasn't carried away by the wave of Italian nationalism that was provoked by the policemen's behavior for, as doctor to the refugees, I was privy to the suffering of the women and I began to identify myself more and more with the Tyroleans, learning their language like a native and otherwise immersing myself in their lives.[29]

Back in 1915 Moreno was one of the many medical students who volunteered and were eventually recruited to assist the health work in one of the largest refugee camps of the empire. His memories described a profound suffering and the on-site chaos, as well as his attempts to build connections with refugees and deeply immerse himself in their lives. Traces of Moreno's activity in the camps are difficult to find in the archives of the time. Furthermore, it is important to consider that these autobiographical notes are highly reflexive and published long after the fact. Thus, it is probable that Moreno projected and even exaggerated the empathy that seemingly defined his relationship with the refugees living in Mitterndorf. Still, these recorded memories give an insight into variations of the role that health workers played in the camp as representatives of the state, as well as their relationships with the local administrators and with the refugees, respectively.

The narrative reports that made their way to the desks of administrators based in the Ministry of Interior told similar stories of intense suffering among refugees, the need to improve measures of assistance, and the implicit and explicit role of health workers on the ground. This was the case in the accounts produced by one Dr. Alfons Foramitti, who repeatedly reported on the infrastructural and organizational insufficiencies in matters of health and hygiene. While visiting the camp of Gmünd in Lower Austria, Foramitti lamented that "sanitary precautionary measures were not taken into account and . . . illnesses were often spread" as refugees were moved from one camp to another because of lack of space.[30] Furthermore, he forwarded complaints about the lack of adequate security personnel and incomplete quarantine which, in his view, brought an "eminent sanitary risk to the population."[31] Notes on poor or incomplete buildings, overpopulation of the camp, lack of adequate water, and a food crisis were found in Foramitti's report of the state of the Gmünd camp.[32]

Foramitti was not the sole voice reporting the dire state of the camps back to Vienna. Indeed, various inspectors of health conditions in the camps criticized the poor administration and improper infrastructure to address the refugees' physical struggles. "The housing conditions are said to be a downright mockery of all laws of hygiene and morality. . . . The sick lie next to the dying and there is so much unspeakable misery that loud wailing can be heard from all sides. . . . One of the officials . . . even said: 'These people are to die anyway.' "[33] This was stated in a report on the conditions in the camp of Leibniz in Styria, for instance, where Polish and Ruthenian refugees were placed. In similar tones, notes about "child mortality of frightening proportions" were recurrent in inspection reports.[34]

The accounts of Moreno and Foramitti, as well as other reports, suggest that some health workers saw the camp as a space of suffering by and large. In using professional standards, they observed and reported the dire health and hygiene conditions. Furthermore, they called for change and advised on measures to improve the refugees' lives in the camps, as they insisted on nutrition improvement, infrastructure expansion, adequate water supplies, as well as a greater work force to assist the refugees. In so doing, the health workers mentioned above, for instance, deemed the camp administrators guilty of omissions in infrastructure and general care of refugees. At the same time, they positioned themselves as empathic toward refugee suffering, claiming a protective and even collaborative rapport. These tensions illustrate the health workers' perception of the camp as a space of distress.

The aforementioned projection of empathy tells, however, an incomplete story of the health workers' experience on the ground. Their role as on-site mediators between the state, its bureaucrats and local representatives, and the refugees themselves undergirded their on-site experiences. Still, the practice of health work in the midst of various crises of epidemics in the camps reveals that the relationship between the on-site worker and the refugee was unequal. Rather, it was paternalistic, driven by formal and explicit agendas of implementation of modern mechanisms of health relief and rehabilitation. This meant expert-generated immediate healing of illnesses, elimination of epidemics, but also addressing the perceived backwardness of the refugees living in the camps.

The collective suffering in these contained spaces provided an ideal laboratory for observational and applied expertise, involving refugees as objects of experimentation.[35] At the time, experts interpreted the camp as a microcosm of the larger society, where novel experiments could be tried and tested. In the process, they announced the development of modern remedies for refugees' health and overall quality of life. For instance, in 1914, the medical director Dr. Josef Reder initiated a study on typhus patients in the camp of Gmünd, on the basis of its intrinsic diversity: "Our observations derive from a camp with civilians who fled. [This] human material differs from that in prison camps in that there are men, women, and children of various ages," wrote Reder in his study.[36] Reder's experiments and analyses lasted until 1917 and included 1,130 cases. Among these were a few healthy refugees brought into the camp hospital, where they were deliberately exposed to the disease and eventually died. In the name of scientific advance and therapeutic interventions, Reder observed, recorded, and published statistics on symptomatology, causes of disease, and potential prophylaxis.[37]

Like Reder, Jacob Levy Moreno used his time in Mitterndorf to observe social relations among refugees. In fact, Moreno later claimed that it was the time spent in the refugee camp itself that lay at the basis of his work on sociometry. According to his writings and autobiography, Moreno used information from Feruccio Bannizoni, a clinical psychologist working in the camp, and his own interactions with the refugees to study various aspects of community life: nationality, politics, gender dynamics, and tension between administrators and refugees. In the name of his study, Moreno moved families around on the basis of their mutual affinities and rearranged work groups in camp factories whenever possible, in order "to create greater harmony and productivity among the workers."[38]

The epidemic crises also enabled the practical mobilization of medical professionals to test and implement different methods of emergency health care in the specific context of World War I. Lack of food and medicine, as well as limited access to proper material resources, saw the emergence of applied expertise on the ground. This was the case in 1915, in the camp of Gmünd, where child mortality caused by measles and typhus called for swift reactions. While the exact number of refugees living in various camps remains poorly documented, evidence suggests that, by May 1916, up to thirty thousand refugees lived in Gmünd.[39] The camp was overcrowded and thus, during the first two years, it was severely hit by multiple epidemics, including aggressive variants of typhus and measles.

In this context, child mortality among refugees living in this camp became a conundrum for local administrators and state authorities. There, tensions between two medical personnel, Dr. Siegfried Weiss and Dr. Johann Cipanowskj, were made the object of several inspections and follow-up reports. The two doctors had conflicting views regarding the best measures to combat measles, particularly the treatment time line, the use of existing barracks or the expansion of infrastructure, as well as the deployment of personnel in general. This alerted officials in Vienna, and the dispute was eventually settled after an inspection by a team of doctors; these experts eventually allowed Weiss to take the reins in combating measles, on the basis that Cipanowskj's methods contradicted long-standing scientific experience.[40]

One of the key figures of this team of doctors was Clemens von Pirquet (1874–1929), a pediatrician and then director of the Kinderklinik in Vienna. Besides settling the Weiss-Cipanowskj feud, Pirquet also spent time addressing the root causes of poor child health and high mortality in the camp. Pirquet was part of Vienna's scientific elite, largely due to his long-standing work on immunology and nutrition for children.[41] Using this knowledge, he assisted the medical personnel to develop a sustainable and practical nutrition plan for children that was adapted to war conditions.[42] Generally, the question of how to feed both child and adult refugees sufficiently and correctly was a frequent matter of debate among health workers in the refugee camps.[43] Pirquet came up with a solution in Gmünd, claiming that children could eat less meat and fat by replacing these with sugar and carbohydrates in order to adapt to conditions of war while improving the immune system. This nutrition scheme was to be implemented primarily in the feeding programs developed in the aftermath of the war.[44] However, Pirquet's ideas also found fertile ground among health professionals tending to the suffering children living in the refugee camps during the conflict.[45]

The observations as well as the tensions around the ideal avenues to heal and improve conditions of life in the Gmünd camp revealed another dimension of health work: the cooperative nature of the relationship between state officials, the scientific center in Vienna, and the on-site administration of sanitary measures. Indeed, this represented a transfer of the authorities' blueprints of health work into a practical setting. Furthermore, it revealed tensions and negotiations around modern methods in the context of extended refugee confinement and demonstrated that in just a few months since the first refugees arrived in Gmünd in late 1914, the refugee camps had transitioned from a haphazard reaction to simply contain potential disease and its foreign carriers into sites of professionalization, largely in response to health crises. In the process the role of the health worker changed and adapted to the demands on-site, from a mere supervisor to an active agent of relief.

The Gmünd case is also an example of the refugee camp as a laboratory, as Vienna-based figures of the scientific world developed or implemented measures to treat and prevent the further spread of epidemics. For experts observing the camps, however, refugees often represented only numbers and statistics, whose collective suffering enabled, in turn, the development of knowledge. In fact, in the process of health work, the experiences of experts and practitioners working on the ground were also shaped by the hierarchical rapport with refugees. This was mirrored in aggressive and interventionist measures to curtail the effects of disease on an emergency basis. In the midst of various epidemiological crises, health workers, alongside the police and local administrators, implemented on-site interventionist relief measures in the name of modern medical standards: quarantines, parent-child separations, and behavior monitoring were leitmotifs of the measures executed and reported by on-site health workers. These often aggressive methods, sanitary authorities claimed, were direct reactions to the emergencies produced by epidemics, the dangers they posed in and outside the camps, and the belief that the refugees' own behavior was, in fact, the seed of contagion.

Various reports claimed that refugees were showing no trust in health workers or simply refusing modern medical care. Some notes reveal the ways in which the belief in the refugees' backwardness was formed in contrast to the health workers' own frame of reference regarding health knowledge and views of medical progress. Several such reports were produced in the case of refugees living in Gmünd, where the measles and typhus epidemics were the causes of high mortality among children. Perceptions of Ruthenians' hostility to progress and rejection of modern healthcare were found in the reports on the work in this camp. In one instance, a note claimed that the epidemiological dimensions were largely caused by the fact that "refugees hid their sick children in the barracks under the straw mats in a quite incomprehensible resistance to the doctors."[46]

Similar reasoning was present in surveys regarding the dire epidemiological situation in other camps. The authorities claimed, for example, that after a relocation of refugees from Gmünd to Steinklamm was completed, new epidemics emerged on the basis of poor behavior. Steinklamm was a camp in Lower Austria, where the large majority of refugees were Slovenian. In their case, inspectors of health and hygiene conditions claimed that there was direct mistrust of medical personnel based on prevailing superstition among the "poorly educated population."[47] They also added that "the fight against disease is all the more difficult when the parents, out of unfortunate prejudices and distrust of hospital care and of the Serbian doctors who, according to the barrack administration, conscientiously fulfill their duties, conceal their children's illness wherever possible."[48]

Comparable worries were expressed in the case of those living in the camp of Bruck an der Leitha, as health workers reported that "refugees defy hospital care."[49] In some cases officials sought to adapt the apparatus of health work to the conditions of the camp. Their notes reveal that state-supported improvement in infrastructure and material resources (i.e., additional barracks, nutrition improvement) helped the overall relief of health and hygiene conditions in the camps.[50] Additionally, the linguistic capacity of practitioners became a significant pillar of organization of health care in practice. Thus, employment or dismissal based on the doctors' knowledge of refugees' language became the norm in camps, as the authorities believed that this was a way to alleviate the seeds of distrust.[51]

Despite adaptations, the authorities also employed measures of intervention on behalf of health and hygiene. Motivated by perceptions of refugees' beliefs in superstitions, their misbehavior, and overall lack of education, local authorities and health workers enforced strict measures of containment, under the guise of relief assistance. This was particularly evident in the case of the camp in Gmünd. In 1915 a proclamation sketched the rules of health work in order to contain the spread and effects of epidemics. This document, presented in German, as well as other "camp languages," represented a detailed exposé of health work in the camp in response to a typhus crisis. For one, infrastructure was developed, a bacteriological laboratory was set up, and new doctors and nurses were employed. But most importantly, administrators mobilized the on-site workers to impose strict measures of disease containment. In this scheme, the doctors, the riot police, as well as the clergy worked together to look for hidden sick people and to monitor the population's reports of cases of illness.[52]

The authorities were alarmed. They reported that "the camp population must in their own interest and that of their children, accommodate the sanitary organs of the camp as far as possible, immediately report any symptoms of illness and not oppose the transfer of individual patients to the hospital."[53] Other orders established a sanitary inspection of the camp at the same time every day, with three guard officers accompanying the doctors. All residents of the barracks would then be shown to doctors. Furthermore, the presence of all barrack residents would be cross-referenced with kitchen records or other aids. The related policy read: "During the sanitary inspection, the barrack exits are to be manned by guards on the accompanying patrol, and no one is allowed to exit the barrack. The commander of the barrack has to accompany the doctor inside and ensure that every single individual is brought to sanitary inspection."[54]

In hindsight, this document illustrates an instance in which the agendas of securitization and containment of refugees explicitly meshed with emergency measures to relieve the sick. What followed was arguably a form of militarization of hygiene, sustained through a collaboration between the on-site health workers and the security bodies, such as the police or the military. If in some of the aforementioned incidents medical personnel reports hinted at fractures between the formal administration and the health workers' methods of assistance, the epidemic crisis in Gmünd showed the collaborative dimension of their rapport. Overall, the health workers' experiences of the camps were heterogeneous. They were determined by the availability of resources, expectations, relationships with administrators, as well as with the refugees themselves. At the same time, the health workers were a common denominator, defined by their role as implementors of modern refugee camps through professionalization and through the use of on-site expertise.

In summing-up his memories of his time in Mitterndorf and his efforts as a young doctor to heal ailing refugees, Jacob Levy Moreno concluded that "although my efforts ameliorated some of the worst problems in the camp, Mitterndorf never became a utopia. There was still hunger, illness, corruptive [sic], abuse of innocent people. There were so many fine, wonderful people there who had to suffer and who had no alternative."[55]

Moreno's retrospective reflections on his experience on the ground, on the needs in this microsociety and on the psychological implications of life in the camps illustrate a belief in the empathic and even heroic ambitions of a health worker assisting refugees, whose sole option was a confined life. Moreno's post facto account was, however, at odds with what the state authorities mapped and presented as a well-oiled mechanism of assistance of ill refugees back in 1915. At the time, state officials had designed and employed an apparatus of health workers, of different status and experience, to contain epidemics, as well supervise, relieve, and control suffering refugees.

The story that this chapter reveals is one of trials and tribulations in the scramble to heal the ill refugees in Austria-Hungary's camps during World War I. It first shows how authorities designed and publicly presented the initial blueprints of health work in the camps. In this scheme, health workers were to be the agents of a seemingly protective state. Concomitantly, they were to ensure securitization of the camps and of the refugees living there. This chapter is also a story of on-site practice, as it highlights the ways in which health workers experienced the situation, as mediators between state officials and the refugees. Here, it illustrates that some health workers immersed themselves in the camp life, as they observed and reported suffering, claimed empathy for the refugees, and called for aid and protection on their behalf. At the same, it shows the hierarchies produced in the way the state and local authorities planned and implemented health work from the outset. This was evident in the interventionist implementation of health and hygiene measures in order to combat epidemics. It was also illustrated in the ways they reported, with a contrast between the multiplicity of voices "at the top" and the refugees' voicelessness.

Overall, the lens of the organization of health work points to the management of refugee camps in Austria-Hungary as a process that officials transferred but also adapted from its blueprint form to the site itself. In this, it points to a shift during World War I: when refugee camps were transformed from a temporary plan to contain outsiders to a permanent fixture of war policy. Thus, the use of experts, professionals, and forms of media to aid, to contain, and also mobilize refugees delineated the making of modern camps in Austria-Hungary during World War I.

Notes

The author thanks the editors of this volume for their constructive feedback and extends her gratitude also to Lukas Schemper, Sielke Kelner, and Oonagh Hayes for their comments. This research is part of the project "Unlikely Refuge? Refugees and Citizenship in East-Central Europe during the Twentieth Century," Masaryk Institute and Archives of the Czech Academy of Sciences. This project has received funding from the European Research Council (ERC) under the European Union's Horizon 2020 research and innovation program (grant No. 819461).

1. Mentzel 1995, 30.

2. For an excellent summary of the quantification of displacement in Austria-Hungary, see Frizzera 2018, 62.

3. Flüchtlingsfürsorge in Salzburg; Anmerkennung als Flüchtlingsgemeinde; Subventionierung des Hilfskomitees, July 25, 1915, Karton 1939, Minsterium des Innern (hereafter MdI), allg. 19, Allgemeines Verwaltungsarchiv (hereafter AVA), Öesterreichische Staatsarchive (hereafter ÖStA), Vienna, Austria.

4. Gatrell 2013, 52–83; Skran 1995; White 2019, 216–36.

5. Arendt 1979, 279; Stonebridge 2018, 46–69.

6. A few examples are Ballinger 2020; Bailkin 2018; Cohen 2012; Malkki 1995, 495–523; Marrus 1985.

7. On refugee camps during the American Civil War, see Taylor 2018. For a recent note on the use of camps for displaced populations in 1848, see Morris 2020.

8. On aspects of civilian and military internment in Austria-Hungary, see, e.g., Stibbe 2018; Rachamimov 2012a; Zaharia 2017.

9. For a further analysis on links between poverty and confinement in camps, see Bohdan Kordan's chapter in this volume.

10. For the name of this West Ukrainian group in the Habsburg monarchy, see Bihl 1980, 555–84.

11. Thorpe 2011, 102–26; Mentzel 1995.

12. Klein-Pejšová 2014, 150–66.

13. "Instruktion betreffend die Beförderung und Unterbringung von Flüchtlinge aus Galizien und der Bukowina, " September 15, 1914, Karton 1921, MdI, allg.19, AVA, ÖStA, Vienna, Austria.

14. K. K. Ministerium des Innern 1915, 4.

15. See Lena Radauer's chapter in this volume.

16. Weindling 2000, 108.

17. Quoted in Healy 2004, 8.

18. "Instruktion betreffend die Beförderung und Unterbringung von Flüchtlingen aus Galizien und der Bukowina," September 15, 1914, Karton 1921, MdI, allg.19, AVA, ÖStA, Vienna, Austria.

19. Flüchtlingstransporte, sanitäre Revisionen, September 19, 1914, Karton 691, Präs "P" 1914, Niederösterreichisches Landesarchiv (hereafter NÖLA), St. Pölten, Austria.

20. "Gmünder Bezirk," *Osterreichische Land-Zeitung*, July 17, 1915.

21. Moll 2014.

22. Herwig 2014, 298–99.

23. K. K. Ministerium des Innern 1915, 15–17; "Zehn Jahre Arbeit des Vereines Soziale Hilfsgemeinschaft Anitta Müller, Wien 1914–1924" (printed pamphlet).

24. Internierte, Gesundheitszustand, Ueberwachung, December 10, 1914, Karton 698, Präs "P" 1915, NÖLA, St. Polten, Austria.

25. Internierte, Gesundheitszustand, Ueberwachung, December 10, 1914, Karton 698, Präs "P" 1915, NÖLA, St. Polten, Austria.

26. Letter from the Provincial Council of Gorizia, March 11, 1916, Karton 1955, MdI, allg.19, AVA, ÖStA, Vienna, Austria.

27. Healy 2000, 57–85.

28. K. K. Ministerium des Innern, *Staatliche Flüchtlingsfürsorge*, 15.

29. Moreno 2011, 72.

30. Report from Dr. Baczynski and Ritter v. Semaka on the Camp in Bruck a.d. Leitha, December 24, 1914, Karton 698, Präs "P" 1915, NÖLA, St. Pölten, Austria.

31. Flüchtlingslager in Gmünd, Verstärkerung [Verstärkung?] der Landsturmwache, July 31, 1915, Karton 1939, MdI, allg.19, AVA, ÖStA, Vienna, Austria.

32. Flüchtlingslager in Gmünd, Sanitäre Inspektion, March 20, 1915, Karton 710, Pras "P" 1916, NÖLA, St. Polten, Austria.

33. Zustände in den steirischen Konzentrationslagern, January 14, 1915, Karton 1924, MdI, allg.19, AVA, ÖStA, Vienna, Austria.

34. Letter from the Provincial Council of Gorizia, March 11, 1916, Karton 1955, MdI, allg.19, AVA, ÖStA, Vienna, Austria.

35. See Nancy Fitch's chapter in this volume.

36. Translation taken from Hermann 2017a, 148–49.

37. Reder 1918.

38. Moreno 2011, 71–73.

39. Hermann 2017b, 38.

40. Flüchtlingslager Gmünd sanitätspolizeiliche Massregeln, October 19, 1916, Karton 710, Präs "P" 1916, NÖLA, St. Pölten, Austria.

41. Burri 2021, 39–70.

42. Clemens von Pirquet, report, October 25, 1916, Karton 710, Präs "P" 1916, NÖLA, St. Pölten, Austria.

43. Luigi Faidutti, letter to Dr. Karl Freiherr Heinold von Udynski, June 7, 1915, Karton 1933, MdI, allg.19, AVA, ÖStA, Vienna, Austria; Milchversorgungsplan für Flüchtlingslager und Vorsorge für das Flüchtlingsvieh in den Gemeinden, October 28, 1916, Karton 16, Kriegsflüchtlingsfürsorge (hereafter KFL), Archiv der Republik (hereafter AdR), ÖStA, Vienna, Austria.

44. Pirquet 1926.

45. Report on Steinklamm camp, September 5, 1918, Karton 340, Präs "P" 1918, NÖLA, St. Pölten, Austria.

46. Flüchtlinge aus dem Bezirke Pola in den Lagern in Gmünd und Leibnitz, Beschwerden, January 13, 1916, Karton 710, Präs "P" 1916, NÖLA, St. Pölten, Austria.

47. Steinklamm Barackenlager, Besuch der Hilfskomitee-Dame Antonie Baronin Beck, December 15, 1915, Karton 340, Präs "P" 1918, NÖLA, St Pölten, Austria.

48. Report from Antonie Baronin Beck on Steinklamm camp, December 10, 1915, Karton 340, Präs "P" 1918, NÖLA, St. Pölten, Austria.

49. Report from Prof. Dr. M. Fabiani on Steinklamm camp, August 22, 1916, Karton 340, Präs "P" 1918, NÖLA, St. Pölten, Austria.

50. Steinklamm Barackenlager, Besuch der Hilfskomitee-Dame Antonie Baronin Beck, December 15, 1915; Bekämpfung der Kindersterblichkeit im Barackenlager in Gmünd, November 19, 1915, Karton 710, Präs "P" 1916, NÖLA, St. Polten, Austria.

51. Report from Michael Gabrijelcic on the Camp in Bruck a.d. Leitha, October 5, 1917, Karton 1997, MdI, allg.19, AVA, ÖStA, Vienna, Austria; Flüchtlingsfürsorge, Neuregelung in Sammelniederlassung, November 16, 1917, Karton 1999, MdI, allg.19, AVA, ÖStA, Vienna, Austria.

52. Mitterndorf Flüchtlingsniederlassung, Abdominaltyphus, July 21, 1916, Karton 743, Präs "P" 1918, NÖLA, St. Pölten, Austria.

53. Barackenlager in Gmünd, Massnahmen zur Bekämpfung der Kindersterblichkeit, November 13, 1915, Karton 710, Präs "P" 1916, NÖLA, St. Pölten, Austria.

54. Barackenlager in Gmünd, Massnahmen zur Bekämpfung der Kindersterblichkeit, November 13, 1915, Karton 710, Präs "P" 1916, NÖLA, St. Pölten, Austria.

55. Moreno 2011, 73.

Chapter 4

Alexandra Palace

A Concentration Camp in the Heart of London

Assaf Mond

On the morning of May 28, 1915, Rudolf Rocker reached the Tube station of Wood Green, London. Before the war, Rocker had lived for many years not very far from there, in the district of Mile End, with his wife Milly and his two sons, Rudolf and Fermin. He worked as a bookbinder and was part of the East Ham Jewish community. During his twenty years of residency in the British capital, the city had become his home. "The sight of the familiar London streets moved me tremendously," he wrote in his memoir about his underground ride on that morning.[1] Rocker, however, was not alone on this trip: he was accompanied by several other civilians of enemy origin and by British guards who watched so they would not try to escape. He was in the city that had been his home for twenty years, but he was no longer part of the civilian life in London—he was excluded, as a prisoner. "We soon reached Wood Green, and got out," he wrote. "We marched slowly up the hill that is topped by the building known as Alexandra Palace. This was our new internment camp."[2] At the foot of the hill, he could have been identified as a civilian using the Tube. But once at the top of the hill, in Alexandra Palace, he was segregated and concentrated with other prisoners—part of "the enemy."

In his memoir, which he started writing a few years after the end of World War II, Rocker referred to Alexandra Palace as an "internment camp." This was not unique: World War I camps, not only in Britain, are often described using this sanitized term and not as "concentration camps"—which are mostly identified with the infamous Nazi camps of World War II. Moreover, preference for the term "internment camp" did not occur in hindsight: British officials were of course familiar with the name "concentration camp," which had been used to describe the camps the British military had set up in South Africa in the beginning of the twentieth century to hold tens of thousands of Boer and African civilians (mostly women and children).[3] Yet, when the practice of interning civilians was used at home during World War I, the term "internment camp" was mostly, though not exclusively, employed (see the contribution of Iris Rachamimov and Rotem Kowner in this volume).

Likewise, works dealing with the history of concentration camps see their roots in the nineteenth-century colonial wars and settings, with titles such as "From Africa to Auschwitz" stressing this trajectory.[4] The discussion regarding the continuity between colonial camps and the camps of World War I focuses on the nature of imprisonment and its implications in terms of international law or conversely on the differences between European and non-European narratives.[5] Research into the role of World War I on later examples of mass incarceration in Europe examines the systematization of the practice and its deployment in the treatment of "undesirable" civilians.[6] Despite some similarities between the camp systems of the two world wars and despite the fact that colonial camps are regularly referred to as "concentration camps," the camps of World War I have been oddly kept out of this trajectory.

One of the key terms in the historiography of concentration camps is "violence." Heather Jones, author of *Violence against Prisoners of War in the First World War*, suggest, based on the work of Stéphane Audoin-Rouzeau and Annette Becker, looking at violence against prisoners during the war as a prism for understanding the escalation of wartime brutalization. Jones argues that the camp system of World War I helped to shape the camp system of World War II, though she notes that because of the different measures of violence "comparison becomes highly problematic." She therefore concludes by stating that "the earlier war provided a logistical model, not an ideological one, for the latter conflict."[7] The violence of the World War II concentration camps, which, in some cases, were also extermination camps, cannot be compared with the treatment of civilians of enemy origin in Britain and in London during World War I. That violence of the World War II camps is one of the reasons why the British camps for civilians in World War I are usually referred to as "internment camps," rather than "concentration camps." There is also a general unease about associating concentration camps with states possessing a strong liberal heritage, as manifested even in 2019 with the public debate in the United States over detention centers for undocumented immigrants. In this chapter, however, I suggest a different prism—one that does not focus on the physical violence within the camp but rather on the spatial concept of concentrating and segregating people.

In her 2017 work, *One Long Night: A Global History of Concentration Camps*, Andrea Pitzer identified some characteristics of the concentration camp from the mid-nineteenth century onward: it holds civilian detainees who had no real trial and are held "outside of the normal legal process"; the detainees have no scheduled date of release; and nearly all concentration camps "extract people from one area to house them somewhere else." The last characteristic is important, according to Pitzer.[8] Pointing out the spatial implications of the imprisonment can be seen as banal, but it uncovers a key element in the philosophy of the camp, as can be noticed in Rocker's process of transformation from civilian to prisoner: the space of the camp and its surroundings shape both the camp and the experience of imprisonment. Spatial elements are therefore important for the story of the concentration camps.

Many historians of World War I, even those who write that some of the camps of 1914–1918 were concentration camps, tend to refer to camps like Alexandra Palace or Knockaloe on the Isle of Man as "internment camps." This testifies both to the term's instability, the lack of consensus about its definition, and the unwillingness to group World War I camps in the same category as Buchenwald or Dachau, not to mention Auschwitz or Bergen-Belsen. The differences between the conditions and levels of violence in the Nazi camps and the camps of World War I make that reluctance reasonable and understandable. This debate was recently, and elegantly, summed up in Matthew Stibbe's book *Civilian Internment during the First World War: A European and Global History, 1914–1920*. "As Annette Becker argues," Stibbe writes, "the use of the language of 'concentration camps,' and evidence of convergences as well as divergences, especially between wartime French and British internment practices, did not mean that there was a 'concentration camp system' anywhere in the world before the 1920s. What can be said with greater certainty is that the 1914–18 conflict, even in its first twenty months, had given rise to various 'models' for concentrating civilians as a part of war governance both in Europe and further afield."[9] The result of such notions, which identify "models of concentrating" but dismiss the usage of the term "concentration camp" because of the lack of "a concentration camp system," is that historical research treats camps like Alexandra Palace in a blurred and noncommittal way.

The term "concentration camp" cannot, and should not, be discussed in disregard of its historical context. The typology of mass incarceration spheres should take into consideration levels of violence and the place of the camps in the collective memory. However, I argue that the historiography of the modern camp system can benefit from a definition of the term "concentration camp" that challenges previous distinctions between the camps in the colonies and the ones in Britain, and between the camps of the "historical enemies," Nazi Germany and Soviet Russia, and the camps that were built in states with a strong liberal heritage. I argue that calling the World War I camp in Alexandra Palace "an internment camp" is not wrong, but neither is it as accurate as it could be—and that calling it "a concentration camp" and looking at it as such can enrich our understanding of World War I camps in Britain.

This chapter places the Alexandra Palace's Great War camp within a wider narrative and historiography of concentration camps, from late nineteenth-century Cuba, Southern Africa, and the Philippines and along with the Nazi concentration camps of World War II and the Soviet Gulags, and within the global history of the World War I camps (for more on World War I as a turning point in the global use of prison camps, see Matthew Stibbe's contribution in this volume).[10] The history identifies a continuous line stretching from the colonial camps of the late nineteenth-century, through the camps of World War I, to the camps of the interwar period, World War II, and beyond.[11] When looking at World War I as a global war with a global history, it is important to view the decision to imprison civilians without a trial as a policy implemented both in the colonies and in Britain.

More specifically, this chapter argues that the camp in Alexandra Palace was a concentration camp not only because it constituted an act of physical violence against the bodies of civilians of enemy origin (albeit a minor one in comparison to the concentration camps of World War II), but also because it was an act of spatial violence—which I define using Pitzer's characteristics of a concentration camp; "the removal of a population from a society with all its accompanying rights, relationships, and connections to humanity . . . followed by an involuntary assignment to some lesser condition or place, generally detention with other undesirables under armed guard."[12] This spatial violence, I argue, shaped the camp and was shaped by it. The concentration camp was defined by the spatial exclusion of population from society into a place that is the ultimate expression of a "state of exception," as explained by the Italian philosopher Giorgio Agamben, where whoever entered "moved in a zone of indistinction between outside and inside."[13] Therefore, I contend that Alexandra Palace was a sphere of liminality—a threshold place, which is neither here nor there—defined through exclusions.

The first part of this chapter surveys the history of Alexandra Palace, from its early days as an entertainment park in the second half of the nineteenth century until the outbreak of World War I, when it was first used as a training ground for the British army, then as a shelter for Belgian refugees, and finally as a camp for civilians of enemy origin. Along with the historical narrative, I examine the reasons for the relative lack of historical research about Alexandra Palace, the thousands of Belgian refugees who found shelter in Britain during World War I, and particularly the treatment of Germans and other civilians of enemy origin in Britain during the war and the eventual decision to imprison them. These multiple uses of Alexandra Palace, I argue, were an expression of its constant exclusion from the city—meaning, its physical and mental separation from the city surrounding it. This, I claim, was part of the place's liminality.

The imprisonment of civilians of enemy origin, which separated them from their lives in the city, expressed another aspect of that liminality: the exclusion of Alexandra Palace from the civil sphere of London—meaning, the "social space," in Henri Lefebvre's term, where the geographical space is defined through the common civil rights and civil perceptions of its inhabitants.[14] The British capital's home front was not a war-free sphere, though not part of the war zone either. This exclusion is discussed in the second part of this chapter, along with an analysis of observations conducted from outside Alexandra Palace and its prisoners, using an official summary, a journalistic report, and a propaganda book. The way the people of London perceived the camp that was erected in the middle of their city is rarely discussed—and it is also part of the change in the city, which for the first time operated a concentration camp within its boundaries. In the third part of this chapter, I explain the exclusion of the Alexandra Palace from the war—meaning, its separation from the experiences of both civilians and soldiers during wartime. The results of this analysis of the nature of the camp express its unique status in London during World War I.

Exclusion from the City

Alexandra Palace is located on the top of a north London hill. The view from the palace covers large portions of the city and most of its northern area. London is seen from Alexandra Palace, and the palace is visible from much of north London, but the two places are separated by the hill on which the palace was erected. Alexandra Palace stands out in the London skyline, and at the same time it is far away, separated from its urbanscape. That is one expression of Alexandra Palace's liminality. "Liminality" is a term that goes back to the anthropological writing of Arnold van Gennep in the early twentieth century. It was part of his theory about "rites of passage," and was later reshaped by Victor Turner. "Liminal entities are neither here nor there," explained Turner. "They are betwixt and between the positions assigned and arrayed by law, custom, convention, and ceremonial."[15] Iris Rachamimov used the concept of liminality to describe the experiences of captured soldiers and life in the camp: "The idea of 'liminality'—the 'no longer/not yet' phase in the passage, when a person has lost one identity but not yet acquired a new one."[16] The liminality of Alexandra Palace, I argue, was expressed through three exclusions: the exclusion of the palace from the city, which characterized it since its earliest days but intensified after the outbreak of World War I, and the exclusions from the civil sphere and from the war.

Not much has been written about Alexandra Palace, and most of the few publications about it have contained little information about its role during World War I.[17] Janet Harris's 2005 *Alexandra Palace: A Hidden History* is the only work that forefronts this chapter in the palace's history, reflecting the general lack of willingness in Britain until the late twentieth century to write about the imprisonment of civilians of enemy origin during World War I.[18] Like the Ruhleben camp near Berlin (see Matthew Stibbe's contribution to this volume) or the Douglas camp on the Isle of Man, the Alexandra Palace camp also replaced a leisure site—a place where the experience was one of escapism, a temporary separation from daily routines in favor of amusement and relaxation.[19]

When World War I broke out, a sign was hung on the closed gates of the palace: "Until further notice the Palace grounds are closed to the public, who are warned that any unauthorized person found in the grounds is liable to be shot. BY ORDER." The reason for the secrecy was revealed within a few days: the army was using the palace and the park to train five hundred horses and men of the 1st King Edward's Horse cavalry regiment. Thus, the area of Alexandra Palace was excluded from the city and became a military zone. This, however, did not last long: the cavalrymen left after less than two weeks; the palace and park were reopened to the public but were soon mobilized again, this time, on September 11, 1914, for humanitarian reasons. The palace was turned into a shelter for Belgian refugees.[20]

Alexandra Palace pertains to the discourse about the "Total War" in London during World War I not only because of its role during much of the war as a concentration camp but also because of its use in the war's first few months as a shelter for Belgian refugees. Two hundred thousand Belgians landed in Great Britain after the German invasion in August 1914, and close to another fifty thousand arrived at later stages of the war. They were all registered in the Central Register of Belgian Refugees, before being transferred to temporary housing that could accommodate simultaneously up to three thousand people. One of the most important of these accommodations was Alexandra Palace. Between September 1914 and the end of October 1914, nineteen thousand Belgians were admitted to the palace before being transferred to permanent accommodation in other parts of London or Britain. The Belgians celebrated Christmas at the palace, but by the end of March 1915, it was once again empty, having hosted thirty-three thousand refugees.[21] Two months later, the palace was once again excluded from the physical surroundings, becoming a camp for civilians of enemy origin. The roots of that decision go back to the late nineteenth century and the early twentieth century.

The declaration of war in August 1914 brought to the surface a hatred of the Germans in Britain and gave the government both the legitimation and the tools to act against them.[22] The Defence of the Realm Act, usually known by its abbreviation DORA, was enacted immediately after the war broke out and was broadened and amended until 1918. It was enacted to compromise individual liberties in the interest of "public safety" and "defense of the realm," and thus allowed the police, for example, to arrest a person just for acting suspiciously or for having a homing pigeon. The Aliens Restriction Act was introduced by the government on August 5, 1914, the day after war was declared, but it was the result of work performed by a subcommittee of the Committee of Imperial Defence, which dealt with the "question of treatment of aliens in time of war." Civilians of enemy origin, according to the new act, were not allowed to enter or leave Britain without a permit and had to register immediately at a local registration office, usually a police station. Those who failed to register were liable to be fined.[23]

That was not enough to calm the British public, however. The popular newspapers fueled Germanophobia, as did the British government, to some extent. This in turn led to several early cases of riots against the German community in the country, the first ones in August 1914 and October 1914, as well as accusations of spying. The calls to arrest all males of enemy origin, and thus exclude them from civil society, intensified after the public learned about the "German atrocities" in Belgium and met the Belgian refugees who had come to Britain. Opposition grew even stronger in May 1915, after a German submarine sank the British ocean liner RMS *Lusitania*, causing the death of more than a thousand of its passengers and crew.[24] Six days later, on May 13, 1915, the government ordered the imprisonment of all civilians of enemy origin. Prime Minister Herbert H. Asquith explained that eight thousand civilians of enemy origin who had become naturalized in Britain would remain free, unless there was evidence of their being a threat, while males of military age, between seventeen and fifty-five, would be segregated and imprisoned.[25] Roughly nineteen thousand aliens of enemy origin were already imprisoned by May 1915, for various reasons. Another twelve thousand enemy aliens remained free even after 1916 for reasons such as having sons fighting in the British army or performing valuable work for the war effort.

With the decision to imprison every civilian of enemy origin of military age, the number of civilian prisoners rose immensely, and a system of mass incarceration started to take shape. Almost six hundred camps operated throughout the war, according to Panikos Panayi, most of them very small and for temporary use only; they usually distinguished between soldiers and civilians. The largest and most important camp was Knockaloe on the Isle of Man, which housed approximately twenty-five thousand prisoners at one time, though there were other large ones, like Frimley and Lofthouse Park. One of the country's largest and most important camps, and definitely the largest and most important in London, was the camp that was opened in May 1915 in Alexandra Palace.[26] The number of prisoners held there at any one time between May 1915 and March 1919 was no more than three thousand, but throughout the entire war seventeen thousand prisoners passed through it, the majority en route to Knockaloe. Some were Austro-Hungarians and Turks, but the vast majority were Germans. The Germans who lived in London preferred to be imprisoned in London, since it offered a convenient option for family visits, unlike the isolated camps on the Isle of Man. The War Office was willing to accept requests to be sent to Alexandra Palace, when possible.[27]

The imprisonment and the separation of the prisoners and their families were just one aspect of the exclusion of Alexandra Palace from London. Another can be found in the recollections of day-to-day life in the camp. Major Pál (Paul) Stoffa was an artillery officer in the Austro-Hungarian army who documented his wartime tale in his 1933 memoir *Round the World to Freedom*. By the end of 1916, Stoffa had become a prisoner in London, but because he was able to hide his military identity, he was taken into the civilian camp. "You'll be all right," he was told by the detective who took him there. "What more do you want than a nice long holiday in a palace?"[28] The conditions of imprisonment in the civilian camps in general, and specifically in North London's Alexandra Palace, were often criticized, and claims were voiced that there was "no hardship in being interned" and that many people in London would gladly change places with them.[29]

These accusations were based upon the fact that, apart from being spared the dangers of the fighting at the front, the Alexandra Palace prisoners were reasonably fed, at least during much of the war and according to official neutral reports, were able to freely practice their religion, organized different kinds of formal educational activities, occupied their time with woodworking, carving, painting, playing music and singing, and were even allowed to work and earn money.[30] Kurt Engler, for example, worked as a dentist and sold paintings he had drawn and toy steamboats he had built, while Benny Cseh worked as a tailor.[31] Life in the camp, therefore, while resembling life in the city, operated in parallel to life on the home front, since the camp was excluded from the civil sphere of London.

Exclusion from the Civil Sphere

The first half of the twentieth century was an age of military imprisonment, with approximately fifty million soldiers captured between the signing of the Hague Convention in 1899 and the signing of the Geneva Convention in 1949.[32] During World War I alone, eight and a half million people were imprisoned, and the vast majority of them were soldiers who became POWs. The number of civilians who were imprisoned during the war was probably several hundred thousand.[33] The imprisonment of civilians during World War I was also a gender-biased issue, since the prisoners were almost all males, and almost all of them were between the specific military ages of seventeen and fifty-five. The camp, not just in Britain, was usually a "town without women," while the wives and families of those prisoners were regarded as the "forgotten victims," suffering separation from their loved ones and calls for repatriation.

This gender prism, therefore, adds another layer to research about Alexandra Palace, since the home front was generally considered to be a place for women and children, while men were considered part of the front.[34] Erroneous as this belief was, it still stressed the difference of the camp's defining characteristic: a place for men of military age, not exactly at the front but also not exactly on the home front. Tammy Proctor refers to this issue in her book about civilians during World War I. "Civilian internment exposed the problems of the civil/military divide," she writes, "creating categories of people who did not fit neatly in either."[35] This interpretation is debatable: the boundaries between civil and military were blurred throughout the front and the home front, with soldiers who were civilians-in-uniform and civilians who became victims of the war machine in their own homes. However, Proctor's notion can be used to describe not the people in the camp, but rather the camp itself, which did not fit neatly in the civil category, nor was it clearly a military zone.

More than that, the exclusion of the camp from the civil sphere was inherent to the way that World War I was fought. That is because the sphere of the camp, along with the prisoners within it, was part of the "Total War" at the home front. Accordingly, the exclusion of the camp from the civil sphere can be explained through the concept of "state of exception," first used by the German political theorist Carl Schmitt and later developed by the Italian philosopher Giorgio Agamben. Schmitt defined "state of exception" (Ger. *Ausnahmezustand*) as part of the sovereign's power to exclude people from the law.[36] Agamben went on to maintain that the concept of "state of exception," as an implement of sovereignty, is critical for an understanding of the concentration camp. "The camp is a piece of land placed outside the normal juridical order, but it is nevertheless not simply an external space," he wrote. "What is excluded in the camp is, according to the etymological sense of the term 'exception' (Lat. *excipere*), *taken outside*, included through its own exclusion."[37]

Agamben highlights that the "state of exception" reflects an interaction between space and people, and he points to the act of exclusion, which I use throughout this chapter to define Alexandra Palace. He also claims that because of the "state of exception" and the spatial characteristics of the camp, prisoners are deprived of their civilian rights, which he defines as "bare life," using a term from Roman jurisprudence, written in reference to Jews in the Nazi concentration camps but nonetheless relevant for the British camps of World War I:[38] they also represented a "state of exception"; they were also in a place outside the normal juridical order that was "included through its own exclusion"; and as such their inhabitants were also excluded from the law.

But how did outsiders perceive the camp? Foreign official authorities, it seems, understood it as a place outside the normal rule of law. After Alexandra Palace became a camp for civilians of enemy origin, when the United States still maintained its neutral status in the war, its embassy in London was chosen to inspect the camp. The German division of the embassy sent delegates to north London, and their impressions were summed up in a report presented to the British minister of foreign affairs, Sir Edward Grey, on May 26, 1915. The eighteen-page report included, along with a ground plan of the place, some short statements about the condition of the baths and latrines ("well and cleaned"), the food ("I inspected the meat, which I found sweet and good"), the sleeping arrangements ("the men sleep in large halls. . . . Each man has a raised board bed . . . covered with straw mattresses") and the terms of correspondence ("if an attempt is made to convey news in a secret matter in a letter or parcel . . . the permission to receive or send letters may be withdrawn").[39]

The American officials were not the only people allowed to witness what was happening within the camp. The journalist Michael MacDonagh had the rare opportunity to visit Alexandra Palace, and the outcome of his visit was an even rarer description of the place as seen by a Londoner who was neither a prisoner nor a military man. On December 28, 1915, he wrote in his diary about his visit to the camp, describing the conditions of imprisonment at length: the four meals that were served every day: "on Friday fish is served instead of meat"; the permission that the prisoners received to work in the camp and even to open barbershops: "the morning charges for hair-cutting is 4*d* and for shaving 2*d*"; the class relations in camp: the reason why "waiting and cleaning-up are done in turns by the poorer class of prisoners, for which they are paid a few shillings a week," and "the better-off . . . have separate cubicles at an extra charge"; and the prisoners' leisure time, in which "circles have been formed for the learning of languages and general study."

His conclusions about the visit were quite positive. "On the whole, the prisoners seem comfortable and contented," he wrote, "as well they may."[40] MacDonagh did not elaborate on the nature of his visit to the camp, but it can be assumed, because of the many details he was given, that it was an official visit, prearranged by the authorities—a look into a different sphere that was organized and planned so that MacDonagh would be willing to sum it up with the notion that "the prisoners seem comfortable and content." By describing the daily routine in the camp, MacDonagh highlighted the differences prevailing there between the civilian prisoners and the civilians in London, thus placing Alexandra Palace outside the home front, and outside the civil sphere.

Another example of the way the camp was perceived from the outside is discernible in a collection of photos taken in different camps in Britain and published in 1916 in England under the title *German Prisoners in Great Britain*. Within its sixty-two pages, the collection contained 106 photos from six different camps in Britain: Alexandra Palace, Donington Hall, Dorchester, Handforth, Lofthouse Park, and Eastcote. It is irrelevant to this research whether the prisoners in Alexandra Palace knew they were being photographed for this collection, agreed to do so, and acted naturally. What is interesting is that the photos in this book received authorization from the British government for publication, if not actually chosen by them, and therefore they were an approved source, which reflected the way the government wanted to present the imprisonment to the British people and to the world. More than that, by presenting a picture of daily life within the camp, British propaganda reflected the perception of the camp as a place different from and outside of the home front, though not really part of the front either because it was safe from the hazards of the war. This, I argue, rendered Alexandra Palace a liminal sphere.

Thus, the first few photos in the book highlight the view from the camp and its surroundings. The first one is labeled simply "view of the grounds" and depicts the city's landscape as seen from the camp.[41] London is not clearly visible in this photo, but it is evident that the British capital can be seen from behind the barbed wire, which is not visible, and that the prisoners are segregated from the city. Another two photos in the first few pages, on the other hand, highlight the exclusion of the camp's sphere from the war by showing the prisoners playing tennis and racing their model yachts.[42] Those activities are not usually identified with the concept of imprisonment, and despite being at least a reflection of a possible authentic scene (the prisoners themselves described these activities in their writings), it is clear that their inclusion in this book was intended to present imprisonment as a bearable experience, perhaps even an enjoyable one, and the camp as a place unaffected by changes on the home front or at the front.

The next photos in the book show the prisoners making toys and running a tailor's shop, followed by a series of photos presenting work in the camp's kitchen.[43] They were included in the book, it can be assumed, in order to claim that there was no lack of food in the camp: the ratio between the number of prisoners and the amount of food expresses comfort and well-being. This feeling is augmented with the next two photos, which display prisoners with hens and pet birds, since the presence of animals attests to their ability to provide food not only for themselves. Only then are the sleeping conditions presented, though they lack one important element: there are almost no prisoners in these photos, only beds.[44] The impression of crowding and density is still strong but much less in comparison with a presentation of the same sleeping hall when it is filled with prisoners. Therefore, it is probable that these photos were not taken in an empty hall by accident. Because of that, I argue that *German Prisoners in Great Britain* aimed at presenting Alexandra Palace as a place that is neither part of London and its urbanscape nor part of the war and its dangers.

Exclusion from the War

The report of the inspection made by the American embassy in the spring of 1915 is revealing. "Situation: On North London heights, about 300' above the valley," it states in the opening of the report, "excellent location and drainage."[45] The unique location was mentioned in another report on inspections of the hilly camp, one written by the Swedish embassy, describing two visits in October and December 1917. The report continues: "The camp is surrounded by vast pleasure-grounds, including a race-course." "The position is very healthy and the view from the palace down to town is very fine."[46] The spatial characteristics of the camp in Alexandra Palace are mentioned because the authors of these reports believed it was important for understanding its conditions, as, indeed, it was. The experience of imprisonment in Alexandra Palace should be analyzed through the prism of its urbanscape and its location in the heart of the British capital. One of the most vivid characteristics of the topography of the camp was its "excellent location," with its very fine view "down to the town," a pastoral surrounding that does not resemble scenes of the war. In that sense, therefore, the liminality of Alexandra Palace lay in its exclusion from the war and its dangers.

The reports made by neutral outsiders provide a rich and detailed description of the camp's facilities throughout the war and the day-to-day life of the prisoners, including the number of prisoners and their ethnic origin. The report dated May 1915, the first month of imprisonment, stated that "there were 1368 prisoners interned in the palace, of whom about 100 were Austrians," and it can be assumed that the others were of German origin.[47] Almost a year and a half later, the population of the camp had almost doubled, as can be learned from a report about a visit held on October 30, 1916: there were 2,554 prisoners, of whom 2,008 were Germans. This ratio is repeated in the report from the following year, on December 20, 1917, when there are 2,946 prisoners in the camp, of whom 2,578 are Germans.[48] Those numbers might not be accurate in terms of cultural research (it is not specified whether they represent the formal identities of the prisoners or the way the prisoners identify themselves), but they are enough to conclude that civilians of German origin formed the vast majority of the prisoners throughout the war.

The sleeping arrangements, for example, did not change much during the war. "The men sleep in large Halls, marked 'A' 'B' and 'C' on the ground plan of the palace," states a report from May 1915. "Each man has a raised board bed, about six foot high, covered with a straw mattress; fresh straw is given each three months. Pillows are provided, and three blankets for each man, if an extra blanket is needed and asked for it is given."[49] Another report, about a visit on December 1916, added, "The battalion have a very high ceiling. . . . There is more than sufficient air space."[50] At least some of the prisoners did not accept that conclusion, a reminder that official reports should be treated carefully.[51]

The question of food can highlight the differences between the official, neutral reports and the prisoners' experience. The reports, as part of the inspection, praised the camp's kitchen and the quality of its products. "I inspected the meat, which I found sweet and good," noted the American embassy report on the May 1915 visit. "Today's dinner consisted of roast beef and vegetables for 500, and an excellent mutton stew for another 500. By way of dessert there was a bread pudding."[52] Another report from August 1916 rejected the claims that the meat served to the prisoners was "unfit for human food," and a report from the following month concluded: "I have seen and tasted the food, and have found it palatable. I have carefully inspected the quality of meat on several occasions, and have always found it sound and sweet."[53] In the Swedish embassy report describing the December 1917 visit, just before the introduction of food rationing for all British civilians, the tone was a bit harsher, though the conclusion was still positive: the prisoners consider their bread and rice allowances "not sufficient," and "also the quality of the other rations is considered poor," but it was hoped that the British authorities would try to increase the allowances, concluding that "the prisoners may be considered averagely well-nourished, taking into consideration the general shortage of food."[54]

This analysis of the prisoners' nutrition in comparison with the nutrition of the rest of the population in Britain stresses the exclusion of the sphere of the camp from both the civil sphere and the war. Some prisoners even tried to calm their loved ones and promised them they were well nourished. Benny Cseh, a long-time Londoner of Hungarian origin, wrote to his wife, Mabel, during the first months of his imprisonment and assured her the conditions were fine. "My dearest Mabel," he wrote on August 11, 1915 in a two-page letter, sent in a special "Prisoners of War" envelope to their home at 39 Charteris Road, Kilburn, London, "you must not worry yourself on my account as I am quite allright [sic]. We get plenty of food & good as well."[55]

The diaries of the prisoners tell a somewhat different story. George Kenner, a prisoner in Alexandra Palace between September 1915 and June 1916, documented in his diary an incident in which the served meat was not even to the taste of a local animal. "The tough meat remained mostly on the table, and a vagabond cat has perhaps spoiled its stomach," he wrote. "For, to everybodies [sic] joke, someone had put a red cross band around her body. Thereafter, she preferred stopping about the canteen to snatch dainty bite."[56] Rudolf Rocker, who was imprisoned in Alexandra Palace from May 1915 until March 1918, described a severe shortage of food in an essay he wrote during his imprisonment. "The general alimentary conditions of the inmates of Alexandra Palace fall far short of the men's bare necessity," he wrote, most probably at the end of 1917 or the beginning of 1918. "The inevitable results of this continued state of malnutrition, and the consequent debilitation, physical and moral, are not absent. Of all the hospital cases, more than

75 percent are stomach and digestive troubles, and not infrequently abdominal ruptures."[57] Richard Noschke, who was imprisoned in the Alexandra Palace camp between February 1917 and February 1918, was even more graphic in the diary he wrote during the war:

> Utensils for cleanliness seemed very scarce, the very buckets in which the soup was served were used for washing up, and in most instances also washing the floor. . . . In summer 1917, we never had no potatoes for nine months, but instead rice, rice, thre [sic] times a day, and shwedes [sic] turnips, also twice salt herrings a week, but they were all foul so that no one could eat them. . . . We found many with warms [sic] in them.[58]

Entertainment had an important role in the experience of liminality and exclusion in the camp but was rarely mentioned in the official reports. Entertainment was needed to pass the time in a place where the general feeling was that time stood still. Alexandra Palace, the former "People's Palace" and a north London amusement center, had probably more to offer than the average camp. "The time seemed to go very quickly as there were many changes," wrote Richard Noschke. "Each battalion had several billiards, there was also a large theatre in which we had regular concerts and cinemetograph [sic], and every week we had some lectures on political and worldly matter."[59] Rudolf Rocker, who himself gave many lectures to the other prisoners during his time at the camp, was especially impressed by the Concert Society, "the Konzertverein," in which the imprisoned musicians participated.[60] "It developed with surprising speed," he wrote. "Since its foundation, the society has given weekly concerts in the theatre, which are for hundreds of the prisoners a wonderful mental recuperation, which cannot be estimated too highly."[61] The quality of the concerts was evident also from the memoir of Pál Stoffa. "There were many talented musicians in the camp who willingly gave their services and were supported by a number of industrious amateurs," he wrote, complimenting the outcome: "It was said at that time in London that the finest orchestra was to be found in Alexandra Palace."[62]

George Kenner played the violin alone and spent most of his time painting, but he also enjoyed what the camp society had to offer him and the other prisoners. "From the earliest morning some studied parts for a theatre play," he described the camp's routine in his journal. "In the mornings were rehearsals of music and singing. Evenings were filled out with theatrical performances, concerts and scientific recitals. Tragedies and comedies were played. Female imitation, comedy singers, and elocutionists were there. The exceptionly [sic] big Alexandra Palace organ was also played now and then."[63]

All those forms of entertainment helped to improve the lives of the prisoners. "I appeared to enjoy whole-heartedly the amusements fostered and encouraged by the authorities," wrote Stoffa. "I never missed a concert, applauded vigorously a brilliant performance of 'Old Heidelberg' and became an assiduous habitué of the cinema, sharing my comrades' childish delight in the antics of Charlie Chaplin."[64] Those amusements, the concerts, theatrical performances and the cinema, were not a unique example of entertainment within a World War I camp, but they emphasize the uniqueness of the imprisonment experience and the exclusion of Alexandra Palace from the war, highlighting the differences between the experience of imprisonment and the experience at the front, which was identified with hardship, pain, and life-threatening missions.

This exclusion can also be noticed in Rocker's description of Alexandra Palace:

> A camp like Alexandra Palace, with its 3,000 civilian prisoners, may be likened to a small town, with all the branches of its inner administration and all the usual class-distinctions and the professional grading of its population. The chief difference is that the town is a natural growth of society, wherein each citizen has his particular sphere of action, and is able, more or less, to satisfy his personal inclinations and necessities, whereas the inmates of Alexandra Palace are a chaos of all kinds of existences, which have suddenly been cut off from their accustomed conditions of life, and by the same law of force, here assembled.[65]

Rocker's comparison between the camp and a small town should be read carefully. He notes that the camp is like a town because its inhabitants are civilians, despite being prisoners, and thus they are excluded from the war sphere. The "chief difference" between the camp and a town, according to Rocker, is that the prisoners are "cut off" from their previous urban life and "assembled" in Alexandra Palace, a "state of exception."

The camp in Alexandra Palace resembled an excluded small town, with an organized administration and different classes among the prisoners. The daily routine started with its strict schedule. "About 6 o'cl. in the morning it began to get lively in our room," wrote George Kenner in his journal, dedicating an entire chapter to describing the timetable in the camp:

> Some shaved, others straightened their beds and blankets. . . . A scent of cologne water spread about, big sash-windows were opened, one after the others awoke, got up from their straw mattresses, went to the wash-room to be ready at the big dining-hall at 7:30 for breakfast. . . .

> After that we put up our plank-beds, swept out, and prepared for the Commander's or Doctor's inspection at 10 a.m. In fair weather we could step out from 9 to 12 a.m. in the wired off part of the Park, and the hilly ground offered sufficient space to run-about. . . . At 11 o'cl. a.m. one could buy English newspapers, which reports we eagerly glanced over until dinnertime drew near. . . . At 2 o'cl. we were again allowed to go out, and before night-fall through whistle signal counted in by pairs by an Officer and Captain. . . . Before bed-time we read, wrote letters, played chess or cards, until the lights were darkened at 10:30 for the night rest.[66]

These lines from Kenner's journal stress the exclusion from the war: the prisoners were counted at least two times a day and had no real civilian freedom, but otherwise, as long as the war continued, could choose how to spend their time. The next component in Rocker's comparison between the Alexandra Palace camp and a small town was the "usual class-distinctions," and the camp indeed did not lack them. "Although all these men are now victims of the same fate, which has suddenly cast them together, their common captivity is by no means able to bridge over, or even partially erase, their former class and intellectual differences, which divided them in their ordinary lives," explains Rocker in his essay about his term of imprisonment. "These differences remain in the camp, though they may take other forms."[67] Pál Stoffa was even more specific about class differences, particularly the ethnic ones. "Society at large and the Central Empires in particular were faithfully reflected in this microcosm," he wrote in his memoir and added:

> Many of the destitute prisoners performed the various fatigue duties, acted as mess-waiters, worked in the laundry and waited on their wealthier comrades. . . . In spite of their solidarity as subjects of the Central Powers, the three nationalities kept their distance, faithful to inbred dislike and tradition: the Germans, capable and efficient, took the lead in all affairs, they were inclined to patronize the Austrians who lacked cohesion, the care-free Viennese element predominating, whilst the Hungarians, an insignificant minority, supplied the bulk of the artistic element and were inclined to keep aloof from the Germans and Austrians.[68]

By using terms that symbolize a fraction of a different concept, a "small" town or a "micro"-cosm, Rocker and Stoffa defined their segregated place in reference to another space, a bigger one. They were part of a place that was excluded from the 1914–1918 war, a threshold sphere between the front and the home front, a liminal sphere.

World War I ended in November 1918, and Alexandra Palace was reopened to the public in March 1920, when the last prisoners were released. This dark chapter in the palace's history reached its end. After being a liminal sphere and excluded from the city, the civil sphere and the war, Alexandra Palace was once again "the People's Palace," as I show here, using Giorgio Agamben's theory of the "state of exception," along with the diaries and memoirs of the prisoners who lived in London before the Great War and became prisoners within their own city. A decade and a half later, a new chapter in the palace's history was written, when the BBC launched from that site the world's first ever television broadcast, on November 2, 1936. In the twenty-first century Alexandra Palace is a place for special events, conferences, and exhibitions, and its main hall, which previously hosted thousands of Belgian refugees and later thousands of German prisoners during the war, now welcomes thousands of people from the UK and across the world for music concerts. The story of the palace's role during the war is commemorated by a blue plaque on its wall, a presentation of the urban sphere's history to its residents.

Notes

The author thanks the Israel Science Foundation (Grant ISF 1190/18) for supporting this study.

1. Rocker 2005, 173.
2. Rocker 2005, 173.
3. Smith and Stucki 2011, 417.
4. Zimmerer 2005, 51–57; Madley 2005, 429–64; Smith and Stucki 2011, 417–37.
5. Rachamimov 2012b, 220–23; Murphy 2017, 23–24.
6. Wachsmann 2015, 8; Audoin-Rouzeau and Becker 2002, 71; Stone 2017, 42.
7. Jones, H. 2011a, 4, 356–62; Forth 2016, 210.
8. Pitzer 2017, 5–6.
9. Stibbe 2019, 115.
10. Hyslop 2011, 251–76.
11. Murphy 2017, 21–25; Pitzer 2017, 296; Stone 2017, 33; Forth 2016, 203, 214.
12. Pitzer 2017, 6.
13. Agamben 1998, 170–71.
14. Lefebvre 2009, 196–97.
15. Turner 1969, 95.
16. Rachamimov 2006, 365.
17. Harris 2005; Carrington 1975; Gay 1992.
18. Panayi 2013, 8.
19. Stibbe 2008a, 2; Panayi 2013, 95–96.
20. Cahalan 1982, 76; Harris 2005, 47–49; Carrington 1975, 159.
21. Cahalan 1982, 76; Harris 2005, 51–60; Carrington 1975, 159–60.
22. Panayi 1991, 1, 11, 17, 22–23; Panayi 2013, 45–46, 52, 167; Panayi 1989, 184–85.
23. Panayi 1991, 45–8.

24. Panayi 1989, 185–93; French 1978, 389.
25. Panayi 2013, 51, 54, 78; Cesarani 1992, 35; French 1978, 368; Engler n.d., 7–8.
26. Panayi 2013, 78–89.
27. Panayi 2013, 69–70, 90–91, 150–52; Panayi 1991, 106–7.
28. Stoffa 1933, 181–82.
29. Harris 2005, 90.
30. Panayi 2013, 140–42, 146, 170, 177, 183–84, 208; Harris 2005, 96–99; Stibbe 2008b, 59.
31. Engler 1922, 11–12.
32. Rachamimov 2012b, 214.
33. Stibbe 2008a, 4; Stibbe 2008b, 49.
34. Proctor 2010, 4.
35. Proctor 2010, 205.
36. Schmitt 1985, 6–7.
37. Agamben 1998, 168–70.
38. Agamben 1998, 170–71.
39. National Archives of the UK, FO 383/333.
40. MacDonagh 1935, 91–92.
41. *German Prisoners in Great Britain* 1916, 14.
42. *German Prisoners in Great Britain* 1916, 14–15.
43. *German Prisoners in Great Britain* 1916, 18–19.
44. *German Prisoners in Great Britain* 1916, 21.
45. National Archives of the UK, FO 383/333.
46. National Archives of the UK, FO 383/469.
47. National Archives of the UK, FO 383/333.
48. National Archives of the UK, FO 383/469.
49. National Archives of the UK, FO 383/333.
50. National Archives of the UK, FO 383/469.
51. Rocker 2002, 52–53.
52. National Archives of the UK, FO 383/333.
53. National Archives of the UK, FO 383/164.
54. National Archives of the UK, FO 383/469.
55. Cseh, Private papers.
56. Kenner, Internment journal.
57. Rocker 2002, 46; Rocker 2005, 201.
58. Noschke 2002, 16.
59. Noschke 2002, 17.
60. Rocker 2005, 179.
61. Rocker 2002, 41.
62. Stoffa 1933, 194.
63. Kenner, Internment journal.
64. Stoffa 1933, 194.
65. Rocker 2002, 31.
66. Kenner, Internment journal.
67. Rocker 2002, 31.
68. Stoffa 1933, 190–91.

CHAPTER 5

Prisoner-of-War Civilian Experience

The Role of Profession among POWs in Russia

Lena Radauer

"It is not the prisoners who work who are to be pitied—it is those who are not allowed to work."

—George P. Conger, YMCA secretary in Siberia, 1917

In 1987 the pioneer of the study of prisoners of war in Russia, Gerald H. Davis, found that life in POW camps during World War I "reflected qualities which the entering prisoners brought with them, their personal qualities as individuals, their national origins, military rank and units, social standing, *levels of professional skill* and education, and war experiences" (emphasis added).[1] In the last three decades, however, scholarship has selectively focused on some of the factors that determine the experience of captivity. Above all, two aspects, both inherent to the POW experience beyond Russia, emerge as crucial for the treatment of POWs: military rank and origin. It is not surprising, then, that the two were used by the Russian authorities to "prescribe treatment, allocate resources, employ POW labor," thereby "influencing all aspects of a prisoner's existence."[2] There, the nationality of prisoners had a major impact, not least on spatial dimensions, determining the place of internment as well as their radius of movement. Those nationalities considered "friendly" to the Russian empire, predominantly Slavs, whose contact with the Russian population was judged innocuous, received privileged treatment. This meant being held in European Russia. On the other hand, remote areas such as Siberia, the Far East, or Turkestan were reserved for the underprivileged POWs, such as Austrians, Hungarians,

Germans, Turks, and a limited number of other captive nationalities. The hierarchic handling of POWs based on nationality was more pronounced in Russia in comparison to other countries, but dividing factors proved to be complex and concessions often remained nominal.[3]

The prisoners' different conditions according to rank were anchored in the multilateral 1907 Hague Convention. The major implication lay in the fact that soldiers could be employed as workforce while officers were exempt from forced labor and instead received monthly salaries to provide for themselves. Based on this fact, the image persists of higher ranks isolated in internment camps while the lower ranks were on labor assignments. With scholars having focused mainly on the situation of POWs in Russia until 1918, important aspects of their fate have been omitted, since for many, their presence in their captor state lasted into the 1920s. Extending the chronological analysis of the everyday lives of prisoners beyond the establishment of Soviet power is at the same time a spatial extension beyond internment facilities.

Research has acknowledged the meaning of POW labor to the belligerent states, with historian of migration Jochen Oltmer even noting that the selection of the POW workforce in Germany increasingly took into account the prisoners' former civilian professions.[4] Nevertheless, studies hardly broach the issue of the professional background of war prisoners and the role it played in the experience of captivity. [5] Part of the reason for this neglect is the predominant practice of identifying POWs exclusively as military personnel.[6] Such a limited definition was especially deceptive in the case of the Habsburg military, which made up the absolute majority of the more than 2.1 million POWs in Russia, no less than 90 percent of them, and counted an exceptionally high number of civilians.[7] Another factor in the underrepresentation of profession is that the work engagements of the higher ranks in captivity await examination.[8] Voluntary POW labor, if at all, has been looked at as a measure against barbed-wire disease.[9]

The systematic deployment of POW labor into the Russian industry and agriculture was implemented in the spring of 1916 and encompassed the majority of captive soldiers by September of the same year.[10] The fact that their civilian occupations played a secondary role in this effort is reflected in reports about the low productivity of POW laborers.[11] However, POWs were also present in commercial sectors requiring specific professional training. By 1919 they made up as much as 50 to 80 percent of skilled workers in those areas of Siberia that were controlled by Alexander Kolchak's (1847–1920) anticommunist government in Siberia.[12] This hints at the fact that profession, too, played a major role. This aspect is also suggested by historian Iris Rachamimov, who asserts that "POWs employed as artisans in their civilian professions usually received the highest wages among POWs."[13]

So, who, exactly, were these artisans, and how did it come about that they earned a living in their line of work? This chapter seeks to answer these questions and thereby illuminate additional factors that determined the treatment of POWs during World War I. It examines the motivations for and consequences of work as well as the implications of profession, thus drawing attention to the civilian characteristics of war prisoners. Leaving aside the fate of the masses of rank and file used as forced laborers, this chapter focuses on those men whose existence was at least initially officially confined to the camps, predominantly in Siberia—that is, POWs of higher ranks and so-called intelligent professions. Based on the abovementioned statement by eyewitness George Conger, the latter's willingness to work lies at the core of this query. The sources for this analysis are, on one hand, administrative records from the central government overseeing the deployment of POW labor. Siberian newspapers as well as POW memoirs disclose the everyday situation on site, with the latter providing valuable insight into the way those war prisoners of privileged categories perceived work.

Distributing Labor—Acknowledging Profession

The use of POW labor in Russia during World War I has been studied in depth, as has their mistreatment. Notably, German historian Reinhard Nachtigal devoted a full monograph to the atrocious conditions of the prisoners forced to construct the Murmansk railroad north of the Arctic Circle.[14] The deployment of rank-and-file war prisoners into Russian agriculture and industry was done on a mass scale, while higher ranks were sent to work less frequently, leading Nachtigal to dismiss the phenomenon, somewhat hastily, as "more or less insignificant."[15] Personal accounts hint that while many members of higher ranks were exempt from labor assignments, a considerable number did, in fact, work.[16] The Hague Convention did not define the category of "officers" who were to be exempt from forced labor, and the conditions for reserve officers, including the large number of one-year volunteers from the Austro-Hungarian army, varied. A separate international agreement between Red Cross delegations from Germany, Austria, Hungary, and Russia in November 1915 stipulated that the ranks occupied by one-year volunteers also not be subjected to work assignments. Their deployment remained an ambiguous matter, however, as their rank was unique to the

Habsburg Army and their attribution to the officer class was not universally recognized.[17] Their relevance to the present study is inherent to their definition: their right to perform a shortened military service was based on academic qualifications, meaning one-year volunteers at least held a degree from secondary school and were thus by default "intellectuals" among POW communities.[18]

In order to employ the labor of over 80 percent of the rank and file, captives underwent certain systems of registration and distribution.[19] In fact, their educational background was taken into account from the start, as lower ranks of "intellectual professions" (Rus. *intelligentnye professii*, as used in sources of the time) were meant to remain in the camps of Siberia instead of being subjected to labor assignments in European Russia.[20] The idea was to limit the influence of POWs on the civilian population by keeping those war prisoners not immediately required for the needs of the Russian economy at bay in internment facilities.[21] Regulations, however, could be skirted in various ways as competencies overlapped and were often transgressed by the various commands in charge.[22] Individual camp administrators effectively decided whether POWs were sent to labor assignments and which benefited from privileged treatment. A trained theologian interned in Spassk, five hundred kilometers south of Moscow, recalled that in the course of 1916, "the Russians had ordered a group of workmen [to weave rush mats]; we were anything but. During roll call we were registered according to profession. There were: teachers, university graduates, merchants, lawyers, theologians, civil servants . . . a comprehensive list of 'intellectual workers.' "[23] This example bears testimony to the fact that POWs with professions not immediately in need for the Russian economy were in fact used as unskilled laborers instead of being isolated in camps.

POWs were generally deployed in large numbers, but small enterprises and private individuals were also able to request manpower, either on a day-to-day or permanent basis.[24] It was very common to relocate prisoners to reach employers in need of their skill sets.[25] Requests for manpower were meant to go through the intermediary of the different ministries or district headquarters (Rus. *shtab okruga*).[26] In certain cities, such as Omsk in southwestern Siberia, designated offices were opened in order to broker POW labor.[27] As early as 1914, the Society for the Improvement of People's Labor (Rus. *obshchestvo ulucheniia narodnogo truda*) actively searched internment camps in order to select POWs with particular professions to be matched with industry demands.[28] Camp commanders were also directly addressed and often took the liberty of allocating POWs without the approval of higher powers. These procedures were widespread, though frowned upon by the authorities.[29] Camp commanders thus assumed the role of agents and were prone to receive favors or even gain financial benefits in return for allocating POW labor. The overseer of one camp in the Russian Far East not only gave out work permits in exchange for money but encouraged a whole team of POWs from various military and professional backgrounds to participate in the development of an urban quarter in which he had personal stakes.[30] These methods led Russian historian Elena Bondarenko to estimate that "20 to 40 percent of all POWs assumed actual honest cooperation with representatives of their captive state in exchange for better conditions."[31]

Because the tsarist empire drafted skilled workers into the war effort despite making exemptions for particular professions, the know-how of POWs became increasingly valuable to the Russian economy.[32] Technical professions were especially sought after, including those in the printing and building sectors, as well as less obvious trades such as dyers and hairdressers.[33] Somewhat surprisingly, the Russian press did not cover up the need to rely on the skills of enemy subjects and actually broached the issue openly and early on. For example, when the Siberian daily *Otkliki Sibiri* (Echoes of Siberia) reported on war prisoners being used to construct a bridge in the western Siberian town of Tomsk in 1914, it specifically mentioned the background of several architects involved in the project.[34]

As early as 1915, a form was distributed among camp commanders to enter the number and nationality of different professions represented among POWs who were fit to work, thereby enabling the systematic employment of war prisoners with specific training.[35] The forms, designed in Saint Petersburg and distributed among camp commanders, listed a diverse series of initially forty-four, then sixty-nine professions, including mainly manual trades and crafts (such as blacksmiths or bricklayers) next to engineers, architects, veterinarians, musicians and artists, and also unskilled workers.[36] Additional professions were noted on a case-by-case basis. The categories confused civilian and military parameters, as they included lower ranks fit to, but free from work (Rus. *trudosposobnye svobodnye ot rabot*), noncommissioned officers, men "knowing different skills" as well as "intellectual professions." Camp administrators were visibly confused as to which POWs were subject to forced labor and thus whether to include noncommissioned officers, majors, and one-year volunteers in the lists.[37]

These forms allow us not only to deduce the professions that had been lacking in the Russian economy, but also to observe changed approaches vis-à-vis POW labor around the turn of the year 1916–17. Some six months after a directive in March 1916 had stipulated not to leave any POW idle in the internment camps, authorities made a push to match the economy's needs with trained POW labor.[38] Henceforth, POWs with manual professions were to be sent to work exclusively according to their training—and not to jobs that could be done by unskilled laborers. This specification points to the fact that while the professions of POWs had been registered previously, this by no means meant that they were actually employed accordingly, though authorities were striving toward this goal. This situation is confirmed in a Siberian newspaper reporting that forty-nine POWs from various professions had been recruited to do sewing work and were later punished for their inaptitude in fulfilling the assignment.[39] In a somewhat desperate move, war prisoners were now even required to be mapped in case they were unfit to work.[40] Shortly thereafter, intent on using POW labor even more effectively, the provisional government launched a call to record "intellectual professions" as well.[41] These, together with one-year volunteers having specialist training, were to be highlighted in the form.[42]

With the training of POWs taking on greater importance in comparison to their rank, a curious system emerged mixing civilian and military factors. Camp authorities now based their main focus on the division between intellectuals (Rus. *intelligenty*) and nonintellectuals (*ne iz intelligentov*), a distinction they applied to noncommissioned officers as well as rank and file.[43] A consequence of this revised emphasis were new guidelines for noncommissioned officers: the junior ranks were to be registered (and thus found placement) independent of whether they wanted to work, while senior noncommissioned officers and officers were to be included only when they expressed in writing a desire to work.[44] Subjecting subalterns (*mladshie ofitsery*) to forced labor was in fact explicitly anchored in the war ministry's regulations.[45] Concern, however, persisted about the war prisoners' presence in local communities, and employers were expected to keep them from partaking in social life and to prevent escapes.[46] Extending the POW workforce to the higher ranks was a major policy change under the short-lived provisional government that replaced the Russian tsar and existed until the 1917 October revolution. This shows that the deployment of POW labor by Russian authorities during World War I was in fact not limited to the rank and file.

The course for widening the POW work base to include all ranks was already set before the Bolsheviks came to power and continued under the anti-Bolshevik "white" rule of Siberia in 1918–1919.[47] In fact, the need for specialized skills, including those of POWs, was particularly tangible at the time when Siberia was cut off from western Russia during the civil war, leading to the introduction of compulsory work for intelligent and technical professions.[48] This stance was further reflected in a policy initiated by the provisional government and upheld under Alexander Kolchak's rule of

Siberia: in deciding applications by war prisoners to become Russian citizens, authorities were interested, among other facts, in their level of education as well as the profession they had held in their home countries.[49]

The incorporation of the workforce of the higher ranks is commonly attributed to the Bolsheviks' introduction of universal labor duty in October 1918, interpreted as forcing all POWs in Russia between the ages of eighteen and forty-five to work.[50] As a matter of fact, POW officers continued to have the (nominal) choice of whether they wished to work.[51] Captive officers who did decide to do so were even treated with suspicion, and procedures were in place to ensure that they be kept in check: the central board of prisoners' and refugees' affairs (Rus. *Tsentroplenbezh*) individually reviewed their trustworthiness while those who already held a job at the time were required to attest to the circumstances of their employment.[52] Captive officers were not allowed to take on administrative duties and ceased to be paid monthly sums by the military authorities as soon as they received salaries. POWs' wages had not been adapted to the significant inflation and were already increasingly insufficient to guarantee their upkeep from late 1916, gradually forcing many POWs who had previously relied on the institutional support infrastructure to seek employment.[53] Despite the common image of POW officers being confined to Russian internment camps for various reasons, be it due to existing conventions or their own sense of superiority, a number of them had actually worked early on following their own wish.[54] POWs' own initiative can be seen in pleas for assistance in their search for an appropriate workplace according to their profession, which they addressed to various available instances such as representatives of relief committees and Russian authorities.[55]

Experiencing the Consequences of Specialist Work

Next to financial incentives work played an important role for captives to make use of the years spent in internment. In the words of a Hungarian painter, while many fellow POWs "languished and disintegrated mentally in their helplessness, those . . . who worked with our hands in the creative field had something to help stabilize the mind and keep it more nearly normal."[56] The emotionally charged role that work played in German society suggests that pursuing their profession was a particularly pressing matter to war prisoners from the German empire. There, for over a century, economists had glorified the concept of work, and an ethos equating work to happiness was shaped through the Protestant church.[57] All captor states agreed on the benefits of engaging their captives in regular, purposeful employment.[58] In fact, even neutral Switzerland subjected those war prisoners interned on its soil to obligated work for "therapeutic and disciplinary reasons."[59] Examining their situation in Germany, theatre scientist Nicole Leclercq found that resuming their profession in captivity was a natural tendency for war prisoners.[60]

Camp life was in many ways defined by POW occupation. In an effort to organize everyday life, the internees in Russia were grouped together in squads, with profession used as a possible denominator. Thus POWs with similar occupations were gathered in "artist squads" in certain camps, as well as broader "intellectuals' squads."[61] One such "intellectuals' squad" was formed in a camp in southern Russia in 1915, grouping together those with high-school diplomas, that is one-year volunteers, majors, as well as "people with intelligent professions, without regard for their rank, which meant any kind of clerk, also instrument makers and musicians."[62] This is a vivid example of how profession could supersede rank as a decisive denominator with a direct impact on POWs' treatment: being classified as belonging to an "intelligent" profession was rewarded with privileges such as superior accommodations and exemption from forced labor. These benefits were coveted among POWs and defended through exams making sure that no professionals from other backgrounds falsely joined.[63] The squads were part of a system of self-organization that developed in internment facilities throughout Russia over the years and turned with time into well-run subcommunities with a distinct cultural and economic life.[64] With the support of relief societies such as the Red Cross or the YMCA, the internment facilities were outfitted with various kinds of workshops where POWs themselves produced their everyday necessities, such as clothes, shoes or soap. Especially in the larger camps this activity developed into a regular industry that saw its height in late 1919. While initially the tradesmen's wages had been sponsored by relief societies, their activities quickly outgrew their initial purposes. One camp in the Omsk military district had artisan studios that were so busy in 1915 that they had a sales and order department.[65] Tradesmen from the POW community were as valuable a resource inside as outside internment camps, and they earned accordingly.[66] Camp industries not only supplied the Russian market but even provided the military with riding and medical equipment, as well as alcohol and cigarettes.[67] The popularity of these workshops can be seen in the coverage they earned in the Russian press, which widely advertised POW production and pointed out the quality of the toys, furniture, leatherwear, or crafts on sale.[68]

The concentration of men of letters and artists in Siberian POW camps was such that according to a contemporary visiting several camps, their cultural activities eclipsed those of Siberian towns.[69] Thus opening a camp theatre was possible, for example, what with "technicians and engineers responsible for building the stage, painters and art historians creating decorations, furniture and costumes, chemists producing paint and makeup[.] From the rank and file, hairdressers, carpenters, shoemakers and tailors were recruited, the camp orchestra and choral societies that were led by successful musicians and composers were . . . at the theatre's disposal."[70] Though introduced for the purpose of serving the POW community, due to their professionalism, many cultural ventures found favor with and gained assignments from local communities.[71] Particularly in Siberia, far from the artistic centers of European Russia, creative professions were highly sought after. By 1916 captive musicians were involved in the opera production of a local composer in Krasnoyarsk. According to musicologist Evgeniia Tsarëva, the cultural life there was kept alive during the civil war solely through the contribution of captive musicians.[72] Painters from the POW community not only easily found work but public recognition as specialists as well.[73] When a pair of Austrian artists who had held a course in etching at an art school were ordered back to the internment camp following a political turnaround, it had to be shut down as no other experts in the field were available in the third largest town in Siberia.[74] Remuneration for their trade was such that by 1920 one painter, Edmund Adler, had amassed twice the worth of his family home through the sale of artwork created in captivity for fellow POWs as well as on the Russian market while his family was living in precarious conditions in postwar Austria.[75] Elsa Brändström goes as far as describing the situation of POWs succeeding to work according to their profession as "carefree."[76] Next to remuneration, providing services entailed privileges, first and foremost personal freedom. This could come in the form of a so-called *propusk*, a document allowing POWs to leave the camp, being housed privately, and being allowed to travel.[77] The topic of privilege through profession was the subject of a humorous sketch entitled "the guard outwitted" by a war prisoner held in Russia. It tells the story of a POW dreaming of leaving camp and finally getting permission as soon as he is equipped with fake paraphernalia and assumed to be an engineer (see figure 5.1).

The occupational group that received, perhaps, the greatest privileges from the earliest point in time were doctors.[78] As medical personnel were crucial in the internment camps to counter the various diseases prevalent among POWs, anyone with medical training was disposed to work in the military hospital or other facilities where POWs were treated, and such individuals enjoyed a highly privileged standing within camp communities. Medical personnel, however, were in demand far beyond camp walls. In order for local, often remote, communities to benefit from treatment, they were

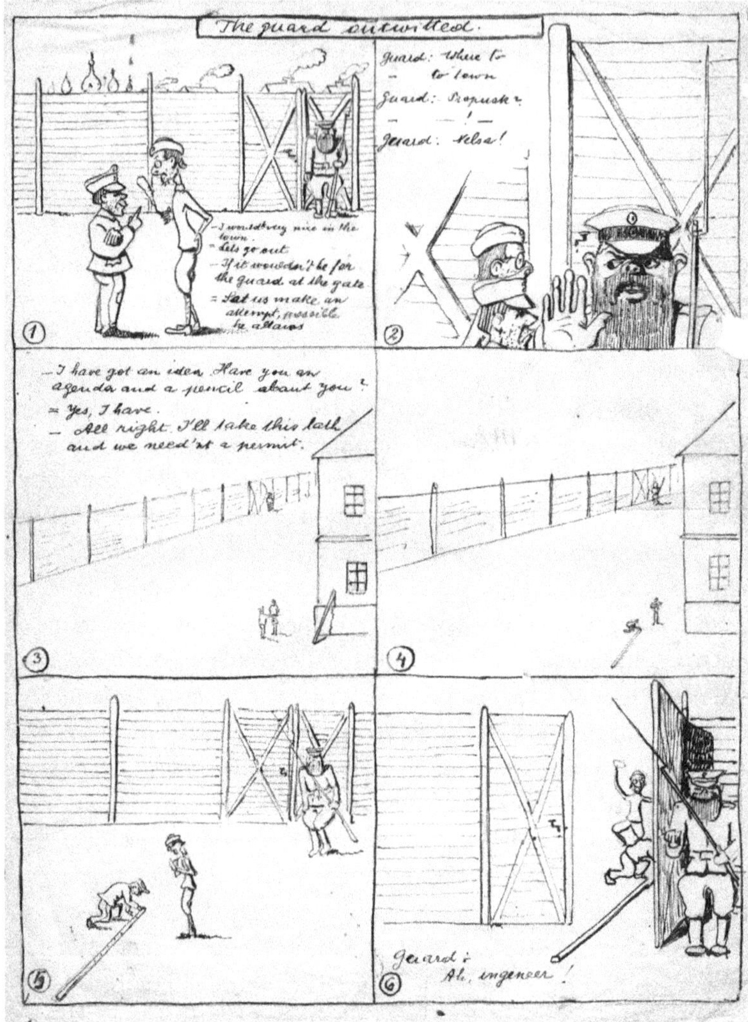

FIGURE 5.1. "The guard outwitted": a caricature drawn by a prisoner of war, Russia, ca. 1919. Courtesy of the Rev. Walter Teeuwissen Papers (unprocessed). Courtesy of Kautz Family YMCA Archives. University of Minnesota Libraries.

granted access to captive medics, who also practiced in civilian institutions. Their indispensability brought these doctors great privileges that included freedom of movement.[79] It also earned them authority, even with Russian officials of different political camps. The Austrian surgeon Burghard Breitner, who spent his entire captivity between 1914 and 1920 in Nikol'sk-Ussuriĭsk in the Russian Far East, is an example of having been able to assert his position throughout several regime changes, assuming the important role of patron among captives and intermediary in their interactions with both their overseers as well as the civilian world.[80]

Working outside camp walls exposed POWs to Russian society and provided them the possibility, to varying extents, to lead a civilian existence. One war prisoner in Ukraine described how, working as a printer during the daytime and an usher at the local cinema at night, he "transformed from '*germanskii*' [German] to '*russkii*' [Russian]," dressing in local clothing and speaking the language.[81] The opportunities of POW specialists in revolutionary Russia can be seen in an example from the Russian Far East. The authorities of an emerging garden town in close vicinity to Vladivostok initially recruited three captive Austrian architects to develop a new residential district.[82] When public money ran out, the war prisoners proceeded to take on private orders and even opened their own architecture office. Theirs is an example of how professionals were able to forge close ties with local communities and establish themselves among the Russian upper class, a situation that was captured in a series of photographs from 1920, showing at least one of the architects mingling with the high society of Vladivostok.[83] In parallel, the military ranks came second to professional standing since they were in a role of authority toward other captives, placing fellow prisoners in their construction projects.[84] However, in certain places higher-ranking POWs were able to move beyond internment facilities and entertain relationships with the local society without working, official restrictions notwithstanding. Preexisting connections were in turn useful to job searches. Social events were a good occasion to interact with potential employers, and patrons were often willing to provide POWs with letters of recommendation or to campaign for them.[85] War prisoners also placed advertisements for their services in newspapers.[86]

Among POWs who were the sole specialist in their field was German prehistorian Gero von Merhart (1886–1959), the sole representative of his specialty in Krasnoyarsk.[87] Merhart himself initiated his employment and used all means at his disposal to be able to take on an occupation in accordance with his training. Initially, his German university with the support of the government had petitioned authorities in Saint Petersburg to this end.[88] While the effort was nullified by the political changes in Russia, it testifies to the fact that the home institutions of the POWs saw the potential for internees to make use of captivity in order to advance their work. In the case of Gero von Merhart, it was actually specifically his place of internment that aroused his professional interest, and the work he was able to accomplish in Siberia served as the basis for his habilitation treatise, which was completed upon his repatriation.[89]

Eventually, it was the Swedish Red Cross nurse Elsa Brändström who arranged a position in the local museum for Merhart, where he was able to work between 1919 and 1921. His post, but also his academic output after his repatriation, bear witness to the fact that he, in the words of prehistorian Hermann Parzinger, was in Siberia "as a war prisoner, but also as researcher and archeologist."[90] Other academics from the POW community were employed in universities, as part of research projects and scientific expeditions.[91] But war prisoners were also able to secure work by feigning expertise. Hans Franta (1893–1983), who eventually became a career painter while captive in Siberia, managed to find employment as doctor's assistant as well as participating in a year-long meteorological expedition of the Institute for the Study of Siberia (*Institut Issledovaniia Sibiri*), citing credentials he did not have.[92]

Both jobs provided Franta with opportunities he would otherwise not have had access to: living at the hospital granted him access to the paper he used for his artwork and allowed him to move around town in civilian disguise during his off-duty hours.[93] The expedition resulted in an invaluable experience that provided inspiration and the opportunity to work artistically.[94] Crucially, his employers pleaded for Franta to receive the salary of a "specialist," on the basis of the challenging circumstances working on a ship travelling to a remote Siberian estuary.[95]

In the context of Bolshevik Russia, work and profession took on a particular role. In a system in which food and housing were linked to the workplace and trade unions, the type of profession was relevant as it could bring crucial benefits, such as additional rations.[96] Not only was labor to act as the basis of socialist society. The construction of the new socialist state relied on the contribution of educated people, and "specialists" were needed in Soviet institutions, regardless of their social background or political affiliation.[97] POWs filled the void in certain professions, and their indispensability was grounds for privileged treatment.[98] When it came to the repatriation of war prisoners in the 1920s, some employers were reluctant to part with their highly skilled workforce, whom they judged indispensable.[99] The POWs' eventual departure left such a palpable void that Soviet institutions regretted their absence long after the fact.[100]

In addition to having an impact on their captivity, work and professional skills had the potential to lend meaning to POWs' lives in a more permanent way, contributing to their prospects after being released. Many camp communities developed courses that allowed those internees serving as instructors to pass on their knowledge and permitted students to receive a professional formation. In "business school," which was developed in Transbaikalia's Berëzovka, almost one hundred students received a solid education first and foremost in engineering and several technical subjects, even arousing the interest of the Austrian war ministry.[101] That said, in 1920 employers in Moscow launched a complaint that among seventy-four technical engineers to be sent from a Siberian POW camp, three were actually former career officers who had received technical training as captives.[102] The importance for POWs to pursue work training led some detaining powers to create special facilities for the purpose.[103] Since the acquisition of new skills improved the chances of returning prisoners to find employment, the receipt of professional training as well as work experience during captivity was in the interest of the POWs themselves and of their states of origin. War prisoners were consequently provided with credentials, both for their participation in camp enterprises as well as from local employers as references to testify to their activities in captivity after returning to their home countries.[104]

The civilian identity of war prisoners played an important role from the beginning of their ordeal. The professional skills of POWs impacted their treatment by Russian authorities as well as their possibilities within the civilian communities with which they came in touch. Notably, in remote areas of the Russian empire, where the higher ranks largely remained concentrated, POWs with specialist training in various sectors aroused the interest of local communities and came to be of great importance to the economies there.[105] This was understood early on by the Russian government, which tried to find ways to skirt international conventions and use the potential of war prisoners exempt from forced labor. In a constant effort to gain workforce, more and more categories of POWs were implicated by applying a curious system of civilian as well as military factors. POW specialists were a valuable asset to all political powers ruling Russia between 1914 and 1920: against the backdrop of a world and civil war, economic needs proved to be more pertinent than questions of enmity or national pride. The presence of war prisoners on the Siberian job market anticipated the important role that foreign specialists were to play in the industrialization of the Soviet Union.[106]

War prisoners were rewarded with money as well as various privileges and were notably able to forge a civilian existence through their work. What is more, POWs themselves put their professions to the fore, organizing within internment camps according to their skills and setting out to find adequate employment. War prisoners were able to build on the qualifications they had gained prior to the war, as well as expanding their skills or acquiring new ones. Other than the military rank they held and the nation they had gone to war for, another affiliation by which to identify themselves was their occupation.

Notes

Epigraph: Conger 1917, 536.

1. Davis 1987, 149.

2. Rachamimov 2002, 55.

3. Stibbe 2008c, 9. For a study of the role of ethnicity in the context of World War I internment, see also Nancy Fitch's chapter in this volume.

4. He goes on to explain how a system of labor administration developed in Germany during the First World War is the precursor of today's employment offices. Oltmer 2006, 81, 87ff.; Jones, H. 2008a, 28; see also Moritz 1998; Nachtigal 2001; Valitov and Sulimov 2014. For a comparative view of the deployment of civilian captives, see Bohdan Kordan's chapter in this volume.

5. A notable exception for the example of Russia can be found in Ikonnikova 2004, 64ff.

6. As leading historians have noted, the fact that most soldiers of the Great War were "civilians in uniform" meant that internment camps were primarily a world of civilians. Audoin-Rouzeau and Becker 2002, 71.

7. Cornwall 2000, 31–32; Deák 1990, 192–93.

8. Some historians, however, have hinted at a shift in POW employment in Russia under Bolshevik rule. See, for example, Moritz 1998, 385.

9. See Panayi 2018.

10. In mid-September 1916, 83.55 percent of the rank and file were employed. Wurzer 2005, 354.

11. Davis 1977, 630.

12. Davis 1983, 174, 176.

13. Rachamimov 2002, 111.

14. Nachtigal 2001.

15. Nachtigal 1995, 203–4.

16. Hackl 2009, 105ff.; Gaiswinkler, n.d., 28.

17. RGVIA f. 1468 op. 2 d. 411 l. 137, 234–35.

18. For a discussion of the process of qualification for one-year volunteers, with the example of a POW held in Siberia, see Nachbaur 2018, especially 72–75.

19. Wurzer 2005, 354.

20. RGVIA f. 1468 op. 2 d. 396 l. 179; see also GATO f. 416 op. 2 d. 4 l. 39–40.

21. See, for example, *Sibirskaia Mysl'* 115 (June 26, 1916), 5; *Sibirskaia Mysl'* 184 (September 24, 1916), 3.

22. Moritz 1998, 383. Matthew Stibbe illustrates the importance of examining local executive practices in addition to government strategies; see his chapter in this volume.

23. Obergottsberger n.d., 65.

24. RGVIA f. 1468 op. 2 d. 417 l. 157; RGVIA f. 1529 op.1 d. 21 l. 37.

25. Ikonnikova 2004, 150–51; RGVIA 2000 op. 9 d. 24 l. 7–7 ob.

26. RGVIA f. 1468 op. 2 d. 396 l. 184.

27. *Otkliki Sibiri* 11 (January 15, 1915), 4.

28. RGVIA f. 2000 op. 9 d. 24 l. 4, 7.

29. RGVIA f. 1468 op. 2 d. 396 l. 178, 181–82 ob., 184.

30. Newald 1938, 250ff.

31. Bondarenko 2002, 11.

32. Sanborn 2014, 93; Moritz 1998, 380–81; RGVIA f. 369 op. 9 d. 2 l. 3, f. 369 op. 9 d. 21 l. 73.

33. Ikonnikova 1999, 94; Bondarenko 2002, 48; GAKK f. r-163 op. 1 d. 4; RGVIA f. 2000 op. 9 d. 24 l. 7–7 ob. Incidentally, hairdressers were also sought after within camp communities; Gaiswinkler, n.d. 18a.

34. *Otkliki Sibiri* 190 (December 5, 1914), 4; *Otkliki Sibiri* 11 (January 15, 1915), 4.

35. RGVIA f. 1468 op. 2 d. 388 l. 311 ob.

36. RGVIA f. 1468 op.2 d. 388 l. 1; RGVIA f. 1468 op. 2 d. 388 l. 80–81.

37. RGVIA f. 1468 op. 2 d. 411 l. 65; RGVIA f. 1468 op. 2 d. 388 l. 35.

38. Moritz 1998, 382.

39. *Znamia Revoliutsii* 26, July 1, 1917, 4.

40. RGVIA f. 1468 op. 2 d. 388 l. 303–6, 311 ob.

41. RGVIA f. 1468 op. 2 d. 411 l. 234–35.

42. RGVIA f. 1468 op. 2 d. 411 l. 334.

43. RGVIA f. 1468 op. 2 d. 409 l. 12.

44. RGVIA f. 1468 op. 2 d. 411 l. 234–5; GAKK f. 161 op. 1 d. 760 l. 105.

45. Valitov and Sulimov 2014, 191.

46. GAKK f. 161 op. 1 d. 760 l. 105.

47. Brändström 1922, 124.

48. See *Eniseĭskiĭ Vestnik* 151 (July 25, 1919), 3.

49. GARF f. r-200 op. 1 d. 643 l. 11.

50. See, for example, Wurzer 2005, 526.

51. GARF f. r-3333 op.1 d. 3 l. 147.

52. For an officer's request for employment in a Soviet Institution, see GARF f. r-3333 op. 3 d. 533 l. 8.

53. Wurzer 2005, 195; see Imrey 1930, 325.

54. Ikonnikova 2004, 28; RGVIA f. 1558 op. 9 d. 10 l. 120.

55. RGVIA f. 1558 op. 9 d. 10 l. 120; RGVIA f. 1558 op. 9 d. 43 l. 134; RGVIA f. 2000 op. 9 d. 50 l. 10. R333 op. 3 d. 550 l. 56; Tsentr. Kollegiia to Sovet Nar. Komissarov (July 31, 1918).

56. Imrey 1930, 352.

57. Campbell 1989, especially 3–4, 8.

58. Davis 1977, 23.

59. Civelli 2017, 197. I would like to thank Dr. Anja Huber for her kind advice.

60. Leclercq 2008, 224.

61. Hackl 2009, 132; Newald 1938, 125.

62. Gaiswinkler, n.d., 18.

63. Gaiswinkler, n.d., 28.

64. Davis, G. 1987. For some insights into the scope of self-organization within the internment camps, see Naoko Shimazu's contribution on civilian internees in Japan in this volume.

65. Kautz Family YMCA Archives, Y.USA, 9–2–1, Box 2, Folder Russia. Correspondence and reports, 1915, "Harte and Day to the hospitals and German prisoners' camps in Siberia, Petrograd, 25 June 1915" initial, unshortened version, 11–12.

66. Wurzer 2005, 483.

67. Brändström 1922, 123.

68. *Eniseĭskiĭ Vestnik* 107 (June 1, 1919), 3; *Svobodnyĭ Kraĭ* 358 (October 23, 1919), 1; *Lel'* 1 (November 15, 1919), 4.

69. Brändström 1922, 98.

70. Karsten 1927.

71. For example, musicologist Evgeniia Tsarëva has studied the importance of POW musicians to the development of a professional music culture in the Siberian town of Krasnoyarsk. Tsarëva 2012, especially 1, 6; For a study of cultural ventures in Russian POW camps and the interest generated among local societies, see Radauer and Egger 2014.

72. see Tsarëva 2013.

73. See Imrey 1930, 318. For case studies of graphic artists held in Siberia, see Radauer 2018; Radauer 2011.

74. GAKK f. 161 op. 1 d. 757 l. 14–16; *Volia Sibiri* 96 (October 23, 1918), 3.

75. Schutzbier 2010, 98.

76. Brändström 1922, 56.

77. Wurzer 2005, 134, 148; for example, Földes 1930, 92.

78. On privileges for doctors, see Wurzer 2005, 156; Baja 1930, 503–6.

79. According to a stipulation from December 17, 1917, trustworthy POW medics were to be allowed to move around town without a guard; however, correspondence shows that in the case of Blagoveshchensk, it took until April 1918 for the four doctors held at the local internment camp to be granted the privilege. RGVIA f. 1558 op. 9 d. 43 l. 35, 36, 52, 114.

80. Breitner 1921, especially 308–11, 234, 257, 272. See also Burghard Breitner, Letters to Peter Panold, 18.10. and 4.11.1916, ÖNB Cod. Ser. N. 37844 Han, 13 and 15.

81. Braun 1930, 51.

82. Newald 1938, 266, 269, 273; Wolf, n.d., 219.

83. Schurz 1986, 11.

84. The photograph of another Austrian architect standing next to the manual laborers he hired from among fellow POWs, including higher ranks, for the construction of a Catholic church in Vladivostok provides a telling visual image of new hierarchies. Scheidl 2014, 167, image 72; Geyling 1919; Newald 1938, 277.

85. RGVIA f. 1558 op. 9 d. 43 l. 202–3; Radauer 2018, 96.

86. *Eniseĭskiĭ Vestnik* 119 (June 17, 1919), 4.

87. Merhart 2008, 34.

88. Merhart 2008, 19.

89. Similarly, Slovenian art historian Hermann / Vojeslav Molè penned his habilitation treatise based on the art collection of the Stroganov family while in Tomsk, the town of the Siberian University, where he arrived as war prisoner, though he subsequently joined the Yugoslav troops.

90. Merhart 2008, 18, 34.

91. Saatzer, n.d., 2; Gaiswinkler, n.d., 28; RGVIA f. 1558 op. 9 d. 1 l. 432 ob.

92. Letter by the geographical section of the Institute for the Study of Siberia on May 10, 1920. GATO f. R-26 op. 1 d. 8 l. 80; Franta 1977, n.p.

93. Franta 1934, 11; Radauer 2011, 19.

94. Franta 1934, 10. For works produced during this period, see Radauer 2011, 46, 47, 72, 105, 113, 130–31, 142–43, 148–49.

95. Protocol Nr. 28, Council meeting of the Institute for the Study of Siberia on May 22, 1920, in *Zhurnaly i zasendaniia soveta instituta issledovaniia Sibiri 1919–1920*, S. 174.

96. See Gillian and Manning 2000, 248.

97. See Finkel 2007, 14; Fitzpatrick 1970, 99.

98. Brändström 1922, 56.

99. GAIO f. r-42 op. 1 d. 8 l. 92 ob.

100. For example, the Soviet section for people's education, GAKK f. r-93 op. 1 d. 42 l. 58.

101. Schreinert 1920.

102. GARF f. r-130 op. 4 d. 512 l. 45–6.

103. Leclercq 2008, 262.

104. For example BAMA Freiburg, MSG 200/1813; Arthur Wolf Papers, certificate from Slaff & Joffe, September 7, 1920.

105. See Kaliakina 2013, 99ff.

106. Graziosi 1988.

Chapter 6

The Face and Race of the Enemy

German POW Photographs as a Weapon of War

Nancy Fitch

When Conrad Hoffman arrived in Germany in 1915 on behalf of the YMCA, he saw dozens of postcards, photographs, and photobooks on sale in German train stations; a lot of these almost certainly featured images of the prisoners of war (POWs) that the German armies had captured in the first year of the war.[1] Thus, it is probably not surprising that two new books about "our enemies" and featuring POW photos appeared in the following year.[2] The country was beginning to feel the effects of two years of grueling warfare, and many of those who remained at home almost certainly wanted to know who their husbands, sons, lovers, and fathers were facing in battle. It might have been startling, however, when they found that both books featured covers portraying the faces of Africans (see figures 6.1 and 6.2). Were they not at war with the English, French, Russians, and now the Italians? What did Africans have to do with the war?

To be sure, a handful of other books appeared in 1916 with "our enemies" in their titles, but these two books are illustrative of the themes I wish to address here. Both were put together by men (adventurer/ethnographer Leo Frobenius and camp commandant Otto Stiehl) who had close connections to the German government and its prisoner-of-war camps. Both purported to be anthropological studies based on careful research of POWs, and both featured portrait photographs so that Germans and others could "see" their enemies.

FIGURE 6.1. Cover of Leo Frobenius, *Der Völker-Zirkus unserer Feinde*.

In fact, I want to argue that photographs of captured colonial subjects from Africa and Asia, as well as those of prisoners from Eastern Europe, played specific roles in shaping Germany's perception of its enemies—and of itself. In both popular accounts and anthropological studies, these photographs in particular were employed in distinctive ways to represent and emphasize Germany's war against "uncivilized" enemies constructed as racial types. Altogether the French deployed almost 440,000 Senegalese, Algerian, Tunisian, Moroccan, and other soldiers from its African colonies, and

Figure 6.2. Cover of Otto Stiehl, *Unsere Feinde: Charakterköpfe aus deutschen Kriegsgefangenenlagern.*

another 44,000 from Indochina and Pacific island colonies, while Britain mobilized almost a million and half Indians.[3] The Germans captured many of these colonial soldiers, turning them into POWs, who were largely housed in special camps in Wünsdorf and Weinberger.[4]

By 1916 the Germans had incarcerated between one and a half and two million prisoners of war, many of them from Europe's colonies and many more from Eastern Europe and Asiatic Russia. For Germany, lacking the colonial troops of its adversaries, the POWs proved to be central in pursuing the war. Germans put them to work as coerced labor at an unprecedented scale; they also cast them as subjects of anthropometric portraits used to construct visual images of the "face" and "race" of the enemy.[5] Since various combatants, including Germany, took millions of prisoners and countless photographs during World War I, the magnitude of wartime incarceration and POW photography contextualized in "anthropological" narratives emerges.[6] Within Germany these images helped to shape perceptions of this nation's wartime role. In the words of one scholar, "There were very few places where Germans' sense of national and cultural supremacy was more powerfully felt than the POW camps."[7]

Scholarship reflecting a renewed interest in both World War I visual representations, including photographs, and POWs blossomed in the 1990s and has continued to be a central focus in how historians now interpret the war.[8] Hence, many today agree with British historian Heather Jones who argued that "far from being a marginal group, prisoners were . . . central to the radicalization of the conflict in Germany, France, and Britain and a fundamental part of each country's wartime self-image."[9] Synthesizing and reinterpreting countless studies and memoirs while providing numerous examples of visual representations, prison camp atrocities, and wartime violence, French historians Stéphane Audoin-Rouzeau and Annette Becker also placed photography and prisoners at the center of questions that need to be answered in order to understand the war and its legacies.[10] Andrew D. Evans in *Anthropology at War: World War I and the Science of Race in Germany* and Britta Lange in a variety of articles and a monograph have provided the most definitive studies on the use of photographs in anthropological research carried out in German POW camps.[11] Finally, several South Asian and Islamic scholars have turned to the visual, oral, and written documents produced in the camps to better understand the subjectivity of Hindu and Muslim soldiers and prisoners during the war.[12] All these studies have emphasized the ways in which anthropological or "scientific" portrait photographs of the POWS contributed to the racialization of Germany's enemies and imbued the nation with biological meaning through linking German ideas of race, nation, and *Volk*.

While I am indebted to and build on this impressive research, I want to complicate these authors' readings of the anthropologic portrait evidence and pay closer attention to the blurred boundaries between publications like those Frobenius and Stiehl produced and the work of institutionally recognized anthropologists like Felix von Luschan, Rudolf Pöch, and Luschan's doctoral student, Egon von Eickstedt. Such an approach suggests the problematic nature of identifying racial "types" from facial photographs, which tended to individualize subjects. It also acknowledges that by examining popular and scholarly publications, one is looking at anthropological practices at a time when anthropology as a discipline was first being institutionalized. Luschan became the first chair of anthropology at Berlin's Frederick William University only in 1911, while Pöch became the first chair of anthropology at the University of Vienna in 1913. Combined with a recognition of the significant extent to which everyone was encouraged to become an anthropologist, or at least think like one, in the popular *Völkerschauen* or "shows of people" featuring colonial subjects before the war, this approach also addresses the relationship between racial ideas that permeated popular culture and those that shaped "scientific" knowledge.[13] Most important, both popular and professional portrait photos circulated widely during the war as weapons that could augment Germans' sense of identity while demonizing their enemies as racial inferiors.

These collections of POW photographs were neither benign nor unique. In fact, POW photographs shaped wartime perceptions of enemies almost from the invention of the camera. During the American Civil War, Union forces used photographs of emaciated POWs to illustrate the brutal treatment that Confederate soldiers inflicted on their prisoners. Colonial powers routinely published photographs of African prisoners in the late nineteenth and early twentieth centuries, while Serbians measured Turkish prisoners during the Balkan Wars.[14] What made the World War I German POW studies both different and significant was the large number of prisoners from different parts of the world gathered together in a single place, as well as the professionalization and standardization of the anthropological methods used in the studies.

The Entente Powers also used prisoners as labor, undertook research on prisoners, and spread their own propaganda,[15] but the German and Austrian governments seem to have been uniquely enthusiastic about setting up social-science researchers in the camps to measure, prod, record, and photograph POWs for scientific and propagandistic purposes. The Austrian Ministry of War even authorized the deployment of soldiers to help take measurements of their human subjects.[16] Because of their easy reproducibility, prisoner-of-war photographs became particularly pervasive during the war. Several mass-produced German publications, such as *The Prisoners of War in Germany* and the serial publication *Der Grosse Krieg in Bildern*, featured POW photographs.[17] Both Pöch and Luschan also began publishing the results of their photography-enhanced POW research while the war raged. When the victorious powers criticized Germany for its treatment of POWs after the armistice, still more German research and propaganda works featuring POW photographs appeared.[18]

Though the direct connection between the POW studies and war photographs is not always clear, there is no question that much of the money for both came from official sources. Evidently, the government and the military had few qualms about letting researchers put together their elaborate laboratories, photographic equipment, and recording studios in the limited space of the camps.[19] Moreover, it appears that researchers were pleased that their scholarly work had military and national value, while journalists and popular writers could point to the POW studies as evidence that the cultural interpretations they propagated were grounded in "science."[20] Most important, such "science" was just as often shaped by the visual representations in the propaganda than by anything social scientists offered to those who wanted to proliferate images of the enemy. It is also clear that the ethnographic portrait photographs, though focusing on groups identified as different races, rarely "spoke for themselves."

Who Are the Barbarians?

War, deportations, and the violence associated with conflict spread faster without victory than anyone imagined in the late summer of 1914, and casualties on all sides reached staggering numbers in the first months of the war. Civilians could not escape the violence. As casualties mounted, millions of civilians and soldiers were either deported or taken as prisoners and marshalled into camps. With the civilian deportations and the shelling and burning of civilian targets, both sides began to call those on the other side "barbarians." From the beginning neither side seemed to accept its own role in the collective calamity of the war. [21] As Stéphane Audoin-Rouzeau and Annette Becker have demonstrated, intellectuals as well as the popular press in France and England began to cast the Germans as barbarians in racial terms as they spread news of German atrocities in neutral Belgium and northern France. For the Entente Powers, German atrocities provided plentiful evidence of the uncivilized nature of their foes, but many Germans believed that their science could show who the barbarians really were. Increasingly drawing on legacies of racial ideas, both sides used nation and race interchangeably, in vague and undefined ways.[22]

In spite of several similar documents from other groups, many writers at the time believed that the opening salvo in this battle over comparative barbarity came with the October 4, 1914, publication of "The Manifesto of the Ninety-three German Intellectuals." Proclaiming that "as representatives of German Science and Art, we hereby protest to the civilized world against the lies and calumnies with which our enemies are endeavoring to stain the honor of Germany in her hard struggle for existence," these scientists, scholars, artists, and writers denied that Germany had committed any atrocities in neutral Belgium. Furthermore, they declared, "*it is not true* that our warfare pays no respects to international laws. It knows no undisciplined cruelty. But in the east, the earth is saturated with the blood of women and children unmercifully butchered by the wild Russian troops, and in the west, dumdum bullets mutilate the breasts of our soldiers." Launching what would become a war of words and images across the globe, this document made clear two points that would inform German propaganda and the POW studies during the war.

First, it suggested that German social scientists as well as photographers, artists, and writers could and would use their talents for the benefit of the German nation and not knowledge or art more generally. It also implied that much of their wartime "science" would focus on demonstrating the physiological basis of the lack of civilized values among both the "wild Russian troops" and the British and French soldiers who used a weapon developed to fight in colonial wars—the dumdum bullets—on cultured and educated Europeans. In case anyone missed the subtlety of their argument, they added that "those who have allied themselves with the Russians and Servians [*sic*], and present such a shameful scene to the world as that of inciting Mongolians and Negroes against the white race, have no right whatever to call themselves upholders of civilization."[23] For this group of professors, which included some of the world's leading scientists, Germany may have inflicted some damage in Belgium and France. However, they argued, these casualties of war were necessary to save German "civilization," which had matured with the advances of German culture and science. Significantly, they linked Eastern Europeans with Asians and Africans as inferior subjects who challenged the superior German race.

While German anthropologists, ethnographers, musicologists, linguists, biologists, and social scientists struggled to persuade the German army and government that their "science" could be useful, in July 1915 the German foreign ministry openly accused France and England of violating international law by using colonial troops against Europeans on the continent.[24] Much of the document charged Africans and Indians with using horrific, primitive weapons and violent and gruesome methods of warfare unknown to "civilized" Europeans. The basic complaint rested on the fact that the Entente Powers had the audacity to use colonial soldiers in "the European theatre of war," that is, in a region that was predominantly white.[25] At the same time, Luschan, Stiehl, and the director of the Municipal Museum of Anthropology in Leipzig, Karl Weule, put together slide shows to illustrate to popular audiences what Germany faced. In Weule's words, "We are fighting the whole world since even the redskins in North America have dug up their hatchets to carry off German scalps." He was most concerned, however, that once colonial soldiers witnessed white men being beaten and mistreated like their colonial subjects, they would lose all respect for their European masters, thereby making it impossible to sustain the colonial order.[26]

As many Germans came to believe they were being encircled by racial enemies, POW photos began to appear on postcards and in the popular press. It is especially useful to explore the popular photobooks produced early in the war because they helped reinforce ideas about the racial nature of Germany's enemies before the "scientists" had an opportunity to begin their work. In 1915 German agricultural professor Alexander Backhaus published a particularly important document in multiple languages that appeared in English as *The Prisoners of War in Germany*. Backhaus worked for the War Ministry, and while he suggested throughout the book that his work was informed by the anthropological studies taking place in POW camps, he was not an anthropologist, and it is not clear who took the photographs he used.[27]

The Prisoners of War in Germany is a strange book. It opens with a full-page colorized photograph of a wooden mosque constructed in the special camp created for colonial prisoners in Wünsdorf. Except for its caption ("Mosk in Mahometan camp Wünsdorf"), there are no clues linking the mosque to POWs and no explanation why the photograph opens the book. Backhaus next explains what he believed his photographs revealed both about the "civilized" nature of Germany and the lack of "civilization" among its enemies. Most of his photographs illustrate clean prison camps with lots of open space or prisoners engaged in sports, religious services, or musical and theatrical productions. The book concludes with Backhaus's main evidence: a handful of photos illustrating the "types" of enemies Germany faced. They were posed and captioned in a way that ostensibly provided a "scientific" answer to the question: who was on the side of civilization? Like Backhaus, many individuals assumed that one could use physiognomy to come to larger conclusions about character by examining facial photos. Notwithstanding this assumption, it seems to have become apparent to those who published POW photos that interpretation of character from an individual portrait or even a posed group photo was far more problematic than anticipated. Thus, Backhaus carefully captioned his photos in five languages, using such headings as "Races Fighting with Our Adversaries" and (ironically) "Champions of Civilization from All Countries." The captions in multiple languages both suggest his international audiences and his understanding that words might be needed to shape the story he wanted to tell with his images.

Moreover, perhaps fearing that even the captions would not suffice to make his argument, Backhaus contextualized his collection of images with a brief anthropological-like narrative that emphasized the racial inferiority of Germany's enemies. Titled "Types of Nations," it explained that "the present German prisoner of war camps, truly, afford a splendid opportunity for anthropological studies and research." While he noted that he included groups in the "Entente Cordiale," mocking the Triple Alliance between France, Britain, and Russia, he acknowledged that "our photos show the great differences existing amongst them." More explicitly, he described Russian prisoners as "partly men of a physique far inferior to that of German troops, and with dull physiognomy." He concluded by pointing out that the last fourteen pages of his book show "with 'what sort of vagabonds Germany has to fight,'" adding that "it is with bitterness and rage that one considers how many a highly educated, promising German soldier and patriot lost his life by the rifle or even the knife of these hords [*sic*]."[28]

Following two hundred photographs of camp life that almost completely excluded them, photographs of these "vagabonds" finally appeared at the end of the book. Eastern European and colonial prisoners were simply absent in almost all the photographs of work, leisure, and play. They existed solely as examples of racial "types." One of the most interesting photo arrangements in *The Prisoners of War in Germany* consists of a group of headshots of French African prisoners. Sarcastically, the caption reads "Champions of Liberty and Civilization" (see figure 6.3). Unlike those in later collections, these portraits were not taken in a standardized format, and the men in them, for the most part, do not seem to have been selected to show the dangers of a specific "type." Significantly, the only feature they have in common is the color of their skin. For Annette Becker, "no additional commentary is needed, the reader is capable of inserting the photographs into his own mental universe and concluding: the barbarians are not those labelled as such." She added that the images worked because such stereotypes had been shared for generations and that identifying these prisoners as black was interpreted as a "sign of intrinsic inferiority, of moral blackness."[29] Andrew D. Evans, too, assumed that "the photographs speak for themselves," expecting that the public could see that the POW photographs provided "proof of savagery and barbarism."[30]

It is quite possible that contemporary viewers easily recognized the racial cues in these images of black men and little else. Becker is correct that images of ferocious Africans had been widely disseminated for generations, most recently during Germany's colonial wars. Even so, it seems difficult to see obvious evidence of savagery and barbarism in these portraits. In fact,

FIGURE 6.3. "Champions of Liberty and Civilization."

even skin color varies, with one man in the lower left light enough to pass as white. Many of the most familiar markings of African "inferiority" are absent. For instance, instead of showing stereotypical dark "peppercorn" hair, six of the nine subjects have covered heads. The man at the center of the page has filed teeth, while the man in the center of the bottom row was photographed to emphasize the stereotypical large lips of Africans. Neither of these characteristics, however, is evident in the other portraits. Two of the men featured are smoking; two are smiling; three of the men are posed with their hands just under their chins, creating natural lines drawing the viewers' eyes to the men's faces, a device commonly used in European portraiture to suggest thoughtfulness. Oddly the skin tones of these men's hands are significantly whiter than their faces, perhaps an effect of camera lighting, but inviting yet additional questions about what the photographer(s) hoped the impression would be. Most of the photos seem lit from the side, which creates some shadows that obscure the subjects' eyes. Taken collectively, especially with Backhaus's narrative, these images clearly suggest significant differences between Africans and Germans. Still, the men portrayed in them do not appear obviously dangerous or violent. Only the man with the pop-out eyes in the lower left (who happens to have the lightest skin) appears at all threatening. Despite its mocking and dismissive caption, the ambiguity and diversity evident in these portraits are as striking as any attempt to portray a racial "type." In short, this layout image is much more complicated than any simple racial typology.

A series of four portraits at the end of the book raises different questions about using prisoners' faces to display racial "types" (see figure 6.4). Featuring Russians and Poles, including a Polish Jewish prisoner and a Tatar, these images suggest the ways in which Eastern Europeans were also racialized in photo publications early in the war. In fact, unlike the mostly neat, well-dressed Africans, these prisoners are often unshaven and sloppily dressed. These are photos designed to show the "Mongol type" in the Russian and Polish soldiers in a pejorative way (with no effort to explain what the "Mongol type" might be).[31] The most racialized and menacing looking portrait in the entire volume is the last one, that of the Polish Jew. The image is dark and posed to suggest that the Jewish prisoner has "shifty" eyes, thick brows, and copious facial hair. This photograph stands out to suggest a potentially dangerous "other," an image that will become far more familiar in the 1930s and 1940s.

Another layout photo from a series of photo books, *Der Grosse Krieg in Bildern*, provides some additional evidence about how Germans viewed their Eastern European enemies and is worth examining in some depth. Figure 6.5 is simply titled "Disinfecting Station in Galicia Where Russian Prisoners Are Freed from Lice." There are many ways to interpret these images. With widespread disease in the German camps, which initially led to thousands of deaths, taking precautions to reduce its spread in the crowded prisons made a great deal of sense. Yet, there is no question that German officials blamed the outbreak of typhus and other serious illnesses on the influx of diseased and

FIGURE 6.4. "European Russian, Pole, Tartar [*sic*], Polish Jew."

uncivilized Russian prisoners. Thus, while the action of delousing was admirable, the way it is portrayed here emphasizes the filthy, unkempt Russians who needed to be cleaned up and "civilized" by their German captors. They look far better once they are "freed," with their crisp white shirts emphasizing their clean-shaven faces. As Oxana Nagornaja argued, late-nineteenth-century German studies had already emphasized "the natural slavishness, dirtiness, and low intellectual development of the Slavs," prejudices that led journalists, photographers, and anthropologists to view Eastern European populations through a colonialist lens. Thus, this photograph focuses on the filth and the savage look of the Russian prisoners rather than the poor, overcrowded conditions in the camps themselves.[32]

By the time anthropologists and other social scientists obtained access to the camps, then, the photographic images of POWS had already been widely disseminated. Notwithstanding the captions and narratives attached to them, the images themselves raise multiple and complex questions. Significantly, in many of these examples, Russians and Eastern European Jews are visually represented as more inferior, different, and dangerous than Africans.

"Our Enemies"

As official teams of government-sponsored social scientists began to set up their laboratories in the POW camps, the two 1916 books on "our enemies" appeared. Both presented readers with more photographs combined with

FIGURE 6.5. "Disinfecting Station in Galicia Where Russian Prisoners Are Freed from Lice."

commentary suggesting that they were serious anthropological studies. Ethnographer and adventurer Leo Frobenius had no institutional position when he visited many POW camps during the war. His book, with its provocative cover and title, described the British and French use of colonial troops as a circus. He essentially denounced many of the racialized African stereotypes found in German and French periodicals but primarily attacked England for treating colonial subjects as both zoo animals and cannon fodder.[33] Frobenius included a variety of photographs and drawings of colonial subjects in no particular order. Many did not appear to be of POWs but presented evidence of the danger that South Asian soldiers posed. For example, one of his photos featured Gurkhas in formation with their dangerous curved knives (*kukris*). No other information is given.[34]

Figure 6.6 is more ambiguous. It features a tall POW from the Sudan and reinforces the concern about the large size of African soldiers. These images are consistent with Joëlle Beurier's argument that photographs in German illustrated magazines usually treated Indians as exotic and dangerous and Africans as "exuberant and excessive." Once again, though exotic, the laughing "giant" of Wünsdorf does not appear to be overtly dangerous or threatening. Frobenius also included numerous photos of Africans with ritual facial scars. While some have interpreted such images as overtly racist representations, this ethnographer suggested that they were simply illustrative of the culture of African soldiers (see figure 6.7).[35]

FIGURE 6.6. "Giant Prisoner, a Sudanese, in the Arab Quarter."

In 1916 POW camp commander Otto Stiehl also published a collection of photographs of "types" of prisoners incarcerated in the Wünsdorf and Zossen-Weinberge camps. Though he had no anthropological training, he used an anthropological narrative to explain his images. As was true with Frobenius, Stiehl's racial biases were much more evident in his narrative than in the photographs themselves. He began with a discussion of French and English prisoners, who he believed were not so unlike Germans racially. Africans were at the bottom of his hierarchy, with Asians, Russians, and Eastern

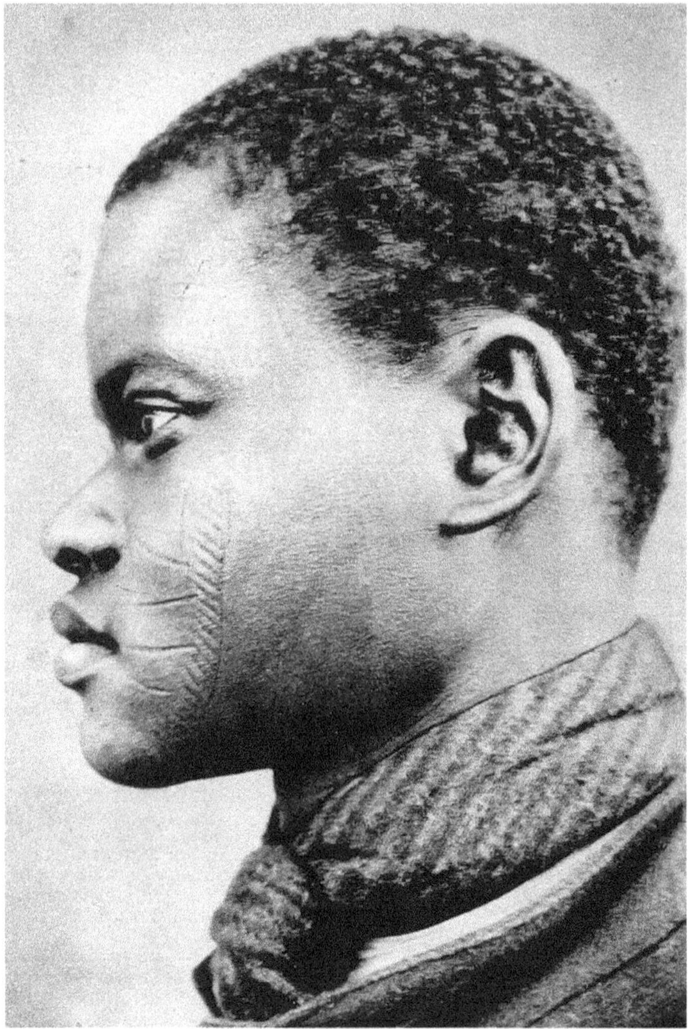

Figure 6.7. "French Marksman from the Volta Region."

Europeans somewhere in the middle.[36] Like Backhaus, Stiehl fully incorporated Germany's European enemies into his discussion of largely colonial subjects. As he wrote in his introduction, "Even if I have made an effort to also do justice to the good sides of the savages and semi-savages which the hatred of our enemies has set upon us, I must not forget to emphasize that in my impression of these exotic masses as a whole, roughness and barbarity outweigh the rest by far."[37] Stiehl described Africans as behaving like "wild animals" or as "savages," but he surprisingly seemed sympathetic to Indians and Tatars.[38]

In contrast to what he wrote, Stiehl used his camera to take mostly sympathetic photographs. He apparently walked around the camp and posed his prisoners against various natural backgrounds. Figures 6.8, 6.9, and 6.10 are examples of his portraits. He photographed both Africans and Indians against walls, probably using outside light in a way that did not cast dark shadows. He did photograph Africans with facial scars, but he also seemed to want to capture the manly quality of an ordinary Senegalese soldier like Sleman Ba (figure 6.8). Though the portrait of this Senegalese soldier was grouped with portraits of other Africans, it could also stand as a portrait of

FIGURE 6.8. "Negro, Sleman Ba, Senegal."

an interesting man. The same is true of the portrait of the Sikh, Digal Singh (figure 6.9).[39] In both photographs Stiehl used a relatively soft light to highlight facial features. Both men, though shown in a group of photographs, are introduced to the reader and viewer as named individuals. Both are photographed in uniform. In spite of what he wrote and how he arranged the photographs to show racial "types," Stiehl took portraits of men with names who only incidentally fit into his racial hierarchy.

FIGURE 6.9. "Indian, Digal Singh, Charumva (Pendschab)."

In this collection, too, the most disturbing images are of Russians and Eastern Europeans (see figure 6.10). Individuals like the Serb Radovan Paitsch are still named, but the portraits of these prisoners were taken against dark backgrounds using harsh lighting and shot from below, which makes them look menacing.[40] Stiehl also used lighting to create dark shadows around the prisoner's eyes, which looked away from the camera in a way that makes them appear "shifty."

FIGURE 6.10. "Serbian, Radovan Paitsch, Stepojevats (Belgrade)."

Ethnologist Monique Scheer sarcastically argued that for Stiehl, "life in a POW camp seemed to make a person knowledgeable about the vast variety of 'natural characters,' just as if one had taken a trip around the world."[41] Pöch, who reviewed Stiehl's book when it came out, assessed Stiehl's anthropological knowledge as limited, though he acknowledged that Stiehl had a "good eye" for choosing photographic subjects.[42] When the professionals began their research in POW camps, however, they soon confronted some of the same obstacles evident in the work of their predecessors in trying to make judgments about the race(s) of their enemies from facial photographs.

Social Science at Work: The Face and Race of the Enemy

As prisoners from all over the world poured into Germany's camps, villagers flocked to the prisons to see what the foreigners looked like. Schoolteachers brought their students to examine the internees like they might have taken them to the zoo for a field trip to watch animals, and scholars from a variety of disciplines began to recognize their good fortune at being able to study such a diverse group of human beings without having to leave Europe. As anthropologist Rudolf Pöch exclaimed, the POW camps were "a *Völkerschau* without comparison," while Luschan wrote, "I finally must concede that the hours I was allowed to spend in our prisoner of war camps were just as pleasant and instructive as any overseas travel."[43]

Receiving large sums of money from the state, the military, and the Royal Academy of Science in Vienna, Pöch's team was the best funded and most well-organized group of scholars studying POWs. His project largely focused on Russian and southeastern European prisoners. The largest German cluster of scholars came together under the direction of psychologist and musicologist Carl Stumpf and a *gymnasium* teacher interested in languages, Wilhelm Doegen. Doegen used his many political connections to garner government support for a linguistically oriented project. It soon expanded to include an anthropology division under the guidance of Luschan. At the time anthropology was a developing field with few professional positions. As historian Evans has argued, the POW studies gave many scholars the opportunity to prove the legitimacy of their field by serving the state. Luschan worked closely with Pöch, and they decided to standardize their methods, including the ways in which they would photograph POWs. Both the German and Austrian groups generally followed the procedures for physical measurements and anthropometric photography outlined in a handbook authored by Rudolf Martin, a Swiss anthropologist who held various professional positions in France, Germany, and Zürich before the war broke out.[44]

A specific form of portraiture, the "type," had become an essential part of anthropological research used to classify races from the 1860s. Martin built on these "type" portraits, but he was most interested in producing photographs that would allow for precise bodily measurements. He therefore wanted all subjects to be photographed naked, insisted that they be a certain distance from the camera, and demanded that they be shot from the front and side like the usual "type" portraits. Pöch added the one-third side photo (in which the head was turned 30 degrees from the frontal position). Pöch also made suggestions to improve the accuracy of the researchers' observations of the shapes of the eyes, nose, and lips. Yet, while the Austrians mostly followed Martin's rules, by contrast, most of the Germans ignored them by photographing men in uniform.[45]

As Evans argued, "German anthropologists involved in the POW studies saw the camera as an objective tool."[46] They believed that if cameras were used correctly according to the guidelines in Martin's manual, they could "represent reality with a great deal of accuracy." Yet, while following Martin's methods, these anthropologists habitually went beyond his idea that anthropometric photos were most useful as a source of body measurements. These scholars, like press photographers, prison guards, and amateur anthropologists, also believed that "because race was essentially a visual phenomenon, the racial 'type' photograph was crucial both to 'seeing' racial difference and to confirming the notion that racial types existed." They never seemed to doubt the verisimilitude of their images and did not seem to reflect much on the photographic elements at work in specific portraits.[47] Nonetheless, they too soon found a host of problems affecting their ability to produce objective representations of racial "types."

The problems with their approach started with the selection of subjects. This, however, was often dependent on whether they got access to particular camps. Originally, most scholars seemed interested in "exotic" prisoners, especially Africans and South Asians. Military officials, however, tended to keep the anthropologists out of the special camps, as they hoped to convince these POWs to fight against the English and the French in the Middle East and India. Eickstedt, for example, hoped to study Sikhs for his anthropology dissertation but ended up studying Russian Jewish prisoners in Gross-Breesen (Gruben) instead. In early 1916 he complained that his Jewish subjects "had little inclination for anthropology" and that they tried "to get around my nice measurements in many ways."[48] He later indicated that he wanted to study Russian nationals who were not Jewish but then changed his mind, asking for permission to investigate Moroccan, French, and English Jews once he moved to the Erfurt camp. At Ohrdurf he measured Tatars, and at

Darmstadt, Algerians and other Africans. He also tried to hone his methodological and photographic skills but constantly complained that the POWs tricked him in spite of his bribes of cigarettes. At this time he wrote that he wanted to measure "Scots, Irish, English, Ukrainians, Poles, ethnic Russians, etc." He argued that it was important to study these POWs because he saw the Entente blockade as "a boa constrictor set upon us by our enemies" and feared it would lead "to the cultural domination of East Asia."[49]

Significantly, Eickstedt was finally able to study Sikhs in late 1916 when he received permission to visit the Wünsdorf camp. Unfortunately for him, just as his research on Sikhs was getting underway, Germany determined that there would be no massive jihad or Indian independence movement. Hence, there was no longer any need for the Wünsdorf camp and its special collection of colonial prisoners. In early 1917 some were moved to labor camps in Germany and others to camps in Romania, where Eickstedt completed his research.[50] Also problematic were the choices of subjects within each camp. With tens of thousands of prisoners to choose from, by the end of 1916, Eickstedt had completed investigations of just a small portion including 743 Russian "citizens" and 353 French "citizens." Ironically, he divided his subjects into two basic categories: one including "Jews from Russia to the peoples of the Caucasus" and the other including "sub-Saharan Africans, Moroccans, Corsicans, Basques and Southern French."[51] Such broad groupings were clearly confounding from the perspective of identifying racial "types."

Eickstedt followed most of Martin's methodological recommendations quite closely, though he recognized some of the method's limitations, including the problem of reconciling visual and measured data before he had an opportunity to analyze the latter. His Austrian counterpart Pöch believed it was possible to be "scientific" in choosing subjects, but he admitted that "while the final decision on the makeup of a population group clearly belongs at the end of the studies [on the basis of careful measurements], it is advisable to begin right away with a provisional list of types, because then the main types . . . are easier for an observer to pick out."[52] Their work followed a circular logic. They intended to use photographs to confirm measurable traits but until they knew what the measurements showed, they could not choose proper photographic subjects to illustrate them.

Eickstedt experienced even more difficulties in obtaining truthful information from his Sikh subjects, who did everything they could to avoid being measured and photographed. He was lucky if the POWs told him who they were or where they were from. He also lacked the money for the materials he needed to photograph everyone he studied. Consequently, he took only a handful of photos of the many individuals he had measured. All were of subjects he believed best represented specific characteristics of a racial "type."[53]

None of his photographs, however, ultimately proved to be valuable. Still, his dissertation advisor, Luschan, used a few in the foreword for a book of the Jewish artist Hermann Struck's drawings of POWs entitled *Prisoners of War: 100 Stone Drawings by Hermann Struck*. Given the book's title, it may have surprised readers that Luschan included photographs of only three prisoners (all Algerians).[54] The example in figure 6.11 emphasizes the eyes, nose, and mouth of one prisoner, who is identified as a Kabyle, a member of a relatively light-skinned Berber ethnic group. Yet, whatever his traits, it is hard to see such an individual as a unique "type."

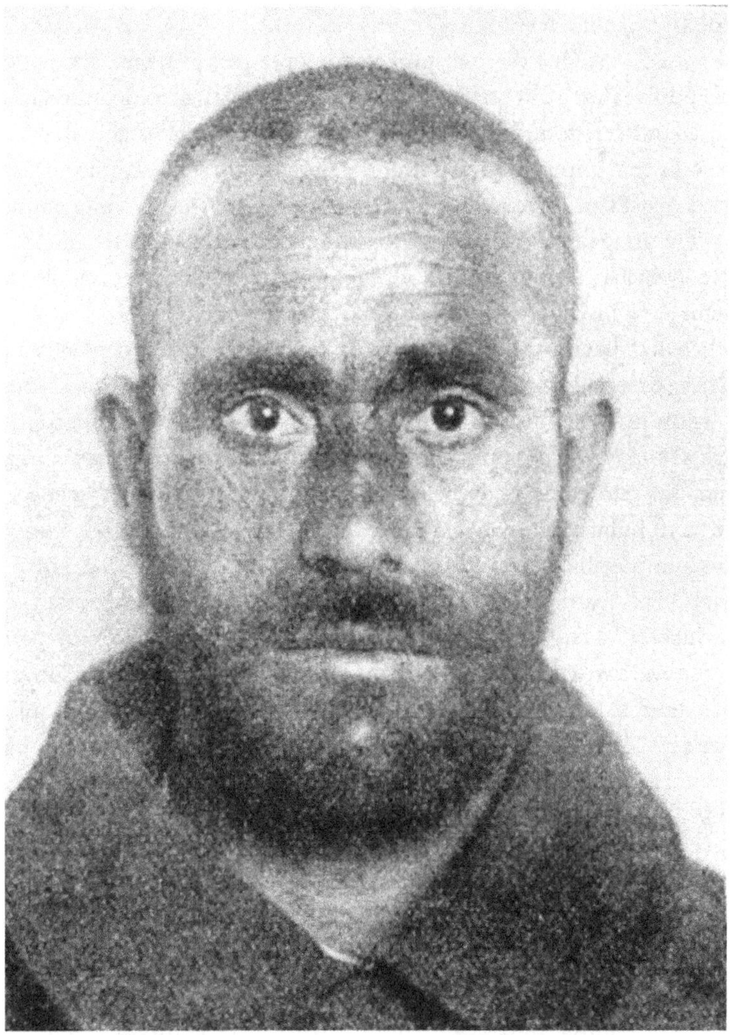

FIGURE 6.11. "Kabyle from Algeria."

To be fair, Luschan wrote nothing more than a foreword to Struck's collection of drawings, though at 117 pages it was a substantial piece. He entitled it "A Contribution of Ethnography/Ethnology during the War," and hoped it could create a more "objective" interpretation of the "anthropology of race." The titles of both the book and the foreword suggest that he would be writing about POWs, but the first photos the reader confronts are of aborigines, one with a bone in his nose. Since the Australians rarely, if ever, recruited aborigines, the photos are quite jarring. In fact, most of them came from Luschan's prewar overseas trips and were used to support his argument that racial differences stemmed largely from geography and climate.[55] Neither the photographs nor the text offer much about the contribution of ethnography to the war effort.

Besides Eickstedt's three examples, the only real evidence about POWs in this book came from Struck's drawings. Once Struck joined the German army, the officers found him useful as a Yiddish interpreter and as an artist, both skills that anthropologists found helpful in the POW camps. Luschan insisted that Struck's drawings had "scientific value" even while admitting they were art. However, in order to strengthen his case, Luschan carefully selected which drawings to use and apparently asked Struck to modify some of them to fit his ideas of racial "types."[56]

Much has been said about the sensitivity that Struck deployed in his sketches, especially those of Jewish prisoners. One can see an emotional expression in these faces that is absent in Eickstedt's "type" photographs. Struck also named these prisoners and located them in their social milieu. Chajim Krasikow, for example, is identified as a Jewish bookkeeper who came from Lubin (figure 6.12). More significantly, he is drawn in a way that makes it impossible to avoid his gaze. One must deal with him as a man, not a "type." This feature is evident in all of Struck's drawings of Jewish prisoners, which led Margaret Olin to argue that this Jewish artist was perhaps being subversive with his lithographs. What seems much less subversive is that the artist drew almost all the POWs like Krasikow in their military uniforms.[57] The uniforms appear to be needed to link these individuals—identified as part of specific "racial" groups—to "national" enemies lined up against Germany.[58]

In this book, taken collectively, both Eickstedt's few wartime photos and Struck's lithographs demonstrate the difficulty of clearly identifying racial "types" based on facial portraits, especially when they are decontextualized from their geographical and cultural settings. The lack of significant cultural grounding within which to place the POW subjects in the camps is what allowed press photographers, agricultural experts, adventurers, camp guards, and artists to produce portraits largely performing the same cultural work.

FIGURE 6.12. "Chajim Krasikov, a Jew from Lubin."

It is, then, probably no accident that when Eickstedt finally published his dissertation in 1920, he used barely any of his own photographs and instead featured on his cover Stiehl's portrait of Digal Singh. To demonstrate the veracity of his measurements, he used some of Struck's drawings. He did include six of the fifteen Sikh photos he took, all shot before he had analyzed his data, when he believed Sikhs constituted a single racial "type." However, he ultimately concluded from his data that there were several racial elements and three racial "types" among the seventy-six Sikhs he measured.[59] Thus, only three of his photos could be used to illustrate specific

Fig. 14.
Sikh Nr. 49: Rassenelement III.

Fig. 15.
Rassenelement II.

Fig. 16.
Sikh Nr. 71: Element IV.

Fig. 17.
Sikh Nr. 34: Untypisch.

Fig. 18.

Fig. 19.

Fig. 18 u. 19. Sikh Nr. 21 und 32: untypische Individuen.

FIGURE 6.13. "Six Sikh Photographs."

racial characteristics, while the other three, which failed to confirm any of his "types," were simply labelled "atypical" (see figure 6.13).

A Visual Time Capsule with Future Messages

Contemporary scholarship, and especially the impressive work of Britta Lange, has uniformly criticized almost all of the racial "science" produced from the POW studies while recognizing that such racialized research helped solidify the careers of some anthropologists like Egon von Eickstedt. Interestingly, others have used the recordings made in the camps to recover "lost" voices, particularly of ordinary South Asians who fought for England. Few, however, have found much value in the photographs taken as part of the German POW research.[60] The largest collection of these photographs appeared in Wilhelm Doegen's 1925 edited book, *Unter fremden Völkern*. Both this volume and a second one published in 1941, *Unsere Gegner damals und heute*, demonstrate the subsequent uses of World War I POW research in promoting German scientific racism during the Nazi era.[61]

Given the difficulties of reconciling anthropometric-portrait photographs either with the preconceived notions of racial "types" or with the results of their analyses of POW data, it would be easy to underestimate the significance of this wartime research. One could also dismiss the collections of POW photographs and drawings published by interested amateurs like Backhaus, Frobenius, Stiehl, and Struck as lacking academic rigor. Taken collectively, however, both the scholarly and popular studies produced a powerful discourse that racialized Germany's enemies and helped shaped Germany's own racial identity and sense of superiority during the war. The widespread proliferation of POW photographs should also be recognized as introducing a new kind of visual wartime weaponry. To be sure, these visual forms still depended upon anthropological narratives to explain their racial and cultural significance. Uniforms and even picture captions rarely sufficed to connect specific racial "types" and their cultural deficiencies with concrete nations identified as enemies.

The narratives profoundly shaped what the authors wanted viewers to see in their portraits; at the same time, the often sympathetic photographs themselves frequently offered critiques of the anthropological narratives and on several occasions may have undermined them. It is also noteworthy that the collections of POW photos emphasized the importance of Germany's struggle in fighting against a world filled with inferior races. The authors of these studies were not necessarily critiquing colonialism, but they deeply resented the fact that France and England had brought over a million men from the rest of the world to Europe. From the start of the war, they also used POW photographs to suggest that the far greater threat might be coming from different "races" of Eastern Europe.

Finally, the use of anthropological narratives to explain the photographs induced viewers to think of the racial inferiority of Germany's enemies from both a visual and a scientific perspective. Much like the *Völkerschauen* that preceded them, POW photographs also emphasized the novelty, diversity, and exoticism evident in the faces of these prisoners. There is little question that those who published these photos were deeply shaped by the racial ideas prevalent at the time, while their work would also help inform new ideas about racial differences in the decades to come. Regardless of their purposes, however, the portrait photographs produced of POWs from around the globe constitute some of the most compelling evidence of the extent to which the "Great War" was truly a world war.

Notes

1. Hoffman 1920, 13.
2. Frobenius 1916; Stiehl 1916.
3. Koller 2008.
4. Kahleyss 2000.
5. Jones, H. 2014, 268–70; Davis, G. 1977, 626–30.
6. Jones, H. 2014, 268–70; Becker, A. 2014b, 16.
7. Grady 2017, 131.
8. Audoin-Rouzeau and Becker 2002, Becker, A. 1998.
9. Jones, H. 2011a, 119.
10. Audoin-Rouzeau and Becker 2002, 70–90, 148–58; Becker, A. 1998, 89–145, 179–336.
11. Evans, A. 2010; Lange 2008a; Lange 2008b; Lange 2010; Lange 2011; Lange 2013; Lange and Gingrich 2014, 599–612.
12. Roy, Liebau, and Ahuja 2011.
13. Evans, A. 2010, 42–55; Berner 2007, 41; Bruckner 1999; Short 2012; Zimmerman 2001, 15–37.
14. Olusoga and Erichsen 2010, unnumbered picture inserts; Górny 2019, 166.
15. Becker, A. 1998, 317–36; Jones, H. 2011a, 362; Avenarius 1916; Jeismann 1997, 261–319; Kuklick 2010, 35–37; Gingrich 2010.
16. Górny 2019, 166–72.
17. Backhaus 1915; *Der Grosse Krieg in Bildern* 1915–1918.
18. Röper 1920; Evans, A. 2010, 189–221; Doegen 1919; Doegen 1925.
19. Lange 2010, 312–15; Evans, A. 2010, 131–38.
20. Evans, A. 2010, 131–38.
21. Becker, A. 1998; Ansky 2004; Reed 1917; Rachamimov 2002.
22. Audoin-Rouzeau and Becker 2002, 142–58; Grady 2017, 132.
23. Audoin-Rouzeau and Becker 2002, 148–49; Church 1915, 27; Le Naour 2003, 7–36.

24. Cf. Jones, H. 2011b.
25. Germany, Foreign Office 1915.
26. Evans, A. 2010, 112–13, 121; Kahleyss 2011; Lange 2011, 172.
27. Backhaus 1915.
28. Backhaus 1915, 21.
29. Backhaus 1915, 111; Becker, A. 1998, 317–33.
30. Evans, A. 2010, 174–75.
31. Backhaus 1915, 21, 112.
32. *Der Grosse Krieg in Bildern* 1915, no. 6, 32; Nagornaja 2009, 477.
33. Frobenius 1916, 3–14.
34. Frobenius 1916.
35. Frobenius 1916; Beurier 2016, 43.
36. Stiehl 1916, 5–32; Kahleyss 2011.
37. Stiehl 1916, 5–32; Scheer 2010, 290.
38. Stiehl 1916, 5–32.
39. Stiehl 1916, 24, 50.
40. Stiehl 1916, 64.
41. Scheer 2010, 290.
42. Lange 2010, 333, 333n.
43. Evans, A. 2010, 131; Struck 1917, 3; Górny 2019, 171.
44. Evans, A. 2010, 131–45; Lange 2011; Martin 1914; Olusoga 2014, 258–68.
45. Martin 1914; Evans, A. 2010, 157–61; Lange 2010, 320–23; Lange 2011, 162–64; Edwards 1990.
46. Evans, A. 2004, 228.
47. Lange 2010; Evans, A. 2004, 228–29.
48. Evans, A. 2010, 144–47; Lange 2010, 319–21.
49. Evans, A. 2010, 145–47; Lange 2010.
50. Lange 2011, 168–69.
51. Evans, A. 2010, 147.
52. Evans, A. 2010, 160; Berner 2010, 248–51; Lange 2010, 323.
53. Evans, A. 2010, 162–64.
54. Struck 1917, 102–11.
55. Struck 1917, 1–117.
56. Struck 1917, drawing 33; Olin 2010, 261; Edelmann-Ohler 2016; Evans, A. 2010, 164–65.
57. Struck 1917, 1–117; Evans, A. 2010, 164–65; Olin 2010, 261–63, 274–77.
58. Olin 2010, 261–63, 274–77; Edelmann-Ohler 2016, 204–5.
59. Lange 2010, 326–33; Eickstedt 1920/1921; Lange 2008b.
60. Evans, A. 2010, 189–221; Lange 2010, 326–33; Lange 2011, 163–66.
61. Doegen 1925; Doegen 1941.

Part II

Internments beyond Europe

Chapter 7

"Enemies of Our Country"

Internment in Canada's Rocky Mountains National Park, 1915–1917

Bohdan S. Kordan

On February 15, 1916, W. J. Roche, Canada's minister of the interior, rose in Parliament to address a question posed by opposition member Frank Oliver as to whether it was the intention of the government to use the labor of prisoners from one of the internment camps recently established in Canada's mountain parks. The minister replied that they would in fact work in accordance with a military schedule and be paid twenty-five cents per day—the wage allotted to prisoners of war. Having them sit idle—"eating their heads off"—would not be countenanced, he said.[1] When pressed about work conditions and to what end, Roche stated the prisoners would build roads, clear brush, and generally clean up the park under military guard to ensure it was properly carried out. He further added that their labor would not be voluntary because only in this way could a lot of work get done.

Oliver reproached the minister, arguing that the compulsory use of internee labor was "a very serious problem." As recent immigrants without jobs, it was inconceivable that they would be treated this way. "These people," Oliver claimed, "have not committed any crime against the laws of the country, and, while I can appreciate the desirability of interning them and offering them the opportunity of employment, when it comes down to compulsory employment at twenty-five cents a day I am afraid that this involves principles which we cannot all subscribe to."[2] For Oliver, these were civilians who happened to be interned. The forcible use of internment labor, he insisted, was unprincipled. Roche, however, was unmoved. Believing that Germany's dreadful treatment of British POWs would offset any criticism, he, for one, did not expect international repercussions. More to the point, by equating their situation to that faced by captured British soldiers and paying them a prisoner wage, Roche made clear that those behind Canadian barbed wire were POWs in every sense of the term. They would work.

The disagreement between Roche and Oliver underscored the difficult position of immigrants from enemy lands.[3] Although civilians and not directly involved in the conflict, they were considered a risk and a liability in war. Yet, they were also jobless and destitute through no fault of their own. How, then, was the government to alleviate the strain of their unemployment and poverty without giving the impression of being unduly charitable and even lenient in its approach? Internment presented a solution: under international agreement, POWs could work for their own health and well-being. But this, too, presented a dilemma. Could noncombatant civilians be considered POWs? An answer to this conundrum was to be found in the notion of "enemy alien."

In the charged atmosphere of war, pervaded by fear and distrust, the term "enemy alien" made foes of all those whose allegiances were presumed to lie elsewhere because of their birthplace.[4] Designated a risk under wartime emergency legislation because of their status as aliens of enemy origin, the contradiction of being both a civilian and a POW was thus squared. But what did an interned enemy alien mean in practice? To the degree that international law was largely silent on the rights of civilian POWs, there was no clear direction.[5] Presented with such an opening, the government would avail itself of the possibilities that followed from the uncertainty. Yet, what did this entail and how was the treatment of interned enemy aliens rationalized? Further, how did their ambiguous status as civilian war prisoners shape the experience of internment, and what effect did this have on the attitudes and actions of those tasked with overseeing them? Moreover, what of public opinion? How did the public come to regard those behind barbed wire and the circumstances of their imprisonment?

In the Rocky Mountains National Park from 1915 to 1917, an internment camp for enemy aliens was established alternating, summer and winter, between Castle Mountain and the town of Banff.[6] The internees' experience there would be defined by the ambiguity in their status as both POWs and civilians. However, being interned as enemy aliens—individuals largely without recognized rights—would have enormous implications for their treatment. The hard labor that occurred at the Castle/Banff camp was typical of the internment experience throughout Canada's frontier regions, where many of the country's twenty-four camps, and the 8,579 individuals interned, mostly civilians, were located.[7] But the experience of internment encompassed more than the labor coerced. As the experience at the camp would show, this was a story of disbelief, betrayal, and loss set against a backdrop of ambition and indifference, brutality and humiliation. It was also, however, a tale of survival and perseverance amid the Rocky Mountain wilderness.

Internment in the Canadian Rockies: "Employed in Remote Regions of the Park"

With the advent of the First World War, immigrants from lands at war with the British empire—aliens of enemy origin—became targets of nativist hostility in Canada, a problem exacerbated by their poor fit within an ailing economy shifting rapidly toward war. Dismissed from places of work, unemployment soared among this cohort, and public attention was drawn to the utility of employing emergency powers under the War Measures Act (WMA). Such powers included expanding the practice of internment, introduced for security reasons during the conflict's opening stages but which heretofore had limited use.[8] Order-in-Council PC 2721, issued October 28, 1914, under the WMA, stated unequivocally that aliens of enemy birth who were without employment or means would be interned and put to work as POWs.

In the months to follow, rising joblessness and privation among enemy aliens led to the internment of hundreds in military prisons and, as the numbers grew, in hastily organized holding facilities. Under pressure, the newly created Directorate of Internment Operations scrambled to secure more permanent spaces. In eastern Canada negotiations with the military as well as the provincial governments of Ontario and Quebec led to the creation of internment camps at Petawawa and Valcartier, and then at Kapuskasing and Spirit Lake. The large number of enemy aliens detained in improvised holding stations at Winnipeg, Brandon, Lethbridge, and Nanaimo spurred a search for partners in Canada's west.

Early on, the idea of using POWs to develop Canada's national parks had been bandied about. When the use of internment labor was authorized under the October 28, 1914, order-in-council, F. H. Williamson, the deputy commissioner of the Parks Branch, sensing an opportunity, quickly wrote a memo touting the benefits that would accrue from the use of prisoners for parks development.[9] Williamson argued that locating internment camps in national parks might address the problem of how to hold POWs securely.

FIGURE 7.1. "New Arrivals," Castle Mountain Internment Camp. Courtesy of the Whyte Museum of the Canadian Rockies, Banff, Alberta, Canada.

In the wilderness, he insisted, escape was impossible. While banishing notions that the initiative could be anything other than a legitimate security concern, the appeal to the priorities of those overseeing internment as a security operation was strategic on Williamson's part. So, too, was the argument that the work would provide employment relief for the many jobless enemy aliens.[10] However, what mattered most for Parks Branch officials was the development of the parks, an enterprise in which internment labor could play a pivotal role. In the context of austerity budgets—the Rocky Mountains National Park faced a two-thirds budget reduction and the national parks system a 50 percent financial cut—internment presented an opportunity.[11] In the process of satisfying multiple constituencies, the goals and rationale for internment in Canada's national parks were laid out. Some aspects of the plan were complementary, while others clashed; all of it, however, was uncharted territory.

Williamson's memo was initially sent to the Department of Justice, under whose authority the newly organized internment directorate fell, and then on to the Department of Militia and Defence, tasked with overseeing the operations. The director of internment, Brigadier-General (later Major-General) William Otter, received the proposal favorably, encouraged by its focus on security and the opportunity to work with partners given the fiscal limitations under which the military operation was placed. On a fact-finding mission to western Canada, Otter arranged to meet with the parks commissioner, J. B. Harkin, at the Banff railway depot on March 12, 1915. Given their mutual interests and the advantages that could be obtained through cooperation, an agreement in principle was struck.

Still, the proposal had to be approved at the ministerial level. Hoping for back channel support, Harkin met with ranking political figures from the province of Alberta, Senator James Lougheed and R. B. Bennett, member of Parliament for Calgary, and impressed upon them the value of the plan. Lougheed was sympathetic to the proposal. So, too, was Bennett, whose federal riding included the Rocky Mountains National Park. Bennett, however, would lend his support only if there were assurances that the prisoners would be "employed in remote regions of the park where they will not come into contact with the population of this province." He further insisted they were not to be coddled. It would have been "monstrous," Bennett tendered, if enemy aliens were better treated than "our own people."[12] That the proposal had civilians deployed as POWs did not warrant comment, underscoring the priority assigned to getting the enemy alien poor off the streets and out of view. With the necessary political support in hand, Harkin persuaded the interior minister of the plan's feasibility and benefits. In early June 1915, it was announced that enemy alien internees would be sent to the parks to work as POWs.

"Work Good and Hard": Internment at Castle Mountain

Some three miles west of Castle, Alberta, a junction on the Canadian Pacific Railway (CPR) line, lay the terminal point of the still-unfinished Banff–Lake Louise motorway. Part of a long-term strategy to increase tourism to the area, the idea was to extend the road from Castle Mountain to Lake Louise, and then on to Field, British Columbia. After some initial difficulties, a site was selected and prepared in the early days of July. An enclosure—120 by 240 feet—was erected, consisting of ten-foot posts supporting twenty horizontal strands of barbed wire spaced six inches apart. Canvas tents for the troops and enemy alien internees were also set up. Scheduled to hold two hundred prisoners, the encampment could accommodate four hundred—the total expected given the anticipated arrest of large numbers of enemy aliens in nearby Calgary. Meanwhile, the provisioning of the camp was contracted out to local Banff businesses, which were "expected to benefit very much, financially, by the arrangement."[13]

With these preliminaries attended to, the first contingent of sixty prisoners arrived from the internment facility at Lethbridge on July 14. More followed within days, for a total of 191. All were of Austro-Hungarian origin, primarily Ukrainians, Poles, Croats, and others from the multinational empire—mostly laborers. Prisoners of German nationality remained at Lethbridge, which was set aside for so-called "first-class" POWs, effectively distinguishing the internment camps, at least initially, on the basis of class and ethnicity. Those newly arrived were put to work immediately, clearing trees and removing dead and fallen timber, not only from the route of the road but also within a hundred feet to either side of the proposed throughway. The remainder were assigned to cut trees within three to four hundred feet of the nearby railway line "to give the valley an open, park like appearance," thus providing train passengers with unobstructed sightlines.[14] Harvested timber was to be set aside for government use on a variety of public projects.[15]

Except for Sundays, the prisoners followed a routine of intense physical labor. Deemed "second-class" POWs (as opposed to an "officer class"), they were expected to work steadily.[16] Save for a thirty-minute repast, the prisoners labored ten hours a day without rest, not including the time spent walking to and from the work site. Declaring the internees "enemies of our country," the local Banff newspaper, the *Crag and Canyon*, insisted that those guarding the prisoners needed to be mindful of this fact and ensure that the prisoners "work good and hard, with long hours."[17] According to the *Crag* editors, the prisoners would come to know their place in the war, having been made to feel the bitter sting of labor.

The regular and constant arrival of arrested enemy aliens placed logistical pressure on the camp's operations. Nonetheless, those immediately responsible expressed satisfaction and welcomed even more prisoners, "feeling that we are doing something the more worthwhile"—a point of view that resonated with a public that saw internment labor as "good business for the Government."[18] Yet, the work was of benefit only if costs were kept to a minimum. Agreeing to cover the allowance for POW labor, the Parks Branch demanded value for money. Schedules and quotas, therefore, had to be closely monitored. But the internment directorate also shared in the costs and it, too, looked to keep expenditures to a minimum. This demanded scrupulous oversight in provisioning the camp. The consequences of the twin imperatives of efficiency and austerity soon became apparent.

With conditions unremitting, escapes soon became commonplace. When several prisoners were caught with wire cutters and hammers in their possession in preparation for their getaway, the *Crag and Canyon* commented: "There must be a screw loose somewhere in the present system of the camp."[19] When eight managed to flee in the days to follow, the paper repeated its assertion that "not all was right." The escape of the odd individual was not the problem, the editors argued; the alarming prospect of four or five hundred "desperate men" marauding about the country, on the other hand, was. There was ample reason for the unacceptable state of affairs. To carry out basic duties, a camp of four hundred prisoners required an estimated 140 soldiers; the existing complement of 113 (NCOs and enlisted men) was insufficient. Twelve-hour shifts of continuous sentry duty combined with other duties were the norm. With little respite from the demanding routine, fatigue and inattentiveness frequently set in, fostering prisoner daring.

Several escapes occurred during August and September, raising doubts about the camp's administration. When five internees fled all at once on October 18, the commandant, Major Duncan Stuart, was forced to explain. The sentries, he claimed, were overworked, while the cutback in rations—following instructions from the internment directorate to reduce costs—resulted in fatigue among the troops. Nonetheless, the commandant assured headquarters that adjustments would be made to prevent further escapes—which by this time numbered twenty-eight. When another five inmates fled three weeks later, the commanding officer admitted that the problem was more deep-seated. The prisoners risked escape, Stuart argued, because of the inclement mountain weather and lack of adequate attire. He had appealed to headquarters for suitable clothing on ten different occasions but was ignored. In the meantime, the situation had become untenable. "During October," Stuart wrote, "the prisoners complained bitterly of want of boots and overalls and having to sleep without fires; one prisoner who escaped left a letter to a friend saying he preferred to take the chance of being shot escaping rather than live under the conditions."[20]

The internees' letters confirmed that the situation at Castle was dreadful—and worsening. Dmytro Tkachyk wrote that to compel them to work, ailing prisoners were shackled and placed in a dark cell on a punishment diet of bread and water for long stretches of time.[21] Nick Olinyk spoke of his ordeal in a censored letter to his wife: "As you know there are men running away from here every day because the conditions here are very poor, so that we cannot go on much longer. We are not getting enough to eat. We are hungry as dogs. They are sending us to work, as they don't believe us, and we are very weak."[22] That Olinyk and others were faint from hunger was unsurprising; the number of calories in a standard internment ration was 2,596 while the estimated energy required for a man at work was 2,903. This shortfall was the consequence of a cut in expenses and the introduction of food substitutes. The cost per meal had decreased from an initial twelve and a half cents to five and one-fifth cents, while meat was replaced with rice or rolled oats, fermented cabbage substituted for vegetables, and unleavened flour or pancake for bread.[23]

The number of escapes at Castle Mountain concerned General Otter, but he believed a change in venue would improve the situation. The approach of winter in the mountains made relocation necessary, and the mineral hot springs at the Cave and Basin, with its bathing pavilion and bunkhouses, was ideal. Major Stuart concurred with the decision, believing that "when we are at Banff, we will be in better circumstances." Following preparations for closing the Castle camp, the inmates were marched the thirty-five kilometers down the road to Banff on November 9. It was reported that while in Banff the prisoners would to be put to work on several municipal and federal park improvement projects.

The Trials of Banff: "Inhumanity Must Not Be Exercised"

Despite the move to Banff and the new quarters, the difficulties did not abate. The American consular representative in Calgary, Samuel Reat—a neutral diplomatic observer—received a smuggled letter from the camp in which internees complained both about their treatment and the camp's conditions, pleading for him to investigate. The consul arrived at the camp and, during inspection, took note of a range of shortcomings: overcrowding, dimly lit quarters, deficient mattresses (the paillasses, normally packed with straw, were left empty), worn footwear, and a lack of gloves, socks, and underwear. Additionally, he chronicled abuses and intimidation at the camp. Sergeant Little freely admitted to firing his rifle at J. Hawrysynyzn but stated that his intention was only to "frighten" the prisoner, not shoot him. Prisoner C. Bota reported sick at the infirmary, but instead of being examined, the medical sergeant, pointing a revolver, instructed him to get back to work. Similarly, prisoner A. Chiskolok, claiming illness, was forced back to work after "the guard struck him with a rifle butt and called him a son-of-a-bitch."[24]

Presented with Reat's report, Otter commented that although the behavior was unfortunate, it was not uncommon. Similar incidents, he explained, took place at other camps. However, the officer commanding Military District No. 13 (Alberta), Brigadier-General E. Cruickshank, was less philosophical, as the issue of excessive force had previously been taken up with the camp's commandant. In a memo to Major Stuart, Cruickshank instructed that the prisoners had to be treated with greater care: "In this connection [I] invite your attention to Chapter 14 of the Army Act as laid down in the Manual of Military Law, 1914, in which the laws and customs for the treatment of Prisoners of War & c. are laid down." The district commander noted that "inhumanity must not be exercised by guards over Prisoners of War."[25] Cruickshank considered the internees war prisoners and entitled to fair treatment. For those overseeing the work of the prisoners, however, this was problematic: without force and intimidation, how would the work get done?

The reports of abuses were disquieting, but it was the growing number of other problems at the camp that convinced Major-General Otter that steps needed to be taken. Inebriated guards had discharged their rifles on the streets of Banff; two soldiers were discovered intoxicated while on duty; and another purportedly gave alcohol to a prisoner work gang. All were found guilty and disciplined. These measures, however, did not appear to register with the detachment; not long thereafter, in a drunken state, two senior noncommissioned officers demolished the camp orderly room and blamed the damage on a fictitious intruder of Chinese origin. An inquiry was also conducted regarding a private who purportedly gave a prisoner money in exchange for favors. This was all too much for the internment director. Feeling compelled to visit the Banff camp in late November, Otter, after an inspection, asked for Major Stuart's resignation.

By Otter's estimation, the situation at the camp was "out of hand"—but the turmoil was not difficult to understand. The fiery destruction of the parliament buildings in Ottawa fed rumors of sabotage, and over two days in early February 1916, soldiers of the Canadian Expeditionary Force (CEF) recruitment battalions in nearby Calgary rioted, destroying establishments identified as "German-owned."[26] Isolated and powerless, the Banff detachment's unhappy fate was to watch over enemy aliens deemed no less suspect and treacherous. Such responsibilities had been neither imagined nor desired by the detachment personnel; many, in fact, were bitter at having been unable to get overseas where the real fight was taking place. Indeed, when a recruiting officer came calling, a full quarter of the men eagerly sought transfers. Such an exodus, however, would have undermined the security of the camp, and the guards, denied and resentful, directed their frustrations at the prisoners. Still, this did not prevent Private George Lomax, whose application had been declined, from boldly and directly making plain his wish in a letter to the military district commander that he be "liberated from this place."[27]

Although every precaution was taken, the internees kept fleeing in large numbers. After escapes took place in January and February, a proposal was made to reduce the ratio of prisoners to guards. But this meant fewer prisoners at work, and from the perspective of the parks officials, their labor was much too valuable. The idea, consequently, was rejected in favor of increasing the number of troops. The addition of ten extra men, however, made no difference; several weeks later, three prisoners escaped, followed by another, and then two more who fled under a withering volley of gunfire. The risk of being shot failed to serve as a deterrent. Indeed, just a few weeks later, seven more prisoners broke free from two separate work gangs on the road project along the Spray River, again under gunfire. The guards' poor marksmanship convinced the new commandant, Major Peter Spence, that the detachment required further training. From that point on, a routine of "shooting competitions" was introduced to help improve the troopers' aim.

Of the fugitives from the Spray River road project, several were recaptured despite assistance from colliers working at the nearby coal mine, who, being ethnic kindred, gave them provisions and directions. Found out, the *Crag and Canyon* reported that these "good Samaritans" were arrested and sent to the Banff camp to supplement the "menagerie" there.[28] Aiding and abetting the enemy was not without risk, and the consequences were well known. Yet, for the colliers—who themselves were confronted daily with the prospect of arrest and internment—the fugitives' predicament resonated and there could be no turning away. Indeed, they understood well the arbitrariness of state-sanctioned measures as these applied to enemy aliens—a point made abundantly clear in the case of John Kondro who was arrested and interned. Being underage at the time his father was naturalized, he claimed that he too had become a citizen and was therefore unjustly imprisoned. Suspicion and disdain, however, meant that his pleas for release as a citizen could be ignored. An enemy he would remain.[29]

The purpose of internment was to have the prisoners work, and work they did on a variety of projects. A large contingent was assigned to a rock

FIGURE 7.2. "To Work," Banff Internment Camp. Courtesy of the Whyte Museum of the Canadian Rockies, Banff, Alberta, Canada.

crusher at the foot of the western face of Mount Rundle, preparing gravel for road construction. Others cut trees and cleared bush for the new St. Julian housing subdivision in Banff. Several gangs labored on constructing a carriage road, pushing it steeply upward through the Sundance Canyon to the Upper Hot Springs, and building a bridge on the Spray River. The fencing of the buffalo paddock near the Cascade River east of Banff and clearing it for pasture was also authorized work, as was filling in a depression, prone to flooding, around the grand Frank Lloyd Wright pavilion at the center of the town's Recreation Park. Near the pavilion, prisoners constructed three "first-class" tennis courts while another group was assigned to repair pavement on Banff's main street.[30]

The impressive number of projects was cited in diplomatic correspondence; but so, too, was the manner in which they were completed, and this elicited criticism and protest. Receiving information that German civilians were now among the internees being forced to work, Berlin determined that the situation at Banff—"a civilian camp"—was unacceptable. The use of compulsory labor negated the assurances previously received from the British government that international provisions were being adhered to and no such thing was taking place in Canada. Unless measures were implemented to address this failing, Germany conveyed, it would be forced to adopt retaliatory measures.[31] Given the gravity of the matter, Berlin also requested that the new US consul in Calgary, Harold Clum, conduct a visit to Banff in May 1916 and provide a detailed report on conditions there. Clum, revealing his prejudices, relayed that there had been nothing remiss in their treatment. This was their lot in life—not only as common laborers, but enemies as well.[32]

If evidence of wrongdoing was ignored and hidden, the sheer number of escapes made plain the distressing reality of the camp. Totaling sixty-one by June 1916, the figure highlighted the extent to which internees were willing to take risks. Deeply worried, Major-General Otter wrote the Banff commander, Major Spence, that stronger measures needed to be introduced to staunch the exodus of prisoners.[33] Otter, however, was acutely aware of the constraints under which the operation was conducted, making robust adjustments unlikely. His plan, for example, to divide the Banff camp into two smaller stations—with the aim of making each more manageable—was opposed by the parks commissioner, J. B. Harkin.[34] Dividing the camp would have unnecessarily complicated and even jeopardized construction of the road to Lake Louise, a scheme that depended on the return of all the prisoners to the Castle Mountain site. The entire group, Harkin insisted, had to remain intact to ensure that as much work as possible could get done during the coming season. Since the Parks Branch paid the POW allowance, its wishes could not be ignored.

Although disappointed, the internment director was not entirely opposed to bringing the prisoners back to the Castle site. The change of venue, Otter felt, might lighten the mood at the camp. He was also persuaded that by concentrating the prisoners on the one job, they at least might be more easily handled. Before this could take place, however, the internees, still in Banff, were put to work on finishing, as much as possible, the road to the Upper Hot Springs and building an access route to the Banff Springs Hotel golf course. A satellite crew was also sent to repair the wharf at nearby Lake Minnewanka, a tourist attraction, and to renew the grounds around the hamlet there. By June's end, the internees, 312 in total, were gathered up and returned to Castle Mountain.

"A Mighty Pleasant Place": Castle Mountain Once More

Upon arrival, the men picked up where they had left off the season before. Road construction had yielded substantial results: 12.8 acres were cleared, 14.7 acres grubbed of tree roots, 11,243 cubic feet of earth excavated, 380 cubic feet of loose and solid rock removed, and 10,600 linear feet of logs prepared—all by hand.[35] Progress for the next four months would be no less appreciable.[36] Out of the thick mountain forest the prisoners carved four miles of road, with 15,700 cubic feet of earth removed. A major permanent bridge consisting of iron beams and concrete abutments was also constructed over Baker Creek. Work on the project was facilitated by the addition of a steam shovel, which proved enormously useful since 136 internees had been released to industry at the end of July, replacing native-born workers who enlisted to join the fight in Europe.

The reduction in the number of enemy aliens held at internment camps across the country led to the closure of several stations, including Brandon on July 30, 1916, from which a final 103 prisoners were transferred to Castle, bringing its total back up to 279. The closure of certain camps and the consolidation of the rest signaled the beginning of a shift in internment policy. In helping to rid municipalities of impoverished, jobless enemy aliens, the policy of internment had delivered. However, now that the economy was improved and the demand for labor high, internment, as it was being conducted, became increasingly knotty. Nevertheless, the initial idea that it was a security measure still held insofar as some of the prisoners demonstrated resistance to their incarceration and were therefore considered "dangerous." Thus, despite the arrival at the camp of company representatives hoping to procure labor (the Canadian Pacific Railway, the Canada Cement Company, and local coal mines), the business of keeping watch remained; so, too, was the business of developing parks infrastructure.

The misery that accompanied internment was especially unsettling in the context of the scheme to use civilian POW labor to develop Canada's parks. Harkin, the parks commissioner, a long-time proponent of the healing power of nature, wrote that during the turmoil of war, Canada's national parks could serve as a balm to help salve the nation's wounds. Places of rest, contemplation, and recreation, the parks had the potential to still angry hearts and broken spirits. Since caring for the country's citizens was as important as defeating the enemy, support for the development of the parks, in his view, was an expression of patriotic duty. Harkin admitted, however, without a jot of irony, that this goal was being achieved, in part, through compulsory labor.[37] The contradiction between the redemptive power of the parks and the perfunctory assignment of civilians as serviceable labor was striking and could only be resolved if such individuals were viewed as existing outside the community and, from a utilitarian perspective, expendable. In the context of war, the meaning of this was explicit, especially where other priorities, such as park development, arose: interned enemy aliens were to be put to work—and by force if necessary. Their dire situation could also as a result be overlooked and even ignored.

Nowhere was this more apparent than in the silence of the visitors who called at the camp. Newspaper reporters, day trekkers, even the governor general and his wife—the Duke and Duchess of Connaught—all made their way to the site and, if invited to stay the night, spent their time marveling at the majestic mountains all about them. Come morning, they were treated to hot buttered toast and coffee or even a hearty breakfast. Some were clearly moved and shared their impressions in the local paper, proclaiming, as one reporter did, that "the fresh, cool air of the morning makes one think that this old world is a mighty pleasant place to live in."[38] But such assessments were possible only if the hundreds of internees in the adjoining compound were conveniently ignored. The belief that this was the fate of the enemy hardly needed stating, and indeed, was not. Yet, they were civilians. So why was it that they were here? The contrast between the serene landscapes and the pitiful sight of inmates listlessly shuffling to and fro behind barbed wire made the question even more pressing. But, insofar as enemy prisoners did not matter, such contrasts went unnoticed.

For the internees, on the other hand, the beckoning expanse and beauty of the mountains seemed all too surreal. A few succumbed to their mental anguish. Mike Penziwater slipped silently away from his workstation on several occasions only to return voluntarily late at night in a state of confusion. He made his final getaway attempt under a hail of bullets—five shots, all missing their mark. Upon returning, he wandered about the camp in a state of agitation, whereupon it was recommended that he be sent to the provincial asylum along with several other inmates who demonstrated signs of instability. No action, however, was taken. Only when Penziwater attacked another prisoner in a fit of uncontrolled rage was he charged with delusional insanity and carted away.[39]

Internment was not easily borne, and Penziwater was but one of those who suffered psychologically from close confinement—a duress felt more deeply for its basic injustice. Indeed, most internees felt aggrieved, believing they were not meant to be in a camp for POWs. Anxious about the future, rumor and speculation fueled their fears. What was to become of them and their families? Such uncertainty would take its toll, though many clung stubbornly to the belief that they were innocent. To the persistent question of what they had done to deserve this fate there was no reply because it was judged none was needed, regardless of circumstances.

The experience of internment cast a long shadow and was felt in more ways than one, even after release. Wasyl Perchaliuk was paroled from the Castle camp, with twenty-five others, to the Canmore Coal Company.[40] Suffering from a debilitating respiratory ailment, he was unable to fulfill the terms of his parole with the mine, at which point, in late November 1916, he enlisted as a private with the 211th Overseas Infantry Battalion. Poised for deployment, Perchaliuk was recognized by a former Castle camp officer as having been one of those interned. Removed from the ranks for questioning, the recruit admitted he was a former internee. Being in violation of the order-in-council prohibiting enemy aliens from enlisting, he was held at the Calgary military detention cells. His return to Castle as a war prisoner was inevitable. The prospect proved too much for Perchaliuk who, alone in a cell and still in uniform, committed suicide. There was no escaping the shame and distress of being designated an enemy alien, a feeling shared among the more than 80,000 who reported regularly to local officials charged with monitoring their whereabouts and status.

There was no hiding from one's misfortune and plight as an enemy alien, either inside or outside the camp. It was an unenviable position, although for those imprisoned what the future might hold was also a matter of chance. Release could occur at any moment. Indeed, between late August and mid-November 1916, eighty-seven internees were freed, begging the question: why risk escape and tempt fate when the prospect of parole was a possibility? After POW No. 290, Petro Konowalczuk, was shot twice in the back and abdomen while attempting to flee, it made sense simply to bide one's time.[41] Still, a few took a chance at flight, being either unable or unwilling to live with the uncertainty. Two leapt from a train during transport, only to be recaptured. Another used wire cutters to slip through the compound fence at night, while a prisoner cook from the field kitchen detail seized the opportunity to disappear under the cover of smoke.

The escapes pointed to the continuing desperate situation at the camp. Worn-out clothing was a constant, as was a lack of boots, socks, and mitts. A scarcity of food was also a problem; in protest, some internees damaged their shovels, resulting in punishment diets (bread and water) and solitary confinement. As for the guards, who became increasingly irascible, a variety of provocations and misconduct took place, including a solider shooting another in the leg. Disciplinary action was meted out for the most severe offences. This sometimes went beyond what Canadian Army regulations provided for, leading to censure by the assistant judge advocate general. Meanwhile, among the internees in the camp's toxic environment, interethnic squabbles turned into full-scale brawls, resulting in serious injuries. But the single greatest menace was the cold. In the open encampment, which consisted of canvas tents, the fierce weather proved challenging. In early fall temperatures hovered around freezing, and the first snow fell on October 17. Throughout that month, some 180 prisoners were assigned to roadwork each day, but by the first week of November and the onset of severe cold, only a handful was sent out to clear snow and cut firewood for the camp. Retreating to Banff once more seemed a sensible if not lifesaving course of action.

Returning to Banff: "Scenic Outlook Not Vastly Improved"

A return to the old quarters at Banff had been discussed in the fall, but a final decision was delayed given looming uncertainties; the diplomatic dispute with Germany continued to dog Canadian officials, complicating the issue of what future awaited the internees. Then there was industry's appetite for more workers, which also led to indecision. Would the camp be emptied, thereby obviating the question of relocation? This was a political matter to be decided independently of the circumstances facing the Castle camp. In practical terms, however, by the first week of November, extreme weather made any further delay dangerous. Once the internment director granted authority, the camp was quickly packed up and the prisoners transferred to Banff. The move was fortuitous. "Banff looked mighty good to both guards and internees," the *Crag and Canyon* reported, noting that temperatures "flirted with the 37 below zero [Fahrenheit] mark . . . and it was an utter

FIGURE 7.3. "Prison Compound," Castle Mountain Internment Camp. Courtesy of the Whyte Museum of the Canadian Rockies, Banff, Alberta, Canada.

impossibility to maintain any appreciable degree of heat in the tents—unless one had a relay of batmen at one's disposal."[42]

Banff was a welcome return for the camp denizens, but the townsfolk were not as enthusiastic. The local paper lamented the fact that little economic benefit had been derived from the operation since provisioning was almost entirely conducted through Calgary, whose Conservative association had greater "pull." The reduced size of the camp was also noted, suggesting that even less value would result from the smaller operation. In the opinion of the *Crag*, however, it did not matter, the paper dismissing the prisoners as a blight that the community would do well to be rid of: "Their diminished number will not be greatly deplored, especially as the majority of our citizens are of the opinion that the scenic outlook is not vastly improved by the presence of the slouching, bovine-faced foreigners."[43]

The paper's sneering characterization of the inmates reflected not only latent xenophobia but also active local hostility toward the prisoners, inflamed, at least in part, by the disheartening news that the affable and well-liked Francis Eykelbosh, a resident of nearby Canmore and former guard at the Banff/Castle Mountain camp, had succumbed to his wounds on the Western front. Shocked that someone they knew had been killed—and by an enemy whose kindred were interned at Banff—local opinion was now solidly against the enemy alien. There was no room for sympathy. During an inspection by the military district's commanding officer, internees lodged complaints of brutal treatment by guards. Upon learning of the protests, the *Crag and Canyon* editors remarked that these "foreign scum" were "best handled with a pickaxe handle."[44] Meanwhile, the bayoneting of a prisoner who refused to walk faster on his way to work was fobbed off as a minor incident. Little was also made of the suicide of prisoner George Budak, who from the moment he was interned, stubbornly insisted that he was innocent and had nothing to do with the war. His pleas ignored, Budak surrendered to melancholy and despair, taking a razor to his throat and abdomen during the night of the Christmas Vigil. The *Crag* spoke disparagingly of the inconvenience presented by this tragedy, as citizens were "yank[ed] . . . from their firesides on Christmas Eve to serve on the coroner's jury."[45]

Despite the *Crag*'s assertion that no benefit was to be derived from relocating the prisoners to Banff, they did in fact perform invaluable service. The Parks Branch had set out ambitious plans for the winter season, assigning the prisoners to projects that would improve local infrastructure and enhance Banff's potential as a winter sporting venue. From mid-January to the end of March, approximately 140 were sent out daily to straighten the "corkscrew" road leading up to the top of Tunnel Mountain with its panoramic view of town and valley. A group was put to work constructing a large retaining rock wall and viewing site at the foot of the Bow Falls, while others built a ski run and toboggan glide. Prisoners were also assigned to certain smaller projects undertaken by private interests to improve the recreation facilities of the park: cutting trails for the Alpine Club of Canada, reclaiming land for a shooting range, and with the onset of spring, ploughing a large tract for growing hay to feed the park's horses used for leisure riding. Then there was the enormous winter carnival ice palace, created for the pleasure and amusement of the local citizenry.[46] Internment labor was available and for the taking—a principle that invited requests from a variety of sources, public and private.

Indeed, once it became known that prisoners could be made available if work was guaranteed, industry turned to the internees for ready and inexpensive labor. Such applications led to regular paroles, at first individually and later in pairs or more. Over time, requests from industry for large groups of prisoners were received. On April 16 the Canmore Coal Company applied for more than fifty men. This was followed by an appeal from the CPR for all the prisoners in the camp. These and other requests were unexpected but favorably received insofar as the problem of enemy alien joblessness—the major factor behind their internment—was being addressed. Still, the internees were enemies and only those judged not to be dangerous would be paroled. Security, in effect, continued to be a consideration.[47]

The tension about the internees' status as both civilians and POWs echoed in the vacillating decision-making regarding their release. As civilians they could be paroled to the extent that jobs were available; but as POWs they were carefully screened and handled, especially as it related to the conditions and terms of their parole. Thus, when it was learned that workers at Canmore were engaged in a strike, the plan to release ten internees to the mine was shelved for fear that they might add to the trouble. On the other hand, when the CPR guaranteed work and provided assurances that there were no labor issues at the company, a total of 109 men were paroled in the final week of April. Meanwhile, for those passed over, anxiousness pervaded the group. Sensing misfortune, some attempted flight. On June 7 a prisoner bolted from the Hot Springs work gang, with guards giving chase. A few weeks later, another prisoner working at the barracks slipped away unnoticed during a favorable moment.

The last desperate escapes underlined what was known to all—that the operations at Banff were winding down. In a final effort to make use of the labor of the remaining prisoners, they were put to work on extending the back nine holes of the golf course at the Banff Springs Hotel.[48] The course, it was felt, would not otherwise get done, at least for the foreseeable future, if the opportunity were missed. Accordingly, the internees were rushed to the site. Shortly after the project was completed, the final group of forty-seven prisoners was gathered up and in the company of twenty-five guards and NCOs sent to the distant Kapuskasing internment camp in northern Ontario to await their fate. With that, in July 1917 the camp was shuttered, and so ended the story of WWI internment at Banff/Castle Mountain.

The designation "enemy alien" was introduced at the start of the war to identify individuals whose origins could be traced to lands at war with Britain and its empire. It prejudged allegiances and reinforced, in the context of war, the more familiar, normative understanding of the term. It denoted adversary. To this end, and under emergency legislation introduced by a government wary of danger and risk, enemy aliens were styled and interned as POWs. Complicating matters, however, was the fact these individuals were civilians and noncombatants. A contradiction, the inconsistency was squared by their status as enemy aliens, which proved advantageous in the absence of a substantive international ruling on the treatment of civilian internees. Behind barbed wire, interned enemy aliens were seen as individuals without rights. As such, they could forcibly be put to work—an issue of useful significance given the levels of poverty and joblessness among the group. Viewed through this lens, the practice of internment would take shape.

Initially introduced as a security measure, internment came to occupy a different role. It facilitated the deployment of civilian POW labor on projects laid out by contracting agencies eager to tap into this pool of available, inexpensive, and reliable labor. The security dimension of internment was thus quickly displaced by economic considerations. Nonetheless, it remained a security operation, and the tension that existed between the economic and security priorities would inevitably become evident. Much of this, however, was resolved by the fact that the internees were enemies to whom nothing was owed or shared. Held in labor camps out on the frontier and away from view, internees would be compelled to work, suffering in silence and subject to abuse and humiliation with little protection or recourse.

As for the officers and guards charged with overseeing the prisoners, their job was simple: put the internees to work and prevent them from escaping. The incongruity of the status of these individuals as POWs and civilians made no impression. That they were the reason, however, behind the hardship being experienced by soldiers and officers alike did have an impact. The prisoners as a result would become the objects of their grievances, underscoring the moral and even psychological danger in which Canada's military were placed—behavior that pointed to the wider meaning and consequences of internment.

The story of the Banff/Castle Mountain camp reflects the circumstances typical of the internment of civilians as POWs. It is a narrative full of misery and despair, recounting a time when immigrants of "enemy" birth were sent into the frontier wilderness and, under military guard and threat of punishment, built a road through the mountain rough, among other things. Attesting to the intolerable situation and the desperation of the internees, scores would flee from a situation that was completely incomprehensible to them. How was it that they could be imprisoned as POWs, their protests of innocence ignored? Why were they being treated this way? Moreover, what had they done to deserve such treatment and what was to become of them? Disquieting questions, these remained unanswered.

No less troubling, however, once deemed enemies and interned as war prisoners, they were put to work in Canada's national parks—in this case the Rocky Mountains National Park. The irony, of course, was thick and the betrayal nowhere more poignant than in Banff, the jewel of Canada's park system. The parks had been created as a comfort to the nation, as places of recovery, contemplation, and relaxation. Expanding and improving access to the parks was an important step in realizing the promise. This work, however, would be carried out at the expense of individuals—civilians—who had come to the country freely and in search of a future. In this regard, the internees' experiences bordered on the surreal but also expected, given their identification and treatment as "enemies" of the country.

Notes

1. Canada, *Hansard* (House of Commons Debates), February 15, 1916, 850.

2. Canada, *Hansard* (House of Commons Debates), February 15, 1916, 850.

3. This difficulty was emphasized by Calgary's mayor, Michael Costello, who also raised the matter of interning enemy aliens and putting them to work, stating that "there was no way out of the dilemma." The matter was an urgent one for Calgary, given its large number of enemy aliens: 36,862 Germans and 26,427 Austro-Hungarians. "Ask Government to Intern All of Teutonic Birth," *Calgary Daily Herald*, February 14, 1915.

4. For a full discussion of the problems associated with political fit during a time of crisis, see Farney and Kordan 2005.

5. The blurring of the distinction between civilian and military status of interned enemy aliens is discussed more fully in Kordan 2020.

6. Later renamed Banff National Park in 1930 with the passage of the National Parks Act.

7. For an overview of the enemy alien experience in Canada, including internment, see Kordan 2016.

8. Internment was introduced to detain those enemy reservists who were inclined to return to their respective homelands to join the colors. In the early stages of the war, Canada followed Britain's lead and its insistence that reservists be detained, although this position was modified by selectively interning those who crossed the US-Canada border.

9. Library and Archives Canada (hereafter LAC), RG 13 A2, vol. 189, file 1639–59, F.H. Williamson, Deputy Commissioner, Dominion Parks Branch, to W. Cory, Deputy Minister, Department of Interior, "Memorandum: Regarding the Employment of German and Austrian Prisoners in the Dominion Parks," October 28, 1914.

10. Canada, Department of the Interior, *Report of the Commissioner of Dominion Parks* (Ottawa, 1916), 11.

11. Hart 2010, 119.

12. Waiser 1995, 12. Bennett's insistence that the prisoners not be coddled, however, ran contrary to convention regarding the treatment of military and civilian POWs, a document with which senior government officials were familiar. See LAC, RG 13, A2, vol. 190, file 117–36, Colonial Secretary to the Governor General, and referred to E. Newcombe, Deputy Minister of Justice, March 2, 1915, "Special treatment to certain classes of interned enemy subjects."

13. "Internment Camp Formed," *Crag and Canyon* (Banff, AB), June 19, 1915. There was some initial speculation that two camps would be created, one to be situated on the flats near Castle Mountain and the other in close proximity, but the idea would be abandoned. "Internment Camp Started," *Crag and Canyon*, June 26, 1915. The setup of the camp is described in a daily diary kept by camp officials. This diary is reproduced in its entirety in Kordan and Melnycky 1991.

14. LAC, RG 24, vol. 4729, file 3, Officer Commanding Castle Internment Camp to Officer Commanding Military District No. 13, July 23, 1915.

15. "Double Number of Prisoners at Castle Internment Camp," *Calgary Daily Herald*, July 29, 1915.

16. The protocol on captured combatants made a distinction between officers and enlisted men. For civilian prisoners, this translated into the difference between men of property and those without means. Following the rule issued by the Colonial Office, the distinction entitled men of a "superior class" to forgo work while also being entitled to better messing and accommodations. LAC, RG 24, vol. 4694, file 448–14–20 (1), "Accommodation. Officers, Prisoners of War," Officer Commanding Internment Operations to Officer Commanding Military District No. 13 (Alberta), February 18, 1915.

17. "Alien Enemies Coming Here," *Crag and Canyon*, June 12, 1915.

18. LAC, RG 24, vol. 4729, file 3, Officer Commanding Castle Internment Camp to Officer Commanding Military District 13, July 23, 1915.

19. "Interned Man Makes Escape," *Crag and Canyon*, July 24, 1915; "Second Escape from Internment Camp," *Crag and Canyon*, July 31, 1915; and "Eight Prisoners Break Away," *Crag and Canyon*, August 4, 1915.

20. LAC, RG 24, vol. 4729, file 3, Major Duncan Stuart to Officer Commanding Military District No. 13, November 4, 1915; and LAC, RG 13 A2, vol. 201, file 533–51, Officer Commanding Military District No. 13 (Alberta) to Major-General Otter, November 5, 1915. On the escapes, see LAC, RG 24, vol. 4729, file 3, "Report of Prisoners of War Escaped from Internment Camp, Castle Alta.," October 1915.

21. *Rabochyi narod* (Winnipeg), no. 31, October 28, 1915.

22. LAC, RG 24, vol. 4729, file 3, letter of N. Olinyk, n.d.

23. LAC, RG 25, vol. 3413, file 1–1–1918/13, "Comparative Statement Showing Caloric Value of Canadian Ration Based on Seven Days Issue for Non-Working Group," n.d.; LAC, RG 24, vol. 4729, file 3, Major Duncan Stuart, Officer Commanding Castle Mountain Internment Camp, to Officer Commanding Military District No. 13 (Alberta), September 13, 1915; and LAC, RG 24, vol. 4280, file 34–13 (4), "Maintenance of Discipline Among Prisoners of War," n.d.

24. Waiser 1995, 21.

25. Waiser 1995, 21.

26. *Crag and Canyon*, February 5, 1916; and *Calgary Daily Herald*, February 7, 9, and 23, 1916. See also Lackenbauer 2001.

27. LAC, RG 24, vol. 4721, file 2, Private George Lomax to Brigadier-General E. A. Cruickshank, 22 April 1916. Private Lomax's wish was granted. He was killed on the Western front a year later.

28. "Late Local Notes," *Crag and Canyon*, April 22, 1916.

29. For a complete description of the episode, see Kordan and Melnycky 1991, 6.

30. The Spray River Road project was described in the Parks Branch's annual report as "one of the most important public works undertaken by the department" insofar as it promised to be "one of the most popular drives in the locality." *Annual Report of the Department of the Interior for the Fiscal Year Ending March 31, 1917* (Ottawa, 1918).

31. LAC, RG 25 G1, vol. 1156, file 48–1, "Note Verbale" to the Embassy of the United States of America, June 23, 1915; and Bonar Law, Colonial Secretary, to the Governor General of Canada, July 5 and 12, 1915.

32. LAC, RG 24, vol. 4721, file 3, H. Clum, US Consul (Alberta), May 25, 1916.

33. LAC RG 24, vol. 4721, file 3, Major-General Wm. Otter to Major Peter Spence, June 22, 1916, "Escapes of POWs from Castle and Banff"; and Major-General Otter to Brigadier-General E. Cruickshank, June 22, 1916.

34. Waiser 1995, 30.

35. *Annual Report of Surveys and Construction of Highways in the Dominion Parks, 1915* (Ottawa, 1915).

36. *Annual Report of Surveys and Construction of Highways in the Dominion Parks, 1916* (Ottawa, 1916).

37. Canada, Sessional Paper No. 25, "Dominion Parks," 1917, 5.

38. *Crag and Canyon*, September 2, 1916.

39. LAC, RG 6 H1, vol. 757, file 3422 (I), Major Spence to Brigadier-General E. Cruickshank, December 12, 1916; and Major Peter Spence to Brigadier-General E. Cruickshank, April 27, 1916.

40. Regarding the Perchaliuk case, see LAC, RG 24, vol. 4729/1, file 3, Major Spence to the Assistant Adjutant General, December 9, 1916; Assistant Adjutant General to Major Spence, December 11, 1916; and Major Spence to the Assistant Adjutant General, December 20, 1916.

41. On the Konowalczuk shooting, see LAC, RG 24, vol. 4728, file 2, Board of Inquiry, August 21, 1916; and *Crag and Canyon*, August 19, 1916.

42. *Crag and Canyon*, November 18, 1916.

43. *Crag and Canyon*, November 18, 1916.

44. *Crag and Canyon*, December 23, 1916.

45. *Crag and Canyon*, December 30, 1916.

46. *Annual Report of the Department of the Interior for the Fiscal Year Ending March 31, 1917* (Ottawa, 1918). See also Waiser 1995, 43.

47. Individual prisoners were identified based on their behavior while interned, and this was cited in a prepared list. See, for example, LAC RG 6 H1, vol. 757, file 3326 (III), "Supplementary List of Prisoners at Banff, Alta.," April 23, 1917.

48. For a discussion of the project, see LAC RG 84, vol. 70, file R313; see also *Crag and Canyon*, April 7 and May 26, 1917.

CHAPTER 8

Globalizing Captivity

"Little Germany in China" in Japan

Naoko Shimazu

"A plaintive letter (*Ein Klagebrief*)
Dear, oh dear, really do try to think about it, dear beloved,
every day passes as though there is nothing, we do not have any free time here.
. . .
At nine, I ask my friend, what he thinks about the Chinese language,
He takes his violin out of the case, and says 'I've got to go to an orchestral practice!' Ordinarily, he would be pleased to keep me company but he hasn't got the time.
. . .
At 2, there is a tea party,
From 3 to 5, there is no body in the house,
Hockey, soccer, Schlagebal, Faustbal,
Tennis, theatre, bird cages, pig sties,
Farm work . . . painting,
Orchestra, billiard, milking cows,
Everyone is pursuing his interest to the fullest,
And nobody has enough time.
At night, it's even worse.

Concerts, casino, beer garden,

Lectures, theatre, cinema

A fun post-bowling party with big barrels of beer. . . .[1]

The above "letter" animatedly captures a day in the life of the prisoner-of-war camp in Bandō, on the island of Shikoku in Japan; it was published in *Die Barracke* (*The Barrack*), an internal newsletter written by the captives, in June 1918. It paints an idealized life of captivity in Bandō, and such rosy perceptions of the Japanese captivity experiences came to dominate popular discourse, at the cost of marginalizing the more varied, and at times not so idyllic, experiences of captivity in other POW camps in Japan. Moreover, the above "letter" may even come across as incredulous for some readers, because so much of what is generally known about the Imperial Japanese Army is conditioned by our knowledge of its well-publicized notoriety over the inhumane treatment of its captives in Japanese camps from World War II. The above "letter," therefore, confounds our preconceptions and challenges us to think beyond the predictable "box" in which we have come to situate uncritically the pre-1945 Japanese war experiences.

In order to make sense of why the Japanese treatment of their captives during World War I differed so dramatically from that of World War II, it is important for us not to fall into the trap of teleological thinking. Instead, we must pay closer attention to the historical evidence of Japan's early twentieth-century wars, especially the Russo-Japanese War of 1904–5. Not many would know that Japan played a leading role in helping to develop international standards for the treatment of POWs in the early twentieth century. In particular, the Russo-Japanese War was regarded by contemporaries as the first significant modern international warfare of the twentieth-century. As such, it was scrutinized by Western military observers and reported widely in global media. In the 1904–5 war, Japan had attempted to put into practice the ideas embodied in the Hague Conference of 1899, which introduced the idea that POWs "should be analogous to that of the troops of the Detaining Power." This was revised as the Hague Convention of 1907 and continued in effect until the Geneva Prisoners of War Convention of 1929. Thus, the treatment of POWs in World War I, which came under the 1907 Hague Convention, was to some extent based on the Japanese experiences in 1904–5.[2] As a way of illuminating this through concrete examples, I have attempted as much as feasible to make a comparison of the captivity experiences of the Russo-Japanese War and those of World War I, as far as the Japan involvement was concerned. In this way, we begin to see the seamless integration of the Japanese narrative into the global narrative of captivity, especially in demonstrating the role Japan played in the development of international standards of POW treatment before the war had even began in 1914.

In unravelling the Japanese narrative, one should note that Japan had been preoccupied with attaining the standard of civilization appropriate for a great power and acceptable to the prevailing Western norms of the day. The "civilization discourse" espoused by the state and the elite at large impacted Japanese attitudes toward its enemies, as evidenced in the harsh treatment of the Qing in the 1894–95 war on the one hand, compared with the notably favorable treatment of the Russians in the 1904–5 war and the Germans in World War I. Hence, it is no exaggeration to say that race mattered greatly to the Japanese at the time, as a significant category that determined nationalities deserving of "civilized" treatment on the part of the Japanese. The pejorative Japanese attitudes toward the Qing were most glaringly manifested in the Port Arthur Massacre of November 1894. Seen comparatively, the Japanese case as evidenced in World War I could fruitfully contribute to the argument that it was part of the global narrative that situated World War I as the last point of the long nineteenth century.

In World War I Japanese POW camps constituted the easternmost fringe of the global map of the camps operated by the Allied powers. One of the most striking dimensions of the captivity of both Germans and Austro-Hungarians during World War I was the comparability of experiences across many different national camps. To this end, this study, which focuses on captives from these two empires in Japan, offers a critical overview of how some of the Japanese camps operated and should be read relationally with the other chapters in this edited volume. This will allow the reader to appreciate fully the comparative value of the Japanese experiences, both in terms of how they constituted a distinct regional experience, while at the same time they shared comparable experiences in the larger global mapping of captives during World War I. The microhistorical approach to examining the Bandō POW camp in Japan offers evidence of the globally shared experiences. Of particular note, the Bandō POW camp shared surprising similarities, for instance, with the civilian internee camp in Knockaloe, Isle of Man.[3] Some of these will be highlighted later on in more detail.

On the other hand, the Japanese case complicates our understanding of the historical situating of World War I captivity experiences. The experiential connection being made by some historians between World War I, during which some of the German POWs in the Soviet Union were subjected to harsh "gulag"-like experiences, and the captivity experiences in the Soviet Union and Nazi Germany during World War II, is not borne out in the Japanese case.[4] Instead, the Japanese case study strengthens the argument made by Iris Rachamimov that the POW experiences in World War I had more to do with "nineteenth-century social thinking than with Auschwitz and the Gulag Archipelago."[5] In fact, there is a clear schism in captor experiences between the two world wars for the Japanese, as the experiences of World War I bear no resemblance to those of World War II. What is often missing in the historiography of wartime captivity during World War I is the Japanese experience gained from the Russo-Japanese War of 1904–5, which helped to establish internationally acceptable standards of treatment of enemy captives by scrupulously attempting to follow the Hague Convention of 1899 and which laid the foundation for the general treatment of captives during World War I through the Hague Convention of 1907.[6] This is why, in spite of the negligible number of captives in Japan, Japanese experiences in World War I remain significant in shaping our general understanding of World War I captivity experiences.

The Bandō Camp

Japan declared war on Germany on August 23, 1914, and mobilized 52,000 troops jointly with the British troops of some 1,320 (of which one-third consisted of Indian troops) to capture Qingdao. The city, the heart of the German concession on the Shandong Peninsula in China, served as a base for the German East Asiatic Squadron, the largest German naval concentration outside Europe. In some sense, it was Japan's participation as an Allied belligerent power in 1914 that made the war truly global by expanding the theater of war into Asia and the Pacific. The fall of Qingdao resulted in 4,689 captives from the German concession.[7] They were transported to Japan and distributed initially across thirteen POW camps.[8] To put things into perspective, the total number of captives held in Japan constituted less than one-thousandth of the total captured by the Allied powers.[9]

Naively, the Japanese government had assumed that the war would be a "European war" and that it would be a short one. Upon realizing the contrary, however, the Japanese Imperial Army in June 1915 instructed regional divisional headquarters to construct purpose-built barracks and amalgamate the thirteen camps into six newly constituted ones, to be situated in Narashino (Chiba prefecture, near Tokyo), Nagoya, Aonogahara (Hyogo Prefecture, near Osaka), Ninoshima (Hiroshima Prefecture), Kurume (Kyushu), and Bandō (Shikoku). The Bandō camp was created by combining the three camps on the island of Shikoku—that is, the Tokushima, Matsuyama, and Marugame camps—and housed some 1,020 captives, becoming the second largest in Japan.[10] Therefore, the Japanese experiences underwent two phases of captivity, which revealed the underlying shift in Japanese thinking on wartime captivity incarceration.

In thinking about places of captivity, the Russo-Japanese War experiences demonstrated an expansive interpretation of what constituted a camp, whereby an entire city would be conceived as a space to house the POWs. To a surprising extent, captives were integrated into the socioeconomic life of the city, and this had a profound impact on their day-to-day interactions with the Japanese people. Since Matsuyama did well commercially from the POW presence in 1904–5, when World War I started the Imperial Army was inundated with requests from municipal authorities to host POW camps. Nevertheless, a shift developed in the Japanese Imperial Army's management of the camps by World War I to favor the separation of captives from the townspeople. In particular, the later phase of captivity was marked by clearly demarcated places of captivity, as most of the captives were transferred to newly purpose-built barracks away from towns. Such a spatial segregation meant that very little gendered interactions took place, for example, between the Japanese women and the German captives, unlike the highly interactive experiences of the Russo-Japanese War.

Thanks to *Die Barracke*, the surviving internal newsletter published by the POWs in the Bandō camp, we can reconstruct a fairly comprehensive view of the everyday life in the camp. The Bandō camp held 815 Germans, 125 Poles, and some eighty "others," representing a wide geographical expanse of ethnicities from Russia, France, Croatia, Denmark, Belgium, Italy, Netherlands, Slovenia, Switzerland, Czechoslovakia, Lithuania, Argentina, and even China and Japan. In any case, there were only three hundred "Austro-Hungarians" captured as POWs by the Japanese, of which 230 were housed in the Aonogahara POW camp in Hyogo Prefecture, most of them from the scuttled Austrian-Hungarian cruiser SMS *Kaiserin Elizabeth*.[11] The captives called themselves the "Bandonese" and referred to the camp as their "country" or their "town." Often lauded by the captives themselves as the "best camp in the world" the Bandō POW camp presents a fascinating episode in the history of World War I. By way of comparison, the 1904–5 war was a much larger war for Japan, and the city of Matsuyama in Shikoku, with a population of thirty-six thousand, ended up hosting some six thousand POWs. Incidentally, the Matsuyama camp in 1904–5 attained the mythical status that the Bandō camp did in World War I as the best camp.

For one, the camp created a unique "space" that enabled a semblance of the continued state of civilization, both for captives and for captors. The Bandō camp was built in a rural area and was officially a fenced enclosure, with an entrance gate. The longest point in the camp enclosure from the gate up to the top of the hill at the other end was 353 meters, and the widest point measured 226 meters, with the entire area including the barbed wire fence measuring 57,233 square meters. Per capita space was rather small with 4.7 square meters (fourth in ranking). Each barrack was seventy-three meters long and 7.5 meters wide.[12] The "town" was divided into Eastern Bandō and Western Bandō, and each section had elected its own "mayor."[13] According to *Die Barracke*, "Eastern Bandō is developing by the day. . . . This area emphasizes the ostentatiousness of the villas, belonging to the well-off upper-class citizens, including merchants, factory owners, engineers, academics, and higher officials."[14] On the grounds, there were two lakes, one of which was a boating lake, and about one hundred small "villas" (pergolas) were built on the hillside with a commanding view of the area; nearby stood an upmarket restaurant called the Crystal Palace, as well as an upmarket bakery, a sausage factory, and a brewery.

The main thoroughfare of the camp was Tapautau (Dabaodao), named after a district in the formerly German-held Qingdao, "a mixed zone of commercial, industrial, and residential activities in which both Europeans and Chinese could live, work, shop, and own property."[15] Similarly, the Tapautau in Bandō had around eighty "shops," including furniture makers, tailors, photo studios, a barber, a repairman for musical instruments, an ice cream maker, music teachers, a bookbinder, ironsmiths, mechanics, and a store that sold eggs, dill pickles, bonbons, and soft drinks.[16] Due to the lack of space, it is not possible here to give a fuller account of everyday life in the Bandō camp. Nonetheless, what Rachamimov adeptly explains about the significance of material culture in affording the POWs the sense of a "small escape" from the reality of wartime incarceration is also true of Bandō.

The cultural activities at the camp turned Bandō, despite its location in a remote area of Japan, into a temple of learning and culture that operated almost like a campus university. The "library" created by the captives boasted some 5,420 books, with an average daily borrowing rate of 170 books.[17] Twice weekly, lectures were given on the "campus" by the captives on a wide range of topics, on German literature, German philosophy including Kant, Ficht, and Nietzsche, on China, local history, prehistoric culture, a series of thirty-two lectures on modern German history to the present war, and an occasional esoteric subject, like the "geological study of German mountains."[18] Many of these lectures were published by one of the two in-house printing presses, which remarkably printed 350,000 sheaves of paper in 1917–18 alone.[19]

There were two printers in the camp; the one located in East Bandō specialized in lithographs, and the other printed materials such as picture postcards as well as doing book binding.[20] On the musical scene the Bandonese could choose from concerts offered by two resident orchestras. The MAK Orchestra (originally known as the Tokushima Orchestra) changed its name to MAK (for M. A. "Tokuschima" Kapelle) in October 1918; its forty-five members held thirty-five concerts in two and a half years at Bandō. In addition, there was a rival orchestra led by Paul Engel (a professional violist from the Shanghai Orchestra) called the Engel Orchestra and a number of chamber music societies, as well as two choirs each boasting sixty members. It was the MAK orchestra that famously gave the first performance of Beethoven's Ninth Symphony on June 1, 1918, to the local public. The tradition of performing the Ninth Symphony at Christmas subsequently took root in Japan and continues to this day. Music played a vital role in providing a sense of well-being to the captives and included little touches like a birthday serenade outside the window of the "birthday boy."[21]

At Bandō, the Japanese wardens knew better than to interfere with internal squabbles between the POWs; an informal court of justice existed among the prisoners, and most problems were resolved by them. As a self-governing community the POWs prided themselves in the efficient, civilized running of the camp.[22] Not all was well, however, as an internal "triad" (gang) of sorts, the "Black Hands," existed among the POWs in the Marugame camp that threatened homosexuals and ran a racket. Some of the so-called punishments meted out by the Japanese guards did not have the intended result due to cultural differences. For instance, one jokingly called "sunbathing" consisted of the culprit having to stand in front of the guard station for two hours in broad daylight. The Japanese were sticklers for the rules; if a guard was not in uniform, then he was not on duty. Once a POW ended up in a brawl with a guard but had gotten off lightly because the guard in question had not been wearing his uniform at the time. The guards also often turned a blind eye to nocturnal "outings" by the POWs to visit prostitutes. When an occasional POW was caught off guard, he was made to demonstrate in front of the other POWs and guards how he had tried to scale up the walls around the camp. If he succeeded in giving a satisfactory demonstration of the escape, he would get away with it. This and other similar instances led one of the captives, Ludwig Wieting, to note repeatedly that, "the Japanese had a real sense of humor."[23]

Interestingly, Wieting claims that the underlying reason why the Bandō camp was seen as a model POW camp during the war in Japan might have had to do with the familiarity of the majority of the captives

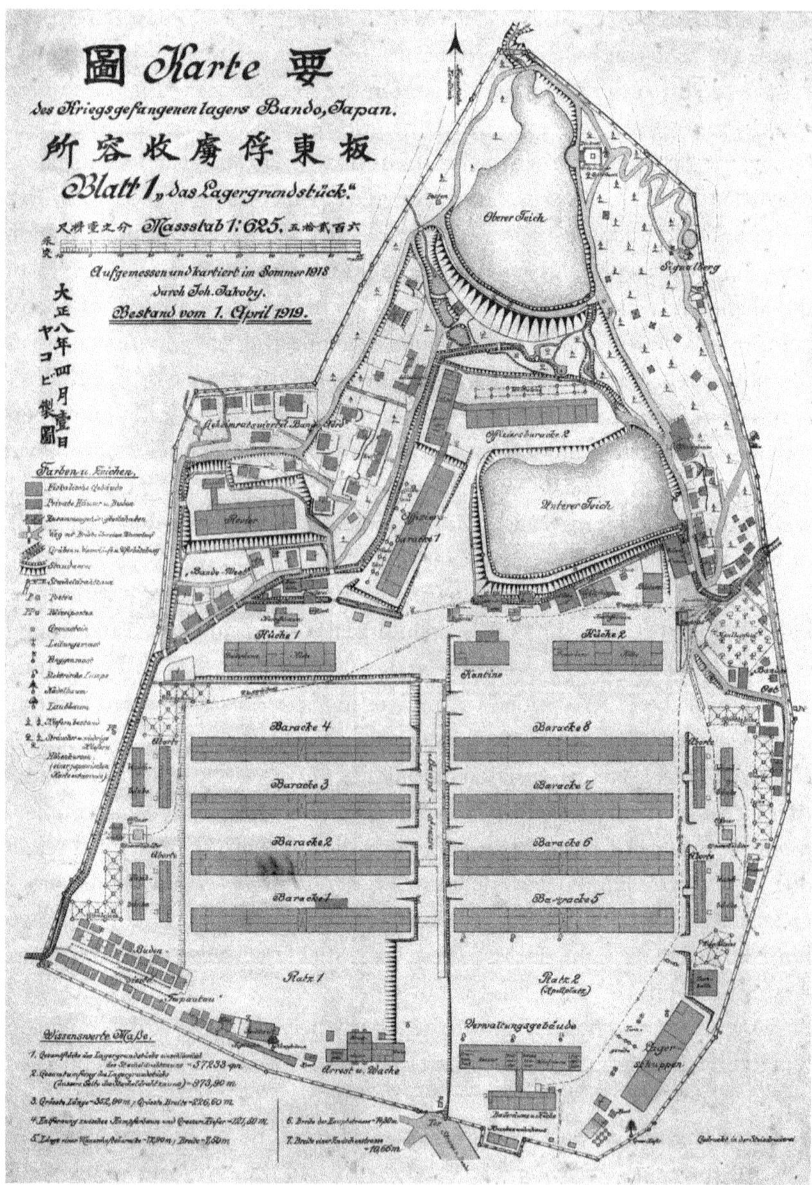

FIGURE 8.1. A map of the Bandō camp drawn by one of its prisoners, 1918–19. Wikipedia Common [online] available at: https://de.wikipedia.org/wiki/Kriegsgefangenenlager_Band%C5%8D#/media/Datei:Lager_Bando_1919.png

with East Asia.[24] They had been living in China or Japan for a while by the time they were mobilized as reserves at the outbreak of the war. Some were even fluent in Japanese and understood "the Japanese mind."[25] In other words, these "Germans" were mostly not Germans from Germany but rather colonial Germans who had already spent some time in Qingdao as residents. They had become accustomed to making their "home" (Ger. *Heimat*) in Asia, being constrained by the geographical boundaries of the foreign concessions in China. Instead of creating a "little Germany" in Bandō, they had effectively created a "little Germany in China" in Bandō—recreating Qingdao in Bandō through such things as the naming of Tapautau—to create for themselves the sense of being at home. Of the Bandō POWs in 1919, only 55 per cent were conscripts; others were reserves and volunteers from East Asia generally, and only 10 per cent were professional soldiers. By age 72 per cent of them were in their twenties, followed by 24 per cent in their thirties; and the oldest captive was forty-eight years of age, and the youngest was sixteen.[26] In this sense the story of Bandō is also the story of a colonial empire in the East and helps to structure an alternative narrative of the "empire" and colonial lives in times of war.

Clearly, Bandō was a shining beacon among the POW camps in Japan during World War I. One POW who was transferred to Bandō from another camp exclaimed: "Where in the world would one find a POW camp like Bandō? Where in the world would one find a POW chief-warden like Colonel Matsue?"[27] Indeed, Colonel Matsue was one of the most liberal and open-minded chief wardens in all of Japan's POW camps. He believed in minimal interference from the authorities in the running of the Bandō camp, and he allowed for maximum freedom in terms of movement, including unsupervised day-long walks outside the camp in the beautiful coastal regions nearby. He created sporting facilities, vegetable allotments, and pastures for tending cows in adjoining fields outside the fence (the unfenced area was as large as the fenced area of camp). This hands-off policy, which left the responsibility of running the camp largely to the POWs, had the effect of nurturing collective responsibility on the part of the POWs, who practiced self-governing, self-censorship, and self-discipline, with much pride and effectiveness. This behavior seems to mirror Brian Feltman's observation that "the manner in which they [Germans] handled themselves on enemy soil was a direct reflection of their national character."[28] Whether or not that was indeed the case, some of the German captives in Japan tended to project their national pride in the way they lived as captives.

The Bandō camp was not unique. It may be instructive at this point to introduce the case of the Nagoya camp, which was considered to be an equally successfully run camp, benefiting from its geographical location in the city of Nagoya, a major manufacturing and commercial center in central Japan. Competitively minded local businesses and industries became interested in tapping into the range of expertise and skills possessed by the "German" POWs. It needs no reminding that Germany had been held in high esteem in Japan at the time, due to the late Meiji preoccupation with wanting to build a modern state not unlike that of Germany, particularly so in the later stages of Meiji modernization. At the Nagoya camp, special skilled POWs were highly sought after, like the engineer who helped to develop the baking oven for Shikijima Flour Company and the skilled engineers who worked for Japanese firms manufacturing automobiles, bicycles, steel, ceramics, textiles, and weaving. At the end of the war, sixty POWs applied to remain in Japan to work in industries; twenty of them alone were employed in the Nagoya area.[29]

Likewise, many of those interned at the Aonogahara camp were skilled engineers, one of them an aircraft engineer, since most of the captives were crew members of the cruiser SMS *Kaiserin Elisabeth* of the Austro-Hungarian Navy.[30] The enthusiasm of local communities to learn from the Germans was evident in the popularity of "handicraft exhibitions" organized by the POW camps, glowingly covered by the local newspapers. In September 1915 a local newspaper in Kobe featured a photograph of a concrete fountain, 1.3 meters high, made by Walter Newiger, a POW in the Himeji Camp. It was built to look like an old castle on the river (probably the Rhine), including details such as gold fish swimming in the fountain.[31] Mirroring the Western fascination with Japanese art and craft in nineteenth-century world expositions, the Japanese were fascinated by the German craftsmanship evident under the highly restricted conditions of captivity.

To what extent was the captives' experience in Bandō or Nagoya reflective of the POW camps generally in Japan? Both were successfully run camps because of the fortuitous convergence of both structural and contingent factors that made them work. To a certain degree, all camps should have been able to achieve the level of general satisfaction that Bandō offered in captivity experiences because structural conditions should have been more or less the same across all of them. However, contingent factors ended up having a substantial impact on the day-to-day running of the camps. For the purposes of our analysis, therefore, the Bandō experience offers a useful model from which management practices and captivity experiences at the other camps can be measured.

Captors' Perceptions of the Captives

By 1914 Japanese captors had already experienced another major war involving the European enemy only a decade earlier, in the Russo-Japanese War. Thus, Japanese wardens took a comparative view of their captives in 1914–1918, judging against those of 1904–5 and providing insightful material for analysis. Their views offer a window into some of the prevalent social norms in contemporary Japanese society.[32] On the arrival of the first cohort of German POWs, the chief warden of the Himeji Camp gave the following speech to welcome them:

> You have fought bravely for your mother country, and have become POWs as a result of sabers breaking and bullets expiring, we express the greatest sympathy to you all. In dealing with you, we shall obey the armed forces code of conduct and, moreover, we shall treat you in the same manner as we would treat our own soldiers and sailors. As soldiers, we should preserve our dignity, and you should also preserve your dignity as German soldiers and as Austrian soldiers.[33]

This pronouncement would have been familiar to contemporary Japanese since such a perspective, recognizing the international convention on the treatment of prisoners of war, dated back to the days of the 1904–5 war. During that war the city of Matsuyama was the site of the most famous POW camp (in the same way as Bandō was famous in 1917–1918), housing nearly five thousand. During World War I, however, the Matsuyama camp was rated unfavorably mainly because of the chief warden, who was nicknamed the Maikaefer (May Beetle) and highly disliked, his orders often ignored by POWs.[34] The "May Beetle" aka Colonel Maekawa gave a lecture illuminating some of his intercultural observations of the German POWs. One of the most striking differences from his previous experience with the Russian POWs was that the Germans had a higher level of literacy and, generally, a higher level of education. Of four hundred privates, more than half had an education beyond the age of fifteen, whereas the Russian soldiers from the 1904–5 war included quite a few who could barely write their own names.

In spite of the fact that Maekawa was disliked by his captives, his lecture was full of praise for them, and the lessons that the Japanese could learn from their captives. Maekawa observed that his captives had diligently followed the progress of the war by posting a map of the European front on the wall and leading endless discussions about the progress of their armies. Moreover, the Germans tended to have a well-developed habit of hygiene, sanitation, and general health. When they became ill, they would voluntarily see a doctor and ask to be quarantined in case they carried contagious diseases. Their daily routine demonstrated their keen interest in exercise and sport, particularly gymnastics. When they would put on variety shows in the camps, gymnastics would be included as part of the entertainment performances. Maekawa argued that the Japanese had much to learn from the German sense of thrift and filial piety. Contrary to what Maekawa had heard about rampant individualism in the West, the POWs seemed to care about their families back home, more so than the Japanese. Another enviable quality was their work ethics; the Germans generally tended to persevere in hard work until they achieved their objectives.[35]

One major lesson that the Japanese had learned from the 1904–5 war was that a multitude of nationalities was present within the so-called Russian Army, including Poles, Finns, and Armenians.[36] The Japanese were taken aback then that many of the captives had openly expressed an anti-Russian sentiment. Such a multiethnic composition of captives no longer surprised the Japanese during World War I, and the Japanese wardens proceeded whenever feasible to keep different ethnic groups away from each other physically, usually by offering separate shelter, to minimize any potential flare up of animosity. Nonetheless, the Japanese were shocked when Italian soldiers in the Himeji camp were killed by the German POWs for demonstrating loyalty to Italy in what became a minor riot when Italy declared war on the Central Powers in May 1915.[37] Moreover, the news of the riot among the Austro-Hungarian soldiers in Bad Radkersburg near Graz reached the POWs at Aonogahara when the war ended in Europe, leading to a greater schism between the Slav and non-Slav POWs and resulting in the occasional flaring up of violence.[38] Not surprisingly, the multiethnic composition of the European imperial armies was considered to be a source of disloyalty and instability by the Japanese Imperial Army, which had experienced it firsthand during both wars.

The Japanese considered the linguistic barrier as one of the biggest problems of managing captivity. Camp guards who occupied the lower stratum of the military hierarchy often knew no foreign language. This linguistic barrier not only impeded communication but led to the problem of censoring the correspondence of the POWs. In fact, the POWs' frustration with their letters being halted for three months or more was often caused by the inability of the Japanese censors to decipher the contents. Italian soldiers in particular expressed dismay at not being able to receive letters; the parcels they received were often devoid of contents.[39] It may not come as a surprise, then, that a German-speaking Japanese officer was stationed at the Bandō camp, no doubt helping to lessen misunderstandings between captors and captives.[40]

Toward the end of the war, the rules were gradually loosened, and often beer parties were held in gazebos built in the compound by the prisoners with merrymaking late into the night—so much so that the monks in the neighboring temples came to complain about the noise. On Christmas day the POWs were allowed to organize a Christmas party in the Buddhist temples, with presents sent from Germans resident in China piled up high, including poppy-seed cakes, nuts, and apples but also fur skins, pocketknives, vests, and socks. The Japanese wardens served herring and potatoes as special treats to celebrate Christmas, and the wardens and guards were invited to partake in the festivities.[41] Much has been made about the "Christmas Truce" between the Germans and British soldiers in Flanders in December 1914. Not many know about the "New Year's Truce," which took place in January 1905 for over one month between the Russians and Japanese officers, when they exchanged gifts and shared fine wine and high-quality tinned food, speaking French as their lingua franca.[42] Here we see another case of continuity between the 1904–5 and 1914–1918 experiences for the Japanese.

On the whole, the Japanese wardens were suitably impressed with the diligence of their "German" captives. Some of the prisoners started studying Japanese and soon became conversant in basic Japanese. Impressed by the civic-mindedness of the POWs who behaved in an orderly manner on outings (such as not littering in parks), the local newspaper exclaimed, "No wonder they are civilized people."[43] Soon local dignitaries started visiting the POWs at the camp, first with the mayor of the city of Himeji—decked out in a white vest, tie, and silk hat, with a private secretary in tow–followed by Buddhist monks who prayed for the well-being of the captives, and then the commander of the Himeji Regiment with an army general. The Austrian priest from Kanazawa City (some 330 kilometers away) visited often, as did a Frenchman who lived in the city of Himeji. Each time these intercultural exchanges took place, the local crowd thronged the nearby streets of the camp to view the POWs and the VIPs visiting them. Even after the experience of the Russian POWs from 1904–5, European POWs remained a highly coveted sight for the locals—mostly arising out of curiosity of "the Other.[44] Indeed, in World War I too (but not in the subsequent conflict twenty-three years later), the Japanese captors had the tendency to regard their captives as hailing from a civilized culture (possibly even more so than that of their own), a perception strengthened by the diligence, discipline, and knowledge displayed by the captives.

International Observers and Captivity Grievances

In spite of the generally positive views of the Japanese treatment of POWs in World War I, as we have seen in some detail in the Bandō and Nagoya camps, captivity experiences seemed to have differed considerably between camps. In Tokyo, the Ministry of the Army set up the Prisoners Information Department (Jpn. *Furyo jōhōkyoku*), to keep abreast of all the details of communications between the authorities and the POWs.[45] Until the American entry into war in 1917, it was the United States that had acted as the key diplomatic channel for communication regarding the POWs held in Japan. An analysis of the observations made by international observers of the POW camps in Japan sheds some useful light on our understanding of the management of respective camps. The POWs in Japan generally felt forgotten by their governments because they had only two official visits in five years, important occasions that provided a safe space to air their grievances.[46] The last camp to close was the Bandō camp on April 1, 1920. In fact, there may have been only four visits made by international observers (two visits by Sumner Wells in early 1916 and in late 1916, one by the Swedish chaplain Neander in January 1918, and another by a Swiss medical doctor, Fritz Palavicini, in June 1918), and a visit by a Japanese delegation headed by Count Yanagisawa in January 1916.[47]

In January 1916 the German government requested the American government to conduct a survey of the POW camps in Japan in response to an anonymous letter received from a POW in the Marugame camp in Shikoku. Sumner Wells, an American diplomat stationed in Tokyo went on a tour of the eleven POW camps, covering a large geographical area from Kanto to Kansai, Shikoku and Kyushu regions, from March 2 to 15, 1916 (an astonishingly short period of time to cover the length of the Japanese archipelago). According to his tight schedule, his visits ranged from 2.5 hours to 5.5 hours per camp. It seems, however, that Wells's report had not yet reached Berlin by the end of June 1916 as a German *note verbale* had been sent to the American embassy in Tokyo to remind them to forward Wells's survey report, as well as to inspect continued complaints from the POWs in Kurume.[48] To this, the Ministry of the Army responded to the Ministry of Foreign Affairs that many of the complaints aired by the POWs at Kurume had not been supported by evidence.[49] Wells's survey offers invaluable insight into the different conditions from camp to camp, and the wide range of issues that complaints covered. In his summary letter to the American ambassador in Tokyo, George W. Guthrie, Wells mentions two camps, Kurume and Osaka, as having the highest number of complaints.[50]

General complaints from most camps centered on the inadequacy of shelter and detention facilities. In the main, this pointed up the gap between European and Japanese expectations about habitat, especially for the lower ranks. In the initial phase of captivity (when Wells made the visits), there was only one newly opened purpose-built camp in Aonogahara (opened in September 1915). Otherwise, the Imperial Army used the existing sheltering facilities from the days of the Russo-Japanese War, when it operated twenty-eight camps around the country. As a result, many of the POWs of World War I were initially housed in draughty temples and dilapidated old barracks. Traditional Japanese houses tended to be cold and draughty in general, though the larger size of the rooms in the temples would have made heating even more difficult. In 1904–5 there were not many purpose-built barracks for POWs; the Matsuyama camp was one of the few with new barracks to house the POWs, and it was considered to be the best camp by many Russian POWs in 1904–5. Moreover, Russian officers rented houses in the city, and often lived with their wives (some even with their children), employed cooks and servants, and practically lived as Russian residents in Japan. In January 1916 Wells commented on the "cramped living quarters" of the lower ranks at many camps, including Matsuyama, Marugame, Tokushima, Fukuoka, Kurume, Osaka, Shizuoka—which led to the construction of Bandō, by combining the first three.[51]

Undisputedly, the Kurume camp was considered the worst camp throughout the entire period, having the largest number of POWs, at 1,107, and at peak times as many as 1,300. The camp was known among the captives as "KZ," (abbreviation of *Konzentrationslager*), the term by which Nazi Germany would later refer to its concentration camps. According to Wells, the camp consisted of sixteen makeshift barracks from the days of the Russo-Japanese War, each with an eighty-person capacity. The buildings were in an unacceptably old condition, with rain and wind blowing through holes in walls, and the POWs were prohibited from fixing them. Many soldiers were crammed into small places, with hardly enough space to sit in their rooms during the day. There was no special provision made for officers in terms of accommodation, though they were allowed at their own expense to renovate the interior in order to make their barracks more habitable.

What marks the Kurume experience is the pettiness of the guards, who intentionally prohibited the lower ranks from fixing their dwellings to make them more habitable. Other related matters, such as the closeness of the distance between the rooms and the latrines, made the living quarters very unpleasant and unhygienic.[52] Furthermore, POWs at Kurume complained about the deplorable condition of the detention cells, which measured fifteen square feet (under 1.4 square meters), with a ceiling height of 5 feet 6 inches and a tiny three-foot-high "closet" with a Japanese-style toilet. In the cells the prisoners were fed only black tea and bread and had no blankets or heating. Every three days they were allowed to wash themselves. One could be incarcerated here from two or three days to three months.[53] The poor housing standards, not just in Kurume but in other camps across the board, led to the construction of purpose-built barracks, starting in 1915. POWs at the Himeji camp were the first ones to be moved into the new barracks in Aonogahara, built on an army drill ground, located in the interior of the Hyogo Prefecture, in September 1915. The new camp provided more room for physical movement, and the facilities were more efficiently heated with iron stoves. Bandō camp was another newly built camp that opened in 1917. In spite of the poor conditions at Kurume, its barracks appear not to have been rebuilt or reinforced.

Other complaints centered on the lack of opportunities for physical movement and exercise, which verged on inhumaneness. The chief warden of Kurume claimed that POWs were allowed an outing three times a month, but in reality they had not been allowed out of the camp for several months, with dire consequences for their physical and mental health. These barracks were so poorly lit that it was impossible to read or do anything in the evening other than going to bed early. The lack of adequate exercise made it difficult to fall asleep readily, and many ended up spending hours lying in the dark.[54] The lack of physical exercise or simply the ability to move around in a larger space had serious consequences on both the physical and psychological well-being of the POWs.[55]

The most serious issue facing the POWs in the Kurume camp was corporal punishment and other disciplinary measures meted out by the wardens, liberally and frequently. A notorious incident occurred on the day of the Taisho emperor's enthronement on November 10, 1915: one German officer refused to accept the gifts of apples and beer made to all POWs in the camp to commemorate this event.[56] The chief warden took this refusal as an insult to the emperor and proceeded to punch and kick the German officer. When questioned about this by Wells, the chief warden admitted that the incident had happened but justified it on the grounds that the refusal was taken as a direct affront to the emperor. Judging from the linguistic ability of the chief warden, Wells thought it highly likely that the incident had arisen from miscommunication. Other instances of violence being meted out to the POWs included a German officer who was punched by a Japanese private and an officer punched by a Japanese guard for having accidentally dropped some cigarette ashes in front of the guard. The chief warden admitted that the guards should not have punched the officers, but he excused himself on the grounds that the guards did not come under his authority and he could not punish them for their misdemeanor. On the other hand, the guards had informed Wells that they had been given orders to punch the POWs for any wrongdoing and were simply doing what they had been instructed to do.[57]

Wells was told by the POWs in the Kurume camp that the relationship between the POWs and the Japanese authorities was acrimonious because the local 46th and 58th regiments were responsible for sending troops to Qingdao to fight against the Germans in 1914.[58] However, historian Imai Hiromasa has argued recently that the root cause of the problems encountered in the Kurume camp might have had more to do with the personality of the successive chief wardens instead of any generalized sentiment of animosity toward the captured enemy soldiers by the local regiment and the local population, as is often assumed to be the case.[59] In January 1916, the Imperial Army entrusted Count Yanagisawa to visit all the camps, particularly paying attention to the escapee problems encountered by the Fukuoka and Kurume camps in 1915, which might have contributed inadvertently to the needlessly harsh treatment of POWs in these camps, since the chief wardens became extra vigilant over their captives to prevent further loss of face.[60]

It did not help that Kurume experienced five different chief wardens during the war (usually there was no change or only one at other camps), causing instability and a lack of coordinated long-term management. Some chief wardens were apparently stricter than others. Two would become full army generals and play a major role in the turbulent politics of Japan during the 1930s. The first was Mazaki Jinzaburō (1876–1956), the chief warden who had caused the incident over the misunderstanding over imperial gifts from the Taisho emperor. He was eventually appointed inspector general of military education, but he also served as a leader of the ultranationalist wing of the Imperial Army in the 1930s, known as the Imperial Way faction.[61] Mazaki was succeeded as chief warden by Hayashi Senjūrō (1876–1943), who later became army minister and even prime minister briefly in 1937.

Another camp that Wells noted as difficult was Osaka, which housed 509 POWs. What broke the little trust that had existed between the POWs and the wardens involved an attempted escape by a few POWs. Instead of punishing the individuals, the Japanese wardens decided to punish collectively by imposing severe restrictions of movement on all the POWs. Henceforth, the chief warden at Osaka became highly suspicious of the POW activities, including correspondence, which was curtailed substantially.[62] From June 30 to July 16, 1918, a Swiss medical doctor based in Yokohama, Fritz Palavicini, was asked to represent the International Red Cross and visit all the POW camps in Japan. Contemporary records show that Palavicini had been on the police watch list during the war as a doctor who frequented the households of Germans in Yokohama. Even though Palavicini tended to be generally positive about the Aonogahara camp, he did report that there was disgruntlement among the German officers, who had to deal with wardens of lower caliber at Aonogahara, compared with wardens at Nagoya.[63] Those at Aonogahara hardly understood German, which made communication difficult.[64]

Clearly, as we have seen in the case of Bandō, the personality of the chief warden had a substantial impact on the way the camp was run. The Bandō camp, which arguably had the most liberal-minded chief warden in Colonel Matsue, scored the highest in POW morale and satisfaction. As we have seen, Matsue's policy was to give as much freedom of movement as possible and to encourage manual and intellectual engagement, in order to give a sense of purpose to the prisoners' daily existence. Wells noted that the relationship between the POWs and the Japanese wardens, to a varying degree, tended to be good, apart from the Kurume and Osaka camps. Aonogahara and Ninoshima fared reasonably well, while Nagoya and Narashino fared very well, as did Bandō. Wells concluded that Kurume had problems because of the personality of the chief wardens.[65]

All the problems of excessive discipline at Kurume ultimately came down to the chief warden's interpretation of the regulations on running the camp. Furthermore, over the period of five years of captivity from November 1914 to December 1919, there was a marked evolution in the Japanese management of the camps as the Japanese government responded to reports of substandard conditions of POW accommodation in the first year of their captivity in Japan. To this end, we can regard the process of transferring POWs to the new purpose-built barracks from September 1915 as the Imperial Army's response to the problem of inadequate housing by modernizing accommodation, as well as an attempt at rationalization of the structure of management from thirteen camps to six camps.[66]

In Japan there is a tendency to idealize the Bandō camp in World War I, mainly because the Japanese understanding of the history of captivity is colored predominantly by the harsh experiences of World War II. This study has shown that Bandō was not an exception, nor was it the norm. There was a wide range of captive experiences, from "excellent" in the Bandō and Nagoya camps to "abysmal" in the Kurume camp. Opening up the field of inquiry by situating the Japanese experiences in the wider global mapping of

World War I captivity experiences, we can deepen our understanding of how modern warfare affected different societies around the world. In this intellectual quest, we may find more similarities than differences, as the Japanese case has pointedly shown in this study.

What we have learned about captivity experiences in Japan during World War I is that they resonated with some of the other European experiences that were still strongly embedded in the civilizational discourse, dating back to the late nineteenth century. In order to truly appreciate the value of the Japanese experiences, it is important to pay attention to the fact that Japan was acting as an international standard bearer at the time, as it had set an important precedent with its captivity experiences a decade before in the Russo-Japanese War of 1904–5. This may fly in the face of our conventional understanding of the Japanese Imperial Army and its treatment of the enemy during World War II. By globalizing the study of captivity during World War I, the early twentieth-century experiences of Japan contribute positively to making these experiences more polycentric and diverse, firmly locking Japanese society into discourses on modern societies at war.

Notes

1. Selected passages from a poem written by a captive in the Bandō camp, available as an online resource from the German Institute of Japanese Studies, Tokyo, http://bando.dijtokyo.org/. All references to *Die Barracke* are from this web source. *Die Barracke*, no. 38, 228–31.

2. Shimazu 2009, 168.

3. Rachamimov 2018.

4. Pastor 1983, 113–17.

5. Rachamimov 2002, 123.

6. For the treatment of Russian captives by the Japanese during the Russo-Japanese War, cf. Shimazu 2009, chap. 5.

7. It is worth pointing out that this number paled in comparison to some eighty thousand soldiers of the Imperial Army and Navy captured by the Japanese during the Russo-Japanese War of 1904–5, of whom 72,418 men were held in prisoner camps in Japan. See Kowner 2017, 431–33.

8. These were Kurume, Oita, Fukuoka, Kumamoto, Marugame, Matsuyama, Tokushima, Nagoya, Narashino, Tokyo, Shizuoka, Himeji, and Osaka.

9. Otsuru 2007, 8, 28–29; Hoshi 2006, 52–53. For Otsuru's work in English, see Otsuru 2019. I wish to thank Jan Schmidt for the draft of the chapter for consultation.

10. The pioneer in the study of the Bandō camp is Tomita 1991.

11. The total number of "Austro-Hungarian" captives was 2.77 million. See Rachamimov 2002, 31.

12. Tamura 2010, 47.

13. *Die Barracke*, no. 41, July 7, 1918, 279–81.

14. *Die Barracke*, no. 32, May 5, 1918, 99–100.

15. Steinmetz 2009, 8.

16. Deutsches Institut für Japanstudien, http://bando.dijtokyo.org/?page=theme_detail.php&p_id=38, accessed October 8, 2017.

17. Most of the books held were popular literature, followed by science, war literature, English literature, French literature, newspapers, and classical literature. *Die Barracke*, no. 34, May 9, 1918, 152.

18. Tamura 2010, 56–57.

19. *Die Barracke*, no. 31, April 28, 1918, 81–84.

20. Narutoshi doitsukan n.d., 4–5. I would like to thank the director of the German House (Jpn. Doitsukan) for his assistance during my research trip there.

21. On one's birthday a birthday performance was given under the window of the POW. See Tamura 2010, 62.

22. Tamura 2004, 31, 34, 37; Ido 2007, 59.

23. Tamura 2004, 31, 34, 37.

24. Tamura 2004, 31, 34, 37.

25. Tamura 2004, 31, 34, 37.

26. Tamura 2004, 38–41.

27. Tamura 2010, 50.

28. Feltman 2015, 3.

29. Menjō 2003, 37–41, 47.

30. Otsuru 2007, 89–96.

31. Otsuru 2007, 45–52; see also Kobe daigaku daigakuin jinbunka kenkyu chiiki renkei senta 2016, 12, for the photograph. On Walter Newiger, cf. "Chintao doitsugun furyo gaiyō," http://koki.o.oo7.jp/Kriegsgefangene_seto.htm, accessed July 15, 2019.

32. For information on the Russo-Japanese War and the Japanese treatment of Russian POWs, cf. Shimazu 2009, chap. 5.

33. Otsuru 2007, 30–37.

34. Guenther 2004, 9.

35. Mori 2003, 53–57.

36. Matsuyama furyo shūyōjo 1906, 137.

37. Otsuru 2007, 74–80.

38. Otsuru 2007, 140–43.

39. Takahashi 2003, 23–26.

40. Tamura 2010, 53.

41. Otsuru 2007, 45–52.

42. Shimazu 2014.

43. Otsuru 2007, 38–39.

44. Otsuru 2007, 74–80.

45. "Furyo johokyoku jorei seitei ni kansuru ken." In Nichidoku sensō no sai furyo jōhōkyoku setchi narabi Doitsu koku furyo kankei zassan, dai issatsu, taishō 3-nen 9-gatsu, Archives of the Ministry of Foreign Affairs, Tokyo.

46. *Die Barracke*, no. 42, July 14, 1918, 305–6.

47. Mahon Murphy 2009, 13, 17–18; Takahashi 2003, 4.

48. "Note Verbale," Berlin to the American Embassy in Tokyo, June 30, 1916. In Nichidoku sensō no sai furyo jōhōkyoku setchi narabi Doitsu koku furyo kankei zassan, dai issatsu, taishō 3-nen 9-gatsu, Archives of the Ministry of Foreign Affairs, Tokyo.

49. Army Vice Minister Yamada to Vice Minister Shidehara (Ministry of Foreign Affairs), December 13, 1916, Correspondence 1081. In Nichidoku sensō no sai furyo jōhōkyoku setchi narabi Doitsu koku furyo kankei zassan, dai issatsu, taishō 3-nen 9-gatsu, Archives of the Ministry of Foreign Affairs, Tokyo.

50. Takahashi 2005, 108–10.

51. Takahashi 2003, 3–4, 29–30.

52. Takahashi 2003, 3–4, 29–30.

53. Takahashi 2003, 23–26.

54. Takahashi 2003, 10–12.

55. Takahashi 2003, 23–26.

56. Japanese imperial enthronement ceremonies usually do not take place immediately on accession due to the period of mourning after the demise of the previous emperor. Hence, the Taisho emperor acceded to the Chrysanthemum Throne on July 30, 1912, but his enthronement did not take place until November 10, 1915.

57. Takahashi 2003, 11–13.

58. Takahashi 2003, 11–13.

59. Imai 2012, 31.

60. Murphy 2009, 13.

61. Seto 2011, 92, 98.

62. Takahashi 2003, 23–26.

63. Ikeyama 2012.

64. Otsuru 2007, 140–43.

65. Takahashi 2005, 108–10.

66. The Kumamoto camp was absorbed by Kurume in June 1915; Osaka moved to Ninoshima in February 1917; Tokyo in 1915 and Shizuoka and Oita in 1918 transferred to Narashino. Himeji was transferred to Aonogahara in September 1915; all three camps in Shikoku (Matsuyama, Marugame, Tokushima) merged into Bandō in April 1917, whereas Fukuoka was distributed to Narashino and Kurume in April 1918, http://www.cf.city.hiroshima.jp/rinkai/heiwa/heiwa008/german%20prisoners%20camp.html#2%20nihonkakuchino.

Chapter 9

German Propaganda and the African and Asian Theaters of the War

Mahon Murphy

World War I was a truly global conflict and so was the experience of internment. The outbreak of war in 1914 resulted in an estimated thirty thousand German civilians and soldiers in Germany's African and Asian colonies being uprooted, imprisoned, or deported by British, French, and Japanese forces. The internment of these former colonial settlers posed a logistical challenge as well as a challenge to the structures that underpinned nineteenth-century imperialism. How one imperial power took over another's colonies during war had a serious impact on the notion of a common European "civilizing mission." The outbreak of World War I also posed questions about the future of Germany as an imperial power and the nature of empire in general. For Germany, the extension of the war into extra-European theaters was not a total loss, it provided the German government with ammunition for its propaganda campaign. The objective of this chapter is to investigate how the loss of Germany's colonies and the internment of German colonial settlers integrated with Germany's overall propaganda campaign during the war.

However, getting information was problematic. The *Frankfurter Zeitung* noted that one of the main problems for Germans and Austrians held in captivity or fighting in the theaters outside Europe was the distance from home, the separation from families, and the difficulty of maintaining communications with their home countries.[1] Propaganda relating to the camps was an important part of how those who were not interned could conceptualize the internment experience. With the cutting of telegraphic lines, how did Germany receive information from its former protectorates, and what role did those who were interned or repatriated to Germany play in developing the propaganda narrative? To answer these questions this chapter will rely on data collected from returning prisoners of war and an analysis of how this information was used to influence domestic and international opinion. From World War I the image of the camp as a series of barracks surrounded by watchtowers and barbed wire became engrained in the public imagination. Propaganda itself focused on the local, national, and global aspects of the camp systems of the belligerent powers, helping to create a common, albeit skewed, image of what internment during World War I was like. This chapter will show that the various fronts of that war were interconnected, and even the often referred to "sideshow fronts" of the war formed an important part of the overall fighting of the war.

Atrocities committed by the enemy played the central role in propaganda stories on both sides during the Great War. In order to successfully mobilize people, propaganda had to connect to the values and ideals of its target audience.[2] Propaganda stories during World War I were aimed at belligerents and neutrals alike reaching across the global audience. For example, Allied atrocity propaganda that accused Germany of boiling prisoners of war down to make glue featured in the Japanese architect (and part-time cartoonist) Itō Chūta's graphical collection of the key events of the war.[3] The Allies also sought propaganda in the extra-European theaters of the war. The *African World* in September 1916 carried stories describing British women in German East Africa being sexually mutilated and British men having limbs broken by German soldiers.[4] As with propaganda focused on the fronts in Belgium and France, British stories on the extra-European theater focused on sensational stories of alleged sexual crimes that at times overshadowed real and well-documented violence against civilians.[5] Officials at the British Foreign Office saw no reason to disbelieve these stories although this may have been because they were keen to seize upon them for their propaganda value.[6]

The war outside Europe has been featured more and more in current historiography. World War I created not only a second imperial scramble for Africa but also a scramble in the Pacific as Allied powers mobilized to take over Germany's overseas empire. While Germany's colonies were not financially important, the occasion of war presented an irresistible opportunity for Britain, France, and Japan to take over German territory and preserve their security as well as expand their imperial reach.[7] When war broke out on the Western Front in August 1914, the French, British, and Japanese empires rushed to take over Germany's overseas possessions. German Samoa fell to New Zealand forces in September, quickly followed by Australia's takeover of German New Guinea. From there the Australians worked their way through the German islands until they met their allies, the Japanese, who had been picking off Germany's Pacific possessions north of the equator and the prize port of Tsingtao (Qingdao) on mainland China.

In Africa, the British and French swiftly took over Togo, but German forces held out until early 1916. The British campaign in German South West Africa suffered complications, with many Afrikaners initially refusing to fight for the Union of South Africa Army against fellow whites, before being brought to a successful close in 1915. In German East Africa General Paul von Lettow-Vorbeck's troops maintained a guerrilla campaign until after the armistice in Europe. World War I mobilized millions of Africans as carriers and soldiers and redrew the imperial map; it also created a new global network of concentration camps to house enemies captured in the former German colonies and "enemy aliens" captured on the home fronts.[8] While Germany's empire may not have been financially attractive, the acquisition of German territory was important for each ally in terms of international prestige and cultural mobilization.[9]

It is important to note that internment in concentrated areas had a proposed humanitarian origin and was regulated by international agreements. Camps during World War I were inspected by the International Committee of the Red Cross and were an important aspect of the attempt to "civilize war."[10] Previous historiography has underplayed the role of international law in controlling the conduct of belligerent powers in favor of a focus on the propaganda war that developed during the conflict. It is important to review the role of international law and how it informed this propaganda and how belligerents adhered to it.[11] International law had to compete with war propaganda. Legal norms largely proved powerless against claims of national security, and demonized images of the enemy fueled fears of "enemy aliens," leading to the mass internment of not just military prisoners but also civilians.

The propaganda campaigns attacked "enemies within" in order to maintain morale and provide an opportunity for those on the home fronts to participate in the war, resulting in "enemy aliens" becoming victims of oppressive policies from above and populist xenophobia from below.[12] In Britain, the press portrayed enemy civilians living in Britain as "fifth columnists" who were plotting the destruction of Britain from within. This growing xenophobia led to anti-German riots in East London, as discussed in Asaf Mond's contribution to this volume for example, with the first beginning as early as September 1914.[13] In relation to Germany's colonies, German propaganda focused on the break with the imperial norm of upholding the civilizing mission, which was claimed, incorrectly, to be enshrined in law. This propaganda singled out the Berlin/Congo Act of 1884/85 as having enshrined colonial neutrality in the case of a European war. In reality the conference made no such provision but was put in place to regulate trade and the expansion of European colonialism in Africa.[14]

Propaganda and World War I

The creation of the concentration camp was one of the key innovations in modern population control. It is most closely associated with warfare and the Holocaust, although its origins lie outside Europe. As discussed in Asaf Mond's contribution to this volume, the term "concentration camp" was not widely used by the interning powers. However, in the minds of German colonial settlers in internment in Africa during World War I, the concentration camps from the Second South African War (1899–1902) provided a pertinent point of reference. It was during this conflict that the concept of the camp became imbedded in common imagination, depicted through images of barbed wire, sentry towers, and ordered barracks. It must be noted that these images came mainly from artistic impressions rather than actual photographs; typical of these were the sketches by the French artist Jean Veber.[15] The sketches fed the imagination and helped to provide a distancing of the camps from civilization, much more than photographs ever could. The camps would join other vague images of violence in the colonial world to create a common "European colonial archive" of barbarity in the extra-European world. Germany showed keen interest in the camps, with 358 German-language titles published on the subject of the Boer War and its camps.[16]

Indeed, the Boer War formed part of Germany's propaganda campaigns during World War I, as the German air force dropped images of the camps into British trenches in France in an attempt to expose alleged British hypocrisy in its presentation of itself as a civilized power. It is unclear whether or how this was intended to sway the loyalties of those who received such handbills. By the outbreak of war in August 1914, the internment camp was already a well-used tool in propaganda, and images of camps were already imbedded in the European imagination and connected to images of barbarity in the colonial sphere. In the September 30, 1915, edition of the *Kölnische Zeitung*, a report on an internment camp in Pretoria made a *"tragikomisch"* (tragicomic) comparison of the camp to not just the Boer War but also the brutal conditions experienced by black laborers in diamond mines, with the camp completely surrounded by barbed wire so that nothing could get into or out of it.[17] This comparison of an internment camp to the compounds used to house black workers was also another way to highlight the supposed intentional racial role reversal employed by Britain in its treatment of German soldiers and civilians.

In Germany, Britain's internment of "enemy aliens" represented a key part of the eradication of German control and influence from Britain and areas of British influence. The British propaganda campaign became central, as Panikos Panayi notes, to a state and an empire saturated with Germanophobia.[18] Even before the sinking of the *Lusitania*, the British and colonial press pushed for the internment of Germans as "enemy aliens." The South African newspaper the *Star* in December 1914 ran a sensational article on Germans on parole in Durban. The story centered around accusations of sexual misconduct, the paper alleging that Germans were running amok in the town: two Germans had left a bar and exchanged some remarks that caused the barmaid considerable "excitement." The paper claimed that seven hundred women had signed a petition to have their parole rescinded on the basis of this report.[19] In the immediate post-armistice periods there were further petitions to ban Germans from returning to the Dominion after the war.

The use of propaganda during World War I was primitive by modern standards but developed rapidly as the armies of both sides of the trenches dug deep and the war dragged on beyond its initial winter. Official German propaganda did not focus on the war in its colonies but recycled and deployed common tropes about the barbaric conduct of non-European troops against German forces on the Western Front. In addition to the "Manifesto of the Ninety-Three German Intellectuals" highlighted in Nancy Fitch's contribution to this volume, one of the key documents in this instance was "Employment Contrary to International Law of Coloured Troops on the Western Front upon the European Area of War by England and France" (issued by the German Foreign Ministry in 1915).[20]

It is important to note that this document was originally published in English, as it was intended primarily for an overseas (American) audience. It cataloged a series of accusations against the Entente Powers relating to uncivilized methods of warfare apparently deployed by the French and British empires' non-European forces, which made up a sizable proportion of each army. It focused on the use of machetes by these troops, to signify their backwardness. The machete was not just used as a tool for killing, the document claimed, it was also used to hack trophies such as arms and ears from the bodies of German soldiers. This stereotyped image of the African solider was often repeated in the German press, most notably in the crude caricatures in the satirical magazine *Kladderadatsch*. The cover of the July 1916 edition depicted an African soldier, barefoot and savage, with a human skull strung around his neck, above the caption "The Civilizing of Europe."[21]

It is also important to note, although this chapter does not have space for discussion, Germany's own propaganda revolving around the concept of the German *Schutztruppe* or *Askari* soldier fighting in Africa, who was loyal to the German empire until death. The image of the well-trained and drilled German African troops served as contrast to that of the violent and out-of-control troops deployed by France and Britain on the Western Front. The enemy did not share this image of course. Captain A. J. Molloy, a member of the 5th South African Infantry fighting in German East Africa, noted that the African soldier was "a brute and does not hesitate to mutilate and kill all wounded or prisoners."[22] While it was impossible for Germany to deploy colonial troops on the Western Front, it could still make the claim that it would not deploy its colonial troops to Europe. This was a propaganda trope that gained particular prominence in Germany during the interwar years.[23]

Indeed, it was not just non-European troops who were accused of barbaric practices. Germany had chosen to attack France by invading Belgium through the Schlieffen Plan (which had been modified to refrain from attacking through the Netherlands). However, the German army met unexpected resistance from the Belgians, and the German high command sought a way of explaining this. German military leaders made direct comparisons between the Belgian forces, who were not recognized as such but rather as *Franc-tireurs* (civilian irregular soldiers or guerrillas), and the Herero of South West Africa, whom Germany had starved to death a decade previously in what have sometimes been described as concentration camps, such as the infamous camp called "Shark Island" off the coast of Lüderitz in German South West Africa.[24] Just like the Herero, the Belgians were said to be behaving outside the established rules of warfare, and the German army were justified in their reprisals against them. It is difficult to establish causal relations between Germany's treatment of the Herero and the Belgians, but as John Horne and Alan Kramer argue, the experience of colonial warfare gave German politicians greater freedom for experimentation in military and political conduct. Crucially, it also lowered the threshold for violence against European civilians during World War I.[25] In Entente reports on these reprisals, the "European Colonial Archive" was deployed to equate the Germans with barbaric behavior, such as the rape of women, the execution of civilians, and the hacking off of limbs of Belgian children. Mutilation, which had been synonymous with Belgian conduct in the Belgian Congo before the war, was now used to show the Belgians as the victims.

World War I marked a turning point in the development of modern propaganda: the need to mobilize opinion not only at home but also abroad in neutral countries became an essential weapon in the national arsenal.[26] Propaganda based on German abuses in Belgium found a receptive audience across the globe, and it was clear that Germany's behavior after the violation of Belgian neutrality was not going to win it any favor among neutral countries. Therefore, the German government sought to create its own counter-propaganda of which the document "Employment Contrary to European Law of Coloured Troops on the Western Front" was a spearhead. However, these instances related to atrocities on the battlefield and did not receive the response that the German government had hoped, although it found an audience in areas of the United States with large German populations.

Another arm of this propaganda was the publishing of stories of German civilians who had been mistreated at the hands of European and extra-European soldiers. Material for this could only be sought in occupied German territory, that is, Germany's overseas colonies of Togo, Cameroon, German South West Africa, German East Africa, Qingdao, New Guinea, Samoa, and the Pacific islands under German protectorates. The *Deutsche Kolonialgesellschaft* (the German Colonial Society) was the natural choice to be the leader of this propaganda drive, which was careful to make clear the comparison between the war that Germany was fighting on the Western Front and the simultaneous war in the colonial sphere as one where the Entente Powers not only dared to arm non-European troops to fight against Germans in Europe, they were also deploying "colored" troops to fight against "whites" in the colonies and elsewhere, thus treating "the native population in Africa and elsewhere to the spectacle of white i.e. German, men and women being subjected to the utmost degradation."[27]

The propaganda narrative in Germany was straightforward: by turning against Germany in Africa, the Entente Powers had, according to this narrative, turned their backs on the collective Christian civilizing mission. This fear was present among white settlers in the colonies regardless of nationality. In July 1915 the *Berliner Illustrierte Zeitung* published a report on the treatment of German prisoners of war in French West Africa, claiming that the prisoners were being treated worse than common criminals in a murderous climate and forced to engage in hard labor. Even worse, the prisoners were being guarded and mistreated by African guards. The accompanying sketch depicted these themes, the white prisoners holding pickaxes and one man collapsed from heat under the watch of black guards: The prisoners were "treated worse than common criminals and toiled in the murderous sun and mistreated by blacks."[28]

A similar report from the *Frankfurter Zeitung* noted that the prisoners had to build their own huts and were not provided with mosquito nets. German newspapers also accused the French authorities of allowing medieval-style torture to be used on prisoners. The *Deutsche Kolonialzeitung* from 1917 published sketches of the thumbscrews supposedly put on prisoners by black guards.[29] Joseph Carl Postel, a prisoner captured from Cameroon, compiled a report intended for publication on his experience in captivity, titled " 'The White Man's Grave." He objected strongly to having been guarded by black guards from the West Indies (Jamaica) but noted that they could at least be bribed. This is a rare account of positive interactions between guard and prisoner. However, this understanding soon came to an end after a guard shot one prisoner for trying to negotiate a bribe.[30]

Propaganda relating to the mistreatment of German prisoners of war and civilian internees in the former German colonies did not have the impact hoped for by those who had created it, but it highlighted an important aspect of World War I, the connections between the various fronts. The battles in the extra-European fronts of the war were not sideshows, as often described. They were certainly not sideshows to those fighting them, and they played important military roles, as well as freeing up communications and providing material for the eventual victors. From a propaganda perspective, footage of Britain's capture of Jerusalem in December 1917 was arguably more important than any recordings of fighting on the Somme. The short film "General Allenby's in Jerusalem' proved to be much more of a hit with audiences in India, the Middle East, and even China than any of the screenings of the film *The Battle of the Somme*.[31] In Germany the surrender of General Paul von Lettow-Vorbeck's troops in East Africa two weeks after the armistice in Europe would provide the usual interwar narrative of the indomitable German fighting spirit.[32] Germans captured in the former German colonies during the war would also find an audience for their propaganda narrative in postwar publications relating to the "Black Shame on the Rhine," the posting of "Senegalese" troops in Germany by the French forces occupying the Rhineland. [33]

The image in German propaganda of violence conducted by colonial troops on the Western Front stemmed from pre–World War I colonial war zones. So too did the images of atrocities committed by the Germans in occupied France and Belgium, some of which focused on mutilation, among several other strands of Allied propaganda. Allegations that African and Indian soldiers engaged in brutal practices, such as mistreating or killing prisoners of war, hunting for "trophies," and using unlawful weapons became the principal accusation in German propaganda.[34] This propaganda was not just limited to colonial troops on the Western Front; the image of the colonial soldier acting outside the accepted norms of "civilized warfare" also extended to the extra-European theaters.

Hermann Röseler, a prisoner of war from the East African theater, recounted the treatment of his fellow prisoners by black guards during their transport to Egypt from internment. His account is colored with images of colonial violence no doubt intended to stir the emotions of the reader. He wrote of a wounded prisoner, a missionary, being shot out of hand by a black soldier, his corpse left to be devoured by hyenas. In some cases both sides had bayoneted or shot wounded prisoners to spare them from the worse fate of being mauled to death by animals, but Röseler claimed that cannibals had eaten some of the killed and wounded.[35] Richard Meinertzhagen, who served as chief of British military intelligence for the East Africa theater between 1915 and 1916, mentions writing propaganda articles on the brutality of warfare in the African theater to increase recruitment in Britain.[36] Although incidents of cruelty by colonial troops were isolated, they could be exaggerated to provide the basis for propaganda myths published in Europe. (Meinertzhagen was an expert at this.) Prisoners, such as Röseler, returning from the colonies wrote about their experiences of the war in the extra-European theater through these images of colonial violence.[37]

It is important to note that while the main strand of propaganda portrayed a negative image of the enemy's colonial troops, there were exceptions. For example, in an article on the treatment of internees, the *Frankfurter Zeitung* noted with surprise that in Lagos internees were treated well and not all those taking care of internees were "barbarians."[38] However, these accounts remained an exception. More typical was a letter from Oberleutant Engelbrechen, held at camp Mbanga-Mujuka in Cameroon, who noted: "We are fighting amongst beasts, our soldiers as well as the British and the negro beasts of the country make use of the war to rob and maltreat. The most difficult piece of work will be after the war. This war called up by the British not only destroys all European values here, but stirs up the whole infamous negro soul."[39] There was still a question of how to gain information from the colonies for use in the propaganda campaign.

Gathering Information for the Propaganda War

One of the key strategic objectives of the Allied forces that took over Germany's overseas possessions was to disable wireless communications. Radio transmitters at Kamina, Togo, and German New Guinea were targeted at the beginning of the war, and Germany quickly lost its ability to independently contact its colonies and its overseas navy. This in turn made it difficult to receive reliable information on the condition of prisoners of war and civilian internees. Communication with Europe from the internment camps of the extra-European theater was additionally restricted through the difficulties in sending letters over long distances during wartime, limits on the frequency and length of prisoner letters, censorship, and reprisal punishments. The inability to communicate effectively increased prisoners' isolation and their fear of being forgotten in Germany.

While interned some prisoners attempted to wage their own propaganda war among the local population to disrupt their captors. One such example is Reverend Jakob Hofmeister, interned in Cameroon. Hofmeister was a missionary and a German reservist who had quickly rallied around the German flag to defend Cameroon. During a brief spell in captivity (he did not state exactly how long), he hatched a plot to sow fear into the British over the future administration of the colony. Fluent in the local languages, he wrote letters to the converts at his mission base, encouraging, even threatening, them not to side with the British but to remain loyal to Germany. At this stage of the war, a British victory was certainly not assured, and many Cameroonians remained fighting with the Germans in the hopes of a German victory. However, Hofmeister's letters were intended to be captured by the British, which they duly were. As a result, the British took measures to prevent agitation by German internees in the colonies (one of which was to deport Hofmeister to Germany), feeling it unwise to allow the spread of inflammatory anti-British propaganda.[40]

In French camps in Morocco, German and Austrian prisoners on regular exercise duty outside the camp attempted to appeal to the "Senegalese" troops stationed to guard them.[41] They expressed solidarity and attempted to impress on the guards the idea that France was only using black troops as "cannon fodder" on the trenches in Europe.[42] Former prisoners held in Morocco claimed that the reason they had been sent there by the French was so that they could be used as a kind of physical propaganda with which the French could impress on the locals the superiority of the French industry over the German. The display of defeated German troops as POWs was intended to hammer home this message.[43] In the Moroccan and Algerian cases we see prisoners being taken from the Western Front to the colonies, creating a home front in North Africa where local anger was taken out on German prisoners of war, such as throwing stones on prisoners as they passed under bridges on their way to the camps.[44]

In India British authorities took measures to cut communication between prisoners and the local population for fear of the potential for agitation. In the main internment camp in India, Ahmednagar, facilities were provided for the teaching of English, French, and other European languages in the camp, but none were provided for Turkish, Arabic, Persian, or other Asian languages. The ban on the study of certain languages was aimed at making escape more difficult, but more importantly, to prevent German prisoners from agitating against the Crown, as in the case of Hofmeister. This fear of German agitation was far from illusory. The Allies knew that Germany had set up special camps for the recruitment of would-be Indian agitators and spies among prisoners of war captured on the Western Front.[45] The Berlin India Committee chaired by Virendranath Chattopadhyaya, established by the Ghadar Party and financed by the German Foreign Office, shortly after the outbreak of war recruited prominent Indian activists in Europe and the United States with the express goal of creating unrest in the subcontinent and beyond. In February 1915 the Singapore Mutiny broke out, resulting in Britain's brutal suppression of the rebellion of the Indian Army's 5th Light Infantry. While the mutineers targeted the prison camp in Tanglin to free German prisoners of war, only a few took the opportunity to make good their escape during the chaos. Julius Lauterbach, an officer from the SMS *Emden* was able to reach Germany and publish his memoirs in 1917.[46] The mutiny ended with 202 court-martials, including forty-three death sentences.[47] The Singapore Mutiny was a significant event in Britain's relationship with its colonies.

Repatriated prisoners of war and civilian internees provided a reliable source of information for the German government in its attempt to create a propaganda campaign from the war in the colonies. In an effort to gather intelligence, the German government organized a questionnaire for returning civilian internees from Togo and Cameroon, who had been briefly interned in 1915. Questionnaires for returning internees was standard practice in most belligerent states, as they wished to compile such information as point of capture, address in home country, and assets. The questions asked, however, show the interest the government had in the way captivity created racial inversion in the colonies—in particular, the interest in whites being mistreated by blacks. Of the twenty-two questions, four made explicit reference to skin color. The final question wished to clarify whether rumors were true that Britain was offering a bounty to African troops on Germans captured in Africa.[48]

This had been a constant accusation by German troops and would make for good propaganda if proven. However, the results proved disappointing.

Responses to the question were usually left blank or answered in terms of hearsay, as in this example from Albert Rexter, a priest in Cameroon: "I have heard rumors of the capture and killing of German soldiers for a bounty but I do not have direct evidence of such." Gustav Schwab, another missionary from Cameroon, had heard through a source of the murder of Arms and Lehning, two German businessmen who were killed in Spanish Guinea, and a British offer of bounties, which were paid upon the presentation of ears.[49] The idea of mutilation as proof that one has carried out orders had its roots in King Leopold's Congo and was well documented in prewar Europe.

The murder of Arms and Lehning caused an outrage. The bodies of the two men were discovered in Ayamiken in Spanish Guinea, south of the Cameroon border. The governor of the colony, Ángel Barrera y Luyando, launched an investigation into the murders. Barrera had been markedly pro-German even before the war, and Karl Ebermaier, the German governor of Cameroon, felt that Barrera could be paid off; they had had good relations before the war, and reports from Britain were suspicious of Barrera's motives.[50] The colony's periodical, *La Guinea Espanola*, noted after Germany's defeat in Cameroon that a "great époque just ended in the Cameroons with tenacity and frigid calculation on the part of one (Britain and France), with gallantry and like heroes on the part of the other (Germany)."[51] Although Spanish Guinea had only a small European population, *La Guinea Espanola* was also published in Spain itself, which had a strong pro-German press. Though a neutral country Spain was known to have many pro-Germans among its military, but there is no evidence to suggest that the Spanish investigation was falsified in any way.[52] The outrage at the murder lay in the fact that the two bodies had been mutilated, the left hand and both ears of each having been severed. The method of mutilation further cast doubt on local involvement, as Barrera claimed that, had it been locals they would more than likely have removed the heart rather than limbs.[53]

A Spanish report to the British Foreign Office in January 1916 accused a party of "five natives" under the command of a British officer, Lieutenant Law, of the murders. Law had been in charge of a vessel harbored at the small island of Dipikar in the Campo River, dividing the two colonies, which was monitoring Germans crossing the Campo River from Cameroon into neutral Spanish Guinea. Law was accused of ordering the "natives" to follow the Germans into Spanish territory to seize documents. Responsibility was judged to lie with Lieutenant Law. Barrera requested that the naval officer in charge be reprimanded for neglect of his duties and that the soldiers responsible for the murders be handed over to the Spanish authorities for trial. In response, the British launched an investigation into the incident.

Although unwilling to hand over British soldiers to Spain, Britain promised a thorough investigation and punishment of those responsible. Lieutenant Law was ordered to write up a report. Law denied that any reward had been offered to the patrol. They had been ordered merely to bring in any weapons, ammunition, and books or diaries that they could capture. The party returning to him reported that "they had killed the European Germans and 4 natives, producing some ears to prove they had done so."[54] No mention was made of the severed hands, and the soldiers responsible were said to be detained elsewhere.

The murders fulfilled European preconceptions of colonial brutality, with its echoes of mutilation in King Leopold's Congo. While I have not found any explicit reference to Arms and Lehning in the German press, many similar horror stories were reported there, often written by returning prisoners, and it can be said with some confidence that the murders inspired other stories that did appear in German newspapers relating to murder and mutilation. An article entitled "England's Price for Assassins" in the *Weser Zeitung* in February 1915 claimed that two Germans from the ship *Kamerun*, had been murdered for a fifty-shilling bounty. This article, along with similar newspaper reports and petitions, were collected by the British government and translated into English for rebuttal in a white paper titled "Alleged Ill-Treatment of German Subjects Captured in the Cameroons." In this folio British complicity in "native" attacks on Germans was often highlighted, as in the example of one German who was slashed across the head with a machete in the train station at Duala in front of white British soldiers. Further articles claimed that German workmen were attacked, robbed, murdered, and their hands brought to the British authorities to be exchanged for money.[55] These claims were dismissed by the British, but with the evidence from the murder case in Spanish Guinea, they appear to have at least some basis in reality.

For Germans in the colonies, extending the war to Africa only served to undermine the basis of European rule and destroy the positive example of moral values that they believed had been set by the whites, values that would be completely impossible to recreate. A. Haberlein detailed this alleged breakdown in colonial social structures in his memoirs: "Black gangs and black soldiers brutally raped white women. They took white women from their beds, tied them, beat them and threw them on the ground."[56] Sexual violence appears in narratives on the European fronts, and fear of miscegenation was especially strong on the Eastern Front, with German soldiers assuming that Russian soldiers would commit rape if they occupied German territory.[57] The advent of war in the colonies, the narrative argued, was against the interest of all whites, whose duty it was to maintain peace among each other and to keep control of the Africans. The fear of the white settler was a dual one and was deployed in German propaganda. First, the spectacle of Europeans fighting one another in the colonial sphere would reduce their status in the colonies. Second, arming black soldiers to fight and kill Europeans would forfeit white racial supremacy and radically alter the imperial balance of power.[58]

German-language missionary publications on the war focused on the complaint that Britain had extended the conflict outside Europe, thus irreversibly damaging the European Christian mission in Africa. They claimed that with the internment or expulsion of German missionaries Britain had halted the civilizing mission and, in some cases, even reversed it. There were accusations that some previous converts had reverted to witchcraft. For example, Otto Wienecke, a prominent member of the Basel mission in Cameroon, delivered a lengthy list of complaints to the British Foreign Office, focusing on the negative effects that ill treatment of German captives had had on the local population. The main thrust of Wienecke's argument was that the placing of prisoners under black guards was completely unacceptable in terms of white dignity and the overall European civilizing mission in Africa.[59] Other members of the Basel mission supported Wienecke's complaints. The mission's director, Dr. Theodor Oehler, argued that Britain had purposely "carried the war into the colonies, and so made a world war out of the war of nations. England has turned the war into a fight against the guiltless and women. They have been made prisoner, drafted away and treated with revolting brutality." He claimed that missionaries and civilians in Duala, Cameroon, were rounded up and kept for twenty-four hours under the watch of black soldiers who treated the captives roughly. Britain's extension of the war into Africa had torn families asunder, all with the goal of plundering German property.[60] For these missionaries, the extension of the war to Africa had turned a war of nations into a world war and irreparably altered the foundations of the imperial system.

Ultimately, during the war the propaganda campaign involving the maltreatment of German colonial settlers never gained traction and did not have a coherent structure. Domestically, the German audience was more interested in the battles on the Western and Eastern Fronts; the perceived hardships of those in Africa and Asia paled in comparison to the hardships on the home front as Germany ran short of supplies. The reporting and sensationalism of atrocity stories did lead to some policy changes on the ground. The British cessation of incentives for levies in May 1915 was a direct result of this propaganda and the fear of misinterpretation in Europe with ensuing negative consequences for Britons held in German captivity.[61] Through attempts to equate the barbarity of the war in the colonies with that on the Western Front, repatriated German colonial settlers sought to integrate themselves into the German narrative of the war. The war in the colonies did, to some extent, stir the imagination of the metropole with its references to mutilation, torture, and the ill treatment of white women by black soldiers.

However, in the postwar period the narrative of maltreatment in the colonies did gain a more receptive audience. The experience of World War I captivity in Africa became directly linked to "black shame on the Rhine" propaganda related to the stationing of French African troops in the occupied Rhineland. In 1920 forty-two thousand French colonial troops were stationed on the occupied Rhine.[62] They were presented in the German media as being dangerous and primitive, with uncontrollable sexual instincts. Campaigners constantly pushed the concern that the use of black troops to watch a "white nation" would seriously undermine and threaten the ideology of white domination.[63] A former prisoner of war held in Morocco, Max Militzer, complained in his memoirs of having being interned for eight days in a black prison, "Negergefängnis," for having taking a break from his work.[64] Punishments such as these, he felt, were calculated to lower the image of Germany in the colonial world. Those Germans who had experienced internment under the watch of black guards in Africa now had a receptive audience for their stories, and their racially colored memoirs, magazine and newspaper articles proved popular. In this period stories particularly relating to the treatment of prisoners in French West Africa connected to the "black shame" propaganda and would remain part of the narrative of colonial irredentism in Germany until the 1940s.

The image of the war in Africa as an eccentric sideshow has been challenged by recent scholarship as the extra-European fronts of the war are woven into the overall narrative of a global war. Britain saw victory in extra-European theaters as essential to the survival of the empire and essential to maintaining the passage to India through possession of Mesopotamia, Palestine, and German East Africa.[65] Contemporary German colonialists saw the loss of their colonies as a radical shift in the balance of power that was carried out through violence. This violence, either real or imagined, was the determining factor through which they described their experience of capture and the loss of their plantations. German writers hoped that reports of and publications about mutilations of Germans in the colonies would connect with a European audience well versed on colonial violence. The notion of a common western "colonial archive" as conceptualized by historians can be applied to propaganda on the treatment of German prisoners of war and civilian internees in the colonies: clearly these activated common ideas of the "colonial."[66]

The war had overturned conventional ideas of racial solidarity. A case in point is an article written by K. Takahashi and published in the *Japan Times* in December 1918. It noted that, on the one hand, the white races had been at war with each other, and on the other, the British brought Indians to fight in Europe, as did the French with Africans and South East Asians. Japan was allied to Britain, and Turkey to Germany and Austria-Hungary.[67] Takahashi's prediction that the spirit of comradeship would displace racial prejudice was soon shown to be optimistic. Germany's portrayal of Britain as reneging on the European civilizing mission through its treatment of German colonial settlers fit with such ideas and triggered older images of colonial barbarity that internees sought to exploit in their reports. The post-war "black shame on the Rhine" propaganda highlighted how clear racial divisions remained, even gaining support from British liberals such as E. D. Morel, who campaigned against King Leopold's abuses in the Belgian Congo.[68] In South Africa there were fears that the development of Garveyism in the United States would lead to airplanes loaded with black Americans who would arrive preaching universal black brotherhood to supplant the Europeans living there.[69] This led to a massacre of members of the Independent Church of Israel, a millennialist group that believed black Americans were coming to their aid.[70] Indeed, Germany had lost its overseas colonies but not the racist and imperialist sensibilities that emerged alongside them.[71]

Notes

1. Bundesarchiv Lichterfelede (BA), R67/251, *Frankfurter Zeitung*, April 11, 1915.
2. Paddock, 2014, 9.
3. Itō 1920.
4. National Archives, Kew, London (thereafter, NA) FO 383/204, *African World*, September 1916.
5. Kramer, Alan, 2007, 245.
6. NA, FO 383/204 249459, December 11, 1916.
7. Nasson 2014, 131.
8. For the creation of the global camp network, see Murphy 2017.
9. Fogarty 2014, 115.
10. Kurosawa 2013, 7.
11. Hull 2014, 12.
12. Bauerkämper 2018, 64.
13. NA, HO 45/10944 257142 Anti-German Riots in London, September 17, 1914.
14. For full text of the "General Act of the Berlin Conference on West Africa," see https://www.thoughtco.com/general-act-of-the-berlin-conference-4070667, last accessed November 8, 2019.

15. Forth 2017, 217.
16. Forth 2017, 214.
17. BA, R67 / 1365, *Kölnische Zeitung*, September 30, 1915.
18. Panayi 2005, 17.
19. NA, FO383 / 103 101510, *Star*, December 15, 1915.
20. "Employment Contrary to International Law of Coloured Troops on the Western Front upon the European Area of War by England and France" (Auswärtiges Amt, Berlin, 1915).
21. *Kladderadatsch*, July 23, 1916.
22. Jeffries 2015, 225.
23. For this discussion, see Moyd 2014, 208–9.
24. Wachsmann 2015, 6.
25. Horne and Kramer 2001, 169.
26. Sanders and Taylor 1982, 11.
27. BA, R8023 / 88, A Protest of the German Colonial Society of Berlin, October 1917.
28. The prisoners were *"schlimmer als gemeine verbrecher behandelt wurden in die mördischen klima hart arbeiten und von schwarzen Aussehern misbehandelt."* BA, R67 / 24, Dahomey, *Berliner Illustrierte Zeitung* April 4, 1915.
29. "Ein Dokument des französischen Sadismus," *Deutsche Kolonialzeitung*, February 20, 1917.
30. NA, FO 381 / 81, Joseph Carl Postel, "The White Man's Grave" (unpublished), 37.
31. See McKernan 2006.
32. For his memoirs, see Lettow-Vorbeck 1920.
33. Most French African troops were erroneously referred to as Senegalese, regardless of their true origin.
34. "Employment Contrary to International Law of Coloured Troops on the Western Front upon the European Area of War by England and France," 1.
35. Röseler, 1931, 105.
36. Samson 2013, 145–46.
37. For Richard Meinertzhagen, see Garfield 2011.
38. BA, R67 / 251, *Frankfurter Zeitung*, April 11, 1915.
39. NA, WO 1581 / 552, Engelbrechen to Gaisser, October 24, 1914.
40. BA, R1001 / 3947, Jakob Hofmeister, "Bericht über meine Dienstleitung in Kamerun," June 6, 1916.
41. Although the troops were officially referred to as Senegalese, they hailed from various parts of French Africa.
42. Militzer 1931, 94.
43. Militzer 1931, 102.
44. BA 67 / 181, Algeria Letter from POW "Jakob" to his wife, "Marie," May 20, 1916.
45. Steuer 2014, 172.
46. Lauterbach 1917.
47. For an account of the mutiny, see Streets-Salter 2017.
48. BA 1001 / 3946, *Krieg in Kamerun 1914–1918*.

49. BA 1001/3946, *Krieg in Kamerun 1914–1918*.

50. NA, ADM 116/1494, Germans Interned at Fernando Po. Proceedings of SNO West Coast of Africa.

51. NA, FO 383/213, *La Guinea Espanola*, February 25, 1916.

52. Romero Salvadó 1999.

53. NA, WO 158/25, Extracts from reports on the killing of Messrs. Arms and Lehning, March 13, 1915.

54. NA, WO 158/25, Extracts from reports on the killing of Messrs. Arms and Lehning, March 13, 1915.

55. Imperial War Museum (IWM) [K] 6248, Correspondence Relative to the Alleged Ill Treatment of German Subjects Captured in the Cameroons, November 1915.

56. BA, R1001/3794, A. Haberlein, "Erlebnisse in Kamerun in den Kriegsjahren 1914/1915," August 27, 1915.

57. Kramer, Alan, 2007, 244.

58. Strachan 2001, 496.

59. IWM [K] 6248, Correspondence Relative to the Alleged Ill Treatment of German Subjects.

60. IWM [K] 6248, Correspondence Relative to the Alleged Ill Treatment of German Subjects.

61. NA, WO 158/525, Dobbel to Harcourt, May 1, 1915.

62. Ogawa 2015, 313.

63. Wigger 2010, 35.

64. Militzer 1931, 98.

65. Stevenson 2017, 338.

66. Das 2011, 18.

67. Lake and Reynolds 2008, 282.

68. Morel 1920.

69. Nasson 2014, 151.

70. Bonner 2011, 281.

71. Hoesen 2014, 303.

Part III

Interwar Repercussions and Beyond

CHAPTER 10

Internment after the War's End

"Humanitarian Camps" in the POW Repatriation Process, 1918–1923

Hazuki Tate

The repatriation of prisoners of war at the end of the Great War was slow and complex. To be sure, it was not a simple physical displacement to their homelands and to the place where they had been before the war for the simple reason that the world's external circumstances had changed significantly during their captivity.[1] Consequently, even after the war ended POWs often endured further internment and a lengthy transport before reaching their final destination. The return of the POWs was meant to provide them with, and at times even impose on some of them, a new place in the postwar world. In this respect, the repatriation of POWs represented both a direct consequence of the Great War, which had just ended, and one of the issues of a new international order under construction with new actors. With this in mind, the present chapter analyzes the patterns of POW movements and internments on the Eastern Front immediately after the war. This is done in order to both facilitate the examination of the purpose and significance of internment as well as the link between the POWs' repatriation and the experiences of displaced persons in the larger context of the war during this period. This examination is guided by a number of questions, such as the identity of those who organized and controlled the POW's repatriation process and the grounds they used for determining and legitimizing their intervention on the POWs' behalf.

The return of the five million POWs incarcerated on the Eastern Front began earlier than the return of those on the Western Front due to the March 1918 Treaty of Brest-Litovsk.[2] Nevertheless, it ended much later, in 1923, as a result of both the larger number of POWs held on this front as well as the more complicated postwar situation in Eastern Europe and Russia. As a whole, that repatriation process can be divided into three successive periods. The first period was between the conclusion of the Treaty of Brest-Litovsk and the November 1918 armistice. The second period was when the Allied countries intensified their interference in the repatriation of Russian POWs alongside their intervention in the Russian civil war. Until early 1920 the Western great powers not only attempted to regulate the POWs' movements but also to control them in accordance with international security concerns. Finally, the third period lasted from the League of Nations' (LoN) participation in the repatriation program to 1923. During this phase, such humanitarian actors as the Geneva-based International Committee of the Red Cross (ICRC) operated the POW camps directly in order to address the needs of a new type of internment that emerged during the postwar era.

The ICRC had actively participated in the POW issue during the war. For example, it organized the Agence internationale des prisonniers de guerre for the purposes of collecting POW information for their families, inspecting the prisoners' camps, and making combatant countries conclude bilateral agreements for the better treatment of prisoners. Accordingly, the ICRC perceived helping their repatriation at the end of the war as an extension of these activities during the conflict. At the same time, the aftermath of the war was a crucial moment for the organization's future as it experienced a sort of identity crisis despite having been awarded the Nobel Prize for peace in 1917 due to the prospect of ending its mission by ending war. Being involved in the POW repatriation question thus provided the ICRC with an opportunity to reorganize its activities in the new postwar circumstances by using its experience in caring for POWs during the war.

By focusing on the return of the POWs on the Eastern Front and the ICRC's role in this process, the present chapter further stresses the role of modernization and internationalization of humanitarianism during the Great War and its aftermath.[3] In addition, it analyzes the ways in which POWs were identified in a postwar international order based on nation states, an order that gave rise to many paradoxes, as Eastern European POWs often possessed multiple identities or expressed indifference to national identities, as recent studies have pointed out.[4] Structurally speaking, the present chapter is made up of three parts. The first examines how the POW issue was dealt with by various actors in the postwar circumstances and how it became a political problem. The second part, in turn, traces the movement and internment of Russian POWs in Germany and the adjoining countries in order to investigate their changing significance and status. Finally, the third part examines the transit camps organized and managed by the ICRC, which were labeled as "humanitarian" and "international," in order to understand how the POW repatriation issue had changed by the end of the process.

Political and Military Significance of POWs in the Postwar Era

The Treaty of Brest-Litovsk in March 1918 could not provide for a smooth and successful repatriation of POWs between Russia and the Central Powers, even though article 17 in the agreement, supplementary to the treaty, stipulated the exchange of prisoners "with the greatest possible speed." The rhythm of transporting POWs was varied according to the geographical and political conditions of each captivity. In Russia, the tsarist authorities held some 2.5 million POWs belonging to the Central Powers. The authorities sought to control their prisoners by dividing them according to nationalities. The Germans, Austrians, Hungarians, and Turks were mostly sent to Turkestan or Siberia to work in mines or rail construction sites, while the Slav prisoners, such as the Poles, Czechs, Slovaks, and Serbians, remained in European Russia, although economic necessities occasionally offset these considerations.[5] In the wake of the Treaty of Brest-Litovsk, one million POWs, especially those held in European Russia, were repatriated throughout 1918 despite transportation problems and other difficulties associated with the outbreak of the civil war; most of the POWs held in Siberia and in Central Asia were unable to take advantage of this opportunity.[6]

On the other side of the Eastern Front, in the territories belonging the Austro-Hungarian empire, there were some 1.2 million Russians.[7] Given the diplomatic frictions between Vienna and Moscow as well as the monarchy's lack of financial and material capacity, any repatriations through official channels were extremely delayed. In fact, only a small portion of the prisoners had been returned to their homeland by October 1918. Disorder was even more prominent after the collapse of the Dual Monarchy since many Russian POWs now left the camps freely, without waiting to be officially repatriated. In the tumultuous conditions of postwar Eastern and Central Europe, many of these former prisoners wandered throughout the dissolved monarchy's vast territory without reaching the Russian frontier. As for Germany, since combat was still taking place on the Western Front, the repatriation of POWs on the Eastern Front continued to be considered a wartime issue. The kaiser's government was extremely reluctant to repatriate the 1.5 million

Russian POWs under its control since they were used as workers in various sectors in order to sustain the German war economy. In these circumstances, only 140,000 prisoners, the majority of whom were disabled or terminally ill, were sent back to Russia.[8]

After the November 1918 armistice, the new German republic decided to repatriate the Russian POWs in its territory, which led to the quick transport of 600,000 prisoners to Russia during the winter of 1918–1919.[9] At the time, the ICRC delegates dispatched to Germany observed the harsh conditions of the Russian POWs' internment and transport when compared to the Allied POWs, whose repatriation was almost complete by the end of January 1919. In particular, the ICRC reported that some camps in the eastern border regions had already been abandoned, and that no authorities were aiding the POWs or organizing their border crossings.[10] Many prisoners thus lacked any means of continuing their journeys, and some were left to die in this vulnerable situation. On the other hand, the Russian POWs who remained in the camps located in the interior regions of Germany were no better off. With the Spanish flu ravaging Germany and the Allied economic blockage still in force, these POWs were among the first to succumb to contagious diseases and food shortages. According to camp inspectors, the "Russians died like flies," since "no one wanted to take care of them."[11]

Furthermore, the outbreak of the German revolution in November 1918 and its spread made many camps uncontrollable and unruly.[12] Accordingly, the large number of nonrepatriated prisoners inevitably raised significant concerns about the peace process in these areas and in Europe in general. In early 1919, more than 650,000 Russian POWs remained in German territory, a fact that caught the attention of the Allied countries, as Ferdinand Foch, commander-in-chief of the Allied armies, noted "It is for the Entente Powers a duty of humanity to protect [the] livelihoods of soldiers who were fighting with us. It is also in our interest to enable them to avoid Bolshevik influence."[13] Though humanitarian concerns regarding the prisoners' desperate situations were certainly an important motivation,[14] the Allies were especially concerned that Russian POWs might be used to reinforce the anti-Allied force under the Bolshevik army. With this in mind, the Allies chose to restrict POW repatriation from Germany to Russia.

This particular decision was inserted as an official and legally justified condition to the prolonged armistice of January 16, 1919.[15] The Inter-Allied Control Commission (IACC) was also established in Berlin in order to organize the supply and repatriation of the Russian POWs based on the principle that the "Allied Governments reserve the right to adjust their repatriation to the particular region that they judge to be the most stable." [16] In this regard, it is not surprising that the "stable" region for the Allies meant areas under non-Bolshevik control, such as southern Russia, which was controlled by General Anton Denikin.[17] This policy led to strong opposition from both the German government as well as the Bolshevik authorities, who considered this position to be an intervention in their internal affairs. Furthermore, the Germans did not want to prolong the Russian POWs' detention in their territory, whereas the Bolshevik government criticized the adopted policy as an "absolutely unspeakable violation of the most elementary rights."[18] Meanwhile, the Russian POWs were disappointed, since they had been politically manipulated by both their imprisoners and their supposed liberators.[19]

The repatriation of Russian POWs was rapidly politicized under postwar circumstances. What should have been a technical military operation without political interference, as stipulated in article 20 of the Hague Convention, the first international law mentioning the conditions of POWs in 1899, and revised in 1907, turned into a long and muddled process.[20] In order to supervise this situation, the POW camps in Germany were placed under the control of the Allied armies. Surveillance and food distribution were handled by IACC officers (approximately eight hundred in number) and by the workers of the American and British Red Cross Societies respectively. In order to provide moral support to the internees, the IACC also decided to dispatch Russian officers to the camps. The food stocks that remained after the departure of the POWs from other nationalities were also distributed to the Russians in the camps. After their depletion, it was the Supreme Economic Council, the Allied organ founded in February 1919, that dealt with the POWs' provisions.[21] The politicization of the Russian POW issue placed the ICRC in a difficult position with respect to its work with Russian POWs in Germany. The Allied military mission tended to treat neutral humanitarian organizations, such as the ICRC, as accessory agencies of its own mission. The delegates of the ICRC were thus obliged to be prudent in order to ensure that their activities would not be construed as political and regarded as a violation of its principle of neutrality.[22] The ICRC also acted in this particular manner because the Allied countries not only aimed to control the POWs' destinations but also sought to organize an anti-Bolshevik expeditionary force consisting of POWs.[23] Nevertheless, the potential use of the POWs as soldiers in Allied anti-Bolshevik combat immediately turned out to be dubious. Indeed, the POWs' situation in Germany and other Central European countries was more chaotic than the Allies had imagined.

In early 1919 ICRC fact-finding missions on the POW issue were organized with French financial support, and representatives were sent to Kiev, Prague, Warsaw, Budapest, Bratislava, and Munich under the slogan of "information, control, and protection."[24] The ICRC representatives found that many POWs suffered from tuberculosis and other contagious diseases, whereas others who had attempted to reach home on their own had become wanderers in the countries that bordered Germany and Russia. These border countries were newly independent following the collapse of their respective empires. They thus experienced unstable and disorganized conditions, which allowed the POWs to move freely across poorly defended borders.[25] The situation changed rapidly. In July 1919 some seven hundred thousand individuals, including many former POWs, were wandering in the border countries, while the number of POWs interned in German camps had decreased to roughly two hundred thousand, due in part to the POWs' individual departures as well as to some repatriation organized by the German authorities without Allied permission.[26] Such circumstances had transformed the POWs' significance in two ways. First, they were no longer potential soldiers capable of fighting Bolshevism but rather uprooted persons abandoned in the vast territory of Central and Eastern Europe. Secondly, the issue of Russian POWs went beyond German territory, the IACC's area of responsibility. With this in mind, in April 1919 the ICRC delegates sent an alert to the Allied authorities regarding "an urgent humanitarian need" and proposed that provision camps be established in the border countries. They also noted that the situation was beyond the powers of the IACC in Berlin.[27]

In May 1919 the Allied leaders gave up their attempt to organize an anti-Bolshevik expeditionary force of Russian POWs. Instead, they focused their efforts on "repatriation by all means"[28] under the responsibility of the German government and under Allied supervision. However, the German government criticized this as an irresponsible withdrawal. Furthermore, this "green light" did not necessarily indicate a smooth repatriation process, since finding safe and efficient routes was particularly difficult on account of the political and military disorder in the border countries. For example, the route via Poland was highly dangerous due to successive conflicts such as the Polish-Ukrainian war (November 1918–July 1919) and the Russo-Polish war (February 1919–October 1920). In addition, the planned route via the Danube River was also abandoned after the Hungarian revolution of March 1919.[29] Meanwhile, Western governments were unable to negotiate this issue since they did not always maintain open channels with the Soviet authorities.

The POWs' Movement and Their Changing Status

While the politics of repatriating the Russian POWs had reached a "dead end" in 1919, the POWs themselves continued to move or chose certain actions based on their own priorities, including remaining in camp or starting a new life in their present location. With this in mind, the present section provides more details about the Russian POWs' internment and movement in Germany and its bordering countries in order to determine how the authorities, including the ICRC, attempted to control the POWs and how the POWs themselves reacted to these attempts at control. Another issue to be explored is the POWs' changing status, which reflects the complex transition from war to peace (*sortie de guerre*).[30] In this case, we might wish to ask whether the POWs were always considered POWs and whether they were always categorized as "Russians."

While the term "Russian POWs" was constantly used in general discussions even after the war, their postwar situation became increasingly detached from what it had been in the camps during the war. Some prisoners were reclassified according to their new nationalities. Following the collapse of the tsarist empire, the label "Russian POW" was no longer applicable to everyone, and there was some discontent about being recognized as Russian. The IACC fully understood that a person's nationality was a sensitive question in the postwar era, and it used this point to demonstrate the new international order that the Allies were planning to establish. The different attitudes of the Allies to the Poles and the Ukrainians is a case in point. Since it was widely agreed that Poland was independent and that "Poles are not Russians,"[31] the Polish POWs in Germany (115,000 in total)[32] could be repatriated earlier than the others. It was the consulate general of Poland in Berlin that classified who was a Pole with Allied consent—those who were originally from the territory of Congress Poland and its large confines, provided that they were Catholic, had a certain "Polishness," and at least one Polish ancestor.[33] In contrast, the desire of Ukrainians who identified themselves as such to be treated as Ukrainian POWs was rejected by the Allies due to their nonrecognition of the Ukrainian state, which had been recognized by the Treaty of Brest-Litovsk. As a result, they were simply categorized as "Russian POWs."

The lack of control and discipline in the camps meant the POWs gained a certain amount of freedom and thus acted more independently even as they were becoming more vulnerable. Some chose to remain in the camps for various reasons, while others risked their lives and left the camps in an attempt to return to their homeland on their own or started a new life in Germany. Among the Russian POWs who remained in Germany in 1919, the officers, whose number was proportionally very low, constituted a group of their own, and most of them categorically refused to return to Bolshevik Russia. In fact, they were motivated to fight against Bolshevism and actively approached the inter-Allied authorities for the purpose of organizing an anti-Bolshevik force.[34] Meanwhile, the rank-and-file soldiers, who made up the majority of the POWs in Germany, disliked the idea of joining the anti-Bolshevik force, stating that they wouldn't "march against their brothers."[35]

The rank-and-file POWs were not a homogenous group either. Those who were able to earn a living or were married to local women did not want to return to homelands that had fallen into chaotic situations. In mid-1919 Germany, for example, approximately fifty thousand POWs expressed a wish not to be repatriated to Russia for various reasons.[36] Conversely, those who remained in the camps had to endure minimal food rations, and some of them tried to escape from the camps in order to return to Russia on their own. When the Treaty of Versailles came into force in January 1920, the German soldiers and guards operating in German camps were demilitarized, leading to a notable deterioration of discipline in the camps and to widespread corruption, such as trade in contraband and illegal commerce.[37] There were also people who joined the revolutionary movement and engaged in hunger strikes, since Soviet activists had penetrated many German camps, after which their Bolshevik propaganda had influenced some prisoners.[38]

The POWs who had escaped from German camps found it difficult to continue their journeys, often not knowing where to go and wandering aimlessly. Furthermore, it was not only ongoing military operations or a broken-down transport system but also the political intentions of some authorities that restricted the POWs' movements. For example, the Allied military missions stationed in Eastern and Central European countries attempted to control the movement of POWs, especially those who showed strong Bolshevik tendencies, by refusing to issue passports.[39] Although some eventually managed to reach Russian soil, some among them actually returned to Germany, since they were unable to find "their place" in the homeland.[40]

POWs were not the only individuals who wandered during this period. Their itineraries often overlapped with other displaced people. This was especially true for movement between Poland and Ukraine, such as Polish workers who had been deported to western Prussia during the war and were now attempting to return home.[41] All these wanderers were able to receive elementary aid and provisions from missions at principal railway stations or at camps established by state or local authorities, and in some cases they were interned when severe weather or the territory's devastation made their journey impossible.[42] Moreover, POWs and other displaced people were often the first victims of such epidemics as typhus, smallpox, and syphilis. Under these circumstances, all displaced people were considered refugees or fugitives, regardless of their motives for wandering.

In the meantime, the Russian POWs who had been held in the former Austro-Hungarian empire underwent a change of status that differed from their counterparts in Germany. Once attaining independence, the new states in Central and Eastern Europe declared that the Russian POWs would no longer be considered as prisoners as it was not the new states who had captured them during the war. Some POWs were nonetheless detained in the camps for security reasons, while others were set free, since some governments (Hungary is a case in point) did not care about their safe travel. Being set free meant that the former prisoners lost the benefits they had received as POWs, such as postal services and identity certificates.[43] In this respect, an ICRC delegate in Budapest who tried to persuade POWs not to move for the time being for their safety's sake, reported that he was told as follows:

> Please issue us a document which clearly states our prisoner of war status. This legitimation is enough for us. That is all what we want. We will leave individually at the risk of our lives. We won't be afraid of either deprivation, which we have already suffered for several years, or the distance to travel on foot, even if it means walking several hundred kilometers. We'd like to arrive home, even if it's just to die there. But please, give us the paper today, tomorrow at the latest.[44]

POWs were well aware of the necessity for papers in order to prove their identities and status for their journey, which they knew would be difficult but at least less risky with the papers. At the same time, the many POWs who had escaped from the camps and attempted to return home on their own, perceived their postwar nationality as less important than their prompt return to their homeland. Without knowing their new nationality (or the new rules for crossing borders), the POWs experienced difficulties in proving their identities to the state/local authorities and to the humanitarian agents. The ICRC reported that some of them even attempted to benefit from such confusing situations in order to expedite their return or simply to survive:

> Organizing the repatriation of isolated Russians faces huge difficulties on account of the inability to identify the Russians, who look like comical bandits. Furthermore, while the Hungarian POWs who escaped from Russia and Siberia arrived with Russian clothes and spoke Russian, the Russian prisoners often looked like Hungarian soldiers and spoke Hungarian. Given their objectives—obtaining some food or avoiding a journey they didn't want to undertake—the Russians pretended to be

> Hungarians and vice versa. There were also Poles, Yugoslavians, and members of all nationalities on this route to Budapest. The Russian prisoners were often accompanied by Hungarian women, while the Hungarian prisoners were often accompanied by Russian women.[45]

This passage indicates that some POWs deliberately blurred their identities in order to attain their objectives. In addition, many prisoners "lied" about their final destinations in order to continue their journeys. Did the "Russian" POWs always lie about their identity and destination? It could be that the ICRC delegates simply did not understand the complexity of the identity question in Eastern Europe. They also lacked the means to examine the information provided by the POWs. According to one report, "most of the Russians don't have any identity documents ["sans papiers"]. Some believed themselves to be Poles, while others saw themselves as Czechoslovakian. Almost everyone could speak a bit of German."[46] The ICRC delegates had only geographical data about new frontiers, while the national identification of POWs originated from ancient empires implied far more complexity associated with other criteria such as languages and religions.

On the other side of the front, many POWs still remained in Russia, especially in Siberia. Moreover, following the ineffective peace negotiations at the Paris Conference, since late 1918 the Allied countries had prohibited the German, Austrian, and Hungarian governments from engaging in the repatriation of POWs from Russia without Allied permission.[47] As a result, some POWs joined the anti-Bolshevik forces and formed units according to their nationalities, while others joined the Red Army. Meanwhile, there were other POWs who suffered from the harsh living conditions in Siberia, as revealed by numerous testimonies obtained by the ICRC. However, their situations did not draw a great deal of attention, unlike those of their counterparts on the western side of the Eastern Front.[48] In the autumn of 1919, the Allies eventually decided to start evacuating the POWs from Russia according to their nationalities due to the constant retreat of the anti-Bolshevik army and the end of Allied intervention. In this respect, the former POWs who had joined the anti-Bolshevik units in the civil war were the first to be chosen, followed by the Polish, Czechoslovak, and Yugoslav prisoners, and then the German, Hungarian, and Austrian prisoners. Nevertheless, the Allies found it extremely difficult to execute a smooth repatriation plan due to the rapidly changing political and military circumstances in Russia and the fact that many of the POWs in Siberia were under the control of Bolshevik forces.

From Inter-Allied to International: "Humanitarian Camps" and the National Identification of POWs

On both sides of the Eastern Front, the impasse regarding POW repatriation continued throughout 1919. In addition, the presence of impatient and non-repatriated prisoners throughout Central Europe and Russia caused disarray in many societies and gave rise to security and public-hygiene problems as well as an economic burden. It should be noted that the nonrepatriated POWs on the Eastern Front in 1919 were no longer considered prisoners of the Great War, and their repatriation had to be conducted in the context of restructuring the concerned areas, drawing the frontiers of new countries, and dealing with ongoing regional conflicts. A dramatic transformation was thus necessary for resolving this politically tangled POW issue. Moreover, the enforcement of the peace treaties in early 1920 made it impossible for the Allies to deal with POW repatriation without the express consent of the countries concerned. At this stage the humanitarian and international aspects of the issue required a comprehensive solution. As a result of the above, the Russian POWs in Germany and the POWs in Russia and Siberia, who had previously been treated separately according Allied interests, were now reexamined as a whole.

The German government asked the ICRC to act as an intermediary in the exchange between the Russian POWs in Germany and the German POWs in Russia, and to control Russian POW camps in German territory until their departure.[49] The ICRC accepted this proposal with the condition that the exchange would also pertain to POWs from the former Austro-Hungarian empire who were stuck in Siberia. At the time, the Dual Monarchy's successors lacked sufficient funds for dealing with their interned nationals. The Allies, who wanted to withdraw from the prisoner repatriation process as soon as possible, welcomed the ICRC's initiatives.[50] In order to support the ICRC's repatriation of all POWs regardless of nationality and in order to deal with the financial issue, the League of Nations, founded in January 1920, nominated a high commissioner for the repatriation of POWs: the renowned Norwegian scientist and politician Fridtjof Nansen (1861–1930).[51] In April 1920 the ICRC successfully mediated a repatriation program agreement between the German and Soviet governments,[52] and the first exchange of POWs occurred in Narva, Estonia, a month later.

The ICRC had proposed the installation of transit camps along the repatriation route to offer accommodations and provisions to returning POWs since the emergence of the POW issue. However, the unstable political conditions in bordering countries, the shortage of funding, and the lack of cooperation from local authorities had prevented the project from becoming a reality. The subsequent internationalization of the issue and the League of Nations' intervention in the spring of 1920 finally made it possible to establish the repatriation routes and transit camps on a large scale. The ICRC immediately began negotiating with the countries between Germany and Russia in order to obtain their permission for POWs crossing into their territories. Devastated by the war and still suffering from ongoing conflicts, most of these countries were somewhat hesitant about accepting the arrangement, at least in the beginning. The harsh weather conditions in these regions were another obstacle in the way of finding appropriate locations for the transports. However, the ICRC persevered and eventually succeeded in establishing several routes across the Baltic Sea.[53]

More specifically, the POWs were to embark from and to Russia at four ports: Björkö in Finland, Narva and Baltischport (modern day Paldiski) in Estonia, and Riga in Latvia. Alternately, Swinemünde (Świnoujście) and Stettin (Szczecin), near the Polish border, were selected on the German side (see figure 10.1). The transit camps established around these ports functioned between May 1920 and June 1922. While the prisoners only spent a short time at the camps (usually between several hours and a week), they were still fed and disinfected as they waited for their departure to the homeland. All in all, a total of 460,091 prisoners were repatriated via these camps.[54] The management of the transit camps was a significant challenge for the ICRC since it lacked experience in this particular domain. The ICRC had only started actively dispatching inspection missions to the POW camps in belligerent countries since the beginning of the Great War, and missions of a more operational nature were only organized after the war. However, in order to complete the POWs' repatriation on humanitarian grounds, and in order to stand out among the other philanthropic organizations, the ICRC had to both establish and manage the transit camps despite its lack of expertise and experience.

The most important point for the ICRC was to establish "international" camps that differed from ordinary wartime POW camps.[55] It had no interest in imposing severe military discipline on the POWs, as in some German camps, nor in starving and weakening the internees, as in some Siberian camps. It also did not vary the treatment of the prisoners according to their nationalities or political ideas, as practiced by the Allies. Instead, the ICRC expected these transit camps to serve as prime examples of internment camps managed by humanitarian organizations (see figure 10.2). Nevertheless, the ICRC delegates (often Swiss army officers) had to work under

FIGURE 10.1. The train station in Stettin: Repatriation of Russian prisoners of war via Narva, under the auspices of the ICRC, May 14, 1920. Courtesy of the International Committee of the Red Cross Archives, V-P-HIST-03002-03©ICRC archives.

uncertain conditions, and some expressed severe militaristic attitudes with little respect for the ICRC's principles and neutrality.[56] At the time, when the professionalism of humanitarian agents had not been sufficiently defined or developed, it was difficult to recruit well-trained and suitable personnel for such humanitarian activities.

Material relief was also organized in the transit camps. In cooperation with Nansen, the ICRC arranged material assistance to needy prisoners under the slogan "for all prisoners and not for specific nationalities."[57] The transit camps also held many civilians, such as refugees of different nationalities, and other categories of military persons other than Great War POWs, such as Soviet soldiers who had been isolated in oriental Prussia after the end of the Soviet-Polish war and were later interned in Germany.[58] Many of these sought to follow the same itinerary as the POWs in traveling from Germany to Russia or vice versa (see figure 10.3). In addition, many prisoners were accompanied by wives they had married during their captivity and their children. According to the ICRC's report, 15,067 Russian POWs who were repatriated from Germany between March 19 and April 15, 1921, traveled

Figure 10.2. Transit camp in Riga for Russian and Latvian POW repatriates from Germany and German POW repatriates from Russia, 1920. Courtesy of the International Committee of the Red Cross Archives, V-P-HIST-03052-02©ICRC archives.

with 2,451 women (mainly Germans but also certain Poles) and 1,809 children.[59] Tragically, some women and their children were abandoned by their husbands shortly after their arrival; there were at least one hundred cases of abandoned Russian women who had arrived in Germany with the POWs from Germany or the former Austro-Hungarian empire, all of whom were cared for by the ICRC and returned to Russia.[60]

Nevertheless, the transit camps were more than a simple philanthropic sphere—they were also a method of control. This is primarily because the ICRC believed that the collection of information was always an important task. Its delegates approached educated POWs, mostly officers, and asked them to write reports that not only included their experiences as prisoners but also information about the general situation in Russia.[61] The control of nationality was also exercised at each point. POWs who had been interned in Russia and were originally from Germany and the former Austro-Hungarian empire arrived after being checked in Petrograd or Moscow. In order to avoid a delay, the transit camps bordering the Baltic Sea were managed by the ICRC delegates, and the presence of national representatives was prohibited. It was thus the responsibility of the ICRC delegates to register the arrival and departure of POWs and to issue them a certificate of nationality, even if the delegates only had vague information about the postwar conditions in these areas. Determining the nationalities of POWs was not an easy task for

FIGURE 10.3. Transit camp at Narva, July 1921. Courtesy of the International Committee of the Red Cross Archives, V-P-HIST-03054-10©ICRC archives.

the ICRC because the majority of prisoners lacked official documents and usually declared their nationalities verbally; the ICRC delegates in the transit camps were unable to verify their words.[62] They were also surprised by the POWs' lack of knowledge and indifference with respect to their new national identities. Sometimes POWs could provide the name of their village, but not the name of their country. In some cases Jews claimed that they were merely Jews.[63] Situations such as the following were also common:

> A Hungarian could, for example, declare himself as Romanian when arriving in the Narva camp, and then become a Czechoslovakian after being examined by the Commission in Stettin. Finally, a border check reveals that he is actually Hungarian.[64]

These cases happened as there were many native Hungarian speakers who also used other languages in Romania and Czechoslovakia and could be categorized as Czechoslovak or Romanian due to the new borders, though they could also be categorized as Hungarian according to their language. This was a situation that ICRC delegates had not considered because they believed that a person should have a single precise nationality. National identification was a very complicated issue, however, especially for the POWs originating from the former multinational Austro-Hungarian empire; the new states born after the collapse of the monarchy remained multiethnic, multilinguistic, and multireligious.[65] After staying in the transit camps near the Baltic ports, the POWs were transported to Stettin in Germany, where the national representatives of each state were waiting to determine their nationalities and destinations. It is possible that these representatives refused to accept the prisoners who pretended to possess the nationality of their country but could not satisfy the conditions demanded by the country.

The determination of a prisoner's nationality was an extremely important task for the concerned governments, since the financial burden of each country was calculated according to the number of POWs via the International Committee for Relief Credits, an organization established in 1920 for the purpose of providing food and raw material aid to the independent countries formed from the former Austro-Hungarian empire for reconstruction purposes. Under such circumstances, where the state could freely exercise powerful political measures, the ICRC delegates suspected that some representatives, especially the Hungarians, would arbitrarily refuse certain prisoners belonging to their state for political reasons.[66] Moreover, the countries that did not want to accept many Jews tried to impose them on each other.[67] There were also many Germans from the territory belonging to Czechoslovakia or former Hungarian subjects who had lived in the Hungarian territory and had become Romanian by nationality. Nansen referred to these prisoners whose nationality and homeland did not match because all countries were reluctant to pay for them as "unfortunate people" or "*sans patrie*" (Fr. without homeland).[68] Conversely, nationality was not the main concern for prisoners who wanted to return to the country that did not correspond to their newly ascribed nationality or to reserve their decision until their arrival in the former Austro-Hungarian empire; this led to cases of intentional identity confusion. Table 10.1 presents the number of self-declared nationalities at Stettin and at the borders by the end of September 1920.

According to this table, the number of Austrians and Hungarians who registered in Stettin decreased by approximately 25 percent by the time they reached the border camps. The disappearance of roughly two thousand prisoners during the journey must have been intentional. However, the decrease in the number of Austrian and Hungarian POWs, and the increase in the number of POWs of other nationalities can possibly be explained by the confusion at the new borders as well as by the lack of precise information. As a nationality-based census was complicated and sometimes even arbitrary in each newly independent country,[69] it is hardly surprising that completing that task in the camps within a limited period of time was extremely difficult.

During the spring of 1922, the transit camps in the Baltic countries and Finland began to close since the number of nonrepatriated POWs was decreasing and the League of Nations realized that the operation was becoming

Table 10.1 The self-declared nationalities at Stettin and at the borders before September 30, 1920.

NATIONALITY	NUMBER IN STETTIN	NUMBER AT THE BORDERS	DIFFERENCE
Austrian	7,720	5,709	−2,011
Hungarian	13,064	9,956	−3,108
Czechoslovakian	7,234	8,309	+1,066
Yugoslav	5,232	5,703	+476
Polish	2,467	2,732	+256
Italian	391	492	+101
Ukrainian	126	147	+21
Bulgarian	21	21	0
Turkish[a]	98	2	−96
Total	38,647	36,470	−2,177

Source: Gegenüberstellung der bis zum 30 September 1920 in Stettin eingetroffenen nichtreichsdeutschen Heimkehrer mit den bis 30 September 1920 auf den Grenzstationen eingetroffenen Heimkehrern, ACICR, MIS 33/5–26.

a. These Turks were interned in Germany, since the official route to Turkey had yet to be organized.

too large and expensive, given the increasingly smaller number of travelers. Nansen himself declared the end of the collective repatriation program at a League of Nations council meeting held in September 1922.[70] However, the ICRC continued carrying out individual repatriations of isolated prisoners dispersed throughout the vast Russian territory until 1923. As part of the closing process, various tools—such as disinfection machines—as well as leftover materials and food supplies were either resold or distributed to local philanthropic organizations. These materials and supplies were then used by vulnerable people, particularly children, who were suffering from contagious diseases and malnutrition.[71] The League of Nations also used the leftover resources in dealing with the Russian refugee issue[72] and other related humanitarian problems.[73]

While the transit camps were in operation, the POW repatriation process—originally a military issue caused by the Great War—was gradually linked to other humanitarian crises, most notably to the issues of Russian refugees and widespread epidemics, both of which were recognized as international problems in the postwar era.[74] The POW transit camps also handled the cases of some civilians who were returning to or escaping from Russia and provided material relief and medical care to such individuals. At the time, the presence of the POWs classified as "sans patrie" predicted the politically and judicially ambiguous status of refugees and minorities that would be largely problematized in the 1920s. Finally, the fate of prisoners who did not return to Russia was incorporated with that of Russian refugees in general. In this respect the ICRC's delegate in Berlin stated that, at the humanitarian level, the question of former prisoners should subsequently be treated as a part of the more general Russian refugee problem.[75] When the Soviet government denied the nationality of Russian refugees by decree in December 1921, it declared explicitly that this measure would include the category of former prisoners of war who had not registered their identity with the Soviet authorities within the specified time frame.[76]

The internment of prisoners of war on the Eastern Front was radically transformed after the war had officially ended. Following the conclusion of the Treaty of Brest-Litovsk, the disorganized and poor repatriation programs prepared by state authorities stimulated the free movement of prisoners longing to return home. The armistice only intensified this tendency: the camps continued to function as poorly managed internment camps for the POWs who had no other choice but to remain there while the Allies tightened their control of the movement of POWs for their own political purposes. In these circumstances some POWs lost their status as prisoners, and their subsequent fate depended on other criteria that were more meaningful in the postwar world (e.g., nationality). In addition, the condition of POWs became increasingly similar to that of other displaced persons in the region. At the time, stronger initiatives to protect such individuals were expected from various international and humanitarian organizations.

This, in turn, raises the question of the significance of humanitarian organization (e.g., ICRC) intervention in the process of POW repatriation. With an apparent neutral and nonpolitical position, which the ICRC took extreme care to prioritize, this organization was able to exercise a multifunctional operation for POW repatriation. Despite the many obstacles in its path, the ICRC, along with the League of Nations, managed to reduce the hardships of the (former) POWs significantly and succeeded in repatriating five hundred thousand prisoners of diverse nationalities. The organization's camps were prime examples of effective "humanitarian camps" while they served not only as a space for protecting the internees from the exterior environment—severe cold, food shortages, continuing conflicts, contagious diseases—but also as a space of governance in which the internees were surveyed and controlled according to the required norms of the postwar international order.

Notes

1. As mentioned in the introductory chapter of this volume, since the 1990s historians have increasingly become interested in POWs of the Great War from diverse perspectives. For POW studies on the Western Front, see, e.g., Becker, A. 1998; Abbal 2001; Jones, H. 2011a; and others. Regarding the POWs on the Eastern Front, see, e.g., Yanikdağ 1999; Fayet 2000; Karpus 2001; Rachamimov 2002; Pastor 2012. Nonetheless, POW repatriation has not been treated as a major theme in most of the studies, except for Housden 2007; Nachtigal 2008; Tate 2015, 2017.

2. Nachtigal 2008, 159.

3. For this perspective, see., e.g., Kévonian 2004; Cabanes 2014; Watenpaugh 2014.

4. See, e.g., Zahra 2008.

5. Rachamimov 2002, 107–15

6. Rachamimov 2002, 191–96; Nachtigal 2008, 169.

7. Moritz and Leidinger 2005, parts 3 and 4.

8. Nachtigal 2008, 169.

9. Oltmer 2005, 269.

10. Rapport du capitaine Hjort et de M. Albert Mussard sur leur voyage en Lithuanie [*sic*], December 1918, Archives du Comité international de la Croix-Rouge (hereafter referred to as ACICR), MIS 6/5 Berlin, Rapport 1.

11. Exposé de la situation des prisonniers de guerre russes, December 21, 1918, ACICR, C G1 A 19–32.

12. Télégramme du général Nudant, February 8, 1919, Service Historiques de la Défense de la République française (hereafter referred to as SHD), 15NN 73.

13. Note au sujet des prisonniers internés en Allemagne, provenant du Commendant en chef des Armées Alliés, January 5, 1919, SHD, 10N 215.

14. Note au sujet des prisonniers russes internés en Allemagne, May 5, 1919, SHD, 7N 640; Télégramme du MAE à l'Ambassade britannique, s. d. (probably at the beginning of December 1918), Archives du Ministère des affaires étrangères de la République française (hereafter referred to as AMAE), Série Z: URSS 41.

15. Note au sujet des prisonniers russes internés en Allemagne, January 5, 1919, SHD, 10N 215; Convention: prolongation de l'Armistice du 16 janvier 1919, SHD, 10N 215.

16. Note pour le général Nudant: une résolution du 13 janvier, AMAE, Série Z: URSS 42.

17. Rapport de la mission de Budapest, January 27, 1919, AMAE, Série Z: URSS 43.

18. Télégramme de Tchitcherine, January 21, 1919, AMAE, Série Z: URSS 42.

19. Rapport du général Dupont, March 29, 1919, AMAE, Série Z: URSS 44.

20. On the POWs' status in the international law, see Neville Wylie and Sarina Landefeld's chapter in this volume.

21. Conseil suprême économique, February 10, 1919, AMAE, Série Y: International 151.

22. Rapport de la mission de Berlin, January 2, 1919, ACICR, MIS 6/5 Berlin, Rapport 1.

23. Note de l'Ambassade britannique, December 2, 1918, SHD, 7N 640; Rapport du MAE à Clemenceau, January 23, 1919, AMAE, Série Z: URSS 42.

24. Communications du chef de la Mission, February 11, 1919, ACICR, MIS 0.

25. Sammartino 2010, 145.

26. Rapport au sujet des moyens de rapatriement des PG russes actuellement au chargé des Alliés en Allemagne, July 25, 1919, SHD, 7N 640.

27. Rapport écrit par M. Blanchod, délégué du CICR, à son retour de Budapest, April 4, 1919, Archives Nationales de la République française (hereafter referred to as AN), F12 8091.

28. Rapport du capitaine Bauchard de la Mission française de Berlin, December 24, 1919, SHD, 7N 640.

29. Rapport de la Mission de Budapest, March 25, 1919, AMAE, Série Z: URSS 45.

30. Regarding this idea of "sortie de guerre," the French historiography is abundant, especially Cabanes 2004; Audoin-Rouzeau and Prochasson, 2008. Gerwarth referred to this period as a time of "chaotic peace"; see Gerwarth 2016, 6.

31. Rapport de Dupont, January 23, 1919, AMAE, Série Z: URSS 42.

32. This number does not include 209,724 Polish POWs who crossed German-Polish borders before the establishment of the IACC (between November 15, 1918, and January 20, 1919). Karpus 2001, 20.

33. Rapport de Dupont, January 23, 1919, AMAE, Série Z: URSS 42.

34. De l'Ambassade russe à MAE, January 18, 1919, AMAE, Série Z: URSS 42.

35. Rapport de Dupont à Nudant, January 20, 1919, SHD, 15NN 73; Compte-rendu de la séance du 19 avril 1919 de la Commission interalliée, SHD, 15 NN 75.

36. PV de la Réunion des Ministres des Affaires Etrangères tenue dans le cabinet de M. Pichon, May 14, 1919, SHD, 10N 215.

37. Rapport de Wildbolz, March 25, 1920, ACICR, MIS 33/5–01.

38. Nagornaja 2009, 491.

39. Rapport de la mission de Budapest, January 27, 1919, AMAE, Série Z: URSS 43.

40. Liste de tous les anciens prisonniers de guerre russes actuellement sur le territoire du Cercle de Deux-Ponts, November 9, 1919, SHD, 7N 638.

41. Mission de Varsovie: Rapport no. 1 concernant l'arrivée des ouvriers de saison au camp de Powonsky, AMAE, Série Z: URSS 42. The ICRC estimated their number between three hundred and four hundred thousand.

42. Rapport de la Mission de Varsovie concernant le rapatriement des prisonniers et la formation d'un cordon sanitaire, May 20, 1920, AMAE, Série Z: URSS 45.

43. Rapport d'ensemble de la mission de Budapest, 29/03; April 12, 1919, AMAE, Série Z: URSS 44.

44. Rapport sur l'état d'esprit régnant actuellement parmi les prisonniers de guerre russes, February 23, 1919, AMAE, Série Z: URSS 44. Translated into English by the author.

45. Rapport sur les prisonniers de guerre russes isolés en Hongrie, 05/03/1919, AMAE, Série Z: URSS 44. Translated into English by the author.

46. Liste de tous les anciens prisonniers de guerre russes actuellement sur le territoire du Cercle de Deux-Ponts, November 9, 1919, SHD, 7N 638.

47. Du plénipotentiaire de la République d'Autriche à Clemenceau, November 5, 1919, AMAE, Série Z: URSS 50.

48. Annexe de l'Appel du CICR en faveur des prisonniers en Sibérie, AMAE, Série Z: URSS 50.

49. La liste des demandes de la part du Gouvernement allemand, January 26, 1920, ACICR, MIS. 33/5–01.

50. Commission interalliée spéciale de Paris pour les prisonniers de guerre russes détenus en Allemagne, procès-verbal no. 4, séance du 9 février 1920, AMAE, Série Z: URSS 47.

51. Procès-Verbaux de la 4e session des 9–11 avril 1920 à Paris, *Journal officiel de la SDN*.

52. Abkommen zwischen dem Deutschen Reich und Russischen Sozialistischen Föderativen Sowjet-Republik über Heimschaffung der beiderseitigen Kriegsfangenen und Zivilinternierten, April 16, 1920, ACICR, MIS 33/5–04.

53. CICR, *Rapport général du Comité international de la Croix-Rouge sur son activité de 1921 à 1923*, Genève: CICR, 1923, 77–134.

54. *Journal Officiel de la Société des Nations*, November 1922. For land transport to and from these ports, the ICRC organized nine routes with railway companies and customs houses and established timetables and other conditions for the passage of the special trains.

55. PV de la Commission des missions, October 11, 1920, ACICR, B MIS.

56. Rapport de Watteville, n. d. (probably in the beginning of August 1920), MIS 33/5–18; Rapport de Wildbolz, June 16, 1920, ACICR, MIS 33/5–11.

57. Rapport de Watteville, February 4, 1921, ACICR, MIS 33/5–31.

58. CICR, *Rapport général*, 94–95.

59. Rapport mensuel PG russes en Allemagne, April 18, 1921, MIS33–5/34.

60. CICR, *Rapport général*, 128.

61. See the reports from the Mission of Narva, ACICR, MIS 35/5.

62. Rapport de Watteville, June 16, 1920, ACICR, MIS33–5–11; De Frick à Bonner, November 19, 1920, Archives de la Société des Nations (hereafter referred to as ASDN), C1112.

63. PV de la Commission des missions, July 11, 1920, ACICR, B MIS.

64. De Watteville à Bonner, May 27, 1921, ASDN, C1112.

65. Rosenblit 2004, 184.

66. Rapport de Watteville, June 16, 1920, ACICR, MIS 33/5–11.

67. Rapport de Watteville, March 31, 1921, ACICR, MIS 33/5–34.

68. From Nansen, August 25, 1920, ASDN, C1111.

69. Zahra 2008, 117–26.

70. Annexe 400: Rapport du Dr. Nansen, soumis au Conseil le 1er septembre 1922, *Journal Officiel de la Société des Nations*, November 1922.

71. De Lucien Brunel à Nansen, March 21, 1922, ASDN, R1705.

72. Russian refugees were those who escaped from Russia after the revolution and during the civil war and dispersed all over the world. They constituted the first international refugee question treated under the League of Nations.

73. Lettre de Nansen à Watteville, April 10, 1922, ASDN, R1709.

74. Kévonian 2004; Gousseff 2008; Piana 2009.

75. Rapport de Watteville, July 13, 1921, ACICR MIS 33/5–39.

76. Gousseff 2008, 87.

CHAPTER 11

POWs, Civilians, and the Postwar Development of International Humanitarian Law

Neville Wylie and Sarina Landefeld

This chapter takes as its starting point a discussion that took place at the first postwar conference of the International Law Association (ILA), held in Portsmouth, England, in May 1920. While the founding of the League of Nations the previous January provided the assembled jurists with plenty to debate, the conference organizers were eager to progress thinking on two areas of law that had been found wanting in the Great War: the law of the sea and the law governing the treatment of prisoners of war (POWs). As Lord Younger, the conference chair, noted in his opening remarks, the existing regulations dealing with POWs—the 1899/1907 Hague rules—had proved utterly "powerless to prevent in innumerable notorious instances the suffering, undeserved, gratuitous, heartrending beyond expression, which thousands of prisoners had to endure through these tragic years of horror."[1] To help sharpen the discussions, two of Britain's foremost international lawyers, Hugh Bellot and George G. Phillimore, were invited to table a draft convention for POWs.

Grounded on the agreements negotiated between the belligerents in the final years of the war, Bellot and Phillimore's code was a thoroughly sober document. One of their more surprising recommendations, though, was the suggestion that the prisoners' well-being might best be met by "civilianizing" them; transferring them into the custody of the civil administration and employing them on non-war-related tasks. This, the two authors suggested, would prevent their falling prey to the physical and psychological illnesses associated with prolonged captivity and would give the detaining power a vested interest in maintaining their health. If accepted, the authors argued, the measure would assure POWs "a definitely fixed status placed under the protection of international law and beyond the power of their captors to treat them as hostages or as instruments to be used against their native country."[2]

Although the proposal struck a chord in certain quarters, it was never formally taken up.[3] Bellot and Phillimore's draft code fed into subsequent discussions in the United Kingdom and elsewhere and in time helped pave the way to the first dedicated POW convention in July 1929, but at no time, either then or since, has any serious consideration been given to depriving POWs of their military status.[4] Quite the reverse. The 1929 POW convention, and its updated version in 1949, insisted that POWs remained bound by the rules, regulations, norms, and hierarchies of the nation's armed forces.[5] The onset of the Cold War strengthened this trend, intensifying expectations around what was appropriate "conduct after capture." Meanwhile, for civilians caught up in warfare, little substantive progress was made during the interwar period to either clarify their position or accord them any specific rights or privileges. A draft convention emerged at the Red Cross conference in Tokyo in October 1934, but the matter was not put before a diplomatic conference before war returned to Europe in September 1939. As a result, save for a handful of articles in the 1907 Hague rules governing conditions of military occupation, "civilians" remained outside international humanitarian law until the conclusion of the fourth Geneva convention in 1949.[6]

It is, nevertheless, worth asking why military and civilians prisoners fared so differently in legal debates following the end of the Great War and questioning the extent to which the fate of the civilian "regime" was influenced by thinking toward POWs. The war had, after all, seen civilians emerge as both important contributors to the war effort and as war victims subject to the levels of violence and intimidation that had hitherto been reserved for those directly involved in the fighting.[7] As Amanda Alexander has shown, the "citizen," whom prewar codes had left open to abuse if his location or conduct so warranted, gave way to the concept of the "civilian," a vulnerable, hapless victim of war deserving of protection.[8] As several chapters in this volume have shown, there was considerable symmetry in the belligerents' treatment of military and civilian prisoners over the course of the war. Regulations governing the administration of military prisoners were routinely applied to their civilian counterparts and "civilian POWs" made the subject of agreements concluded between the belligerents that covered conditions of internment, arrangements for repatriation and exchange, and the right to receive correspondence, medicines, and spiritual aid. Some of these agreements even touched on such thorny subjects as hostage taking and the right of reprisal.[9] "Enemy aliens" were, moreover, often treated with generosity, and their internment justified, with some reason, on the grounds that it was required for their own protection.[10] Even in the midst of a titanic struggle governments were clearly ready to adapt legal norms to meet the humanitarian needs of civilians.

In exploring these questions, we seek to make two points. First, although the legislative trajectories of military and civilian prisoners quickly diverged, the two processes remained closely aligned. The 1929 POW convention provided a template for the development of a civilian code and had a marked influence on the way civilians were conceived as legal subjects. This was perhaps a natural development but, we suggest, it was not entirely to the benefit of civilians, and it hampered innovative thinking on how to provide legal protection to this important category of war victim. Secondly, while the attempt to secure agreement on a civilian code was ultimately wrecked by the downturn in international politics in the 1930s, the project's supporters had always struggled to forge the kind of broad consensus necessary to assure themselves success. But for a brief period in 1929–1930, the tenor of opinion was always critical to developments in this area. In order to understand why the project was pursued as far as it was, culminating in a draft code in 1934, we need to look at the internal drivers at work in the International Committee of the Red Cross (ICRC), the principal "norm entrepreneur" in this area.

Emergence of an Idea: Civilians and POWs under International Law

Although historically the ICRC had been associated with the Geneva conventions and the task of tendering aid to sick and wounded soldiers on the battlefield, the cause of civilians was not new to the organization at the start of the Great War. The committee's first humanitarian action had seen its delegates administer aid to refugees during the Balkan insurrection in 1875–76. Yet both the scope of its practical activities in the first fifty years of its existence and its written reflections on the nature of war were limited.[11] The principal champion for civilian interests in the Red Cross movement before 1914 was the American Red Cross Society, which had, over the course of several decades, developed a brand of humanitarianism that worked to mitigate the effects of natural disasters at home and, increasingly, abroad. This saw the American society send aid to famine-stricken Russian peasants and Armenians in Turkey, to Cuban war refugees, and to flood victims in China.[12] The plight of Boer civilians during the second South African War likewise spurred some European societies into following Washington's lead and shifting from administering medical services to Boer fighters to providing relief aid to Boer farmers.

The ICRC was, however, initially slow in extending its services to those caught up in the mass evacuations triggered by the outbreak of war in July 1914. A civilian division was opened in the International Prisoner of War Agency, but it took the personal efforts of the division's head, Dr. Frédéric Ferrière, in tracing civilian evacuees, to more or less shame his colleagues into resourcing it properly, dispatching delegates to visit civilian internment camps, and pressing the belligerents to include civilians in their wartime agreements.[13] Ferrière's campaigning had the desired effect, and by late 1917 civilian protection arguably topped the committee's agenda. Senior officials freely acknowledged that the detention of civilians was the "most shocking . . . even the most odious" of the war's many innovations.[14] Tackling excesses in this area and calling a halt to the remorseless proliferation of categories (civilian internees and hostages, evacuees, refugees, and deportees) that ran roughshod over the rudimentary prewar legal regime were widely seen as some of the principal issues in need of attention after the return of peace.[15]

The fact that the belligerents had voluntarily negotiated improvements in the treatment of enemy aliens and civilian internees naturally gave heart to those who were eager to construct a legal regime for civilians once peace returned. Within a month of the close of the war, internal ICRC documents show that the organization was keen to explore any option that might further this aim.[16] At the same time, it is clear that there were other factors also at play. The brutal redrawing of Europe's borders ensured that the plight of civilians remained a live issue long after the armistice had brought formal fighting to an end in November 1918. By 1923, in the "shatter zones" of former empires stretching across Eastern and Southeastern Europe, the Middle East, and central Asia, as many as four million people died and many more were forced to flee their homes to avoid the endemic violence.[17]

The issue likewise played into the ICRC's own institutional interests. The emergence of a League of Red Cross Societies under American patronage in 1919 challenged the committee's "primacy" within the Red Cross movement and called into question its vision of the Red Cross as an institution dedicated to aiding "privileged" combatants in times of war.[18] With the League pledging to tackle the social and health needs of populations at peace, it was hardly politic for the committee to turn its back on the humanitarian needs of civilians in times of war. ICRC officials were reluctant to openly admit to the League's influence on their thinking toward a civilian convention, but their sensitivity on the issue was evident in the efforts made to publicize the committee's wartime and postwar work on behalf of civilian populations and in the release of films on the subject at the 1921 and 1923 Red Cross conferences.[19]

If the committee entered the postwar negotiations with some nervousness, reactions to its initial practical and legislative forays into civilian protection were nevertheless positive.[20] At the movement's meeting during March and April 1921, representatives from the national Red Cross societies endorsed a series of recommendations that amounted to a "dramatic break [from] previous policies." The resolutions not only stipulated that civilian prisoners should be accorded the same rights as military prisoners of war but insisted that these rights were guaranteed by the "immutable moral principles of humanity, not reciprocal agreements between states."[21] As a consequence, any violence against these prisoners, including reprisals and their use as hostages, was expressly prohibited. These rights were, moreover, to apply to all armed conflicts, including civil wars, and not just those between sovereign states. In closing, the conference tasked the ICRC to advance discussions on updating the 1907 Hague regulations and align the laws governing the treatment of civilian deportees, evacuees, and refugees with those accorded to prisoners of war.[22]

The lofty idealism exhibited at the 1921 conference did not long survive contact with reality. It is generally assumed that the fate of a "civilians" convention was sealed by the events of the 1930s, but in truth the project was dealt blows in the 1920s from which it never really recovered. Indeed, the objections raised at the Red Cross conferences in 1923 and 1925 were sufficiently profound to call into question the wisdom of the entire enterprise. The first casualty was the aspiration to create a "*code des prisonniers de guerre, déportés, évacuees et réfuges*," i.e., a set of legally binding restrictions governing state treatment of a country's own nationals, not just enemy POWs. As Boyd van Dijk notes, the rejection of this code at the 1923 conference essentially compelled the ICRC to exclude from the frame the very groups who had been subjected to the most extreme violence after 1914—"persons lacking nationality [e.g., stateless persons], those imprisoned for political reasons [such as conscientious objectors], and the state's own nationals [for instance, Ottoman Armenians]."[23] The hope of extending protection to these categories was quietly shelved and did not resurface until the emergence of "human rights" law in the latter half of the century.[24]

From 1923 attention focused not on "civilians" per se but rather on the more discrete categories of civilians of enemy nationality who found themselves in the hands of their adversaries, either by dint of being residents of or present in enemy states at the outbreak of hostilities or those who fell into enemy hands by virtue of invasion and armed occupation. The conceptual benefit of narrowing discussion to civilians of "enemy nationality" did not end the debate over what the term "civilian" actually entailed. We will expand on this matter below, but here we need merely note that concern over the difficulty of reaching an agreement on civilians was sufficiently great to convince delegates at the 1925 Red Cross conference to uncouple civilians from discussions of a code for prisoners of war. By this date Swiss officials were already alarmed by French and Italian comments over the wisdom of concluding a POW convention.[25] Protracted negotiations over civilian issues might, it was feared, embolden these critics and jeopardize the chances of securing a timely agreement on a prisoner-of-war code. It was therefore only after the conclusion of a POW convention in July 1929 that the ICRC, the Swiss government, and the international community more broadly felt able to return to the subject of civilians.

With the benefit of hindsight, such caution was clearly wise. The practical and legal issues posed by a civilians' convention were infinitely more complex than those confronting military prisoners. By the late nineteenth century nobody questioned a belligerent's right to reduce its adversary's military power by detaining members of its armed forces.[26] But could a similar argument be made for enemy civilians, and if so, what criteria should govern the selection of those to be detained and the length and nature of their detention? At what point did "innocent civilians" justify treatment normally reserved for regular "combatants"?[27] Furthermore, while military POWs were, as members of the armed forces, bound by an oath of allegiance to their state, the same was not necessarily the case for civilians, especially those who had voluntarily chosen to reside abroad. It was not clear whether their detention could be justified on grounds of security or their repatriation on the grounds of humanitarianism. Finally, there was the question of resources. Resident aliens could be left to fend for themselves without being made destitute, but the same could not necessarily be said for enemy nationals who unwittingly found themselves in enemy hands at the start of war and for whom some kind of state intervention might be required for their own good.

None of these issues was itself inherently intractable. Many of these subjects had been addressed as practical problems in the wartime agreements, and when internal discussions resumed in the early 1930s, the ICRC made rapid progress in establishing the criteria for selecting which categories of civilians could be legitimately detained or denied their liberties. The real obstacle to a civilian code was not legal or conceptual but political. The confidence that Ferrière, in particular, placed in the powers' willingness to translate their ad hoc wartime agreements into permanent legally binding conventions was misplaced. Paul Dinichert, as head of the Swiss political department, had hosted the belligerents' negotiations in 1917 and 1918; in December 1923 he astutely observed that the wartime agreements were not ultimately motivated by the spirit of humanity but rather by the need to satiate the demands of the prisoners' next-of-kin at home. In the absence of this political imperative, there was little chance of governments' signing up to their former pledges.[28] Dinichert's view was shared by Lord Younger, one of the architects of the 1917 Anglo-German accord, who admitted that when issues were dealt with as existing difficulties, "belligerents were prepared to come to a far more elaborate arrangement than you could ever have committed them to in advance."[29]

The state that voiced the most strident opposition to the idea of a civilian code in the 1920s was France, though the Italian government harbored similar concerns. As the premier military power on the continent, French views carried particular weight, though for cultural as well as historic reasons, the ICRC had long deferred to the opinions of the French government and its national Red Cross society.[30] While few in the 1920s considered the Hague or Geneva conventions applicable to the subjects of colonial rule, the entry of French forces into the Ruhr on January 11, 1923, brought state practice into direct contact with the nascent ideas raised in Geneva and gave a piquancy to the debates at the eleventh Red Cross conference when it opened in August of that year. Paris was naturally determined to discourage any discussions over refining civilians' legal rights under "alien" rule, lest they incite civil disobedience and resistance in the Ruhr. The French Red Cross delegate, Baron d'Anthouard, not only spoke out against eliding the two categories of prisoners—the civilian and the military—but pointedly warned the committee against exceeding its remit as an "expert in charity" and encroaching on matters that were the preserve of sovereign states. French attitudes on this matter did not materially soften after their forces withdrew from the Ruhr in August 1925.[31]

So opposed was Paris to the whole question of a civilian convention that the committee felt it wise to tread carefully in subsequent discussions, despite receiving assurances from other quarters, notably Swiss, Dutch, and German, that its right to initiative in this and similar areas was recognized and welcomed.[32] The committee heeded French advice and limited itself to merely collating the key principles underpinning the wartime agreements, rather than pulling the individual clauses together into a draft code.[33] The exercise had its merits and resulted in a set of principles that later resurfaced in the 1934 Tokyo "project," but it left many of the more detailed provisions from the wartime agreements unexplored and added little momentum to the wider drafting process. The committee was also mindful to keep discussions within Red Cross circles and maintain foreign governments at a distance. Instead of directly approaching current or retired officials for their views, the committee left these discussions in the hands of Julien Lescaze, who could claim to speak in a private capacity as a lawyer and doctoral candidate at the University of Geneva, rather than as secretary to the ICRC's "commission des civils."[34] Needless to say, Lescaze's discussions did not progress very far and exasperated those, like Ferrière, who wanted to inject pace into the project and craft an international consensus behind the initiative.[35]

The ICRC was not alone in treading warily on the subject of civilian internees. Many of the early postwar attempts to reflect on the wartime experiences and draft codes for POWs sought to tackle the two subjects in parallel. The British Grotius Society debated the issue at some length in the years immediately following the conclusion of hostilities, while the ILA maintained a lively interest in the matter throughout the first half of the 1920s, picking up on Bellot and Phillimore's paper of 1920 and devoting substantial time to the subject at its conferences in The Hague in 1921 and Stockholm in 1924.[36] In contrast to the ICRC, the ILA focused on civilian prisoners and remained silent on the question of civilians under enemy occupation. At the close of its 1924 conference, members expressed the hope that a draft code, consisting of twenty articles, might form the basis of discussion at a future diplomatic conference. Two years later the association specifically brought the issue of civilian prisoners to the attention of a committee of legal experts at the League of Nations. Yet, notwithstanding the growing interest in the issue, none of the efforts of the international legal community to shift attitudes made much headway, nor were the lawyers able to overturn the entrenched reluctance of states to accept legal restrictions on their dealings with civilian populations in time of war.[37]

The Geneva Conference, July 1929

Against this backdrop the unanimous support expressed at the 1929 conference in Geneva to the idea of pursuing a code for civilians might seem rather odd. The initiative was prompted by discussions over whether to include article 91 of the ICRC's draft code into the final POW convention. The article proposed allowing certain categories of civilians who found themselves in enemy territory at the start of hostilities to be assimilated to the position of POWs. When the matter came up for debate, the British and German delegations both spoke out against introducing an issue that lay beyond the delegates' competencies and the original remit of the conference. The widespread sympathy for the sentiments behind the draft article nevertheless persuaded the Italian and Danish delegations to push for the inclusion of a nonbinding resolution (Fr. *vœu*) in the Final Act of the Conference, calling on the international community to draw up, as soon as possible, a code protecting the rights of individuals who found themselves in enemy hands.[38]

The 1929 "vœu" could be dismissed as simply a rhetorical device, permitting those present to brandish their humanitarian credentials without committing them to any firm action. It conveniently suppressed further discussion on the subject and meant that the ICRC's article was never put to a vote. Expressions of sympathy were a poor substitute for the ICRC's hope of assimilating civilians by default to the POW code. The vœu also avoided apportioning responsibility for the preparatory work required to bring the matter to a diplomatic conference. Still, the breadth of support in favor of a civilian code is impressive and suggests at least some softening of opinions on the issue. There is little doubt that to many delegates the oft-rehearsed objections against the idea of a civilian convention no longer rang true.[39] This was certainly the case with the political tensions that had blighted earlier discussions. The delegates themselves appear to have been heartened by their success in negotiating the Red Cross and POW conventions. The chief British delegate later spoke of the "cooperation and harmony" that marked the conference and the surprising (to him) extent to which the former enemies found themselves occupying similar positions on the major areas of debate, aided in part by the need to deflect some of the wilder suggestions aired by delegates from neutral or nonbelligerent states.[40]

While a sense of collegiality may well have encouraged the belief that a civilian convention lay within reach, there were also important initiatives introduced into the new POW convention that materially improved the chances of securing agreement on civilian code and helped frame discussions in the years leading up to the Tokyo conference in October 1934. The first and most obvious was the success in prizing POWs from the Hague tradition of the "laws and customs of war" and situating them within Geneva law, with its focus on humanitarianism and providing succor to the victims of war.[41] This reflected a broader recognition that POWs were not merely "disarmed combatants" but "humanitarian subjects," deserving of a discrete set of rights and privileges derived from their status as privileged combatants.[42] There was still a conceptual gulf to be crossed before civilians could be equated with military prisoners, but some of the objections to bestowing privileges on civilians under humanitarian law, and the involvement of the ICRC in this process, were weakened by the emergence of a dedicated POW code in 1929. If POWs could be extracted from the laws of war, why not select categories of civilians deemed especially vulnerable?

This conceptual shift was further strengthened by subtle changes in the way the new convention extended protection and privileges to POWs. The new convention went farther than many had expected in protecting POWs from acts of deliberate victimization. Although the 1921 Red Cross conference had, as we have seen, condemned as inhumane hostage taking and the use of civilians in reprisals, by the middle of the decade opinions had shifted, partly in recognition of the valuable deterrent effect that reprisals could play and partly from doubts over the wisdom of questioning an issue of such importance to state sovereignty and security.[43] ICRC officials came away from the 1925 Red Cross conference convinced that the question of hostage taking was best omitted from any future convention. They also agreed to delay judgment on reprisals until states had shown their hand in negotiating a POW convention. Discussions in 1929 did little to clarify the issue of hostage taking, but article 2's prohibition on reprisal measures against POWs represented a major advance and inevitably fanned hopes that similar concessions could be won for civilians.[44]

The new POW convention was also significant in shifting the site of humanitarian protection and refining its territorial focus. Under the Red Cross Conventions for the Amelioration of the Condition of the Wounded and Sick in Armies in the Field of 1864, 1906, and 1929, the principal site of humanitarian action lay on the battlefield. The 1929 POW convention, by contrast, shifted the locus of action away from the battlefield and into the POWs' camps and places of employment. Although the conference saw some dissension over precisely when and where the POW convention should apply, the wartime agreements were quite explicit about the need to remove POWs from the front line and zone of operations.[45] The events of the Great War had, of course, eroded the distinction between the "front line" and the "home front" under the pressure of economic blockade, aerial bombardment, and the expanding ideas of "total" war. But in 1929 delegates reverted to classical understandings of the battlefield; attention was directed toward framing humanitarian standards for spaces explicitly located outside a defined battle space and which were essentially "at peace."[46] At the same time, while POWs were accorded general rights as humanitarian subjects (the right to humane treatment, to protection from acts of violence, insults, and public curiosity, for example), the new POW convention also granted rights and standards of treatment to POWs in defined geographical areas (POW camps and work detachments). In the process it established a precedent for linking the bestowal of privileges and protections not just to categories of individuals (in this case, military prisoners) but to specific localities and spaces. These spaces of "exception," to use Agamben's phrase, were exceptional not just for the restrictions they imposed on their inmates but for the protective regime they permitted as well.[47]

The final innovation introduced in 1929 that went on to influence subsequent discussions over a civilian code was the decision to call on the services of neutral "protecting powers" to supervise the application of the POW convention. While not unknown before 1914, over the course of the Great War, the belligerents had increasingly called upon protecting powers to hold their adversaries to their obligations under the Hague regulations and wartime agreements and to help administer the distribution of relief aid to civilian populations under enemy control.[48] In agreeing to the involvement of external sovereign authorities in the functioning of the POW regime, the 1929 convention not only effectively made belligerent powers accountable to the international community for their treatment of military prisoners but also put in place an authoritative body to whom the belligerent governments, and their captured servicemen, could appeal to defend their interests and investigate alleged infringements of the convention.[49] They gave hope to those who wished to underscore the humanitarian status acquired by POWs under the convention and strike a more equitable balance between the prisoners' interests and the political and security concerns of the detaining power. The benefit that such arrangements could bring to any convention that sought to mediate relations between state authorities and enemy civilians was self-evident.

The one area where the 1929 convention disappointed advocates of a civilian convention was in its failure to advance debate on who was entitled to protection as a POW. Despite criticism of the German army's ferocious response to "*francs-tireurs*" in Belgium and northern France, no attempt was made in 1929 to clarify what might constitute a "legitimate combatant." Instead, the 1929 convention reserved POW status for those who satisfied the traditional criteria for combatant status as set down in the fourth Hague convention of October 18, 1907.[50] This did little to help define the position of civilians. As Helen Kinsella reminds us, the modern concept of a civilian only emerged over the course of the nineteenth century, while the concept of combatant status has been in continuous development for over eight hundred years.[51] Under such circumstances it was clearly unhelpful to consider "civilians" as being the linear opposite of "combatants," just as it was unwise to equate "civilian internees" and "political prisoners" with "POWs," or "civilians of conscription age" with "combatants."

Discussion on these matters over the 1920s had revealed striking variations in opinion. For some in the ICRC, like Mlle. Suzanne Ferrière, who took the lead in championing civilian interests after the death of her uncle, Frédéric Ferrière, in 1924, it was perfectly appropriate to assign the rights attached to POWs to any males of military age detained by their adversary or denied the right to return home. The fact that they had not "yet" taken up arms was irrelevant. To others, even inside the organization, "the principle of complete assimilation of a civil prisoner and a military prisoner [was] false and contrary to the spirit of modern law."[52] Such views resonated powerfully in official and legal circles abroad.[53] The ILA settled upon a definition in 1924, an "enemy national who is not subject to their country's military jurisdiction," but this hardly captured the complexity of identities, positions, and loyalties of civilians caught up in conflict.[54]

From Geneva to Tokyo

The results of the 1929 Geneva conference clearly emboldened the ICRC to return to the issue of civilian protection, despite the absence of a clear mandate. Its "civilian commission" was speedily reconstituted, and in keeping with earlier practice, steps were taken to secure Swiss approval for this strand of work. The influence of the POW convention on the development of thinking over the next five years was unmistakable and entirely deliberate.[55] The draft convention presented to the 1934 Red Cross conference in Tokyo evoked many of the principles established in 1929. Besides protections against acts of violence and intimidation and insistence on humane standards of treatment and conditions of detention, measures of reprisals against enemy civilians in the territory of a belligerent were specifically prohibited (article 10), as was the general right to deport or take hostages from the civilian population of an occupied territory.[56] Article 17 stipulated that the POW convention would be applied "by analogy" to civilians, thus setting a benchmark for what constituted an acceptable level of treatment. Finally, neutral protecting powers were given extensive powers to oversee the application of the code, inspect places of internment, represent prisoners' interests with the camp authorities, and offer their good offices to resolve disputes.

The advantages in taking the 1929 POW convention as a template for drafting a civilian code were obvious, but there were also significant downsides. For one thing, the 1934 draft code followed the POW convention in ignoring the confusion around definitions. The code updated the 1907 Hague regulations for civilians living under foreign occupation and for the first time covered enemy civilians in the territory of a belligerent. But it ducked responsibility for clarifying precisely what constituted a "civilian" in these circumstances, defining them as merely anyone who failed to fulfill the Hague criteria for combatants. Civilians were therefore denied the status of lawful belligerents, while at the same time they were assured "by analogy" the same rights accorded to legitimate "combatants" under the POW convention.

There was, as we have seen, much to be gained from aligning the draft civilian code with the earlier POW convention. At the same time, however, in continuously genuflecting to the POW convention, those tasked with crafting a civilian code may have inadvertently closed down fruitful lines of inquiry. One such initiative was the suggestion by Edmond Boissier, president of the ICRC's "commission des civils," that the issue be reframed into one that juxtaposed a set of ideas and principles applicable to those "on campaign" (concerning the rights of "combatants") and one designed for those who were "not on campaign" (dealing with the rights of "noncombatants").[57] Boissier's proposal clearly lacked precision and harked back to traditional and (by the 1920s) largely anachronistic assumptions about the nature of warfare. Yet, the possibility of conceptualizing the way enemy aliens could be treated outside zones of active military operations certainly piqued the imagination of some inside the ICRC. Over the 1920s thinking about the treatment of aliens had begun to evolve beyond the traditional norms governing a state's right to extend diplomatic or consular protection to its citizens living abroad.

By the end of the decade, the international community had crafted an increasingly sophisticated web of bilateral agreements governing the treatment of foreign nationals in different jurisdictions, based, ostensibly, on the reciprocal exchange of social and welfare rights and protections.[58] The period had also seen states sign up to the 1926 international convention outlawing slavery and imposing strict constraints on the use of forced and compulsory labor, echoing some of the ambitions Ferrière had championed for his "civilians" code in the early 1920s.[59] Taken collectively, these treaties, though designed for times of peace, provided a framework for considering how the rights of aliens could also be applied to the context of "enemy nationals" in times of war, one that, critically, was divorced from the 1929 POW convention or the Hague regulations governing armed occupation. It was precisely this kind of paradigm shift that was required to give substance to Bellot and Phillimore's radical ideas about the "civilianization" of military prisoners. The nearest the Tokyo "project" came to admitting to this possibility was its insistence that enemy civilians should "receive the treatment to which aliens are ordinarily entitled."[60]

Following the close of the Geneva conference in the summer of 1929, the ICRC was left in comparative peace to develop its ideas. The subject was ignored by the ILA. Beyond the rarefied confines of the ICRC, most observers fixed their attention on the deepening economic crisis, the outbreak of fighting in East Asia, and the fate of the world disarmament talks, which opened in Geneva in February 1932 and reached their denouement in June 1934. These unfolding events clearly colored the work of the ICRC's "commission des civils" and eroded the sense of optimism that had briefly characterized deliberations in 1929. By the time officials convened in early 1934 to prepare materials for the Red Cross conference in Tokyo that autumn, Hitler had already announced his intention to withdraw Germany from the disarmament talks and the League of Nations.

Under the circumstances, it is legitimate to ask whether the ICRC had any real faith in the draft civilian code it presented in Tokyo. While Red Cross delegates in Tokyo might be expected to applaud the idea, the fracturing of international politics cast serious doubts over whether state support would ever be forthcoming, notwithstanding the growing number of ratifications for the 1929 POW convention, including Germany's on February 21, 1934. These doubts resonated with particular force in discussions over the new code's scope and ambition. Members of the "commission des civils" settled on the view that the code should content itself with outlining key principles, leaving it to belligerents to thrash out details as required. Others, including the committee's legal expert, Paul des Gouttes, wished to replicate the line pursued in 1929 and tie states to a comprehensive set of policies and standards based on those elements of the POW convention and the 1907 rules that had applied to civilian prisoners during the last war. While both approaches had their merits, it was their reading of the external environment that ultimately convinced the ICRC to embrace the commission's view.[61] The draft code thus remained at the level of generalities; the nature of any detail provisions were merely alluded "by analogy" to the 1929 POW code (article 17) and by reference to the 1907 Hague rules (article 18). To those who had hoped for a more expansive convention, the sense of frustration was palpable: "One day," des Gouttes wearily noted on learning of the decision, "the convention will be tested in war, and when it is found to be insufficient, we will then have to complete it in the way we have done for prisoners of war."[62]

Whatever its doubts over the robustness of the draft code, there were a number of external pressures at play that help account for the ICRC's approach to the Tokyo conference. In contrast to the situation facing the committee in the early 1920s, relations with the League of Red Cross Societies were cordial and little threat was thought to exist from this quarter.[63] What concerned the committee, however, was the thought that its work might be overtaken by developments elsewhere. Throughout the 1920s the committee had kept a wary eye on the Dutch government, lest it reassert its position as guardian of the laws of war and resume the series of Hague "peace" conferences that had stalled after the outbreak of war in 1914. This never occurred, but the collapse of the Geneva disarmament conference in June 1934 tempted the Belgian government down a similar path, donning the mantle of champion of international law that it had last worn in 1874. In July 1934 Brussels dispatched letters to the major powers, offering to convene a conference the following year to discuss a convention for the humanization of warfare. The proposal may have been, in the words of ICRC president Max Huber, "disjointed and incoherent," but when the German Red Cross signaled that it would not stand in Brussels's way, the committee was forced to reassess its position.[64] Not only did it need to defend its right to initiate discussion on the question of civilian protection, a right it had painstakingly built up over the last fifteen years, but it had also to guard against the possibility of having its draft code hijacked by the Belgians and subsumed into a process over which it had no control—and whose chances of success were at best slim. In Tokyo, then, the ICRC delegation found itself promoting a highly circumscribed, abridged code that amounted to little more than a statement of basic principles and a framework for future discussions between the belligerents. ICRC delegates were animated less by the thrill of finally presenting a civilian code to the Red Cross community, or even a conviction in the intrinsic practical merits of their endeavors, than by the need to protect the ICRC's standing and avoid being ensnared in Belgian diplomatic maneuvers.

The fate of the Tokyo "project" is well known.[65] In the short term, the Red Cross conference was a marked success. Max Huber's opening appeal for unity was heeded, the Japanese Red Cross society proved exemplary hosts, and most items on the agenda progressed without provoking serious dissent. The ICRC's draft civilian code was warmly received, and delegates called on the ICRC to work with the Swiss authorities and bring the matter back to a diplomatic conference in Geneva. The longer-term consequences were, however, less positive. Although Berlin and Rome reacted favorably to Swiss inquiries, few could ignore the duplicity of Berlin's appeals to humanitarianism by this date, and when Berne's note went unanswered in London and was firmly rebuffed in Paris, Swiss officials opted to suspend further action until the diplomatic atmosphere improved. The ICRC tried to resurrect the matter after the Red Cross conference in 1938, but Germany's invasion of Poland in September of the following year wrecked any chance of convening a diplomatic conference in Geneva. With confidence in the civilian code ebbing, ICRC officials increasingly pinned their hopes on the "Lieux de Genève," which worked to secure recognition for the creation of safe havens for civilians and medical personnel. These initiatives failed to develop any traction, and although the ICRC called upon the belligerents to abide by the Tokyo project at the start of the conflict, references to the draft civilian code became progressively less frequent in ICRC public statements as the war progressed.

The Great War may, then, have marked a key moment in the evolution of civilian internment practices, but it did not bring about any substantive improvement in the legal or normative framework governing this activity. Those involved in advancing the matter have been criticized for failing to stand up to the blatant self-interest of state authorities or to predict the horrors that awaited civilian and military prisoners after 1941. Given the context, it is perhaps fairer to fault them for leaving intact a legal regime that had been so woefully exposed during the Great War and its immediate aftermath. That some measure of reform was at least possible after 1918 is evident from the successful negotiation of the 1929 POW convention and the 1925 Geneva protocol banning the use of poisonous and asphyxiating gases, both of which imposed significant restraints on the exercise of state power. The history of the civilian code is not simply, therefore, the story of a worthy initiative floundering on the rocks of political realism. What lay at the root of the code's demise was a failure to manage the negotiation process and build coalitions and networks of experts in support of the proposal.[66]

It was also a failure to conceive of the project in terms other than those set out in the POW convention. Opportunities were lost to frame civilian protection as part of the new rights-based paradigm that had permeated thinking over the protection of minorities and children in the early 1920s or the norms governing the reciprocal treatment of alien nationals that came to the fore at the same time.[67] For all the ambiguity around what constituted a "civilian," drafters remained wedded to the Genevan tradition of bestowing rights and protections to particular "privileged" groups occupying particular locations, rather than to individuals. The limitations of both the approach and the assumptions that underpinned it were laid bare over the course of the 1930s and 1940s by states intent on not just defeating their enemies on the battlefield but annihilating their entire societies and political systems. These experiences forced the ICRC to reconsider the wisdom of attaching rights to privileged categories and, for the first time, tempted the leadership into basing their action on an appeal to the "droits des gens."[68] In the process, it began a dialogue between international humanitarian law and human rights that continues unabated to this day.

Notes

The authors would like to thank Kimberly Lowe, Romain Fathi, and the editors for their comments on earlier drafts. The ideas were initially aired at a workshop, "Dialogues among Experiences and Representations of Major Wars of the Twentieth Century," hosted by the University of Seville/University of Buenos Aires (September 2017).

1. ILA 1920, 249.
2. ILA 1920, 274.
3. See memo by M. S. Prichard, "Draft Regulations for the Treatment of Civilian Prisoners of War," June 28, 1924, Institute of Advanced Legal Studies (IALS), London, Archives of the International Law Association, ILA/3/11/1.
4. Wylie 2010a, 44–47; Tate, 2017.
5. See Beaumont 1983, 67–94.
6. See Best 1994; articles 42–56 of the "Regulations concerning the Law and Customs of War on land," annexed to the fourth Hague Convention of 1907.
7. See Becker, A. 2012.
8. Alexander 2007, 369.
9. The following agreements covered civilian affairs: Russia-Austria-Germany (Stockholm, December 1915, May and December 1916; Christiana, November 1917; Petrograd, January 1918); Austro-Hungary-Romania (May 1917); U.K.-Germany (Hague, July 1917; Berne, May 1918; Hague, July 1918); Germany-Austria-Romania-Russia-Turkey (Copenhagen, October–November 1917); Bulgaria-Serbia (Geneva, November 1917); U.K.-Turkey (Berne, December 1917); France-Turkey (Berne, March 1918); France-Germany (Berne, March 1918, April 1918); Belgium-Germany (Berne, March–April 1918); Italy-Germany (Berne, May 1918); Austria-Hungary-Serbia (Berne, June 1918); Austria-Hungary-Italy (Berne, September 1918); U.S.-Germany (Berne, November 1918).
10. This was especially so in Austria-Hungary, where some Entente nationals enjoyed considerable liberty and freedom of movement; see Stibbe 2018, 61–84.
11. Palmieri 2012, 1278; Holmes 2018, 119.
12. Irwin 2017, 36–49.
13. Ador 1915, 5–8. See Stibbe 2006 and, in general, Bugnion 2018; Durand 1984, 83–89.
14. Eduoard Naville, September 10, 1917, "Conference des Neutres," September 14, 1917, AICRC, CS 4.
15. See the remarks of the ICRC president in September 1917, cited in Becker, A. 2015, 1039.
16. See propositions by M. Huber on revision of the Geneva Convention of 1906, December 6, 1918, AICRC, CR93/24.
17. See Gerwarth 2016.
18. For the League's "challenge," see Hutchinson 1996.

19. See Palmeiri 2018 and Piana 2015.

20. See Lowe 2014 and Rodogno 2014.

21. Lowe 2019, 84–93.

22. ICRC 1921; Tate 2017, 205–9.

23. Van Dijk 2018, 561. Russia provides an extreme case; see Gatrell 2000; Lohr 2003.

24. For a survey of this development, see Bates 2010; Hitchcock 2012.

25. For French and Italian objections to the POW code, see meeting with M. Dinichert, February 12, 1926, AICRC CR119/11, and meeting of the ICRC, November 3, 1927, AICRC C2.

26. Neff 2010.

27. For contrasting policies during the Crimean and Franco-Prussian wars, see Dixon 2016; Caglioti 2013.

28. Meeting with M. Dinichert, December 15, 1923, AICRC.

29. ILA 1920, 241–42.

30. See Cotter 2017, 124–30.

31. See Girardet to Lescaze, November 23, 1923, CRI 15; minutes of commission de civils, August 29, 1923, AICRC 1925.

32. For German support, see Frankfurter Verein vom Roten Kreuz to Lescaze (ICRC), December 4, 1923, AICRC, CR119/7; "Le problem des civils et la procedure a suivre," n.d (probably February 1926), AICRC, CR119/11.

33. Commission des civils, November 28, 1923, AICRC, CR119–7.

34. See Commission des civils, November 28, 1923, AICRC, CR199.

35. F. Ferrière to E. Boissier, November 20, 1923, AICRC, CR199.

36. See ILA 1922 and ILA 1924; Phillimore and Bellot 1919; Phillimore 1920.

37. For a discussion of this process, see Landefeld 2021, chap. 4.

38. ICRC 1930, Première Commission, July 19 (Italian intervention) and July 26, 1929; Deuxième Commission, July 22 and 24, 1929 (Danish intervention).

39. See remark by Des Gouttes, Meeting of the International Committee, October 31, 1929, AICRC, CR119 GV.

40. Sir Horace Rumbold, July 31, 1929, cited in Wylie 2010b, 102; Wylie and Cameron 2019, 1349.

41. The Russian delegate at the 1863 Geneva conference and Henri Dunant in 1873 both proposed extending the Red Cross idea to cover prisoners of war, though neither development took hold.

42. For a wider discussion, see Wylie and Cameron 2019.

43. "Memorandum concernant le problème des prisonniers civils et l'élaboration éventuelle d'un projet d'une Convention internationale règlant la situation des civils tombés à la guerre au pouvoir de l'ennemi" (c. July 1925), 11–12, AICRC, CR119/7.

44. Wylie and Cameron 2019, 1336–43.

45. For the "thirty kilometers" rule, see Jones, H. 2008b.

46. For law's spatial dimension, see Mégret 2011/12. The 1923 Hague Draft Rules of Aerial Warfare also implicitly tied civilian protection to different territorial spaces; Alexander 2007, 374–75.

47. For camps as "states of exception," see Agamben 2005, and for their historical evolution, Greiner and Kramer 2013, and as "spaces of hyper-jurisdiction with multiple, overlapping legal codes applying," Jones, H. 2016, 33.

48. See Henn 1986 and Stibbe 2006.

49. See Wylie 2010b, 98–101; Wylie and Cameron 2019, 1343–46.

50. Article 1. Convention relative to the Treatment of Prisoners of War. Geneva, July 27, 1929; the only advance was the assimilation of aerial and maritime warfare to the original 1907 rules governing the conduct of war on land.

51. Kinsella 2011, 29, passim. See also Scheipers 2015, 33–104.

52. Comment by M. Drachenfels, "Prisonniers Civils. Visite de MM. Cramer & Drachenfels à M. Dinichert le 30 juillet 1925," AICRC, CR119–7.

53. See note by J.E.G. de Montmorency, July 25, 1924, IALS, ILA/3/11/1.

54. ILA 1924. For the civilian experience, see Proctor 2010, Barros and Thomas 2018.

55. Commission des Civils, November 23, 1931, AICRC, CR119/11.

56. Draft International Convention on the Condition and Protection of Civilians of enemy nationality who are on territory belonging to or occupied by a belligerent. Tokyo, 1934. The taking of hostages was forbidden unless in "exceptional" circumstances and when deemed "indispensable." They were, however, to be treated humanely and not executed or subjected to corporal punishment.

57. Commission des Civils, June 23, 1931, AICRC, CR119/GV.

58. The French government signed agreements on immigration and migration with Poland, Italy, Czechoslovakia, and Yugoslavia. See Pachowicz 2017, 136–37.

59. Ferrière 1923; The Convention to Suppress the Slave Trade and Slavery, September 25, 1926.

60. Article 6. This was made subject to "measures of control or security," such as compulsory residence and internment.

61. Commission des Civils, February 27, 1934, AICRC, CR119/11.

62. See Commission des Civils, March 12, 1934, AICRC, CR119/11.

63. See Procès-verbal de la séance tenue par la Délégation à Tokio, August 16, 1934, AICRC, CRI/15, Folio 197.

64. Memoire établi pour les membres de la Délégation du CICR en vue de la XVme Conference, à Tokio (August 28, 1934); Draudt (Vice President, German Red Cross) to Brown (ICRC), July 25, 1934 (handwritten), AICRC, CRI 15, Folios 204, 180.

65. Durand 1984, 288–92.

66. For the successful techniques used in the 1925 Geneva protocol, see Holmes 2018, 127.

67. See Cabanes 2014; Van Dijk 2018, 559–62.

68. For the ICRC's "Appel sur les violations du droit des gens," see Favez 1999, 84–89.

Conclusion

World War I and Its Internments: Final Remarks

Iris Rachamimov and Rotem Kowner

Some four years after the Great War had ended, the Italian sculptor Paolo Boldrini unveiled a grand memorial in the Austro-Hungarian camp of Mauthausen where he had formerly been interned as a prisoner. Boldrini used Carrara marble for his 4.5-meter-high memorial and dedicated it to the 1,831 Italian prisoners of war who had died in Mauthausen, but he did not forget to mention the dead inmates of other Allied nationalities.[1] The *Kriegsgefangenenlager Mauthausen* (POW Camp Mauthausen) had opened its gates in October 1914 and within two months grew to house more than fifteen thousand Serbian POWs in what quickly became one of the largest camps in Austria-Hungary, encompassing eight subcamps and sixty barracks.[2] During the first months of 1915, a deadly typhus epidemic swept through Mauthausen, killing an estimated twelve thousand people, mostly prisoners of war, but also guards, civilian workers, and even the Bishop of Linz, Rudolph Hittmair, who had visited the camp for a few hours. The Italian POWs memorialized by Boldrini only arrived in Mauthausen after Italy became involved in World War I in May 1915, after which the camp population swelled within a year to encompass some forty thousand inmates.

Despite its massive size and tragic history very few people associate the name "Mauthausen" with World War I. The SS concentration camp Mauthausen, which existed between August 1938 and May 1945, completely overshadows the historical writing about the place and its memory. A search for the keyword "Mauthausen" in a scholarly database would consequently yield thousands of academic texts on the latter camp and almost none on the former.[3] Two hundred thousand visitors call on the memorial for the victims of the Nazi camp (*KZ-Gedenkstätte Mauthausen*) annually, while hardly anyone visits the Boldrini memorial located a mere few kilometers away.[4] Granted, the fact that the SS camp was much deadlier, that over ninety thousand inmates perished in it, and that it was meant to be a particularly brutal instrument of repression from its very establishment makes it far better known.[5] However, as we argued in the introduction of this volume, the latter camp is also better known because internment—military, civilian, and political—is inherently connected with World War II and is perceived as one of its salient features. In contrast, mass internment during World War I does not seem to possess the same resonance, despite the memorialization efforts of former prisoners in the interwar years, the legal discussions about wartime internment that have never abated since World War I, and the efforts of historians in the past few decades.

However, as demonstrated by the contributors to this volume, World War I was an important stage in the long-term evolution of the internment camp, and it is still crucial for understanding its usage by modern states. Although the institution of the internment camp emerged before World War I as a means for dealing with unruly, needy, or uprooted populations—primarily in colonial settings—it only became a global fixture during World War I. It became the default space in which to place millions of people who seemed to be either "out of place" or "out of line." Consequently, it was used by a plethora of political powers: imperial and national states, militaristic monarchies and democratic republics, internationally recognized governments and newly formed revolutionary regimes. By the same token, it was also used by neutral countries during the war and by international organizations after the cessation of fighting. Put differently, the internment camp served different purposes and it still does in many parts of the world.

The present volume has sought to offer a fresh perspective on mass internments during World War I, on the meanings of their global proliferation, and on understanding their postwar repercussions. Its narrative, divided into eleven thematic chapters, was bound by several lines of investigation on the nature of internment during this long conflict.

Categories of Internment

Our introduction argued that the conventional categories that separate military, civilian, and political interments and treat them as sui generis do not offer a sufficiently nuanced description of the complexity found in World War I. These ostensibly different forms of internment, we proposed, were much more fluid in nature and often overlapped. From an experiential perspective, similar living conditions and camp regimes could be found across all three categories, and at times holding powers opted to obfuscate the difference when it suited them. Several of the chapters in this volume confirmed this argument. Bohdan Kordan, for example, shows how destitute and unemployed enemy aliens in Canada were interned and put to work as prisoners of war. Disregarding the distinction between "civilian" and "military" categories, they would be viewed as "enemies" without recognized rights. This ambiguity enabled them to be utilized as forced labor, constructing roads through the dense wilderness of the fabled Canadian Rocky Mountain National Park. It also led to abuse and neglect, mistreatment being commonplace. But so too was resistance among the internees, a great many of whom found it inconceivable they would be treated this way. The experience at Castle Mountain/Banff approached what was occurring at other internment camps on the frontier. Yet, as Kordan maintains, where it did differ was in the poignancy of the work, undertaken for the purpose of developing the national park as a place of rest, relaxation, and contemplation—a place of comfort for the nation. In this regard, the work was carried out on the understanding that the internees neither could nor ever would be part of the nation.

The distinction between civilian, military, and political prisoners was also blurred as a result of a growing military involvement in civilian affairs. This state of affairs developed in Germany, Russia, and Austria-Hungary, where the armies acquired an increasing influence over the economy, infrastructure, politics, and social policy. As André Keil and Matthew Stibbe show in their respective chapters, this military expansion took place during the war within the prewar territory of Germany and even more clearly in the occupied territories administered by the German military. In Austria-Hungary, as Doina Anca Cretu demonstrates, camps for fleeing civilians offered securitized protection but were transformed from a temporary plan to contain outsiders to a permanent fixture of war policy. The blurring of categories also continued in the aftermath of war as ex-prisoners began returning home. As Hazuki Tate shows in her chapter, the Allies tightened their control over the movement of returning prisoners for their own political purposes. In Germany, for example, Russian military prisoners found themselves manipulated politically by both their former captors as well as their supposed liberators.

In other places delegates of the International Committee of the Red Cross (ICRC) discovered that certain countries arbitrarily refused to admit prisoners who had been dwelling in their prewar territory for political and national reasons. Tate also makes plain that classifications changed because of the new international configuration. Certain identity labels—such as "Russian" or "Austrian" prisoners—were no longer applicable in the same way. The profound changes in the international state system after 1918 undermined previous categories of internment and made political and national markers reign supreme. Still, the unprecedented involvement of neutrals and, to some extent, global international organizations like the League of Nations, from 1919 onwards managed to reduce the hardships of many POWs and succeeded in repatriating more than five hundred thousand prisoners.

The Global Dimension of Internment

A central contention of this book has been that World War I made internment a global and universal phenomenon. Although various types of camps had already emerged in the latter part of the nineteenth century and the first decade of the twentieth century, they were mostly limited to colonial settings. These colonial camps were designed to control the actions and movements of recalcitrant subjects, whether in times of famine and plague—as in British India—or because of rebellions—as in Cuba, the Philippines, South Africa, and southwest Africa. At the same time, military POW camps were set up before the war to detain captured enemy personnel who were to be treated according to international regulations as envisioned in the Hague Conventions of 1899 and 1907. In spite of the fact that there were a few important wars in the decade preceding World War I, most notably the Russo-Japanese War of 1904–5 and the Balkan Wars of 1912–13, these were mostly regional affairs. World War I and its accompanying pressures—military, economic, social, political, and moral—seemed to have established the internment camp as a useful tool for controlling many of these challenges. As a result, camps were erected throughout the world, from New Zealand in the east to British Columbia in the west, and from Cape Town in the south to Murmansk in the north.

Thousands of camps dotted the globe, some very small and temporary and others large and long lasting. Millions of people experienced internment firsthand, while many others acclimated themselves grudgingly or willingly to the camp as a seemingly unavoidable bio-political tool. Put differently, mass internment became a universal phenomenon, not merely in a geographical sense but also in a political and a social sense. This had far-reaching repercussions; it led to the continued use of camps for various purposes by interwar regimes while simultaneously giving rise to attempts to standardize and regulate internment practices. As Neville Wylie and Sarina Landefeld discuss in their chapter, the 1920s ushered in an international discussion seeking to create more robust protections for military and civilian prisoners. It drew inspiration from bilateral agreements formulated during the war by various belligerents and sought to universalize their lessons. In this context, the ICRC became what Wylie and Landefeld refer to as the main "norm entrepreneur" pushing for international agreement. The successful negotiation of the 1929 POW Convention is a testimony to the possibilities existing at the time. However, the failure to agree on a civilian code led to disastrous consequences in the decades that followed.

Naoko Shimazu's contribution shows that Japan not only treated its prisoners much better during World War I than during World War II but also that the Japanese played a leading role in establishing internationally acceptable standards of treatment for enemy captives in the decades preceding the war. Despite playing a limited part in the Great War and not being involved in the land clashes in Europe, Japan's earlier experiences with Russian captives during the Russo-Japanese War had laid the foundation for their general treatment of captives during World War I. As Shimazu emphasizes, however, the category of race mattered a great deal to Japan at the time, and the question of which racial group attained a "proper" developmental stage and thus merited "civilized" treatment was central in the thinking of its ruling elites. The Bandō camp, which contained German and Austro-Hungarian prisoners, was viewed by the prisoners "as their 'country' or their 'town'" and was very similar in organization to the camps in Knockaloe (Britain) and Ruhleben (Germany). Inmates regarded it as the "best camp in the world." The Matsuyama camp, on the other hand, was less liked by its German-speaking prisoners.

Likewise, Nancy Fitch's chapter discusses how the global dimension of internment amplified ethnic stereotypes, racial prejudice, and—by extension—national strife. Britain had deployed 1.5 million soldiers from India while France mobilized 440,000 colonial troops from Africa and tens of thousands from Indochina and the Pacific Islands. Imperial Russia raised troops in the Caucasus and in its central and East Asian territories. When these non-European soldiers fell into the hands of the Central Powers their images were used for constructing a racialized view of the enemy and for showing "the true face" of Allied scheming, i.e., to attack the racial integrity of white Europe. As Fitch shows, the German and Austrian states were uniquely enthusiastic about "setting up social science researchers in the camps to measure, prod, record, and photograph POWs for scientific and propagandistic purposes." The presence of colonial prisoners in Europe and European prisoners across the globe, in turn, had diverse outcomes: it sharpened the tone of racist propaganda in Europe even as it demonstrated the vulnerability and weaknesses of the ostensibly superior "West" to non-European people. This would prove a stimulus for bitter struggle along ethnic and racial lines after the war but would lead eventually to future liberation too.

Mahon Murphy's chapter, in turn, analyzes the role of internment in the propaganda war of both sides. He argues that World War I marked a turning point in the development of modern propaganda as the need to mobilize support at home and in neutral countries increased during the prolonged conflict. The fate of fellow citizens in enemy hands struck a sympathetic chord among home audiences, and sensationalized stories about racial and ethnic degradations helped to divide the world into forces of "good" and "evil." As Murphy shows, the different theaters of war were interconnected from a propagandistic perspective, and stories from one area were avidly consumed in other areas. Thus, for example, Richard Meinertzhagen, who served as the chief of British military intelligence for the East African theater between 1915 and 1916, wrote propaganda pieces on the brutality in the African theater in order to increase recruitment in Britain.

The Determinants of Treatment during Internment

One of the common threads of this collection has been that the actual treatment of prisoners was influenced by a multitude of factors. Internees were not treated equally during World War I, and there was a very broad spectrum of camp regimes within different countries and between them. Previous historiography on World War I internment has already provided examples of the wide divergence in treatment, and several chapters in this collection underscore this point well. For example, Matthew Stibbe argues that we have to look beyond broad issues if we want to understand German internment practices and why they differed so markedly in specific contexts. Although "*große Politik*" (high politics), labor shortages, migratory considerations, and reciprocity between belligerents exerted an impact in this respect, it was frequently narrow issues that played a decisive role. The views and priorities of local military commanders could determine the well-being of prisoners, as could the guards' material and psychological drives.

Naoko Shimazu shows that Japan's largely positive treatment of POWs was embedded in a civilizational discourse dating back to the late nineteenth century. This discourse would weaken during the 1930s, resulting in a much more severe treatment of prisoners in World War II. She also shows how local officials were granted a certain leeway to decide on the de facto treatment of POWs despite the general policy framed by the state authorities.

The different behavior and personalities of the Japanese chief wardens in the Bandō and Kurume camps impacted the well-being of the internees, and in this respect Hazuki Tate's chapter discusses how the "legibility" of nationality—the authorities' capacity to assign a definite national identity to a prisoner—became an important determinant in deciding on the treatment and rights of returning prisoners. In order to accomplish repatriation, the ICRC and its delegates first had to determine a particular prisoner's actual patria, not always an easy task in the fluid boundaries of post–World War I. Prisoners from the former multinational empires could often speak a few languages and their self-identification was often complex or at odds with official categories.

Lena Radauer's chapter, in turn, shows how the prisoners' civilian professions could often exert a great influence on their experiences and fates. In her case study of German-speaking prisoners in Russia, Radauer shows how a captor state inquired about the civilian occupations of military prisoners and assigned them importance. In this respect, expert knowledge was critically needed in all sections of the Russian economy in order to replace the expertise of the millions of men who were recruited into the army. It is therefore hardly surprising that expert prisoners made up a significant proportion of the skilled workforce in certain parts of Russia. This was especially apparent in Siberia from 1918 onward, where professionals among the prisoners often provided sorely needed expertise. In this sense, camp industries provided a wide variety of products from medical supplies and riding equipment to alcohol and cigarettes.

Race proved to be a significant factor in some cases. This is not particularly surprising, as race had already played an important role in determining internment practices before 1914, as evidenced by British, American, and German policies in India, the Philippines, and southwest Africa respectively. World War I continued this trend, as revealed by Nancy Fitch, Naoko Shimazu, and Mahon Murphy in their chapters. In this matter, photographs, illustrations, and texts worked in tandem to disseminate the notion that the world is divided into unequal races whose humanity and cultural potential is inherently different. With this in mind, anthropologists, journalists, and artists used prisoners as grist for the mill in the construction of racial fantasies.

While gender has not been the main focus of this volume, it is nonetheless important to point out that it did play a role in determining treatment. Internment in World War I was largely a male experience. The great majority of military POWs were men, and most civilian internees were "enemy-alien" men of military age. As recent scholarship has shown, many everyday activities in officer and enemy-alien camps were designed to maintain a sense of productive masculinity, and prisoners often equated their mental well-being with performing these activities.[6] That said, it is crucial to emphasize that there were many women among the Belgian, French, and Eastern European forced laborers working in Germany, and women figured very prominently among refugees who fled the front lines. As Mahon Murphy shows in this volume, allegations of maltreatment of women internees, their sexual abuse in particular, were used as propaganda on both sides. Moreover, women and children predominated among the Armenian civilians sent to concentration camps in the Syrian desert, with many of them exposed to sexual violence.[7] Put differently, even though the great majority of those interned in the Great War were men, those who were the least protected and most brutalized included a disproportionately large number of women. This aspect of World War I internments should be further explored, especially vis-à-vis the Armenian genocide.

Internment and the End of the War

In most accounts, the Great War ends in November 1918, when the guns fell silent on the Western Front. However, as Robert Gerwarth and others have pointed out, fighting, conflict, and violence did not stop in many other parts of the world; Central and Eastern Europe, the Middle East, Turkey, Siberia, and the Caucasus were all hot spots of continuous battles.[8] Due to these conflicts and the logistical constraints involved in repatriating prisoners, the human tragedy associated with internment lasted long after the war officially ended. This is not a unique phenomenon, of course, and it commonly characterizes large-scale conflicts, World War II in particular.[9] Nonetheless, historians seeking to understand the global aspects of this war and to take seriously the "world" in World War I, should go beyond conventional periodization and examine what was referred to as "the Greater War."[10] Many of these post-1918 conflicts did not pit the armies of two internationally recognized sovereign states against each other. Instead, the conflicts frequently involved imperial forces battling local militias, paramilitary groups fighting each other, and armed ideological formations nicknamed "Reds," "Whites," or "Greens." The Russian Civil War is perhaps the best-known case of a war that drew state and nonstate actors into the mix, but significant fighting also continued for five years at what has been referred to as "the shatter zones of empires" i.e., in the areas previously controlled by the Ottoman empire, the Russian empire, the Habsburg empire, and the German empire.[11]

The post-1918 conflicts led to the capture and internment of many prisoners—military, civilian, and political. These were prisoners of war in a literal sense but seldom acknowledged as prisoners of war as defined by international law. Prisoners did not have the clout of a sovereign state to care for their rights and their well-being, and the level of violence inflicted on them by various armies appears to have been horrific. This is still a subject that has not been well researched and has not been integrated into the study of global internment at all. However, as discussed earlier with regard to Soviet concentration camps, the long-term legacies of 1918–1923 on the history of internment has been enormous. As new states and regimes attempted to create order and establish their legitimacy, they used internment as means to enforce their real and symbolic power.

Moreover, such humanitarian actors as the International Committee of the Red Cross (ICRC) and the newly formed League of Nations attempted to regulate this flow of people via transit camps.[12] At first these camps were established to facilitate the return of five million prisoners of war who had been captured on the Eastern Front. These returnees were initially viewed as ex-soldiers, as well as potential soldiers in the political struggles sweeping the region, but they soon became uprooted persons abandoned by both their governments and their captors in the vast region. It was not always clear to which country they belonged or should belong, as one confused ICRC delegate observed in his report. Writing from Budapest, he noted that "Russians pretended to be Hungarians and vice versa. . . . Russian prisoners were with Hungarian women, while the Hungarian prisoners were with Russian women."[13] Given these porous conditions and the epistemological instability, the bio-political device of an internment camp continued to make sense. Regardless of whether the people in the camp were civilians or soldiers, or whether they constituted a political, social, or demographic threat, they still needed to be stopped, sorted out, and classified. In many cases internment camps continue to fulfill this function to this very day.

This volume demonstrates that for a large number of internees the war ended much after an armistice with Germany had been signed on November 11, 1918. There was a wide gap between the official cease-fire date and the actual denouement of the internees' plight, regardless of their civil status. Their actual war experience was much longer than that of demobilized soldiers or civilians who worked in war-related jobs. For some prisoners, the experience lasted eight years. As is often the case, large-scale wars generate local conflicts and minor wars that do not necessarily terminate once the main conflict ends. This occurred in many regions between 1918–1923, as discussed in the present volume from several angles. Hazuki Tate's chapter, for example, provides a powerful reminder of the ordeal that many prisoners and internees experienced after the war ended, especially in countries such as

Russia, whose regime had collapsed, whose territory had been divided into new national entities, and whose population witnessed the outbreak of civil war or local conflicts.

Internees often carried the memories of their life behind barbed wire with them for years and decades to come. In this respect, the Swiss psychiatrist Adolf Vischer coined the term "barbed-wire disease" to describe the mood swings, irritability, and mental anguish of many prisoners; he believed that such powerful experiences were bound to affect home societies. "Europe," he warned alarmingly, "will thus be infiltrated with individuals of abnormal psychical tendencies, who will not presumably be without influence on the collective psychology of the community."[14] The understanding that their experiences brought them together led many ex-prisoners to form associations and mutual-aid groups. Like other participants of World War I, they sought to ascribe meaning to their unique stories and did so through word, stone, and ritual. However, their efforts often fell on deaf ears or, in some cases, clashed with an explicit decision to erase the memory of internment from the collective narrative. As Assaf Mond shows in his chapter, Alexandra Palace, the London camp that housed thirty-three thousand Belgian refugees and seventeen thousand internees, though never more than three thousand simultaneously, was almost completely blotted out from the English capital's urban history. However, whether Alexandra Palace was indeed "a concentration camp in the heart of London," as Mond asserts, is open for debate. What is certain is that we would be hard pressed to find any indication of the camp in a city that is otherwise very conscious of its illustrious history. In March 1920 the last prisoners were released from Alexandra Palace, and the venue reverted to its prior function as an entertainment center. As chance would have it, Alexandra Palace was also the location of the BBC's first television broadcast on November 2, 1936.

Impact on Future Internments

The well-being of POWs seemed better than ever twelve years after the war, and a year after the conclusion of the Geneva Convention of 1929. "Prisoners of war!" Winston Churchill lamented in his early memoir that year, "That is the least unfortunate kind of prisoner to be, but it is nevertheless a melancholy state. You are in the power of your enemy. You owe your life to his humanity, and your daily bread to his compassion."[15] Soon, however, Churchill's view of the tough but bearable fate of POWs proved premature if not naive. The outbreak of the second Sino-Japanese War in 1937 dispelled any illusion that some acute observers and well-wishers entertained about the treatment of prisoners in the future. If anything, the opposite was true, as demonstrated by Japan's deteriorating treatment of its prisoners. During the Great War, the Japanese empire had meted exemplary treatment upon its European POWs, resulting in one of the lowest mortality rates (merely 1.9 percent) during that war. But this humanitarian goodwill did not last long. After refusing to ratify the Geneva Convention of 1929, Japan was turning now into a serial abuser of any acceptable standard of treatment, even that maintained by the World War I belligerents.[16]

The harbinger of Japan's new attitude leaked during its initial campaigns in the summer of 1937.[17] Nevertheless, it was the cold-blooded massacre of tens of thousands of surrendered Chinese soldiers shortly after the nationalist capital Nanjing had capitulated (the "Nanjing massacre") that shocked the world.[18] Two years later, as World War II broke out in Europe, the remaining buoyant interwar expectations of the humane treatment of POWs were not met either. By then it was clear that the Japanese mistreatment of Chinese POWs was a precursor of a widespread phenomenon, rather than an aberration or an isolated case limited to Asian soldiers. The final checks in this respect were removed upon the outbreak of Operation Barbarossa in June 1941 and the Asia-Pacific war in December of that year.[19] Never before in human history were so many POWs mistreated in enemy hands. Indeed, the mistreatment of POWs in these World War II arenas was staggering—even by premodern standards. While countless combatants were killed in cold blood upon their surrender, millions of others were spared but then left to die of hunger, disease, hardship, or execution in prisoner camps.

To what extent has World War I served as a precedent? Historians have been debating for the past three decades whether World War I internments presaged the internment practices of totalitarian regimes like the Soviet Union, Nazi Germany, and to some degree imperial Japan, or whether they were comparatively more benign institutions that were very far removed from Auschwitz and the gulag camps of the Kolyma region.[20] In her magnum opus *The Origins of Totalitarianism*, Hannah Arendt argues that "concentration camps are the most consequential institutions of totalitarian control" and that a direct line connects the camps established in India and South Africa in the late nineteenth century with those of the Third Reich.[21] Curiously, she has very little to say about the issue of World War I internments; perhaps they complicated her notion that all camps could be sorted "to the three basic Western conceptions of a life after death: Hades, Purgatory, and Hell."[22] World War I introduced forms of internment that went beyond simplistic divisions of seclusion / inclusion, civilian / military, and oppression / care.

Some camps were tightly connected with the societies around them, while others were separated and remote. A few camps for officers and civilian internees had better food and richer cultural choices than those available to the majority of people living outside. Other camps, however, were horrendous death traps due to epidemics and mismanagement or, in a few cases, due to the genocidal intent of their captors, as the Armenian civilians sent to the Bab or Meskenah camps (in the vicinity of Aleppo, present-day Syria) witnessed in 1915–16.[23] But in general, despite the fact that the notion of international law, and humanitarian law in particular, was only beginning to globalize, the internments of World War I were paradoxically both a promising experiment in humanitarianism and a step forward to the exceptional inhumanity experienced in the next total war.

This book demonstrates that the unprecedented scale of internment during World War I habituated the practice of interning people in camps and made it malleable enough to be adopted in different political configurations and settings. Internment became as ubiquitous and modern as mass surveillance, propaganda, and emergency powers. It is against this backdrop, as Wylie and Landefeld argue in their chapter, that the end of the war witnessed calls to devise a new and "modern" legal regime for dealing with the many new aspects of war captivity. The Geneva Convention of 1929 was one outcome of these calls, but the associated discourse encompassed far more than military captivity.

Notes

1. Gusenbauer 1997.
2. Gusenbauer 1997, 13–14.
3. For more on this, see Mayr 2016.
4. Mayr 2016, 1.
5. Wachsmann 2015, 163–66, 626.
6. Rachamimov 2006; Rachamimov 2012a; Feltman 2015; Rachamimov 2018.
7. Mouradian 2019, 146–52.
8. Gerwarth and Manela 2014b.
9. See, e.g., Hilger 2000; Watts 2009; Kowner 2020.
10. See Oxford University Press series "The Greater War."
11. Bartov and Weitz 2013.
12. See Hazuki Tate's chapter in this volume.
13. See Hazuki Tate's chapter in this volume.
14. Vischer 1919, 25.
15. Churchill 1930, 259.
16. For this transition, see Kowner 2009.
17. Van de Ven, 2017.

18. Timperley 1938; Hata 1986; Fogel 2000.
19. Porter 2009; Daws 1994; Weingartner 1996.
20. See Rachamimov 2002; Jones, H. 2008b.
21. Arendt 1951 440–41.
22. Arendt 1951, 445.
23. Mouradian 2019.

References

Archives

Archives du Comité International de la Croix-Rouge [ICRC Archives], Geneva, Switzerland.

Archives of the International Law Association, London, United Kingdom.

Archives du Ministère des affaires étrangères de la République française [Diplomatic Archives], Paris, France.

Archives de la Société des Nations [Archives of the League of Nations], Geneva, Switzerland.

Bayerisches Hauptstaatsarchiv, Abteilung IV: Kriegsarchiv [Bavarian State Archive, Section IV: War Archive], Munich, Germany.

Bundesarchiv Militärarchiv Freiburg, Germany [BAMA; German Federal Military Archive].

Gaimushō Gaikō shiryōkan [Archives of the Ministry of Foreign Affairs], Tokyo, Japan.

Gosudarstvennyĭ Arkhiv Krasnoiarskogo Kraia [GAKK; State Archives of the Krasnoyarsk Region], Krasnoyarsk, Russia.

Gosudarstvennyĭ Arkhiv Tomskoĭ Oblasti [GATO; State Archives of the Tomsk Oblast], Tomsk, Russia.

Kautz Family YMCA Archives, University of Minnesota Libraries, United States.

Library and Archives Canada, Ottawa, Canada.

Manx National Heritage Library and Archives.

National Archives, Kew, London, United Kingdom.

Oesterreichische Staatsarchive, Vienna, Austria.

Prikhod Presviatoĭ Bogoroditsy [PPB; Parish of the Mother of God], Vladivostok, Russia.

Rossiĭskiĭ Gosudarstvennyĭ Voenno-Istoricheskiĭ Arkhiv [RGVIA; Russian State Military History Archives], Moscow, Russia.

Printed Sources

Abbal, Odon. 2001. *Soldats oubliés: les prisonniers de guerre français*. Esparon: E&C.

Ador, Gustav. 1915. "Egalité de traitement pour les prisonniers de guerre militaires ou civil." *Revue internationale des Sociétés de la Croix-Rouge* 46, 181: 5–8.

Agamben, Giorgio. 1998. *Homo Sacer: Sovereign Power and Bare Life*. Stanford, CA: Stanford University Press.

——. 2005. *State of Exception*. Chicago: Chicago University Press.

Alexander, Amanda. 2007. "The Genesis of the Civilian." *Leiden Journal of International Law* 20: 359–76.

Ansky, S. 2004. *The Enemy at His Pleasure: A Journey through the Jewish Pale of Settlement during World War I*. Translated by Joachim Neugroschel. New York: Henry Holt.

Applebaum, Anne. 2003. *Gulag: A History*. New York: Doubleday.

Arendt, Hannah. 1951. *The Origins of Totalitarianism*. New York: Harcourt.

——. 1979. *Origins of Totalitarianism*. San Diego: Harcourt Brace.

Audoin-Rouzeau, Stéphane, and Annette Becker. 2002. *Understanding the Great War*. Translated by Catherine Temerson. New York: Hill & Wang.

Audoin-Rouzeau, Stéphane, and Christophe Prochasson. 2008. *Sortir de la Grande Guerre: le monde et l'après-1918*. Paris: Editions Tallandier.

Avenarius, Ferdinand. 1916. *La calomnie par l'image: quelques remarques sur l'art d'inciter les peuples à la haine*. Berne: Ferd. Wyss.

Backhaus, Alexander. 1915. *The Prisoners of War in Germany*. Siegen: Hermann Montanus.

Bailkin, Jordanna. 2018. *Unsettled: Refugee Camps and the Making of Multicultural Britain*. Oxford: Oxford University Press.

Baja, Benedek, ed. 1930. *Hadifogoly Magyarok Története*. Vol. 2. Budapest: Athenaeum.

Ballinger, Pamela. 2020. *The World Refugees Made: Decolonization and the Foundation of Postwar Italy*. Ithaca, NY: Cornell University Press.

Barkhof, Sandra. 2018. "The New Zealand Occupation of German Samoa during the First World War, 1914–1918: Enemy Aliens and Internment." In *Internment during the First World War*, edited by Stefan Manz, Panikos Panayi, and Matthew Stibbe, 242–68. London: Routledge.

Barros, Andrew, and Martin Thomas, eds. 2018. *The Civilianization of War: The Changing Civil-Military Divide, 1914–2014*. Cambridge: Cambridge University Press.

Barton, Susan. 2019. *Internment in Switzerland during the First World War*. London: Blumsburry.

Bartov, Omer, and Eric D. Weitz. 2013. *Shatterzone of Empires: Coexistence and Violence in the German, Habsburg, Russian, and Ottoman Borderlands*. Bloomington: Indiana University Press.

Bates, Ed. 2010. "History." In *International Human Rights Law*, edited by Daniel Moeckli, Sangeeta Shah, and Sandesh Sivakumaran, 3–21. Oxford: Oxford University Press.

Bauerkämper, Arnd. 2018. "National Security and Humanity: The Internment of Civilian 'Enemy Aliens' during the First World War." *German Historical Institute London Bulletin* 40: 61–85.

——. 2021. *Sicherheit und Humanität im Ersten und Zweiten Weltkrieg: Der Umgang mit zivilen Feindstaatenangehörigen im Ausnahmezustand*. 2 vols. Berlin: De Gruyter.

Beaumont, Joan. 1983. "Rank, Privilege and Prisoners of War." *War & Society* 1: 67–94.

——. 1996. "Protecting Prisoners of War, 1939–1995." In *Prisoners of War and Their Captors in World War II*, edited by Bob Moore and Kent Fedorwoich, 277–98. Oxford: Berg.

Becker, Annette. 1998. *Oubliés de la Grande Guerre: humanitaire et culture de guerre, 1914–1918: populations occupées, déportés civils, prisonniers de guerre*. Paris: Editions Noêsis.

——. 2012. *Oubliés de la Grande Guerre: humanitaire et culture de guerre, 1914–1918*. Paris: Pluriel.

——. 2014a. "Captive Civilians." *The Cambridge History of the First World War, vol 3: Civil Society*, edited by Jay Winter, 257–81. Cambridge: Cambridge University Press.

——. 2014b. *Voir la Grande Guerre: Un autre récit*. Paris: Armand Colin.

——. 2015. "The Great War: World War, Total War." *International Review of the Red Cross* 97/900: 1029–45.

Becker, Jean-Jacques. 1973. *Le Carnet B. Les pouvoirs publics et l'antimilitarisme avant la guerre de 1914*. Paris: Éditions Klincksieck.

Becker, Jean-Jacques, and Annie Kriegel. 1968. *Les inscrits au "Carnet B." Dimensions, composition, physionomie politique et limite du pacifisme ouvrier*. Paris: Association Le Mouvement Social.

Berner, Margit. 2007. "From 'Prisoner of War Studies' to Proof of Paternity: Racial Anthropologists and the Measuring of 'Others' in Austria." In *"Blood and Homeland": Eugenics and Racial Nationalism in Central and Southeast Europe, 1900–1940*, edited by Marius Turda and Paul J. Weindling, 41–53. Budapest: Central European University Press.

——. 2010. "Large-Scale Anthropological Surveys in Austria-Hungary, 1871–1918." In *Doing Anthropology in Wartime and War Zones: World War I and the Cultural Sciences in Europe*, edited by Reinhard Johler, Christian Marchetti, and Monique Scheer, 233–53. Bielefeld: Transcript Verlag.

Best, Geoffrey. 1994. *War and Law since 1945*. Oxford: Clarendon Press.

Beurier, Joëlle. 2016. *Photographier la Grande Guerre: France-Allemagne, l'héroïsme et la violence dans les magazines*. Rennes: Press Universitaire de Rennes.

Bicheno, Hugh. 2004. "Total War." In *The Oxford Companion to Military History*, edited by Richard Holmes, Charles Singleton, and Spencer Jones. Oxford: Oxford University Press.

Bihl, Wolfdieter. 1980."Die Ruthenen." In *Habsburgermonarchie 1848–1918*, Vol. 3: *Die Völker des Reiches*, Part 1, edited by Adam Wandruszka and Peter Urbanitsch, 555–84. Vienna: Verlag der österreichischen Akademie der Wissenschaften.

Bird, John Clement. 1986. *Control of Enemy Alien Civilians in Great Britain, 1914–1918*. New York: Garland Publishing.

Black, Dan. 2019. *Harry Livingstone's Forgotten Men: Canadians and the Chinese Labour Corps in the First World War*. Toronto: James Lorimer.

Bondarenko, Elena Iur'evna. 2002. "Inostrannye voennoplennye na Dal'nem Vostoke Rossii (1914–1956)." PhD diss., Dal'nevostotchnyĭ Gosudarstvennyĭ Universitet.

Bonner, Philip. 2011. "South African Society and Culture, 1910–1948." *The Cambridge History of South Africa*, edited by Robert Ross, Anne Kelk Mager, and Bill Nasson, 254–318. Cambridge: Cambridge University Press.

Boswell, Laird. 2000. "From Liberation to Purge Trials in the 'Mythic Provinces': Recasting French Identities in Alsace and Lorraine, 1918–1920." *French Historical Studies* 23: 129–62.

Brändström, Elsa. 1922. *Unter Kriegsgefangenen in Rußland und Sibirien, 1914–1920*. Berlin: Deutsche Verlagsgesellschaft für Politik und Geschichte.

Braun, William Hermann. 1930. *Unter Zarenherrschaft und Sowjetstern: Erlebtes und Erschautes in Rußland und Sibirien während des Weltkrieges und der Revolution*. Graz: Köstenberger.

Breitner, Burghard. 1921. *Unverwundet gefangen. Aus meinem Sibirischen Tagebuch*. Vienna: Rikola.

Bruckner, Sierra Ann. 1999. "The Tingle-Tangle of Modernity: Popular Anthropology and the Cultural Politics of Identity in Imperial Germany," 2 vols. PhD diss., University of Iowa.

Bugnion, Francois. 2018. *Confronting the Hell of the Trenches. The International Committee of the Red Cross and the First World War*. Geneva: ICRC.

Burrell, Kathy, and Panikos Panayi, eds. 2006. *Histories and Memories: Migrants and Their History in Britain*. London: Tauris Academic Studies.

Burri, Michael. 2021. "Clemens Pirquet: Early Twentieth-Century Scientific Networks, the Austrian Hunger Crisis, and the Making of the International Food Expert." In *Remaking Central Europe: The League of Nations and the Former Habsburg Lands*, edited by Peter Becker and Natasha Wheatley, 39–70. Oxford: Oxford University Press.

Cabanes, Bruno. 2004. *La victoire endeuillée: La sortie de guerre des soldats français (1918–1920)*. Paris: Seuil.

——. 2014. *The Great War and the Origins of Humanitarianism, 1918–1924*. Cambridge: Cambridge University Press.

Caglioti, Daniela L. 2013. "Waging War on Civilians: The Expulsion of Aliens in the Franco-Prussian War." *Past and Present* 221 / 1: 161–95.

——. 2018. "Colonial Subjects and Enemy Aliens: Confinement and Internment 134 in Italy, 1911–1919." In *Internment during the First World War: A Mass Global Phenomenon*, edited by Stefan Manz, Panikos Panayi, and Matthew Stibbe, 134–59. London: Routledge.

Cahalan, Peter. 1982. *Belgian Refugee Relief in England during the Great War*. New York: Garland.

Campbell, Joan. 1989. *Joy in Work, German Work: The National Debate, 1800–1945*. Princeton, NJ: Princeton University Press.

Caplan, Jane. 2005. "Political Detention and the Origin of Concentration Camps in Nazi Germany." In *Nazism, War and Genocide: Essays in Honour of Jeremy Noakes*, edited by Neil Gregor, 22–41. Exeter: Exeter University Press.

Cardozo, Ian. 2019. *The Indian Army in World War I, 1914–1918*. Milton: Taylor & Francis.

Carrington, Ron. 1975. *Alexandra Park and Palace: A History*. London: Greater London Council.

Carsten, Francis L. 1992. *War against War: British and German Radical Movements in the First World War*. Berkeley: University of California Press.

Cesarani, David. 1992. "An Alien Concept? The Continuity of Anti-Alienism in British Society before 1940." *Immigrants & Minorities* 11, no. 3: 24–52.

Christoph, Jürgen. 1988. *Die Politischen Reichsamnestien, 1918–1933*. Frankfurt: Peter Lang.

Church, Samuel Harden. 1915. *The American Verdict on the War: A Reply to the Appeal to the Civilized World of 93 German Professors*. Baltimore: Norman Remington Co.

Churchill, Winston S. 1930. *A Roving Commission: My Early Life*. New York: Scribner's Sons.

CICR. 1921. *Rapport général du Comité International de la Croix-Rouge sur son activité de 1912 à 1920*. Geneva: Comité International de la Croix-Rouge.

Civelli, Ignaz. 2017. "'Platz wäre in der Dependance bequem': Zivil- und Militärinternierte im Kanton Zug im Ersten Weltkrieg." *Tugium* 33: 181–209.

Cohen, Gerard Daniel. 2012. *In War's Wake: Europe's Displaced Persons in the Postwar Order*. Oxford: Oxford University Press.

Cohen-Portheim, Paul. 1932. *Time Stood Still: My Internment in England, 1914–1918*. London: Duckworth.

Conger, George P. 1917. "In the War Prisons of Eastern Siberia." In *The European War*, vol. 13: 533–37. New York Times Current History. New York: New York Times Company.

Connolly, James E. 2018. *The Experience of Occupation in the Nord, 1914–18: Living with the Enemy in First World War France*. Manchester: Manchester University Press.

Conrad, Sebastian. 2010. *Globalisation and the Nation in Imperial Germany*. Translated by Sorcha O'Hagan. Cambridge: Cambridge University Press.

Cook, Tim. 2006. "The Politics of Surrender: Canadian Soldiers and the Killing of Prisoners in the Great War." *Journal of Military History* 70: 637–65.

Cornwall, Mark. 2000. *The Undermining of Austria-Hungary: The Battle for Hearts and Minds*. New York: St. Martin's Press.

Cotter, Cédric, 2017. *(S)Aider pour survivre. Action humanitaire et neutralité Suisse pendant la Première Guerre Mondiale*. Chêne-Bourg: Georg.

Crawford, Emily. 2010. *The Treatment of Combatants and Insurgents under the Law of Armed Conflict*. Oxford: Oxford University Press.

Creswell, Yvonne. 2010. *Living with the Wire: Civilian Internment in the Isle of Man during the Two World Wars*. 2nd ed. Douglas: Manx National Heritage.

Crouthamel, Jason. 2014. *An Intimate History of the Front: Masculinity, Sexuality, and German Soldiers in the First World War*. Basingstoke: Palgrave Macmillan.

Cseh, Benny. Private Papers. London: The Imperial War Museum, Documents. 15168.

Das, Santanu. 2011. "Introduction." In *Race, Empire and First World War Writing*, edited by Santanu Das. Cambridge: Cambridge University Press.

Davis, Belinda. 2000. *Home Fires Burning. Food, Politics, and Everyday Life in World War I Berlin*. Chapel Hill: University of North Carolina Press.

Davis, Gerald H. 1977. "Prisoners of War in Twentieth-Century War Economies." *Journal of Contemporary History* 12: 623–34.

——. 1983. "The Life of Prisoners of War in Russia, 1914–1921." In *Essays on World War I: Origins and Prisoners of War*, edited by Samuel R. Williamson and Peter Pastor, 163–96. New York: Columbia University Press.

——. 1987. "Prisoner of War Camps as Social Communities in Russia: Krasnoyarsk 1914–1921." *East European Quarterly* 21: 147–63.

Daws, Gavan. 1994. *Prisoners of the Japanese: POWS of World War II in the Pacific*. New York: William Morrow.

Deák, István. 1990. *Beyond Nationalism: A Social and Political History of the Habsburg Officer Corps, 1848–1918*. New York: Oxford University Press.

Deist, Wilhelm, ed. 1970. *Militär und Innenpolitik im Weltkrieg 1914–1918*, 2 vols. Düsseldorf: Droste.

——. 1991. "Vorraussetzungen innenpolitischen Handelns des Militärs im Ersten Weltkrieg." In *Militär, Staat, Gesellschaft. Studien zur preußisch-deutschen Militärgeschichte*, edited by Wilhelm Deist, 103–52. Munich: R. Oldenburg Verlag.

Deutscher Reichstag, ed. 1927. *Das Werk des Untersuchungsausschusses. Reihe 3: Völkerrecht im Weltkrieg, Bd. III, 2. Teil*. Berlin: Deutsche Verlagsgesellschaft für Politik und Geschichte.

Dittmann, Wilhelm. 1917. *Belagerungszustand, Zensur und Schutzhaft vor dem Reichstage: Drei Reichstagsreden, geh. 1916*; Nach d. amtl. Stenogramm. Leipzig: Verlag der Leipziger Buchdruckerei.

Dixon, Simon. 2016. "Allegiance and Betrayal: British Residents in Russia during the Crimean War." *Slavonic and East European Review* 94, no. 3: 431–67.

Doegen, Wilhelm. 1919. *Kriegsgefangene Völker: Der Kriegsgefangenen Haltung und Schicksal in Deutschland*, vol. 1. Berlin: Verlag von Dietrich Reimer.

——, ed. 1925. *Unter Fremden Völkern: Eine neue Völkerkunde*. Berlin: Otto Stollberg Verlag für Politik und Wirtschaft.

——, ed. 1941. *Unsere Gegner damals und heute; Engländer und Französen mit ihren europäischen und fremdrassigen Hilfsvölkern in deren Heimat, an der Front und in deutscher Gefangenschaft in Weltkriege und im jetzigen Kriege: Grossdeutschlands koloniale Sendung*. Berlin-Lichterfelde: O. F. Hübner.

Dornel, Laurent. 2018. *Les Chinois dans la Grande Guerre: des bras au service de la France*. Paris: Les Indes savantes.

Douglas, Mary. 1966. *Purity and Danger: An Analysis of Concepts of Pollution and Taboo*. London: Routledge & Kegan Paul.

Douki, Caroline, and Philippe Minard. 2007. "Histoire globale, histoires connectées: un changement d'échelle historiographique?," *Revue d'histoire moderne et contemporaine* 54–55: 7–21.

Dove, Richard, ed. 2005. *Totally Un-English? Britain's Internment of Enemy Aliens in Two World Wars*. Amsterdam: Rodopi.

Durand, André. 1984. *From Sarajevo to Hiroshima: History of the International Committee of the Red Cross*, vol. 2. Geneva: Henry Dunant Institute.

Edelmann-Ohler, Eva. 2016. "Exclusion and Inclusion: Ethnography of War in *Kriegsgefangene* (1916) and *Das ostjüdische Antlitz* (1920)." In *Writing Jewish Culture: Paradoxes in Ethnography*, edited by Andreas Kilcher and Gabriella Safran, 181–207. Bloomington: Indiana University Press.

Edwards, Elizabeth. 1990. "The Image as Anthropological Document: Photographic 'Types': The Pursuit of Method." *Visual Anthropology* 3: 235–58.

Eickstedt, Egon von. 1920/1921. "Rassenelemente der Sikh: Mit einem Anhang ober biometrische Methoden." *Zeitschrift für Ethnologie* 52: 217–394.

Engler, Kurt. n.d. *Dual Nationality* (a memoir written by his son, Karl). The Imperial War Museum, The Private Papers of Kurt Engler. Documents. 1644.

Evans, Andrew D. 2004. "Capturing Race: Anthropology and Photography in German and Austrian Prisoner-of-War Camps during World War I." In *Colonialist Photography*, edited by Eleanor M. Hight, 226–56. London: Routledge.

——. 2010. *Anthropology at War: World War I and the Science of Race in Germany*. Chicago: University of Chicago Press.

Evans, Richard J. 2003. *The Coming of the Third Reich*. London: Allen Lane.

Farney, James, and Bohdan S. Kordan. 2005. "The Predicament of Belonging: The Status of Enemy Aliens in Canada, 1914." *Journal of Canadian Studies* 39 (Winter): 74–89.

Favez, Jean-Claude. 1999. *The Red Cross and the Holocaust*. Cambridge: Cambridge University Press.

Fayet, Jean-François. 2000. "En attendant la fin de la guerre: la [sur]vie des soldats et des civils allemands détenus en Russie pendant la Première Guerre mondiale." In *Guerres et Paix,* edited by Michel Porret, Jean-François Fayet, and Carine Fluckiger, 147–62. Geneva: Médecins & Hygiène.

Feldman, Gerald. 1966. *Army, Industry and Labor in Germany, 1914–1918*. Princeton, NJ: Princeton University Press.

Feltman, Brian K. 2015. *The Stigma of Surrender: German Prisoners, British Captors, and Manhood in the Great War and Beyond*. Chapel Hill: University of North Carolina Press.

Ferguson, Niall. 2004. "Prisoner Taking and Prisoner Killing in the Age of Total War: Towards a Political Economy of Military Defeat." *War in History* 11: 148–92.

Ferrière, Frédéric. 1923. "Projet d'une Convention internationale réglant la situation des civils tombés à la guerre au pouvoir de l'ennemi." *Revue internationale des Sociétés de la Croix-Rouge* 54: 560–85.

Finkel, Stuart. 2007. *On the Ideological Front: The Russian Intelligentsia and the Making of the Soviet Public Sphere*. New Haven, CT: Yale University Press.

Fitzpatrick, Sheila. 1970. *The Commissariat of Enlightenment. Soviet Reorganization of Education and the Arts under Lunacharsky, October 1917–1921*. London: Cambridge University Press.

Fogarty, Richard S. 2014. "The French Empire." In *Empires at War, 1911–1923*, edited by Robert Gerwarth and Erez Manela, 109–29. Oxford: Oxford University Press.

Fogel, Joshua A., ed. 2000. *The Nanjing Massacre: In History and Historiography*. Berkeley: University of California Press, 2000.

Földes, Jenő. 1930. *Hadifogoly-Karrier*. Budapest: Szerző.

Forth, Aidan. 2016. "Britain's Archipelago of Camps: Labor and Detention in a Liberal Empire." In *The Soviet Gulag: Evidence, Interpretation and Comparison,* edited by Michael David-Fox, 199–223. Pittsburgh, PA: University of Pittsburgh Press.

——. 2017. *Barbed-Wire Imperialism: Britain's Empire of Camps, 1876–1903*. Berkeley: University of California Press.

Franta, Hans. 1934. "Aus der Werkstatt Heimischer Künstler." *Welt und Heimat (Illustrierte Beilage zur Linzer Tages-Post)*, April 21.

——. 1977. *Hans Franta zum 84. Geburtstag*. Linz: Trauner Verlag.

French, David. 1978. "Spy Fever in Britain, 1900–1915." *Historical Journal* 21: 355–70.

Frizzera, Francesco. 2018. "Population Displacement in the Habsburg Empire during World War I." In *World War I in Central and Eastern Europe: Politics, Conflict and Military Experience*, edited by Judith Devlin, Marina Falina, and John Paul Newman, 60–72. London: Bloomsbury.

Frobenius, Leo. 1916. *Der Völker-Zirkus unserer Feinde*. Berlin: Eckart.

Funk, Albert. 1985. *Polizei und Rechtsstaat. Entstehungsgeschichte der preußischen Polizei, 1848–1914*. Frankfurt: Campus.

Fyson, Robert. 2000. "The Douglas Camp Shooting of 1914." *Proceedings of IoM Natural History and Antiquarian Society* 11: 115–27.

Gaiswinkler, Adolf. n.d. *Memoirs*. Dokumentation Lebensgeschichtlicher Aufzeichnungen, Universität Wien.

Garfield, Brian. 2011. *The Meinertzhagen Mystery: The Life and Legend of a Colossal Fraud*. Lincoln: University of Nebraska Press.

Gatrell, Peter. 2000. *A Whole Empire Walking: Refugees in Russia during World War I*. Bloomington: Indiana University Press.

——. 2013. *The Making of the Modern Refugee*. Oxford: Oxford University Press.

Gay, Ken. 1992. *Palace on the Hill: A History of Alexandra Palace and Park*. London: Hornsey Historical Society.

"German Imperial and State Citizenship Law, 22 July 1913." 1914. *American Journal of International Law* 8, no. 3 (July): 217–27.

German Prisoners in Great Britain. 1916. Bolton: Tillotson & Son.

Germany, Foreign Office. 1915. "Employment, Contrary to International Law, of Colored Troops upon the European Arena of War by England and France, July 1915." In World War I Pamphlet Collection, University of Colorado, Boulder Library, accessed September 27, 2017, http://cudl.colorado.edu/luna/servlet/detail/UCBOULDERCB1~58~58~445124~127847:Employment,-contrary-to-internatio.

Gerwarth, Robert. 2016. *The Vanquished: Why the First World War Failed to End, 1917–1923*. London: Allen Lane.

Gerwarth, Robert, and Erez Manela. 2014a. "The Great War as a Global War: Imperial Conflict and the Reconfiguration of World Order, 1911–1923." *Diplomatic History* 38: 786–800.

——, eds. 2014b. *Empires at War 1911–1923*. Oxford: Oxford University Press.

"Gesetz über den Kriegszustand vom 6. Dezember 1916." In *Reichsgesetzblatt* 1916: 1329–31.

Geyer, Martin H. 1998. *Verkehrte Welt: Revolution, Inflation und Moderne. München 1914–1924*. Göttingen: Vandenhoeck & Ruprecht.

Geyer, Michael. 2006. "Rückzug und Zerstörung 1917," In *Die Deutschen an der Somme 1914–1918: Krieg, Besatzung, Verbrannte Erde*, edited by Gerhard Hirschfeld, Gerd Krumeich, and Irina Renz, 163–201. Essen: Klartext.

Geyling, Rolf. 1919. "Brief an die Nachwelt." PBB, no catalog number.

Gillian, Pascall, and Nick Manning. 2000. "Gender and Social Policy: Comparing Welfare States in Central and Eastern Europe and the Former Soviet Union." *Journal of European Social Policy* 10: 240–66.

Gingrich, Andre. 2010. "After the Great War: National Configurations of Anthropology in Late Colonial Times." In *Doing Anthropology in Wartime and War Zones: World War I and the Cultural Sciences in Europe*, edited by Reinhard Johler, Christian Marchetti, and Monique Scheer, 355–79. Bielefeld: Transcript Verlag.

"Gmünder Bezirk." 1915. *Österreichische Land-Zeitung*. July 17.

Górny, Maciej. 2019. *Science Embattled: Eastern European Intellectuals and the Great War*. Translated by Antoni Górny. Germany: Ferdinand Schöningh.

Gousseff, Catherine. 2008. *L'exil russe: la fabrique du réfugié apatride*. Paris: CNRS Éditions.

Grady, Tim. 2017. *A Deadly Legacy: German Jews and the Great War*. New Haven, CT: Yale University Press.

Graziosi, Andrea. 1988. "Foreign Workers in Soviet Russia, 1920–40: Their Experience and Their Legacy." *International Labor and Working-Class History* 33: 38–59.

Greiner, Bettina, and Alan Kramer, eds. 2013. *Welt der Lager: Zur "Erfolgsgeschichte" Einer Institution*. Hamburg: Hamburger Edition.

Grosse Krieg in Bildern, Der. 1915–1918. Berlin: Georg Stilke.

Grundlingh, Albert. 2017. "Pleading Patriots and Malleable Memories: The South African Cape Corps during the First World War (1914–1918) and Its Twentieth-Century Legacy." *Wicazo sa review* 32: 29–47.

Guenther, Dierk. 2004. "Tokushima shinpō, Lagerfeur, Barracke—shikoku no doitsuhei furyo shūyōjo shinbun no hikaku kentō." *Chintaosen doitsuhei furyo shūyōjo kenkyū* 2 (October): 3–22.

Gumz, Jonathan E. 2014. "Losing Control: The Norm of Occupation in Eastern Europe during the First World War," In *Legacies of Violence: Eastern Europe's First World War*, edited by Jochen Böhler, Włodzimierz Borodziej, and Joachim von Puttkamer, 69–87. Munich: De Gruyter Oldenbourg.

Gusenbauer, Ernst. 1997. "Auf den Spuren einer vergessenen Zeit. Das Kriegsgefangenenlager in Mauthausen 1914 bis 1918." *Oberösterreichische Heimatblätter* 51: 13–23.

Gutsche, Willibald, ed. 1977. *Herrschaftsmethoden des deutschen Imperialismus 1897/8 bis 1917. Dokumente zur innen- und aussenpolitischen Strategie und Taktik der herrschenden Klassen des Deutschen Reichs*. Berlin: Akademie-Verlag.

Hackl, Erich. 2009. "Erinnerungen an Sibirien. Memoiren aus der Gefangenschaft 1914–1920." In *Quelle zur Geschichte Oberösterreichs 7*, edited by Alexander Smutni. Linz: Oberösterreichisches Landesarchiv.

Harris, Janet. 2005. *Alexandra Palace: A Hidden History*. Stroud, Gloucestershire: Tempus.

Hart, E. J. 2010. *J. B. Harkin: Father of Canada's National Parks*. Edmonton: University of Alberta Press.

Hata Ikuhiko. 1986. *Nankin Jiken: Gyakusatsu no kōzō*. Tokyo: Chūō Kōron Shinshō.

Healy, Maureen. 2000. "Exhibiting a War in Progress: Entertainment and Propaganda in Vienna, 1914–1918." *Austrian Yearbook* 31: 57–85.

——. 2004. *Vienna and the Fall of the Habsburg Empire: Total War and Everyday Life in World War I*. Cambridge: Cambridge University Press.

Henn, Charles. 1986. "The Origins and Early Development of the Idea of Protecting Powers." PhD diss., University of Cambridge.

Herbert, Ulrich. 1986. *Geschichte der Ausländerbeschäftigung in Deutschland 1880 bis 1980: Saisonarbeiter, Zwangsarbeiter, Gastarbeiter*. Bonn: Dietz.

Hermann, Martina. 2017a. "'Cities of Barracks:' Refugees in the Austrian Part of the Habsburg Empire during World War I." In *Europe on the Move: Refugees in the Era of the Great War*, edited by Peter Gatrell and Liubov Zhvanko, 129–55. Manchester, UK: Manchester University Press.

——. 2017b. "Die hölzerne Stadt. Das Barackenlager Gmünd 1914–1918." PhD diss., University of Graz.

Herwig, Holer H. 2014. *World War I, Germany and Austria-Hungary 1914–1918*. London: Bloomsbury.

Hilger, Andreas. 2000. *Deutsche Kriegsgefangene in der Sowjetunion 1941–1956. Kriegsgefangenschaft, Lageralltag und Erinnerung*. Essen: Klartext Verlag.

Hinz, Uta. 1999. "Die deutschen 'Barbaren' sind doch die besseren Menschen: Kriegsgefangenschaft und gefangene 'Feinde' in der Darstellung der deutschen Publizistik, 1914–1918," In *In der Hand des Feindes: Kriegsgefangenschaft von der Antike bis zum Zweiten Weltkrieg*, edited by Rüdiger Overmans, 339–61. Cologne: Böhlau.

——. 2003. "Internierung." In *Enzyklopädie Erster Weltkrieg*, edited by Gerhard Hirschfeld, Gerd Krumeich, and Irena Renz, 582–84. Paderborn: Ferdinand Schöningh.

——. 2006. *Gefangen im Großen Krieg: Kriegsgefangenschaft in Deutschland, 1914–1921*. Essen: Klartext.

Hitchcock, William. 2012. "Human Rights and the Laws of War: The Geneva Conventions of 1949." In *The Human Rights Revolution: An International History*, edited by Akira Iriye, Petra Goedde, and William I. Hitchcock, 93–112. Oxford: Oxford University Press.

Hoesen, Brett M. van. 2014. "The Rhineland Controversy and Weimar Postcolonialism." In *German Colonialism in a Global Age*, edited by Bradley Naranch and Geoff Eley, 302–29. Durham, NC: Duke University Press.

Hoffman, Conrad. 1920. *In the Prison Camps of Germany: A Narrative of "Y" Service among Prisoners of War*. New York: Association Press.

Hofmann, Hasso. 2005. "'Souverän ist, wer über den Ausnahmezustand entscheidet'." *Der Staat* 44, no. 2: 171–86.

Holmes, Ben. 2018. "The *International Review of the Red Cross* and the Protection of Civilians, c. 1919–1939." *International Review of the Red Cross* 100: 115–41.

Hörath, Julia. 2014. "'Arbeitsscheue Volksgenossen': Leistungsbereitschaft als Kriterium der Inklusion und Exklusion," In *Arbeit im Nationalsozialismus*, edited by Marc Buggeln and Michael Wildt, 309–28. Munich: De Gruyter Oldenbourg.

Horne, John, and Alan Kramer. 2001. *German Atrocities, 1914: A History of Denial*. New Haven, CT: Yale University Press.

Horvath, Agnes. 2013. *Modernism and Charisma*. Basingstoke: Palgrave Macmillan.

Hoshi Masayuki. 2006. "Furyo no Heimatsort no hitei ni tsuite." *Chintaosen doitsuhei furyo shūyōjo kenkyū* 4: 49–54.

Housden, Marthyn. 2007. "When the Baltic Sea Was a "Bridge" for Humanitarian Action: The League of Nations, the Red Cross and the Repatriation of Prisoners of War between Russia and Central Europe, 1920–1922." *Journal of Baltic Studies* 38: 61–83.

Howard, Michael, George Andreopolous, and Mark Shulman, eds. 1994. *The Laws of War: Constraints on Warfare in the Western World*. New Haven, CT: Yale University Press.

Hull, Isabel V. 2005. *Absolute Destruction: Military Culture and the Practices of War in Imperial Germany*. Ithaca, NY: Cornell University Press.

——. 2014. *A Scrap of Paper: Breaking and Making International Law during the Great War*. Ithaca, NY: Cornell University Press.

Hutchinson, John F. 1996. *Champions of Charity: War and the Rise of the Red Cross*. Boulder, CO: Westview.

Hyslop, Jonathan. 2011. "The Invention of the Concentration Camp: Cuba, Southern Africa, and the Philippines, 1896–1907." *South African Historical Journal* 63: 251–76.

ICRC. 1921. *Dixième Conférence Internationale de la Croix-Rouge, tenue à Genève du 30 Mars au 7 Avril 1921: Compte Rendu*. Genève: Albert Renaud.

——. 1925. *XIIme Conférence internationale de la Croix-Rouge, Genève, 7 octobre 1925. Annexe au Rapport Général du Comité international de la Croix-Rouge. La Situation des civils se trouvant sur territoire ennemi*. Geneva: ICRC.

——. 1930. *Actes de la Conférence Diplomatique de Genève de 1929*. Geneva: Journal de Genève.

Ido Keiji. 2007. "1918nen roku-gatsu futsuka, Tokushima ni okeru 'Tokushima furyo sōgakudan' ensōkai." *Chintaosen doitsuhei furyo shūyōjo kenkyū* 5 (October): 57–60.

Ikeyama Hiroshi. 2012. "Sekijūji kokusai iinkai ni yoru chintaosen doitsuhei furyo shūyōjo no shisatsu—Kurume furyo shūyōjo to Nagoya furyo shūyōjo to no taihi." *Chintaosen doitsuhei furyo shūyōjo kenkyū* 10 (December): 21–69.

Ikonnikova, Tat'iana Iakovlevna. 1999. "Voennoplennye Pervoĭ Mirovoĭ Voĭny na rossiĭskom Dal'nem Vostoke." *Rossiia i ATR* 1: 90–94.

——. 2004. *Voennoplennye Pervoĭ Mirovoĭ Voĭny na Dal'nem Vostoke Rossii (1914–1918 gg)*. Khabarovsk: GOU VPO.

ILA. 1920. *Report of the Twenty-Ninth Conference, May 27th to 31st, 1920*. London. Sweet & Maxwell.

——. 1921. *Report of the Thirtieth Conference, 30th August to 3rd September, 1921*. London. Sweet & Maxwell.

——. 1924. *Report of the Thirty-Third Conference, September 8th to 13th, 1924*. London: Sweet & Maxwell.

Imai Hiromasa. 2012. "Mō hitotsu no furyo shūyōjo: Kurume to doitsuhei, 1914–1920." *Kindai chiiki shakaishi kenkyū* (Fukuoka Daigaku Kenkyūbu Ronshū) A 11: 5, 29–36.

Imrey, Ferenc. 1930. *Through Blood and Ice*. New York: E. P. Dutton.

Irwin, Julia. 2017. *Making the World Safe. The American Red Cross and the Nation's Humanitarian Awakening*. New York: Oxford University Press.

Itō Chūta. 1920. *Ashura-Cho*. Tokyo: Kokusai Shuppansha.

Jahr, Christoph. 1999. "Zivilisten als Kriegsgefangene: Die Internierung von 'Feindstaaten-Ausländern' in Deutschland während des Ersten Weltkrieges am Beispiel des 'Engländerlagers' Ruhleben," In *In der Hand des Feindes: Kriegsgefangenschaft von der Antike bis zum Zweiten Weltkrieg*, edited by Rüdiger Overmans, 297–321. Cologne: Böhlau.

Jahr, Christoph, and Jens Thiel. 2019. "Adding Colour to the Silhouettes: The Internment and Treatment of Foreign Civilians in Germany during the First World War," In *Internment during the First World War: A Mass Global Phenomenon*, edited by Stefan Manz, Panikos Panayi, and Matthew Stibbe, 41–60. London: Routledge.

Jeffries, Keith. 2015. *1916: A Global History*. London: Bloomsbury.

Jeismann, Michael. 1997. *La patrie de l'ennemi: la notion d'ennemi national et la représentation de la nation en Allemagne et en France de 1792 à 1918*. Translated by Dominique Lassaigne. Paris: CNRS.

Jones, Heather. 2008a. "A Missing Paradigm? Military Captivity and the Prisoner of War, 1914–18." *Immigrants & Minorities* 26: 19–48.

——. 2008b. "The German Spring Reprisals of 1917: Prisoners of War and the Violence of the Western Front." *German History* 26: 335–56.

——. 2011a. *Violence against Prisoners of War in the First World War: Britain, France and Germany, 1914–1920*. Cambridge: Cambridge University Press.

——. 2011b. "Imperial Captivities: Colonial Prisoners of War in Germany and the Ottoman Empire, 1914–1918." In *Race, Empire and First World War Writing*, edited by Santanu Das, 175–93. Cambridge: Cambridge University Press, 2011.

——. 2014. "Prisoners of War." In *The Cambridge History of the First World War*, vol. 2: *The State*, edited by Jay Winter, 266–94. Cambridge: Cambridge University Press.

——. 2016. "International Law and Western Front Prisoners of War in the First World War." In *Wartime Captivity in the Twentieth Century: Archives, Stories, Memories*, edited by Anne-Marie Pathé and Fabien Théofilakis, 30–44. Oxford: Berghahn.

Jones, Mark. 2016. *Founding Weimar: Violence and the German Revolution of 1918–1919*. Cambridge: Cambridge University Press.

K. K. Ministerium des Innern. 1915. *Staatliche Flüchtlingsfürsorge im Kriege 1914/15*. Vienna: Aus der K. K. Hof- und Staatsdruckerei.

Kahleyss, Margot. 2000. *Muslime in Brandenburg-Kriegsgefangene im 1 Weltkrieg: Ansichten und Absichten*. Berlin: Museum Europäischer Kulturen.

——. 2011. "Indian Prisoners of War in World War I: Photographs as Source Material." In *"When the War Began We Heard of Several Kings": South Asian Prisoners in World War I Germany*, edited by Franziska Roy, Heike Liebau, and Ravi Ahuja, 207–30. New Delhi: Social Science Press.

Kaliakina, Aleksandra Viktorovna. 2013. "Ispol'zovanie truda voennoplennykh v Saratovskoĭ Gubernii v 1914–1917 godakh." *Izvestiia Saratovskogo Universiteta* 13, no. 2: 99–101.

Karpus, Zbigniew. 2001. *Russian and Ukrainian Prisoners of War and Internees Kept in Poland in 1918–1924*. Toruń, Poland: Adam Marszaek.

Karsten, Julius. 1927. "Der Plenny spielt Theater." *Neues Wiener Tagblatt*, January 29.

Kashima, Tetsuden, 2003. *Judgment without Trial: Japanese American Imprisonment during World War II*. Seattle: University of Washington Press.

Keegan, John. 1998. *The First World War*. London: Hutchinson.

Keil, André, and Matthew Stibbe. 2020. "Ein Laboratorium des Ausnahmezustandes: Schutzhaft während des Ersten Weltkrieges und der frühen Weimarer Republik in Preußen und Bayern, 1914–1923." *Vierteljahrshefte für Zeitgeschichte* 64, no. 4: 535–73.

Kellogg, Robert H. 1867. *Life and Death in Rebel Prisons*. Hartford, CT: L. Stebbins.

Kenner, George. Internment journal. London: Imperial War Museum. Art.IWM ARCH 27.

Ketchum, Davidson J. 1965. *Ruhleben: A Prison Camp Society*. Toronto: University of Toronto Press.

Kévonian, Dzovinar. 2004. *Réfugiés et diplomatie humanitaire: les acteurs européens et la scène proche-orientale pendant l'entre-deux-guerres*. Paris: Publication de la Sorbonne.

Kinsella, Helen M. 2011. *The Image before the Weapon: A Critical History of the Distinction between Combatant and Civilian*. Ithaca, NY: Cornell University Press.

Klein-Pejšová, Rebekah. 2014. "Beyond the 'Infamous Concentration Camps of the Monarchy': Jewish Refugee Policy from Wartime Hungary to Interwar Czechoslovakia." *Austrian History Yearbook* 45: 150–66.

Kōbe daigaku daigakuin jinbunka kenkyū chiiki renkei senta, ed. 2016. *Kasai ni furyo ga itakoro: Aonogahara shūyōjo to sono sekai*. Kasai, Japan: Kasai-shi kyōiku iinkai.

Koller, Christian. 2008. "The Recruitment of Colonial Troops in Africa and Asia and Their Deployment in Europe during the First World War." *Immigrants and Minorities* 26: 111–33.

——. 2011. "German Perception of Enemy Colonial Troops, 1914–1918." In *"When the War Began We Heard of Several Kings": South Asian Prisoners in World War I Germany*, edited by Franziska Roy, Heike Liebau, and Ravi Ahuja, 130–48. New Delhi: Social Science Press.

Kordan, Bohdan S. 2016. *No Free Man: Canada, the Great War, and the Enemy Alien Experience*. Montreal: McGill-Queen's University Press.

——. 2018. "The Internment of Enemy Aliens in Canada during the Great War: Rights, Obligations and Diplomacy." In *Internment during the First World War*, edited by Stefan Manz, Panikos Panayi, and Matthew Stibbe, 184–210. London: Routledge.

——. 2020. "First World War Internment in Canada: Enemy Aliens and the Blurring of the Military / Civilian Distinction." *Canadian Military History* 29: 1–28.

Kordan, Bohdan S., and Peter Melnycky, eds. 1991. *In the Shadow of the Rockies: Diary of the Castle Mountain Camp, 1915–1917*. Edmonton: CIUS Press.

Kowner, Rotem. 2000. "Japan's Enlightened War: Military Conduct and Attitudes to the Enemy during the Russo-Japanese War." In *The Japanese and Europe: Images and Perceptions*, edited by Bert Edström, 134–51. Folkestone, UK: Japan Library.

——. 2001. "Becoming an Honorary Civilized Nation: Remaking Japan's Military Image during the Russo-Japanese War, 1904–05." *Historian* 64: 19–38.

——. 2008. "Japan's 'Fifteen Minutes of Glory': Managing World Opinion during the War with Russia, 1904–05." In *Japan and Russia: Three Centuries of Mutual Images*, edited by Yulia Mikhailova and M. William Steele, 47–70. Folkestone, Kent: Global Oriental.

——. 2009. "Imperial Japan and Its POWs: The Dilemma of Humaneness and National Identity." In *War and Militarism in Modern Japan: Issues of History and Identity*, edited by Guy Podoler, 80–110. Folkestone, Kent: Global Oriental.

——. 2017. *Historical Dictionary of the Russo-Japanese War*, 2nd ed. Lanham, MD: Rowman & Littlefield.

——. 2020. "The Repatriation of Surrendered Japanese Troops, 1945–47." In *In the Ruins of the Japanese Empire: Imperial Violence, State Destruction, and the Reordering of Modern East Asia*, edited by Barak Kushner and Andrew Levidis, 121–38. Hong Kong: Hong Kong University Press.

Kramer, Alan. 1997. "Wackes at War: Alsace Lorraine and the Failure of German National Mobilization, 1914–1918." In *State, Society and Mobilization in Europe during the First World War*, edited by John Horne, 105–21. Cambridge: Cambridge University Press.

——. 2007. *Dynamic of Destruction: Culture and Mass Killing in the First World War*. Oxford: Oxford University Press.

Kramer, Arnold. 2008. *Prisoners of War: A Reference Handbook*. Westport, CT: Praeger.

Kruse, Wolfgang. 1994. *Krieg und nationale Integration: Eine Neuinterpretation des sozialdemokratischen Burgfriedensschlusses 1914/15*. Essen: Westphälisches Dampfboot.

Kuklick, Henrika 2010. "Continuity and Change in British Anthropology, 1914–1919." In *Doing Anthropology in Wartime and War Zones: World War I and the Cultural Sciences in Europe*, edited by Reinhard Johler, Christian Marchetti, and Monique Scheer, 29–45. Bielefeld: Transcript Verlag.

Kuncz, Aladár. 1934. *Black Monastery*, translated by Ralph Murray. New York: Harcourt, Brace.

Kurosawa Fumitaka. 2013. *Futatsuno kaikoku to Nihon*. Tokyo: Tokyo University Press, 2013.

Kutzler, Evan A. 2019. *Living by Inches: The Smells, Sounds, Tastes, and Feeling of Captivity in Civil War Prisons*. Chapel Hill: University of North Carolina Press.

Lackenbauer, P. Whitney. 2001. "The Military and 'Mob Rule': The CEF Riots in Calgary, February 1916." *Canadian Military History* 10 (Winter): 31–42.

Lake, Marilyn, and Henry Reynolds. 2008. *Drawing the Global Colour Line: White Men's Countries and the International Challenge of Racial Equality*. Cambridge: Cambridge University Press.

Landefeld, Sarina. 2021. *Combatants and civilians? Individuals as Constructed in International Humanitarian Law, c. 1864–2020*. PhD diss., University of Nottingham.

Lange, Britta. 2008a. "Academic Research on (Coloured) Prisoners of War in Germany, 1915–1918." In *World War I: Five Continents in Flanders*, edited by Dominiek Dendooven and Piet Chielens, 152–60. Tielt: Lannoo.

——. 2008b. "Der Rassenkundler Egon von Eickstedt und sein Gastspiel in Freiburg (1921–1923)," accessed on January 7, 2020, http://www.freiburg-postkolonial.de/Seiten/Egon-von-Eickstedt.htm.

——. 2010. "AfterMath: Anthropological Data from Prisoner-of-War Camps." In *Doing Anthropology in Wartime and War Zones: World War I and the Cultural Sciences in Europe*, edited by Reinhard Johler, Christian Marchetti, and Monique Scheer, 311–35. Bielefeld: Transcript Verlag.

——. 2011. "South Asian Soldiers and German Academics: Anthropological, Linguistic and Musicological Field Studies in Prison Camps." In *"When the War Began We Heard of Several Kings": South Asian Prisoners in World War I Germany*, edited by Franziska Roy, Heike Liebau, and Ravi Ahuja, 149–84. New Delhi: Social Science Press.

——. 2013. *Die Wiener Forschungen an Kriegsgefangenen 1915–1918*. Vienna: Austrian Academy of Sciences Press.

Lange, Britta, and Andre Gingrich. 2014. "Gefangene Stimmen, internierte Körper: Rudolf Pöch, die Wünsdorf-Reise 1917 und die Frage der Geschichte der Völkerkunde." *Anthropos* 109: 599–612.

Lauterbach, Julius. 1917. *1000 £ Kopfpreis—tot oder lebendig: Fluchtabenteuer des ehemaligen Prisenoffiziers S. M. S. "Emden."* Berlin: August Scherl.

Le Naour, Jean-Yves. 2003. *La honte noire: L'Allemagne et les troupes colonials françaises, 1914–1945*. Paris: Hachette Littérature.

Leclercq, Nicole. 2008. "De la culture dans les camps de prisonniers? Allemagne 1914–1918." In *Mémoires et Antimémoires Littéraires au XXe Siècle*, edited by Annamaria Laserra, 219–71. Vienna: Lang.

Lefebvre, Henri, 2009. *State, Space. World: Selected Essays*. Minneapolis: University of Minnesota Press.

Leidinger, Hannes, and Verena Moritz. 2003. *Gefangenschaft, Revolution, Heimkehr. Die Bedeutung der Kriegsgefangenenproblematik für die Geschichte des Kommunismus in Mittel- und Osteuropa 1917–1920*. Vienna: Böhlau.

Lettow-Vorbeck, Paul Emil von. 1920. *Heia Safari! Deutschlands Kampf in Ostafrika*. Berlin: Hase & Köhler.

Levie, Howard S. 1978. *Prisoners of War in International Armed Conflict*. Newport, RI: Naval War College Press.

Levine, Philippa. 1998. "Battle Colors: Race, Sex, and Colonial Soldiery in World War I." *Journal of Women's History* 9, no. 4: 104–30.

Liszt, Franz von. 1920. *Das Völkerrecht*, 11th ed. Berlin: Julius Springer.

Liulevicius, Vejas Gabriel. 2000. *War Land on the Eastern Front: Culture, National Identity and German Occupation in World War I*. Cambridge: Cambridge University Press.

Lohr, Eric. 2003. *Nationalizing the Russian Empire: The Campaign against Enemy Aliens during World War I*. Cambridge, MA: Harvard University Press.

Lowe, Kimberly A. 2014. "Humanitarianism and National Sovereignty: Red Cross Intervention on Behalf of Political Prisoners in Soviet Russia, 1921–3." *Journal of Contemporary History* 49: 652–74.

——. 2019. "The Red Cross and the Laws of War, 1863–1949: International Rights Activism before Human Rights." In *The Routledge History of Human Rights*, edited by Lora Wildenthal and Jean Quataert, 75–96. Abingdon: Routledge.

MacDonagh, Michael. 1935. *In London during the Great War: The Diary of a Journalist*. London: Eyre & Spottiswoode.

Mackenzie, S. P. 1994. "The Treatment of Prisoners of War in World War II." *Journal of Modern History* 66: 487–520.

Madley, Benjamin. 2005. "From Africa to Auschwitz: How German South West Africa Incubated Ideas and Methods Adopted and Developed by the Nazis in Eastern Europe." *European History Quarterly* 35: 429–64.

Mahony, Sean. 1987. *Frongoch: University of the Revolution*. Dublin: FDR Teoranta.

Malkki, Liisa. 1995. "Refugees and Exile: From 'Refugee Studies' to the National Order of Things." *Annual Review of Anthropology* 24: 495–523.

Manifest der Internationale zur gegenwärtigen Lage. Resolutionen am Basler Kongress 24.–25. November 1912. Berlin: Vorwärts Verlag.

Manz, Stefan, and Panikos Panayi. 2020. *Enemies in the Empire: Civilian Internment in the British Empire during the First World War*. Oxford: Oxford University Press.

Manz, Stefan, Panikos Panayi, and Matthew Stibbe, eds. 2019. *Internment during the First World War: A Mass Global Phenomenon*. London: Routledge.

Marrus, Michael. 1985. *The Unwanted: European Refugees in the Twentieth Century*. New York: Oxford University Press.

Martin, Rudolf. 1914. *Lehrbuch der Anthropologie in systematischer Darstellung*. Jena: Gustav Fischer.

Matsuyama furyo shūyōjo, ed. 1906 *Matsuyama shūyōjo rokoku furyo*. Matsuyama: Matsuyama furyo shūyōjo.

Mayr, Julia. 2016. "Der Internationale Soldatenfriedhof Mauthausen—ungleiche Erinnerung an die Toten zweier Weltkriege und KZ-Häftlinge." Master's thesis, University of Vienna.

McConnachie, Kirsten. 2016. "Camps of Containment: A Genealogy of the Refugee Camp." *Humanity* 7, no. 3: 397–412.

McElligott, Anthony. 2014. *Rethinking the Weimar Republic: Authority and Authoritarianism, 1916–1936*. London: Bloomsbury Academic.

McKernan, Luke. 2006. "The Supreme Moment of the War: General Allenby's Entry into Jerusalem." *Historical Journal of Film, Radio and Television* 13: 169–80.

McPhail, Helen. 2000. *The Long Silence: Civilian Life under the German Occupation of Northern France, 1914–1918*. London: I. B. Tauris.

Mégret, Frédéric. 2011 / 12. "War and the Vanishing Battlefield." *Loyola University Chicago International Law Review* 9, no. 1: 131–55.

Menjō Yoshio. 2003. "Nagoya furyo shūyōjo oboegaki." *Chintaosen doitsuhei furyo shuyōjo kenkyu* 1 (December): 36–52.

Mentzel, Walter. 1995. "Weltkriegsflüchtlinge in Cisleithanien, 1914–1918." In *Asylland wider Willen. Flüchtlinge in Österreich im europäischen Kontext seit 1914*, edited by Gernot Heiss and Oliver Rathkolb, 17–44. Vienna: Jugend und Volk.

Merhart, Gero von. 2008. *Daljóko. Bilder aus Sibirischen Arbeitstagen. Ed. Hermann Parzinger*. Vienna: Böhlau Verlag.

Militzer, Max. 1931. "500 Tage in Marokko." In *Feindeshand: Die Gefangenschaft im Weltkriege in Einzeldarstellungen*, edited by Hans Weiland and Leopold Kern, 94–104. Vienna: Bundesvereinigung der ehemaligen österreichischen Kriegsgefangenen.

Miller, Susanne. 1974. *Klassenkampf und Burgfrieden: Die deutsche Sozialdemokratie im Ersten Weltkrieg*. Düsseldorf: Droste.

Moll, Martin. 2014. *Die Steiermark im Ersten Weltkrieg: Der Kampf des Hinterlandes ums Überleben 1914–1918*. Graz: Styria Premium.

Monteath, Peter. 2018. Captured Lives: Australia's Wartime Internment Camps. Canberra: NLA Publishing.

Morel, E. D. 1920. *Horror on the Rhine*. London: Union of Democratic Control.

Moreno, Jonathan D. 2011. *The Autobiography of J. L Moreno (Abridged)*. **United Kingdom:** The North-West Psychodrama Association.

Mori Takaaki. 2003. "Matsuyama doitsu furyo shūyōjo ni kansuru shiryō shōkai," *Chintaosen doitsuhei furyo shūyōjo kenkyū* 1 (December): 53–7.

Moritz, Verena. 1998. "Die Österreichisch-Ungarischen Kriegsgefangenen in der russischen Wirtschaft (1914 bis Oktober 1917)." *Zeitgeschichte* 11 / 12: 380–89.

——. 2005. Zwischen Nutzen und Bedrohung. Die russischen Kriegsgefangenen in Österreich 1914–1920. Bonn: Bernard & Graefe.

Moritz, Verena, and Hannes Leidinger. 2005. *Zwischen Nutzen und Bedrohung. Die russischen Kriegsgefangenen in Österreich (1914–1921)*. Bonn: Bernard & Graefe.

Moritz, Verena, and Julia Walleczek-Fritz. 2017. "Prisoners of War (Austria-Hungary)." In *1914–1918-online. International Encyclopedia of the First World War*. DOI: 10.15463 / ie1418.10374.

Morris, James. 2020. "The European Revolutions of 1848 and the Danubian Principality of Wallachia." PhD diss., University of Cambridge.

Mosse, George L. 1990. *Fallen Soldiers: Reshaping the Memory of the World Wars.* Oxford University Press.

Mouradian, Khatchig. 2019. "Internment and Destruction: Concentration Camps during the Armenian Genocide, 1915–1916." In *Internment during the First World War*, edited by Stefan Manz, Panikos Panayi, and Matthew Stibbe, 145–61. London: Routledge.

Moyd, Michelle. 2014. *Violent Intermediaries: African Soldiers, Conquest, and Everyday Colonialism in German East Africa.* Athens: Ohio University Press.

Murphy, Mahon (Mahon Maafii). 2009. "Daiichiji sekai taisenchū no nihon ni okeru doitsujin furyo: Doitsu biru o nozokeba karerani fujū wa nakatta," *Chintaosen doitsuhei furyo shūyōjo kenkyū* 7 (December): 5–24.

——. 2017. *Colonial Captivity during the First World War: Internment and the Fall of the German Empire, 1914–1919.* Cambridge: Cambridge University Press.

Nachbaur, Ulrich. 2018. "Rudolf Wacker: K.u.k. Fähnrich in Der Reserve." In *Wacker im Krieg. Erfahrungen Eines Künstlers*, edited by Jürgen Thaler and Andreas Rudigier, 69–83. Salzburg: Residenz Verlag.

Nachtigal, Reinhard. 1995. "German Prisoners of War in Tsarist Russia: A Glance at Petrograd/St Petersburg." *German History* 13: 198–204.

——. 2001. *Die Murmanbahn. Die Verkehrsanbindung eines kriegswichtigen Hafens und das Arbeitspotential der Kriegsgefangenen (1915 bis 1918).* Grunbach: Greiner.

——. 2003. *Russland und seine osterreichisch-ungarischen Kriegsgefangenen (1914–1918).* Grunbach: Greiner.

——. 2008. "The Repatriation and Reception of Returning Prisoners of War, 1918–22." *Immigrants & Minorities* 26: 157–84.

Nachtigal, Reinhard, and Radauer, Lena. n.d. "Prisoners of War (Russian Empire)." In *1914–1918-online. International Encyclopedia of the First World War.* http://encyclopedia.1914-1918-online.net/article/prisoners_of_war_russian_empire.

Nagler, Jörg. 2018. "Control and Internment of Enemy Aliens in the United States during the First World War." In *Internment during the First World War*, edited by Stefan Manz, Panikos Panayi, and Matthew Stibbe, 211–41. London: Routledge.

Nagornaja, Oxana. 2009. "United by Barbed Wire: Russian POWs in Germany, National Stereotypes, and International Relations, 1914–22." *Kritika: Explorations in Russian and Eurasian History* 10: 475–98.

Naranch, Bradley, and Geoff Eley, eds. 2014. *German Colonialism in a Global Age.* Durham, NC: Duke University Press.

Narutoshi doitsukan. n.d. *Naruto-shi doitsukan shozōhin mokuroku: Bandō shūyōjo narabi ni daiichi sekai taisenji no zenkoku shūyōjo kanren shiryō.* Nartuto-shi, Japan: Naruto-shi doitsukan.

Nasson, Bill. 2014. "British Imperial Africa." In *Empires at War, 1911–1923*, edited by Robert Gerwarth and Erez Manela, 130–51. Oxford: Oxford University Press, 2014.

Neff, Stephen C. 2010. "Prisoners of War in International Law: The Nineteenth Century." In *Prisoners in War*, edited by Sibylle Scheipers, 57–73. Oxford: Oxford University Press.

Newald, Richard. 1938. "Sibirische Odyssee." MSG 200/1931 Reg. Nr. 27757. BAMA Freiburg.

Nivet, Philippe. 2011. *La France occupée, 1914–1918*. Paris: Armand Colin.

Noschke, Richard. 2002. *An Insight into Civilian Internment in Britain during WWI: From the Diary of Richard Noschke and a Short Essay by Rudolf Rocker*. Maidenhead, UK: Anglo-American Family History Society Publication.

Obergottsberger, Franz. n.d. "Ich hörte noch die Nachtigall. Die Lebensgeschichte des Franz Obergottsberger," vol. 2. Vienna: Dokumentation Lebensgeschichtlicher Aufzeichnungen, Universität Wien.

Ogawa Ryo. 2015. *Daiichiji sekai taisen to nishi Afrika: Furansu ni mei wo sasega kokujin butai (Senegaru hohei)*. Tokyo: Tōsui Shōbo.

Olin, Margaret. 2010. "Jews among the Peoples: Visual Archives in German Prison Camps during the Great War." In *Doing Anthropology in Wartime and War Zones: World War I and the Cultural Sciences in Europe*, edited by Reinhard Johler, Christian Marchetti, and Monique Scheer, 255–77. Bielefeld: Transcript Verlag.

Oltmer, Jochen. 2006. "Unentbehrliche Arbeitskräfte: Kriegsgefangene in Deutschland 1914–1918." In *Kriegsgefangene im Europa des Ersten Weltkriegs*, edited by Jochen Oltmer, 67–96. Paderborn: Ferdinand Schöningh.

Olusoga, David. 2014. *The World's War*. London: Head of Zeus.

Olusoga, David, and Casper W. Erichsen. 2010. *The Kaiser's Holocaust: Germany's Forgotten Genocide and the Colonial Roots of Nazism*. London: Faber & Faber.

Omissi, David, ed. 1999. *Indian Voices of the Great War: Soldiers' Letters, 1914–18*. New York: Palgrave.

Otsuru Atsushi. 2007. *Aonogahara furyo shūyōjo no sekai: Daiichiji sekai taisen to ōsutoria horyohei*. Tokyo: Yamakawa shuppansha.

——. 2019. "The Prisoner of War Camp at Aonogahara near Kōbe—The Austro-Hungarian Empire in Miniature." In *The East Asian Dimension of the First World War. Global Entanglements and Japan, China and Korea, 1914–1919*, edited by Jan Schmidt and Katja Schmidtpott, 349–64. Frankfurt: Campus, 2019.

Pachowicz, Anna. 2017. "Polish Emigration in France at the Beginning of the Twentieth Century." *Istraživanja. Journal of Historical Researches* 28: 134–46.

Paddock, Troy R. E. 2014. "Introduction." In *World War I and Propaganda*, edited by Troy R. E. Paddock, 1–20. Leiden: Brill.

Palmieri, Daniel. 2012. "An Institution Standing the Test of Time? A Review of the History of the International Committee of the Red Cross." *International Review of the Red Cross* 94/888: 1273–98.

——. 2018. "Humanitarianism on the Screen: The ICRC films, 1921–1965." In *Humanitarianism and the Media*, edited by Johannes Paulmann, 90–106. Oxford. Berghahn.

Panayi, Panikos. 1987. "The Imperial War Museum as a Source of Information for Historians of Immigrant Minorities: The Example of Germans in Britain during the First World War." *Immigrants and Minorities* 6: 348–61.

——. 1989. "Anti-German Riots in London during the First World War." *German History* 7: 184–203.

——. 1991. *The Enemy in Our Midst: Germans in Britain during the First World War*. Oxford: Berg.

——. 1993a. "An Intolerant Act by an Intolerant Society: The Internment of Germans in Britain during the First World War." In *The Internment of Aliens in Twentieth Century Britain*, edited by David Cesarani and Tony Kushner, 53–78. London: Routledge.

——. 1993b. *Minorities in Wartime: National and Racial Groupings in Europe, North America, and Australia during the Two World Wars*. Providence: Berg.

——. 2005. "A Marginalized Subject? The Historiography of Enemy Alien Internment in Britain." In *'Totally Un-English?' Britain's Internment of 'Enemy Aliens' in Two World Wars*, edited by Richard Dove, 17–28. Amsterdam: Rodopi.

——. 2013. *Prisoners of Britain: German Civilian and Combatant Internees during the First World War*. Manchester: Manchester University Press.

——, ed. 2014. *Germans as Minorities during the First World War: A Global Comparative Perspective*. London: Routledge.

——. 2018. "Work, Leisure, and Sport in Military and Civilian Internment Camps in Britain, 1914–1919." In *Sport under Unexpected Circumstances: Violence, Discipline, and Leisure in Penal and Internment Camps*, edited by Gregor Feindt, Anke Hilbrenner, and Dittmar Dahlmann, 63–85. Göttingen: Vandenhoeck & Ruprecht.

Pastor, Peter. 1983. "Introduction." In *Essays on World War I: Origins and Prisoners of War*, edited by Samuel Williamson and Peter Paster, 113–17. New York: Columbia University Press.

——. 2012. "Hungarian Prisoners of War in Siberia." In *Essays on World War I*, edited by Peter Pastor and Graydon A. Tunstall, 111–29. New York: Columbia University Press.

Pegram, Aaron. 2020. *Surviving the Great War: Australian Prisoners of War on the Western Front, 1916–18*. Cambridge: Cambridge University Press.

Phillimore, George G. 1920. "Some Suggestions for a Draft Code for the Treatment of Prisoners of War." *Transactions of the Grotius Society* 6: 25–34.

Phillimore, George G., and Hugh Bellot. 1919. "Treatment of Prisoners of War." *Transactions of the Grotius Society* 5: 47–63.

Piana, Francesca. 2009. "Humanitaire et politique, in medias res: le typhus en Pologne et l'organisation internationale d'hygiène de la SDN (1919–1923)." *Relations internationales* 2, no. 138: 23–38.

——. 2015. "Photography, Cinema, and the Quest for Influence: the International Committee of the Red Cross in the Wake of the First World War." In *Humanitarian Photography: A History*, edited by Davide Rodogno and Heide Fehrenbach, 140–64. Cambridge, Cambridge University Press.

Pickenpaugh, Roger. 2009. *Captives in Gray: The Civil War Prisons of the Union*. Alabama: University of Alabama Press.

Pirquet, Clemens. 1926. *Volksgesundheit im Krieg*. Vienna: Hölder-Pichler-Tempsky.

Pitzer, Andrea. 2017. *One Long Night: A Global History of Concentration Camps*. London: Little, Brown.

Polian, Pavel. 2005. "First Victims of the Holocaust: Soviet-Jewish Prisoners of War in German Captivity." *Kritika:* 6: 763–87.

Pollock, Gordon D. 2018. *Black Soldiers in a White Man's War: Race, Good Order and Discipline in a Great War Labour Battalion*. Newcastle-upon-Tyne: Cambridge Scholars.

Porter, Thomas Earl. 2009. "Hitler's *Rassenkampf* in the East: The Forgotten Genocide of Soviet POWs." *Nationalities Papers* 37: 839–59.

Poznakhirev, Vitaliĭ Vital'evich. 2014. Turetskie voennoplennye i grazhdanskie plennye v Rossii v 1914–1924 gg. St. Petersburg: Nestor-Istoriia.

Proctor, Tammy M. 2010. *Civilians in a World at War, 1914–1918*. New York: New York University Press.

Rachamimov, A. (Iris). 2002. POWs and the Great War: Captivity on the Eastern Front. Oxford: Berg.

——. 2006. "The Disruptive Comforts of Drag: (Trans)Gender Performances among Prisoners of War in Russia, 1914–1920." *American Historical Review* 111: 362–82.

Rachamimov, Iris. 2012a. "Camp Domesticity: Shifting Gender Boundaries in WWI Internment Camps." In *Cultural Heritage and Prisoners of War: Creativity behind Barbed Wire*, edited by Gillian C. Carr and Harold Mytum, 291–305. London: Routledge.

——. 2012b. "Military Captivity in Two World Wars: Legal Frameworks and Camp Regimes." In *Cambridge History of War, Vol. 4: War and the Modern World, 1850–2005*, edited by Roger Chickering, Dennis Showalter, and Hans van de Ven, 214–35. Cambridge: Cambridge University Press.

——. 2018. "Small Escapes: Gender, Class, and Material Culture in Great War Internment Camps." In *Objects of War: The Material Culture of Conflict and Displacement*, edited by Leonora Auslander and Tara Zahra, 164–88. Ithaca, NY: Cornell University Press.

Radauer, Lena. 2011. *Hans Franta: Sibirien*. Linz: Nordico Museum der Stadt Linz.

——. 2018. "Rudolf Wacker—(ein) Künstler in sibirischer Kriegsgefangenschaft." In *Wacker im Krieg. Erfahrungen eines Künstlers*, edited by Jürgen Thaler and Andreas Rudigier, 85–101. Salzburg: Residenz Verlag.

Radauer, Lena, and Egger, Matthias. 2014. "Kultur im Lager. Kulturelle Aktivitäten der österreichisch-ungarischen Kriegsgefangenen in Russland 1914–1918." *Österreich in Geschichte und Literatur* 2: 160–78.

Rae, John. 1970. *Conscience and Politics: The British Government and the Conscientious Objector to Military Service*. Oxford: Oxford University Press.

Raithel, Thomas, and Irene Strenge. 2000. "Die Reichstagsbrandverordnung: Grundlegung der Diktatur mit den Instrumenten des Weimarer Ausnahmezustands." *Vierteljahrshefte für Zeitgeschichte* 48: 413–460.

Reder, Josef. 1918. *Das Fleckfieber nach dem heutigen Stande seiner Lehre und nach Beobachtungen in den Epidemien des k. k. Flüchtlingslagers Gmünd*. Leipzig: Deuticke.

Reed, John. 1917. *War in Eastern Europe: Travels through the Balkans in 1915*. New York: Charles Scribner's Sons.

Reisman, W. Michael, and Chris T. Antoniu, eds. 1994. *The Laws of War: A Comprehensive Collection of Primary Documents on International Laws Governing Armed Conflict*. New York: Vintage Books.

Rhodes, James Ford. 1904. *History of the United States from the Compromise of 1850: 1864–1866*. New York: Harper & Brothers.

Roberts, Adam. 1994. "Land Warfare: From Hague to Nuremberg." In *The Laws of War: Constraints on Warfare in the Western World*, edited by Michael Howard, George Andreopolous, and Mark Shulman, 116–39. New Haven, CT: Yale University Press.

——. 2011. "The Civilian in Modern War." In *The Changing Character of War*, edited by Hew Strachan and Sibylle Scheipers, 357–80. Oxford: Oxford University Press.

Rocker, Rudolf. 2002. *An Insight into Civilian Internment in Britain during WWI: From the Diary of Richard Noschke and a Short Essay by Rudolf Rocker*. Maidenhead, UK: Anglo-American Family History Society Publication.

——. 2005. *The London Years*. Edinburgh: Five Leaves Publications.

Rodogno, Davide. 2014. "The American Red Cross and the International Committee of the Red Cross: Humanitarian Politics and Policies in Asia Minor and Greece (1922–23)." *First World War Studies* 5: 83–99.

Romero Salvadó, Francisco J. 1999. *Spain 1914–1918: Between War and Revolution*. London: Routledge.

Röper, August. 1920. *Kriegsgefangene in Deutschland*. Fribourg, Switzerland: Librairie de L'Université Otto Gschwend.

Rosenblit, Marsha L., 2004. "Sustaining Austrian "National" Identity in Crisis: The Dilemma of the Jews in Habsburg Austria, 1914–1919." In *Constructing Nationalities in East Central Europe*, edited by Pieter M. Judson and Marsha L. Rosenblit, 178–91. New York: Berghahn Books.

Röseler, Hermann. 1931. "Bilder aus englischer Gefangenschaft im deutschen-ostafrikanischen Kolonial-gebiet in Ägypten und in England." In *Feindeshand: Die Gefangenschaft im Weltkriege in Einzeldarstellungen*, edited by Hans Weiland and Leopold Kern, vol. 2, 105–9. Vienna: Bundesvereinigung der ehemaligen österreichischen Kriegsgefangenen.

Roy, Franziska, Heike Liebau, and Ravi Ahuja, eds. 2011. *"When the War Began We Heard of Several Kings": South Asian Prisoners in World War I Germany*. New Delhi: Social Science Press.

Saatzer, Josef. n.d. "Sibirien. Erinnerungen an die Gefangenschaft 1915–1917 und Aufenthalt bis 1920." Vienna: Dokumentation Lebensgeschichtlicher Aufzeichnungen, Universität Wien.

Sammartino, Annemarie H. 2010. *The Impossible Border: Germany and the East, 1914–1922*. Ithaca, NY: Cornell University Press.

Samson, Anne. 2013. *World War I in Africa: The Forgotten Conflict among the European Powers*. London: I. B. Tauris.

Sanborn, Joshua. 2014. "The Russian Empire." In *Empires at War, 1911–1923*, edited by Robert Gerwarth and Erez Manela, 91–108. Oxford: Oxford University Press.

Sanders, Michael, and Philip Taylor. 1982. *British Propaganda during the First World War, 1914–1918*. London: Palgrave MacMillan.

Schafft, Gretchen E. 2004. *From Racism to Genocide: Anthropology in the Third Reich*. Urbana: University of Illinois Press.

Scheer, Monique. 2010. "Captive Voices: Phonographic Recordings in the German and Austrian Prisoner-of-War Camps of World War I." In *Doing Anthropology in Wartime and War Zones: World War I and the Cultural Sciences in Europe*, edited by Reinhard Johler, Christian Marchetti, and Monique Scheer, 279–309. Bielefeld: Transcript Verlag.

Scheidl, Inge. 2014. *Rolf Geyling (1884–1952). Der Architekt zwischen Kriegen und Kontinenten*. Vienna: Böhlau Verlag.

Scheipers, Sibylle. 2011. "The Status and Protections of Prisoners of War and Detainees." In *The Changing Character of War*, edited by Hew Strachan and Sibylle Scheipers, 394–409. Oxford: Oxford University Press.

——. 2015. *Unlawful Combatants. A Genealogy of the Irregular Fighter*. Oxford: Oxford University Press.

Schirks, Rhea. 2002. *Die Marten'sche Klausel. Rezeption und Rechtsqualität*. Baden-Baden: Nomos.

Schlotterbeck, John T., Wesley W. Wilson, Midori Kawaue, and Harold A. Klingensmith. 2019. *James Riley Weaver's Civil War: The Diary of a Union Cavalry Officer and Prisoner of War, 1863–1865*. Ashland, OH: Kent State University Press.

Schmitt, Carl. 1985. *Political Theology: Four Chapters on the Concept of Sovereignty*. Cambridge, MA: MIT Press.

Schreinert, Anton. 1920. *Die Kriegsgefangenen-Handelsschule in Beresowka (Sibirien)*. Aussig (Ústí nad Labem), Germany: Tuch.

Schudnagies, Christoph. 1994. *Der Kriegs- und Belagerungszustand im Deutschen Reich während des Ersten Weltkrieges: Eine Studie zur Entwicklung und Handhabung des deutschen Ausnahmezustandsrechts bis 1918*. Frankfurt: Peter Lang.

Schurz, Peter. 1986. *Sigmund Mathias Schiffler: Architekt 1889–1944*. Klagenfurt: Self-published.

Schutzbier, Heribert. 2010. *Edmund Adler—Kriegsdienst und Gefangenschaft im Spiegel seiner Korrespondenz*. Stixneusiedl, Austria: Ecker KG.

Semchuk, Sandra, and Jen Budney. 2018. *The Stories Were Not Told: Canada's First World War Internment Camps*. Edmonton: University of Alberta Press.

Seto Takehiko. 2011. "Nijūyonmei no furyo shūyōjochō." *Chintaosen doitsuhei furyo shūyōjo kenkyū* 9 (December), 91–104.

Shimazu, Naoko. 2009. *Japanese Society at War: Death, Memory and the Russo-Japanese War*. Cambridge: Cambridge University Press.

——. 2014. "Views from the Trenches: New Year's Truce, Bloody Sunday and Japanese Attitudes towards the 1905 Revolution in Russia," *Horizons* 5: 2 (2014): 194–208.

Short, John Phillip. 2012. *Magic Lantern Empire: Colonialism and Society in Germany*. Ithaca, NY: Cornell University Press.

Silkenat, David. 2019. *Raising the White Flag: How Surrender Defined the American Civil War*. Chapel Hill: University of North Carolina Press.

Simpson, Alfred William Brian. 1994. *In the Highest Degree Odious: Detention without Trial in Wartime Britain*. Oxford: Oxford University Press.

Skran, Claudena. 1995. *Refugees in Interwar Europe: The Emergence of a Regime*. Oxford: Clarendon Press.

Smith, Ian R., and Andreas Stucki. 2011. "The Colonial Development of Concentration Camps (1868–1902)." *Journal of Imperial and Commonwealth History* 38: 417–37.

Sondhaus, Lawrence. 2011. *World War I: The Global Revolution*. New York: Cambridge University Press.

Speed, Richard Berry. 1990. *Prisoners, Diplomats, and the Great War: A Study in the Diplomacy of Captivity*. New York: Greenwood Press.

Spoerer, Mark. 2006. "The Mortality of Allied Prisoners of War and Belgian Civilian Deportees in German Custody during the First World War: A Reappraisal of the Effects of Forced Labour." *Population Studies* 60: 121–36.

Springer, Paul J., and Glenn Robins. 2015. *Transforming Civil War Prisons: Lincoln, Lieber, and the Politics of Captivity*. New York: Routledge.

Steinmetz, George. 2009. "Qindao as a Colony: From Apartheid to Civilizational Exchange." An unpublished paper prepared for the Johns Hopkins Workshops in Comparative History of Science and Technology, "Science, Technology and Modernity: Colonial Cities in Asia, 1890–1940," Baltimore, January 16–17, 2009.

Steuer, Kenneth. 2014. "German Propaganda and Prisoners of War during World War I." In *World War I in Propaganda*, edited by Troy R. E. Paddock, 155–80. Leiden: Brill.

Stevenson, David. 2017. *1917: War, Peace and Revolution*. Oxford: Oxford University Press.

Stibbe, Matthew. 2004. "A Community at War: British Civilian Internees at the Ruhleben Camp in Germany, 1914–1918," In *Uncovered Fields. New Approaches in First World War Studies*, edited by Jenny MacLeod and Pierre Purseigle, 79–94. Leiden: Brill.

——. 2006. "The Internment of Civilians by Belligerent States during the First World War and the Response of the International Committee of the Red Cross." *Journal of Contemporary History* 41: 5–19.

——. 2008a. *British Civilian Internees in Germany: The Ruhleben Camp*, 1914–1918. Manchester: Manchester University Press.

——. 2008b. "Civilian Internment and Civilian Internees in Europe, 1914–20." *Immigrants and Minorities*, 26: 49–81.

——. 2008c. "Introduction: Captivity, Forced Labour and Forced Migration during the First World War." *Immigrants and Minorities* 26: 1–18.

——. 2013a. "Ein globales Phänomen: Zivilinternierung im Ersten Weltkrieg in transnationaler und internationaler Dimension." In *Lager vor Auschwitz: Gewalt und Integration im 20. Jahrhundert*, edited by Christoph Jahr and Jens Thiel, 158–76. Berlin: Metropol.

——. 2013b. "Krieg und Brutalisierung: Die Internierung von Zivilisten bzw. 'politisch Unzuverlässigen' in Österreich-Ungarn während des Ersten Weltkriegs." In *Besetzt, interniert, deportiert: Der Erste Weltkrieg und die deutsche, jüdische, polnische und ukrainische Zivilbevölkerung im östlichen Europa*, edited by Alfred Eisfeld, Guido Hausmann, and Dietmar Neutatz, 87–106. Essen: Klartext.

——. 2018. "The Internment of Enemy Aliens in the Habsburg Empire, 1914–1918." In *Internment during the First World War*, edited by Stefan Manz, Panikos Panayi, and Matthew Stibbe, 61–84. London: Routledge.

——. 2019. *Civilian Internment during the First World War: A European and Global History, 1914–1920*. London: Palgrave Macmillan.

Stiehl, Otto. 1916. *Unsere Feinde: 96 Charakterköpfe aus deutschen Kriegsgefangenenlagern*. Stuttgart: J. Hoffmann.

Stoffa, Major Paul. 1933. *Round the World to Freedom: Being the Escape and Adventures of Major Paul Stoffa (of the Hungarian Army)*. London: Bodley Head.

Stone, Dan. 2017. *Concentration Camps: A Short History*. Oxford: Oxford University Press.

Stonebridge, Lyndsey. 2018. *Placeless People: Writings, Rights, and Refugees*. Oxford: Oxford University Press.

Strachan, Hew. 2001. *The First World War: Vol. 1: To Arms*. Oxford: Oxford University Press.

Streets-Salter, Heather. 2017. *World War One in Southeast Asia: Colonialism and Anticolonialism in an Era of Global Conflict*. Cambridge: Cambridge University Press.

Struck, Hermann. 1917. *Kriegsgefangene: Hundert Steinzeichnungen von Hermann Struck*. Berlin: Dietrich Reimer [Ernst Vohsen].

Takahashi Terukazu. 2003. "Samuna Weruzu (Sumner Wells) ni yoru doitsuhei shūyōjo chōsa hōkokusho," *Chintaosen doitsuhei furyo shūyōjo kenkyū* 1 (December): 3–31.

——. 2005. "Weruzu no chōsa hōkokusho no tenpu zumen." *Chintaosen doitsuhei furyo shūyōjo kenkyu* 3 (September): 108–121.

Tamura Ichiro. 2004. "Ruddowiggu Vietingu (Ludwig Wieting) no kaisō kara." *Chintaosen doitsuhei furyo shūyōjo kenkyū* 2 (October): 23–40.

——. 2010. *Bandō furyo shūyōjo no zenbō: Shochō Matsue Toyohisa no mezashita mono*. Tokyo: Sakuhokusha.

Tate, Hazuki. 2015. "Rapatrier les prisonniers de guerre: la politique des Alliés et l'action humanitaire du Comité international de la Croix Rouge (1918–1929)." PhD diss., École des Hautes Études en Sciences Sociales.

——. 2017. "Le comité international de la Croix-Rouge comme architecte du droit international: vers le code des prisonniers de guerre (1929)." *Monde(s): histoire espaces relations* 12, no. 2: 203–20.

Taylor, Murrel. 2018. *Embattled Freedom: Journeys through the Civil War's Slave Refugee Camps*. Chapel Hill: University of North Carolina Press.

Thiel, Jens. 2007. *"Menschenbassin Belgien": Anwerbung, Deportation und Zwangsarbeit im Ersten Weltkrieg*. Essen: Klartext.

Thilmans, Guy. 2012. Les sénégalais et la Grande Guerre: lettres de tirailleurs et recrutement (1912–1919). Gorée: Éditions du Musée Historique du Sénégal.

Thorpe, Julie. 2011. "Displacing Empire: Refugee Welfare, National Activism and State Legitimacy in Austria-Hungary in the World War I." In *Refugees and the End of Empire: Imperial Collapse and Forced Migration in the Twentieth Century*, edited by Panikos Panayi and Pippa Virdee, 102–26. London: Palgrave Macmillan.

Thoß, Bruno. 2012. "Weißer Terror, 1919." In *Historisches Lexikon Bayerns*. Accessed December 12, 2018. URL: http://www.historisches-lexikon-bayerns.de/Lexikon/Weißer_Terror,_1919.

Timperley, Harold John, ed. 1938. *Japanese Terror in China*. New York: Modern Age Books.

Tomita Hiroshi. 1991. *Bandō furyo shūyōjo: Nichidoku sensō to doitsu furyo*. Tokyo: Hōsei Daigaku Shuppankai.

Torpey, John. 2000. *The Invention of the Passport: Surveillance, Citizenship and the State*. Cambridge: Cambridge University Press.

Trarore, Mohamet. 2014. *Schwarze Truppen im Ersten Weltkrieg: Zwischen Rassismus, Kolonialismus und Nationalismus*. Hamburg: Diplomica Verlag.

Tsarëva, Evgeniia Sergeevna. 2012. "Vklad muzykantov-voennoplennykh Pervoĭ Mirovoĭ Voĭny v razvitie professional'noĭ muzykal'noĭ kul'tury Sibiri." *Nepreryvnoe Obrazovanie v Sfere Kul'tury* 9: 18–27.

——. 2013. "Vklad voennoplennykh Pervoĭ Mirovoĭ Voĭny v razvitie professional'noj muzykal'noĭ kul'tury Sibiri (Na primere Krasnoiarska 1914–1920 gg.)." *Kontsept. Nauchno-Metodicheskiĭ Elektronnyĭ Zhurnal* 1: 1–12.

Turner, Victor. 1969. *The Ritual Process: Structure and Anti-Structure*. Ithaca, NY: Cornell University Press.

Valitov, Aleksandr Aleksandrovich, and Vadim Sulimov. 2014. "Trud voennoplennykh Pervoĭ Mirovoĭ Voĭny v Tobol'skoĭ Gubernii." *Izvestiia VUZov, Gumanitarnye Nauki* 3, no. 5: 189–92.

Van de Ven, Hans. 2017. "The Battle of Shanghai." In *China at War: Triumph and Tragedy in the Emergence of the New China, 1937–1952*, edited by Hans Van de Ven, 75–101. Cambridge, MA: Harvard University Press.

Van Dijk, Boyd. 2018. "Human Rights in War: On the Entangled Foundations of the 1949 Geneva Conventions." *American Journal of International Law* 112: 553–82.

Van Galen Last, Dick, Ralf Futselaar, and Marjolijn de Jager. 2016. *Black Shame: African Soldiers in Europe, 1914–1922*. London: Bloomsbury.

Vance, Jonathan. F. 2006. *Encyclopedia of Prisoners of War and Internment*, 2nd ed. Millerton, NY: Grey House.

Vischer, Adolf Lukas. 1919. *Barbed Wire Disease: A Psychological Study of the Prisoner of War*. London: John Bale, Sons & Danielson.

Vu-Hill, Kimloan. 2011. *Coolies into Rebels: Impact of World War I on French Indochina*. Paris: Indes savantes.

Wachsmann, Nikolaus. 2015. *KL: A History of the Nazi Concentration Camps*. London: Little, Brown.

Waiser, Bill. 1995. *Park Prisoners: The Untold Story of Western Canada's National Parks, 1915–1946*. Calgary-Saskatoon: Fifth House.

Walleczek-Fritz, Julia. 2017. "The Social Degeneration of the Habsburg Home Front: 'Forbidden Intercourse' and POWs during the First World War." *European Review of History: Revue Européenne d'histoire* 24: 273–87.

Wang, Haochen. 2014. "A Cleaner, Better, Stronger Land: The Causes of Anti-German Riots in Wartime London, 1914–1918." *Great Lakes Journal of Undergraduate History* 2: 54–75.

Watenpaugh, Keith David. 2014. *Bread from Stones: The Middle East and the Making of Modern Humanitarianism*. Oakland: University of California Press.

Watson, Alexander. 2014a. *Ring of Steel: Germany and Austria-Hungary at War, 1914–1918*. London: Allen Lane.

——. 2014b. "'Unheard-Of Brutality': Russian Atrocities against Civilians in East Prussia, 1914–1915." *Journal of Modern History* 86: 780–825.

Watts, Lori. 2009. *When Empire Comes Home: Repatriation and Reintegration in Postwar Japan*. Cambridge, MA: Harvard University Press.

Weiland, Hans, and Leopold Kern, eds. 1931. *In Feindeshand: Die Gefangenschaft im Weltkriege in Einzeldarstellungen*. Vienna: Bundesvereinigung der ehemaligen österreichischen Kriegsgefangenen.

Weindling, Paul. 2000. *Epidemics and Genocide in Eastern Europe, 1890–1945*. Oxford: Oxford University Press.

Weingartner, James. 1996. "War against Subhumans: Comparisons between the German War against the Soviet Union and the American War against Japan, 1941–1945." *Historian* 58: 557–73.

White, Benjamin Thomas. 2019. "Human and Animals in a Refugee Camp: Baquba, Iraq, 1918–20." *Journal of Refugee Studies* 32, no. 2: 216–36.

Wigger, Iris. 2010. "'Black Shame' The Campaign against 'Racial Degeneration' and Female Degradation in Interwar Europe." *Race and Class* 51: 33–46.

Wilkin, Bernard. 2016. "Isolation, Communication and Propaganda in the Occupied Territories of France, 1914–1918." *First World War Studies* 7: 229–42.

Wolf, Arthur. n.d. "Account of His Life to 1920." Arthur Wolf Papers, Folder 4. Leo Baeck Institute Center for Jewish Studies.

Wolf, Arthur, Papers. Miscellaneous certificates. Documents: 1890–1968. AR 25270. New York: Leo Baeck Institute.

Wurzer, Georg. 2005. *Die Kriegsgefangenen der Mittelmächte in Rußland im Ersten Weltkrieg*. Göttingen: V&R Unipress.

Wylie, Neville. 2010a. *Barbed Wire Diplomacy*. Oxford. Oxford University Press.

——. 2010b. "The 1929 Prisoner of War Convention and the Building of the Interwar Prisoner of War Regime." In *Prisoners in War*, edited by Sibylle Scheipers, 91–108. Oxford: Oxford University Press.

Wylie, Neville, and Lindsey Cameron. 2019. "The Impact of World War I on the Law Governing the Treatment of Prisoners of War and the Making of a Humanitarian Subject." *European Journal of International Law* 29: 1327–50.

Xu, Guoqi. 2014. "Labour (China)." In *1914–1918-online. International Encyclopedia of the First World War*. DOI: 10.15463/ie1418.10389.

Yanikdağ, Yücel. 1999. "Ottoman Prisoners of War in Russia 1914–1922." *Journal of Contemporary History* 34: 69–85.

Zaharia, Ionela. 2017. "For God and/or Emperor: Habsburg Romanian Military Chaplains and Wartime Propaganda in Camps for Returning POWs." *European Review of History: Revue européenne d'histoire* 24, no. 2: 288–304.

Zahra, Tara. 2008. *Kidnapped Souls: National Indifference and the Battle for Children in the Bohemian Lands, 1900–1948*. Ithaca, NY: Cornell University Press.

——. 2016. *The Great Departure: Mass Migration from Eastern Europe and the Making of the Free World*. New York: W.W. Norton.

Zehfuss, Nicole M. 2005. "From Stereotype to Individual: World War I Experiences with Tirailleurs Senegalais." *French Colonial History* 6: 137–57.

Zhong, Yurou. 2017. "'Sacred, the Laborers': Writing Chinese in the First World War." *Cross-currents* 6: 296–324.

Ziemann, Benjamin. 2007. *War Experiences in Rural Germany, 1914–1923*. Translated by Alex Skinner. Oxford: Berg.

Zimmerer, Jürgen. 2005. "Annihilation in Africa: The 'Race War' in German Southwest Africa (1904–1908) and Its Significance for a Global History of Genocide." *Bulletin of the German Historical Institute in Washington* 37: 51–57.

Zimmerman, Andrew. 2001. *Anthropology and Antihumanism in Imperial Germany*. Chicago: University of Chicago Press.

Contributors

Doina Anca Cretu is a research fellow within the European Research Council (ERC) Consolidator Grant project "Unlikely Refuge? Refugees and Citizens in East-Central Europe during the Twentieth Century," Masaryk Institute and Archives of the Czech Academy of Sciences. Her research interests include the history of foreign aid, of migration, and of human rights. She holds a PhD in international history from the Graduate Institute of Development Studies in Geneva, Switzerland. She was a 2019–2020 Max Weber postdoctoral fellow at the European University Institute (EUI). She was previously a visiting fellow at the Institute for Human Sciences in Vienna (2018–2019), the University of Oxford (2017–2018), and the Graduate Center, City University of New York (2015–2016).

Nancy Fitch was a professor of history emeritus at California State University, Fullerton, United States, where she served as chair of the history department from 2014–2017. She specialized in modern European, especially French, history and was interested in the French Revolution, World War I, visual representations in history, and the history of antisemitism. Her articles won several prizes, including the 1986 French Historical Studies' Koren Prize for the best article in French history, the 1993 Western Association of Women's Historians' Judith Lee Ridge Prize, and the 2017 Nancy Lyman Roelker Award for the Best Article in Early Modern French History. Professor Fitch passed away on November 15, 2020, shortly after delivering the final version of her chapter.

André Keil is a senior lecturer of history of modern Europe at Liverpool John Moores University, United Kingdom. Focusing on German, French, and British history between 1850 and 1950, he has published on a wide range of topics relating to British and German history, including the history of trade unionism in Britain, the origins of civil-liberties activism, media and history, and memory cultures of the First World War. He is currently preparing the publication of his first monograph, entitled *The Politics of Endurance: Emergency Government and the Home Fronts in Britain and Germany during the First World War*. Recently he has coauthored (with Matthew Stibbe) a detailed study of "Schutzhaft" in Wilhelmine and Weimar Germany together, which was published in the journal *Vierteljahrshefte für Zeitgeschichte*.

Bohdan S. Kordan is a professor of international relations at St. Thomas More College, University of Saskatchewan, Canada, and director of the Prairie Centre for the Study of Ukrainian Heritage. Over the years he has written on various aspects of World War I Canadian internment. His publications in this area include (with Peter Melnycky) *In the Shadow of the Rockies: Diary of the Castle Mountain Internment Camp, 1915–17* (CIUS, 1991); *Enemy Aliens, Prisoners of War: Internment in Canada during the Great War* (McGill-Queen's University Press, 2002); (with Craig Mahovsky) *A Bare and Impolitic Right: Internment and Ukrainian Canadian Redress* (McGill-Queen's University Press, 2004); and *No Free Man: Canada, the Great War and the Enemy Alien Experience* (McGill-Queen's University Press, 2016).

Rotem Kowner is a professor of history and Japanese studies at the University of Haifa, Israel. A founder of the department of Asian studies at the same university and its first chair, he specializes in early modern and modern Japanese history with a focus on wartime conduct and race. He has led several large projects that examined broad themes in East Asia as a whole within a global context. One of these projects concerned the regional and global impact of the Russo-Japanese War and culminated in several books. Notable among these are *The Impact of the Russo-Japanese War*, editor (Routledge, 2007) and *Rethinking the Russo-Japanese War*, editor (Brill, 2007), the *Historical Dictionary of the Russo-Japanese War* (Rowman & Littlefield, 2017), and *Tsushima* (Oxford University Press, 2022).

Sarina Landefeld is a lecturer in law at De Montfort University, Leicester, United Kingdom. Her PhD, completed in 2021 at the University of Nottingham and funded by the AHRC/Midlands3Cities Doctoral Training Partnership, drew on social constructivism to examine the changing conceptualization of civilians and combatants under international humanitarian law from 1864 to the present day. Her current research focuses on the history of international humanitarian law and the protection of civilians.

Assaf Mond is a postdoctoral fellow at the Minerva Center for the Rule of Law under Extreme Conditions, Faculty of Law and the Geography and Environmental Studies Department, the University of Haifa, and teaches modern history of Europe in Levinsky College of Education, Israel. He received his PhD in 2019 from Tel Aviv University. His article "'It Is at Night-Time That We Notice Most of the Changes in Our Life Caused by the War': War-Time, Zeppelins and Children's Experience of the Great War in London" was awarded the Gail Braybon Prize for Best Postgraduate Paper in the Ninth Conference of the International Society for First World War Studies at Oxford University in 2016 and was published in Routledge's 2018 *War Time: First World War Perspectives on Temporality*. His article "Chelsea Football Club and the Fight for Professional Football in First World War London" was published in the November 2016 issue of the *London Journal*.

Mahon Murphy is an associate professor of international history at the Graduate School of Law at Kyoto University, Japan. He received his PhD in 2015 from the London School of Economics and Political Science and was awarded the German Historical Institute London annual thesis prize. His first book, *Colonial Captivity during the First World War: Internment and the Fall of the German Empire, 1914–1919* (Cambridge University Press) was published in 2017. Since moving to Japan, he has been a member of the Prisoners of War Research Group, which is currently working on an edited volume on Japan's treatment of prisoners of war from the Meiji Restoration until World War II. His most recent publication, "The Heimei Maru Incident 1921: Japan's Diplomatic Intervention in Prisoner of War Repatriation," was published in the *International History Review* in 2020.

Iris Rachamimov is an associate professor of modern history of Central and Eastern Europe at the Department of History at Tel Aviv University, Israel. She received her PhD in 2000 from Columbia University. Her book *POWs and the Great War: Captivity on the Eastern Front* (2002) was awarded the Fraenkel Prize for Contemporary History for a first major work. Her article "The Disruptive Comforts of Drag" was published in the April 2006 issue of the *American Historical Review*, and she has written the chapter on military captivity in the latest edition of the *Cambridge History of War: War and the Modern World* (2012). She has published more than twenty-five scholarly articles, and her work has appeared in six languages. Between the years 2014–2019 she was the chief editor of the Hebrew-language journal *Zmanim: A Historical Quarterly*.

Lena Radauer is a department member at the Institute for the Culture and History of Germans in Northeastern Europe at Hamburg University. She is an advanced PhD student in Eastern European history at the Albert-Ludwigs-

University Freiburg and also holds an MSc in Russian and East European Studies from Oxford University, as well as a degree in Slavic Studies from the Université Libre de Bruxelles. Her thesis deals with painters as war prisoners in Siberia, focusing specifically on questions of transcultural interaction, intellectual transfer, and the materiality of captivity. She has written a number of articles on different aspects of captivity and is working on processes of (forced) migration and transcultural biographies as a consequence of the world wars. She is active in the field of public history and has worked as an exhibition curator since 2011.

Naoko Shimazu is a professor of humanities (history) at Yale-NUS College, and professor at the Asia Research Institute, National University of Singapore. Her major publications include *Russian Revolution in Asia: From Baku to Batavia*, coeditor (Routledge, 2022); *Postcard Impressions of Early-20th Century Singapore: Perspective from the Japanese Community*, coauthor (National Library Board of Singapore, 2020); *Imagining Japan in Post-war East Asia*, coeditor (Routledge, 2013); *Japanese Society at War: Death, Memory and the Russo-Japanese War* (Cambridge University Press, 2009); *Nationalisms in Japan*, editor, (Routledge, 2006); and *Japan, Race and Equality: Racial Equality Proposal of 1919* (Routledge, 1998). She is currently working on the cultural history of global diplomacy, focusing on the Bandung Conference of 1955, as well as exploring methodological issues.

Matthew Stibbe is a professor of modern European history at Sheffield Hallam University, United Kingdom. He has published extensively on World War I internment, in English, German, and Portuguese. His intimate study of a particular group of prisoners, *British Civilian Internees in Germany: The Ruhleben Camp, 1914–18* (Manchester University Press, 2008), has been followed by a more recent monograph, *Civilian Internment during the First World War: A European and Global History* (Palgrave, 2019). He has also edited two volumes of essays on this subject: *Captivity, Forced Labour and Forced Migration in Europe during the First World War* (Routledge, 2009); and (with Stefan Manz and Panikos Panayi), *Internment during the First World War: A Mass Global Phenomenon* (Routledge, 2019).

Hazuki Tate is an associate professor in the department of European Studies at Musashi University, Tokyo, Japan. She received her PhD in 2015 from École des Hautes Études en Sciences Sociales (Paris, France) and subsequently was a visiting postdoctoral researcher at Geneva University (2015–2017). She specializes both in twentieth-century French history and international history, and her current research interests focus on the expansion of the Red Cross movement during the interwar period. She is the author of more than ten articles in several languages, including "Le Comité international de la Croix-Rouge comme architecte du droit international: vers le Code des prisonniers de guerre (1929)," *Monde(s): histoire espaces relations* 12 (2017), 203–20; "Hospitaliser, interner et rapatrier: la Suisse et les prisonniers de guerre," *Relations internationales* 159 (2014), 35–48.

Neville Wylie is a professor of international history and deputy principal at the University of Stirling in Scotland, United Kingdom. His research explores various aspects of modern warfare, drawing on the disciplines of history, international relations, and international law. His more recent work has focused on prisoners of war, the evolution of international humanitarian law, and the history of humanitarianism. His publications include *Barbed Wire Diplomacy: Britain, Germany and the Politics of Prisoners of War, 1939–1945* (Oxford University Press, 2010) and *The Red Cross Movement: Myths, Practices and Turning Points* (Manchester University Press, 2020), coedited with Melanie Oppenheimer and James Crossland. He was a member of the International Committee of the Red Cross's external review panel for the updated "commentary" of the Third (POW) Geneva Convention of 1949.

Index

www.ingramcontent.com/pod-product-compliance
Lightning Source LLC
Chambersburg PA
CBHW020456270326
41926CB00008B/629

* 9 7 8 1 5 0 1 7 6 5 9 0 2 *